ALSO BY DAVID F. SWENSEN

Pioneering Portfolio Management

Unconventional Success

A Fundamental Approach to Personal Investment

DAVID F. SWENSEN

FREE PRESS
New York London Toronto Sydney

FREE PRESS
A Division of Simon & Schuster, Inc.
1230 Avenue of the Americas
New York, NY 10020

FREE PRESS and colophon are trademarks
of Simon & Schuster, Inc.

For information regarding special discounts for bulk purchases,
please contact Simon & Schuster Special Sales at 1-800-456-6798
or business@simonandschuster.com.

Manufactured in Italy

30 29 28 27 26 25 24 23 22 21

Library of Congress Cataloging-in-Publication
Data Control Number: 2005044086

ISBN 13: 978-0-7432-2838-1
ISBN 10:   0-7432-2838-3

I dedicate this book to my children:
my wonderful daughter, Tory,
who even as a teenager shines as my beautiful baby girl;
my golfing partner, Alex, who
teaches me something every day about
the meaning of courage;
and my sports-crazed son, Tim,
who always seems to know how to
bring a smile to my face.

Note to Readers

Unconventional Success contains my opinions and ideas. The strategies outlined in this book will not suit every individual. No warranties or guarantees exist regarding the realization of any particular result. The publisher and I specifically disclaim responsibility for any loss incurred as a consequence of the application of the contents of this book. *Caveat lector.*

Readers should know that I serve as a trustee of Teachers Insurance and Annuity Association, better known as one part of the TIAA-CREF acronym. In a number of instances in the book, I make generally favorable references to TIAA, particularly with respect to the organization's single-minded devotion to its clients. My economic interests in TIAA consist of the customary and usual trustee's fees that I earn and the performance that I expect on my retirement accounts with TIAA-CREF. The views that I express do not necessarily reflect those of the governing boards of management of TIAA and CREF.

Acknowledgments

This book would not exist were it not for the extraordinary efforts of three of my colleagues in the Yale Investments Office—Kimberly Sargent, Randy Kim, and Carrie Abildgaard. Unflagging in their devotion and tireless in their execution, Kimberly, Randy, and Carrie assisted me with every aspect of the production of this manuscript. Their unfailing good humor turned a labor of love into a truly joyful experience.

Dean Takahashi, my friend for nearly three decades and my colleague for nearly two, infuses the work of the Yale Investments team with intellectual rigor and vigor. His influence and thinking permeate this book. Our personal and professional collaboration continues to bring great satisfaction to me and, not incidentally, substantial resources to Yale.

My manuscript benefited enormously from constructive comments made by my colleagues Seth Alexander, Jay Kang, Dan Kilpatrick, and Ken Miller. My brother, Steve Swensen, assisted me from the perspective of an astute, nonfinancial professional. In spite of their help, errors remain, for which I take full responsibility.

Contents

Preface

W hen I began my work on *Unconventional Success*, I contemplated writing a different book. My first volume, *Pioneering Portfolio Management: An Unconventional Approach to Institutional Investment*, drew on my years of experience as Yale University's chief investment officer to provide a template for other institutions to use in managing their funds. *Pioneering Portfolio Management* describes an equity-oriented, broadly diversified, actively managed investment program. I expected that *Unconventional Success* would resemble *Pioneering Portfolio Management*, adjusting only for differences between the resources and instruments available to institutions and to individuals.

As I gathered information for my new book, the data clearly pointed to the failure of active management by profit-seeking mutual-fund managers to produce satisfactory results for individual investors. Following the evidence, I concluded that individuals fare best by constructing equity-oriented, broadly diversified portfolios without the active management component. Instead of pursuing ephemeral promises of market-beating strategies, individuals benefit from adopting the ironclad reality of market-mimicking portfolios managed by not-for-profit investment organizations.

The colossal failure of the mutual-fund industry carries serious implications for society, particularly regarding retirement security for American workers. I share with most economists the bias that free markets generally produce superior outcomes, believing that government intervention often creates more problems than it solves. However, the market failure resulting from the mutual-fund industry's systemic exploitation of individual investors requires government action. Without an appropriate policy response, I worry about the level of resources available to support future generations of American retirees.

Introduction

John Maynard Keynes wrote, "Worldly wisdom teaches that it is better for reputation to fail conventionally than to succeed unconventionally."[1] The profound wisdom of Keynes's statement reaches into every nook and cranny of the investment world. Slavishly following conventional wisdom proves unwise, as the frequently trod path often leads to disappointment. Taking a well-considered unconventional approach generally proves sensible, as the less-traveled route provides greater opportunity for success.

Contrarian Investing

Pursuit of nontraditional strategies poses significant challenges for investors. Human nature prefers the comfort that comes with pursuing a time-honored strategy. Sharing a common outcome with large numbers of fellow citizens creates a mutually reinforcing social bond. Unfortunately, the comfortable rarely produces success.

Millions of mutual-fund investors sleep well at night, serene in the belief that superior outcomes result from pooling funds with like-minded investors and engaging high-quality investment managers to provide professional oversight. The conventional wisdom ends up hopelessly unwise, as evidence shows an overwhelming rate of failure by mutual funds to deliver on promises. A nontraditional approach leads to greater likelihood of investment success.

Unconventional Success: A Fundamental Approach to Personal Investment recommends that investors engage not-for-profit fund management companies to create broadly diversified, passively managed portfolios. Note that most mutual-fund assets rest under the control of for-profit management companies. Not-for-profits represent a contrarian alternative. Note that most individuals' portfolios contain result-dominating allocations to domestic marketable securities. True diversification represents a contrarian alternative. Note that most mutual funds attempt to beat the market. Market-mimicking strategies represent a contrarian alternative.

In the eyes of public opinion, the contrarian investor faces a lose-lose proposition. When contrarian approaches fail to keep pace with the current market darling, more-fashionable players mock the out-of-step independent thinker. When contrarian approaches surpass the alternatives, consensus-oriented players decry the irresponsibility of the unconventional investor. Regardless of the investment outcome, out-of-the-mainstream investors receive cold comfort from outside observers.

Contrarian investors require conviction to implement and maintain an unconventional portfolio. Without a rock-solid belief in the fundamental principles that undergird an intelligently crafted portfolio, weak-kneed investors face the likelihood of a disastrous whipsaw. By abandoning an unconventional strategy in the face of poor performance and implementing a conventional alternative after a run of strong investment results, investors sell low and buy high. At some point after the garden-variety investor abandons the unconventional, rationality prevails. The recently oh-so-attractive conventional alternative falters. The recently out-of-favor contrarian portfolio shines. Investors who sold low and bought high suffer the consequences.

In its most basic form, the message of *Unconventional Success* requires only a few pages to describe the blueprint of a well-diversified, equity-oriented, passively managed portfolio, using not-for-profit investment managers to implement the plan. Unfortunately, a prefabricated version of the recommended strategy provides scant assistance to time-constrained investors. Investment success requires the conviction that comes from a fundamental understanding of the rationale for building the portfolio to certain specifications. Unless investors truly believe in the efficacy and validity of an unconventional approach to asset management, the end result almost certainly fails to withstand the wear and tear of market forces.

Thoughtless, knee-jerk contrarian responses ultimately generate results as dismal as the conventional alternative. Consensus-driven strategies frequently produce attractive returns for extended periods of time, placing the fickle contrarian in a difficult position. Complicating the contrarian's life, in some situations the consensus proves correct. Investment success requires far more than taking the other side of the market's trade of the day. Thoughtful investors build investment programs on a fundamental understanding of the reasons for pursuing a nonconventional approach.

Unconventional Success seeks to provide investors with the knowledge and fortitude to take a contrarian path. Examples of the pitfalls that swallow mainstream investors teach lessons in what to avoid. Descriptions of less-traveled routes that beckon unconventional investors offer alternatives to consider. If understanding leads to conviction, then knowledge proves indispensable to investment success.

Public Policy Issues

Although the primary purpose of *Unconventional Success* concerns the description of a sensible investment framework for individuals, the book touches on important public policy issues central to the retirement security of American workers. Increasingly, individuals shoulder responsibility for accumulating the resources necessary to fund a comfortable retirement. In recent decades, employer-managed retirement programs gave way to employee-directed retirement schemes. The shift in accountability from employer to employee caused a move from reasonably well-managed, low-cost investment programs to generally poorly managed, high-cost investment programs. The increase in employee-directed retirement programs threatens the retirement security of millions of Americans.

The decline in employer-sponsored defined benefit programs seems irreversible. Employers dislike defined benefit plans, because of the large, variable liability associated with a promise to pay remainder-of-lifetime benefits to pensioners and because of the large, variable pool of assets required to fund the liability. Employees dislike defined benefit plans, because the future stream of pension payments lacks definition and immediacy. In popular opinion, defined benefit plans register as unpopular.

Likewise, the increase in employee-directed defined contribution plans seems irreversible. Employers like defined contribution plans because of the limited, well-defined liability. Employees like defined contribution plans because of the clear bottom-line description of account value. In a popularity contest, defined contribution plans beat defined benefit plans, hands down.

Unfortunately, defined contribution plans fail to make the grade. Some employees decline to participate. Other employees participate at levels insufficient to produce adequate retirement savings. When employees change jobs, far too many cash out and spend the proceeds. The voluntary nature of participation in defined contribution plans poses the first challenge to future retirement security.

High-cost investment alternatives pose the second threat to retirement security. Defined contribution menus reflect the investment products promoted by the mutual-fund industry. As a result, investors pay high fees for mediocre performance. The investment tools available to defined contribution participants fall far short of minimal standards of adequacy.

The third impediment to retirement security concerns the investment management expertise of the participants. Most individuals lack the specialized knowledge necessary to succeed in today's highly competitive investment markets. Poor asset allocation, ill-considered active management, and perverse market timing lead the list of errors made by individual investors. Even with a massive educational effort, the likelihood of producing a nation of effective investors seems small.

One appropriate policy response to the retirement savings problem puts defined benefit programs at the center of an individual's retirement program and places defined contribution programs on the periphery. Unfortunately, political sentiment seems to lean in the opposite direction. The Bush administration's proposal to allow "individuals to voluntarily invest a portion of their Social Security taxes in personal retirement accounts" imposes an even greater responsibility on the individual investor.[2] Partial privatization of Social Security causes individuals to decide where to invest a portion of retirement assets, adding another obligation to the already-too-large burden on ill-equipped individual investors.

Nobel laureate Paul Samuelson expresses concern regarding privatization of Social Security:

> In all likelihood post-Bush ideology will permit future workers to withdraw part of their Social Security credits in private self-managed accounts. Why? Because that will work out well for the greatest numbers? No. It is virtually guaranteed to work out expensively for most people. But the finance industries will make out well, doing their usual mediocre job for their clients who have Social Security funds to invest. Lobbyists will grease the skids to favor a system with gratuitous deadweight losses and inefficiencies.[3]

Allowing mutual-fund marketers greater access to American retirement savings benefits Wall Street at Main Street's expense.

Another appropriate policy response limits investment alternatives to a well-structured set of choices. Government-provided tax advantages encourage individual participation in defined contribution programs. Suppose the government were to award tax benefits only to accounts that invest in low-cost, market-mimicking funds. By restricting tax-advantaged investments to passive vehicles, investors face far fewer opportunities to make investment mistakes. Government regulation might address market-timing issues by limiting the number and frequency of moves between funds. Educational efforts might deal with the challenges of asset allocation, encouraging individuals to adopt investment programs that fit their specific risk profiles and time horizons. Acting *in loco parentis,* the government could create powerful incentives to adopt passively managed, appropriately allocated investment programs.

The U.S. government's Thrift Savings Plan, developed for the country's civilian and military employees, serves as a possible model. At the end of 2003, the plan contained $128.8 billion in assets distributed across five funds. Four of the funds track well-known indices, namely the large-capitalization-stock S&P 500 Index, the small-capitalization-stock Wilshire 4500 Index, the developed-foreign-stock MSCI EAFE Index and the broadly inclusive domestic bond Lehman Brothers U.S. Aggregate Index. From a security selection perspective, the U.S. government protects its employees from playing the negative-sum game of active management.

If tax-advantaged investments were limited to passively managed investment vehicles, investors might continue to pursue the futile game of high-cost active management with taxable funds. But the carrot of the government's tax advantages would accompany the stick of limitations on investment choice, forcing investors to choose from among a high-quality set of alternatives and improving the retirement prospects for millions of Americans.

The mutual-fund industry sits at the center of a massive market failure. The asymmetry between sophisticated institutional providers of investment management services and unsophisticated individual consumers results in a monumental transfer of wealth from individual to institution. The case for government intervention rests on the clear inability of market mechanisms to produce satisfactory outcomes for the vast majority of individual investors.

Mutual-Fund Industry Failure

Unconventional Success concludes that the mutual-fund industry fails America's individual investors. Compelling data show that nearly certain disappointment awaits the mutual-fund shareholder who hopes to generate market-beating returns. The root of the problem lies in the competition between a mutual-fund management company's fiduciary responsibility and its profit motive. The contest almost inevitably resolves in favor of the bottom line. Individual investors lose. Mutual-fund managers win.

Evidence points overwhelmingly to the conclusion that active management of assets fails to produce satisfactory results for individual investors. Two factors explain the individual's predicament. The first problem stems from the investment choices available to individuals. High costs and poor execution doom the vast majority of offerings. The second problem concerns responses by individuals to markets. Research shortcomings, rearview-mirror investing, and investor fickleness (in the face of both adversity and opportunity) cripple most investment programs. If the outside investment manager fails to diminish investor assets, then the investor steps in to administer self-inflicted pain.

A distressing tale results. Much of *Unconventional Success* details the shortcomings of the mutual-fund industry, warning investors to stay away from profit-driven investment management organizations. Another significant portion of the book describes the behavioral miscues of individuals, suggesting that investors create a plethora of problems for themselves.

Ultimately, *Unconventional Success* proposes a positive solution to the investments challenge facing individual investors. The investment management world includes a very small number of not-for-profit money management firms, allowing investors the opportunity to invest with organizations devoted exclusively to fulfilling fiduciary obligations. Moreover, the market contains a number of attractively structured, passively managed investment alternatives, affording investors the opportunity to create equity-oriented, broadly diversified portfolios. In spite of the massive failure of the mutual-fund industry, investors willing to take an unconventional approach to portfolio management enjoy the opportunity to achieve financial success.

David Swensen
New Haven, Connecticut
March 2005

OVERVIEW

1
Sources of Return

Capital markets provide three tools for investors to employ in generating investment returns: asset allocation, market timing, and security selection. Explicit understanding of the nature and power of the three portfolio management tools allows investors to emphasize the factors most likely to contribute to long-term investment goals and deemphasize the factors most likely to interfere with long-term goals. Establishing a coherent investment program begins with understanding the relative importance of asset allocation, market timing, and security selection.

Asset allocation refers to the long-term decision regarding the proportion of assets that an investor chooses to place in particular classes of investments. For example, an investor with a long time horizon may opt to place 30 percent of assets in domestic equities, 20 percent of assets in foreign equities, 20 percent of assets in real estate, 15 percent of assets in inflation-indexed bonds, and 15 percent of assets in conventional bonds. The asset-allocation decision represents an infrequently revisited set of targets that defines the benchmark against which investors measure investment results.

Market timing refers to deviations from the long-term asset-allocation targets. Active market timing represents a purposeful attempt to generate short-term, superior returns based on insights regarding relative asset class valuations. For example, an investor who believes that stocks represent good value and bonds represent poor value might temporarily move the domestic stock allocation from 30 percent to 35 percent of assets, while reducing the bond allocation

from 15 percent to 10 percent of assets. The return—positive or negative—from overweighting stocks and underweighting bonds represents the return from active market timing. Passive market timing
consists of inadvertent deviations from long-term targets caused by
the action of market forces on the values of a portfolio's various asset
classes. Whether caused by an investor's active decision or an investor's passive indifference, market-timing returns result from deviations between hypothetical target portfolio returns and actual
portfolio asset class returns.

Security selection refers to the method of construction of portfolios for each of the individual asset classes, beginning with the choice
of passive or active management. Passive management, the baseline
against which other options must be measured, involves replication of
the underlying market. In the case of domestic equities, the S&P 500,
the S&P 1500, the Russell 3000, and the Wilshire 5000 represent
broad-based indices that provide reasonable definitions of the market
and sensible alternatives for investors pursuing passive management.
Active management involves making bets against the market, with the
investor attempting to overweight attractively priced stocks and underweight expensively priced stocks. The returns resulting from the
active manager's deviations relative to the benchmark represent security selection returns.

Asset-allocation decisions play a central role in determining investor results. A number of well-regarded studies of institutional portfolios conclude that approximately 90 percent of the variability of
returns stems from asset allocation, leaving approximately 10 percent
of the variability to be determined by security selection and market
timing. Another important piece of research on performance of institutional investors suggests that 100 percent of investor returns derive
from asset allocation, relegating security selection and market timing
to an inconsequential role.[1] Careful investors pay close attention to the
determination of asset class targets.

Academic conclusions about the importance of asset allocation
lead many students of markets to conclude that some immutable law
of finance dictates the primacy of asset allocation in the investment
process. In fact, the studies cited reflect investor behavior, not finance
theory. Investors gain important insights into questions of portfolio
structure through understanding the forces that place asset allocation

in a starring role, while leaving security selection and market timing in the wings.

Three basic investment principles inform asset-allocation decisions in well-constructed portfolios. First, long-term investors build portfolios with a pronounced equity bias. Second, careful investors fashion portfolios with substantial diversification. Third, sensible investors create portfolios with concern for tax considerations. The principles of equity orientation, diversification, and tax sensitivity find support both in common sense and academic theory. Surprisingly, basic investment principles seem to find little support in real-world asset-allocation activity.

ASSET ALLOCATION

Asset-allocation decisions take center stage in most investor portfolios, because investors generally own portfolios broadly diversified within asset classes (mitigating the impact of security selection decisions) and investors generally maintain reasonably stable asset-class allocations (mitigating the impact of market-timing decisions).* With two of the three sources of return down for the count, asset allocation takes the prize as the last contender standing. Since long-term portfolio targets play such a powerful role in determining investment outcomes, sensible investors pay careful attention to establishing thoughtful asset-allocation structures.

Investment maven Charley Ellis observes that investors generally fail to spend the most time and the most resources on the most important investment decisions. Seduced by the appeal of security-trading decisions and the allure of market-timing moves, investors tend to focus on unproductive and expensive portfolio-churning activities. While hot stocks and brilliant timing make wonderful cocktail party chatter, the conversation-stopping policy portfolio proves far more important to investment success.

The essence of the process that leads to creation of viable portfolio targets involves knowledge of basic investment principles, definition

---

*Unfortunately, well-diversified portfolios and reasonably stable allocations prove insufficient to prevent investors from losing significant assets through chasing yesterday's hot performers (see Part II—Market Timing) and from wasting staggering sums on ineffective active management (see Part III—Security Selection).

of specific investment goals, and understanding of individual risk tolerances. Fundamental investment tenets provide the framework upon which investors build portfolios with the greatest probability of meeting investor needs. Clear articulation of goals defines the task that investors desire to accomplish, while explicit specification of risk preferences outlines the parameters within which investors sensibly operate. Investors armed with basic investment principles, well-defined goals, and reasonable self-awareness increase the likelihood of investment success.

FUNDAMENTAL INVESTMENT PRINCIPLES

Finance theory and common sense support three long-term asset-allocation principles—the importance of equity ownership, the efficacy of portfolio diversification, and the significance of tax sensitivity. Allocations to equity-like assets enhance portfolio characteristics as the superior returns expected from high-risk positions ultimately produce greater wealth. Commitments to a range of asset types that behave differently one from another improve portfolio attributes, as the reduced risk associated with broadly diversified portfolios ultimately produces more stable returns. Attention to the tax characteristics of asset classes and tax consequences of portfolio strategies strengthens portfolio results, as the improved after-tax returns ultimately produce more assets. The wealth-creating equity bias, the risk-reducing portfolio diversification, and the return-enhancing tax sensitivity combine to undergird the asset-allocation structure of effective investment portfolios.

Equity Bias

Finance theory posits that equity investors rightly expect returns superior to those expected by holders of less risky financial assets, albeit at the cost of higher levels of risk. Because equity owners get paid after corporations satisfy all other claimants, equity ownership represents a residual interest. As such, stockholders occupy a riskier position than, say, corporate lenders who enjoy a superior position in a company's capital structure. In the case of marketable securities returns, reality matches theory, as over reasonably long periods of time stock returns exceed those of bonds and cash.

History tells us that equity markets produce handsome returns over long holding periods. Any number of sources provide high quality information on capital markets returns. Ibbotson Associates, founded by Yale scholar Roger Ibbotson, produces a widely used survey of returns covering the past seventy-eight years. Over the nearly eight-decade period from 1926 to 2003, U.S. stocks produced an annual compound return of 10.4 percent, U.S. government bonds returned 5.4 percent, and U.S. Treasury bills generated 3.7 percent. The 5.0 percentage point difference between stock and bond returns represents the historical risk premium, defined as the return to equity holders for accepting risk above the level inherent in bond investments.

Even apparently modest return differentials, operating over long periods of time, translate into staggering wealth differentials. During the seventy-eight years of the Ibbotson series, as shown in Table 1.1, one dollar invested in large-company stocks expanded 2,285 times, while bonds produced a 61 multiple, and cash, an 18 multiple. Small stocks demonstrated even more impressive results, as the 1925 dollar multiplied 10,954 times by 2003. Equity ownership beats holding bonds or cash, hands down.

Similar results can be found in Jeremy Siegel's *Stocks for the Long Run*. The third edition of Siegel's classic study of capital markets returns shows U.S. stocks producing an 8.3 percent per annum compound return over the two centuries spanning 1802 to 2001. In a hard-to-believe statistic, one dollar invested in the stock market at the outset of the nineteenth century, with all gains and dividends reinvested, grows to $8.8 million at the beginning of the twenty-first century!

Table 1.1 Equity Ownership Drives Long-Term Returns

	Cash Return		Long-Term Government Bond Return		Large-Company Stock Return		Small-Company Stock Return	
Period	Percent	Multiple	Percent	Multiple	Percent	Multiple	Percent	Multiple
1926–2003	3.7	18	5.4	61	10.4	2,285	12.7	10,954
1802–2001	4.3	4,500	4.9	14,000	8.3	8,800,000	N/A	N/A

Sources: Ibbotson Associates. Stocks, Bonds, Bills, and Inflation 2004 Yearbook *(Chicago: Ibbotson Associates, 2004); Jeremy Siegel,* Stocks for the Long Run *(New York: McGraw Hill, 2002).*

Bonds generate less spectacular results. The compound annual return for long-term government bonds of 4.9 percent per annum proves sufficient to cause one dollar to produce a portfolio worth $14,000 after a two-century holding period. Predictably, bills bring up the rear. The 4.3 percent compound return causes a dollar to produce a mere $4,500 after two hundred years. Note that the risk premium of 3.4 percentage points in Siegel's two-century study falls in the same neighborhood as the risk premium of 5.0 percentage points in Ibbotson's seventy-eight-year study.

Historical evidence clearly points to a strong equity orientation for long-term investment programs. In fact, a superficial examination of the data might lead to the conclusion that investors should put all of their eggs in the equity market basket. However, a closer look at history illustrates the dangers of a single-asset-class concentration.

Diversification

The stock market crash of 1929 provides the most dramatic example of holding an undiversified portfolio. From the peak of small company stock prices in November 1928 to the trough in 1932, small stock investors suffered an excruciating 90 percent collapse in value. The depression-induced deflation slightly mitigated the purchasing power loss, bringing the price-level-adjusted decline to 88 cents on the dollar. Table 1.2 outlines the terrible tale.

The bear market and stagflation of the 1970s present another example of intolerably poor small-stock returns. In the bull market frenzy of the 1960s, small-stock prices peaked in December 1968, a full four years prior to the peak in large-stock prices. In a seemingly inexorable decline, small stocks fell nearly 60 percent by the time they reached the bottom in December 1974. Adding to the pain of the bear

Table 1.2 Markets Occasionally Crush Concentrated Portfolios

Period	Small Stock Multiple	Purchasing Power Adjusted Multiple
November 1928–June 1932	0.10	0.12
December 1968–December 1974	0.42	0.29

Source: Ibbotson Associates. Stocks, Bonds, Bills, and Inflation 2004 Yearbook (Chicago: Ibbotson Associates, 2004).

market, inflation reduced the purchasing power of a 1968 dollar to just 68 cents six years later. The combination of market action and inflation erosion produced a purchasing-power-adjusted loss of more than 70 percent. Undiversified investors paid the piper.

From a strictly financial perspective, diversification improves portfolio characteristics by allowing investors to achieve higher returns for a given level of risk (or lower risk for a given level of returns). Generations of economics students who learned that "there ain't no such thing as a free lunch" may be surprised to discover that Nobel laureate Harry Markowitz called diversification one of the economic world's rare "free lunches." By diversifying, investors gain risk reduction without return diminution (or gain return enhancement without risk expansion).

Ultimately, the behavioral benefits of diversification loom larger than the financial benefits. Investors with undiversified portfolios face enormous pressures, both internal and external, to change course when the concentrated strategy produces poor results. In the 1930s, as small-stock dollars collapsed to dimes, and in the 1970s, as small-stock dollars shrank to 30 cents, investors declared "no more" and "never again," sold their shares and invested in cash. Of course, the investors' epiphany regarding the risk of small-stock investing came at an inopportune time. A dollar invested in small stocks in June of 1932 grew more than 100,000-fold by December 2003. Unfortunately, diversification provides no guarantee that investors will stay the course through adverse conditions. But, when only a portion of the portfolio suffers from dramatically adverse price moves, investors face a higher likelihood of riding out the storm.

Sensible individuals take care to distribute assets across a range of investment alternatives. The act of diversification provides a free lunch of enhanced returns and reduced risk, increasing the likelihood that an investor will stay the course in difficult market environments.

Investment Principles in Practice

In spite of nearly universal support among investment professionals for equity-oriented, well-diversified portfolios, market practice generally fails to reflect fundamental portfolio management precepts. Consider the average asset allocation of college and university endowments, which represent the best managed of institutional funds. Ten years ago, as portrayed in Table 1.3, domestic equities constituted nearly 50 percent of assets and domestic bonds more than 40 percent. With two asset classes accounting for almost 90 percent of assets, the portfolios flunk the test of diversification. With low-expected-return bonds and cash accounting for in excess of 40 percent of assets, the portfolios flunk the test of equity orientation. In the early 1990s, college and university endowment managers earned dismal grades.

Portfolios dominated by traditional marketable securities exhibit even less diversification than the bond and stock distinction suggests. Under many circumstances, changes in interest rates—one of the most important fundamental drivers of market returns—influence bonds and stocks in similar fashion. When rates rise, the harsh reality of bond math calls for prices to fall. When rates rise, the discount rate applied to future corporate earnings streams rises as well, causing stock prices to fall. The converse holds, too. College and university endowment porfolios of the early 1990s exposed nearly 90 percent of assets to a common determinant of financial market returns.

**Table 1.3 Colleges and Universities
Fail to Follow Basic Investment Principles**
Equal-Weighted Allocations (Percent of Assets)

Asset Class	June 30, 1993	June 30, 2003
Domestic equities	48.6	47.7
Domestic bonds and cash	40.8	29.2
Diversifying assets	10.6	23.1

Source: NACUBO.

Stock and bond holdings prove most diversifying when inflationary expectations fail to match the subsequent reality. For instance, in an environment of unanticipated inflation, the fixed nominal claims of bondholders become worth less. In contrast, higher-than-expected levels of inflation increase the value of a stockholder's residual claim on corporate assets. The converse holds, too. In short, only under unusual circumstances do holdings of stocks and bonds produce substantial diversification.

The 2003 portfolios of colleges and universities show scant progress relative to the 1993 versions. Domestic equity holdings in

2003 amounted to nearly 48 percent of the average endowment, hovering around the same level as the portfolio of a decade earlier. Fixed-income portfolios constituted nearly 30 percent of assets, representing more than a 10 percentage point decline from the 1993 allocation. Obviously, the 1993 to 2003 reduction in exposure to traditional marketable securities improved portfolio characteristics. Yet, in spite of increased allocations to diversifying assets, the 2003 endowment registered neither as particularly well diversified nor as adequately equity-oriented.

Contrast the experience of the broad group of colleges and universities with the best-endowed educational institutions. Harvard, Yale, Princeton, and Stanford lead the endowment world in size and led the endowment world with early adoption of well-diversified, equity-oriented portfolios. As early as 1993 the market-leading quartet allocated only 56 percent of assets to domestic marketable securities, relative to the excessive level of 89 percent for the more inclusive group of educational endowments. By 2003, as shown in Table 1.4, the leading universities further improved endowment diversification, reducing the domestic marketable security allocation to 32 percent, relative to the broader universe's allocation of 77 percent.

Not only did the larger endowments exhibit greater diversification, they showed superior equity orientation as well. Fixed-income allocations for the four top endowments amounted to an average of 20 percent in 1993 and 15 percent in 2003, representing approximately one-half of the respective allocations of 41 percent and 29 percent for the broad group of colleges and universities.

The well-diversified, equity-oriented portfolios produced superior results. For the ten years ending June 30, 2003, Harvard, Yale, Prince-

Table 1.4 Large Endowments Adopt Well-Diversified, Equity-Oriented Portfolios
Equal-Weighted Allocations (Percent of Assets)

Asset Class	June 30, 1993	June 30, 2003
Domestic equities	35.5	17.0
Domestic bonds and cash	20.0	14.6
Diversifying assets	44.5	68.4

Source: NACUBO.
Note: Figures represent allocations for Harvard, Yale, Princeton, and Stanford.

ton, and Stanford generated results that stood in the top 5 percent of
the ranks of endowed institutions, far outpacing the returns of the average college or university. Real-world application of fundamental investment principles produces superior outcomes.

MARKET TIMING

Market timing fails to make an important contribution to institutional
portfolio results, because investors quite sensibly show reasonable
constancy in holdings of various asset types. Perhaps institutions
avoid market timing because they understand the inconsistency inherent in making a speculative short-term bet against a carefully crafted
long-term target portfolio. Or maybe investors keep to policy asset allocations because they recognize the futility of consistently making
the relative asset class valuation assessments necessary for market-
timing success, particularly when such assessments rely on a bewildering collection of unknowable economic and financial variables.
Regardless of the reasons for underlying stability in portfolio allocations, market timing fails to make a major difference in institutional
investment results.

The story differs for individual investors. The available evidence
points to a pattern of excessive allocation to recent strong performers
offset by inadequate allocation to recent weak performers. Possibly,
investors allow inertia to drive portfolio allocations, with asset class
weights flowing and ebbing with the relative rise and fall of markets.
Or maybe investors actively chase yesterday's winners while aggressively abandoning previous losers. The impact of market timing on individual investor portfolios generally falls into the negative category.

The relative insignificance of market timing stems from the behavior of investors, not from the precepts of finance theory. Consider the
market-timing alternative to the generally reasonable behavior of
sticking to long-term asset-allocation targets. If an investor pursued an
exclusive strategy of day trading stock index futures, investment results for the portfolio would have nothing to do with asset allocation
or security selection and everything to do with market timing. The
lack of widespread frenetic trading by investors stems either from a
general sensibility of the investing populace or from a Darwinian win-
nowing of the day traders' ranks.

Perhaps the most frequent variant of market timing comes not in the form of explicit bets for and against asset classes, but in the form of passive drift away from target allocations. If investors fail to counter market moves by making rebalancing trades, portfolio allocations inevitably move away from the desired target levels. For example, if bonds show superior performance relative to stocks, the bond portfolio rises above target levels as the stock portfolio falls below. A rebalancing trade requires sales of the relatively strongly performing bonds to fund purchases of the relatively poorly performing stocks. Since few investors engage in systematic rebalancing activity, most portfolios wax and wane with the markets, subjecting the portfolio to a strange form of market timing. By pursuing a tack that overweights recent strong performers and underweights recent weak performers, investors reduce chances for investment success.

Overweighting assets that produced strong past performance and underweighting assets that produced weak past performance provides a poor recipe for pleasing prospective results. Strong evidence exists that markets exhibit mean-reverting behavior, a tendency for good performance to follow bad and bad performance to follow good. In markets characterized by mean reversion, investors who fail to rebalance portfolios to long-term targets end up with outsized exposure to recently appreciated assets that prove most vulnerable to poor future results. Only by regularly rebalancing portfolios to long-term targets do investors realize the results that correspond to the policy asset-allocation decision.

SECURITY SELECTION

Security selection plays a minor role in investment returns, because investors tend to hold broadly diversified portfolios that correlate reasonably strongly with the overall market. The high degree of association between investor security holdings and the market reduces the importance of security-specific influences, causing portfolio returns to mirror market returns.

Consider the security selection alternative to the generally sensible investor behavior of holding broadly diversified portfolios. If an investor were to hold a single stock instead of a diverse portfolio of stocks, the idiosyncratic character of that particular security would drive equity portfolio performance. In the single-stock portfolio scenario, security selection plays a critical role in portfolio results.

Investors need to hold only a small portion of the market to achieve market-like levels of diversification. According to a group of scholars that includes investment guru Burton Malkiel, in years past "[a] conventional rule of thumb . . . [was] that a portfolio of 20 stocks [attained] a large fraction of the total benefits of diversification."[2] In more recent years, research shows that to achieve the same reduction in nonmarket risk, investors required a portfolio of fifty securities. Regardless of the specific number needed to produce a portfolio that embodies market-like risk, the total falls far short of the thousands of stocks in the U.S. market.

Consider the systematic market-related risk and unsystematic nonmarket-related risk associated with portfolios of various numbers of randomly chosen securities. Systematic risk constitutes risk inherent in the market, while unsystematic risk consists of security-specific variability. Note that a portfolio containing a single security contains a high degree of nonmarket, idiosyncratic risk. In contrast, a comprehensive, market-capitalization-weighted index fund contains only market, systematic risk. With a single-security portfolio and the market portfolio describing the extremes, as the number of securities in the portfolio increases, the nonmarket-related (or unsystematic) risk declines and the market-related (or systematic) risk rises.

According to a well-constructed study covering three roughly equal periods from 1963 to 1997, a two-security portfolio carries double or triple the risk of the market. In contrast, a portfolio of twenty securities contains a risk level of roughly one-third or two-thirds higher than the overall level of market risk. Finally, a portfolio of fifty securities exhibits risk characteristics quite similar to the market as a whole, showing very little diversifiable risk.[3] Stated differently, the typical well-diversified equity portfolio with dozens or even hundreds of securities produces results driven largely by the market.

The relative unimportance of security selection in determining the aggregate of portfolio returns corresponds to the predictions of academic theory. Consider the U.S. equity market. Since the market encompasses the value of all securities held by all investors, the aggregate return to the entire group of investors in U.S. equities must be the return of the market. If each investor pursued a passive management strategy of holding the market portfolio, then each investor would receive the market return. Security selection would count for nothing.

Of course, large numbers of investors pursue active management strategies, attempting to generate excess returns by beating the market. But an active investor can overweight a stock only if other market players take offsetting underweight positions. By definition, the sum of overweight positions must equal the sum of underweight positions, allowing the market weight to remain the market weight.

Obviously, based on subsequent performance, the overweighters and underweighters turn into winners and losers (or losers and winners). If the stock in question performs well relative to the market, the overweighters win and the underweighters lose. If the stock performs poorly relative to the market, the overweighters lose and the underweighters win.

Before considering transaction costs, active management appears to be a zero-sum game, a contest in which the winners' gains exactly offset the losers' losses. Unfortunately for active portfolio managers, investors incur significant costs in pursuit of market-beating strategies. Stock pickers pay commissions to trade and create market impact with buys and sells. Mutual-fund purchasers face the same market-related transactions costs in addition to management fees paid to advisory firms and distribution fees paid to brokerage firms. The leakage of fees from the system causes active management to turn into a negative-sum game in which the aggregate returns for active investors fall short of the aggregate returns for the market as a whole.

Security selection may provide substantial excess returns to skilled investors, but those excess returns come directly from the pockets of other players who suffer poor relative returns. When aggregating the returns for all actively managed portfolios, the combined results inevitably mimic the market, less a discount equal to the amount paid to play the game. For the investment community as a whole, security selection plays a return-reducing role in investment performance.

TAX SENSITIVITY

Taxation of income and capital gains introduces enormous complexity into asset-allocation and security-selection decisions. Tax-exempt endowment, foundation, and pension portfolios simply evaluate expected risk and return characteristics of investment alternatives without regard to the expected tax consequences of the nature of the income or the length of the holding period. In contrast, taxable individuals must consider tax implications of various asset allocation, security selection, and portfolio structuring alternatives.

MIT economist James Poterba observed that "the tax rules that apply to income from capital are the most complicated part of most modern income tax systems."[4] He nonetheless made some simplifying assumptions to create a head-to-head comparison of pre-tax and after-tax historical asset returns. Even though after-tax returns depend on an individual's particular tax bracket and the timing of gain and loss realization, Poterba's estimate of the gap between pre-tax and after-tax returns provides some sense of the magnitude of the role that taxes play in the portfolio decisions. According to Poterba's calculations, shown in Table 1.5, taxable investors in stocks might lose as much as 3.5 percentage points per year to taxes. In the context of a pre-tax return of 12.7 percent per year, the tax burden dramatically reduces the rewards for investing in equities.

The absolute level of the tax impact on bond and cash returns falls below the impact on equity returns, but taxes consume a greater portion of current-income-intensive assets. According to Poterba's esti-

Table 1.5 Taxes Materially Reduce Investment Returns
Pre-Tax and After-Tax Returns (Percent) 1926 to 1996

Asset Class	Pre-Tax Return	After-Tax Return	Tax Burden
Large stocks	12.7	9.2	3.5
Long-term government bonds	5.5	3.4	2.1
Treasury bills	3.8	2.2	1.6

Source: James M. Poterba, "Taxation, Risk-Taking, and Household Portfolio Behavior," NBER Working Paper Series, Working Paper 8340 (National Bureau of Economic Research, 2001), 90.

mates, 28 percent of gross equity returns go to the tax man, while taxes consume 38 percent of bond returns and 42 percent of cash returns.

Tax laws currently favor long-term gains over dividend and interest income in two ways: capital gains face lower tax rates and incur tax only when realized. The provision in the tax code that causes taxes to be due only upon realization of gains allows investors to delay payment of taxes far into the future. Deferral of capital gains taxes creates enormous economic value to investors.*

When investors hold taxable investments, future tax rates and individual tax circumstances determine a particular investor's after-tax results. While individuals face unknowable future tax regimes, some insight into the future comes from the past. Over the last quarter century, as outlined in Table 1.6, dividends and interest incurred taxes at rates significantly higher than long-term capital gains. Short-term gains, currently defined as gains from positions held less than a year and a day, received the same harsh treatment as dividend and interest income. The Internal Revenue Code provides tax-sensitive investors with strong incentives to favor long-term holding of equity securities.

Note the significant reduction in the tax rates in recent years. Long-term capital gains rates declined from 28 percent in 1980 to 15 percent in 2003. Short-term gains rates halved, dropping from 70 percent in 1980 to 35 percent in 2003.

Table 1.6 Historical Federal Tax Rates Favor Long-Term Capital Gains

Year	Long-Term Gains Rate	Short-Term Gains and Current Income	Dividends
1980	28.0	70.0	70.0
1985	20.0	50.0	50.0
1990	28.0	31.0	31.0
1995	28.0	39.6	39.6
2000	20.0	39.6	39.6
2003	15.0	35.0	15.0

Sources: American Council for Capital Formation website; Congressional Budget Office website; Poterba[5].

---

*In the most extreme case, if individuals hold appreciated securities in their estate, the heirs enjoy a stepped-up basis on the inherited securities, resulting in no tax paid on the appreciation during the individual's lifetime and a fresh start from a tax perspective for the heirs.

Dividends exhibit the most impressive rate reduction. After decades during which long-term capital gains enjoyed a dramatic tax advantage over dividends, in 2003 the two forms of income achieved tax parity. The significant changes in absolute and relative levels of tax rates contain an important lesson in uncertainty. No one knows the future tax liability associated with various forms of investment income.

The data in Table 1.6 represent the maximum rates applied to various forms of investment income. Individuals making investment decisions must consider not only the structure of future tax regimes, but the character of their individual circumstances. Overly precise estimates of the future may prove of little use, while more general concepts might serve a useful purpose. For example, the expectation that after retirement an individual will be in a lower tax bracket contains important implications for current financial planning.

Tax Deferral

The significant burden that taxes impose on security returns causes investors to seek ways to reduce the gap between the pre-tax and after-tax returns. The single most important method available to individual investors lies in the alphanumeric soup of tax-deferred investment vehicles. Individual Retirement Accounts (IRAs), 401(k) accounts, 403(b) accounts, Keogh accounts, and Simplified Employee Pension (SEP) accounts provide individuals with the means to save for retirement in a tax-advantaged fashion.

Higher education trusts, so-called 529 plans, allow savings for a child's higher education expenses to accumulate tax-free. If funds from the trust pay for tuition or other qualifying uses, the tax deferred becomes tax forgiven, making the trusts an extraordinarily powerful tool for tax-conscious investors.

In structuring investment portfolios, investors should stay in the mainstream, avoiding tax-related exotica. The gap between tax rates on ordinary income and long-term capital gains prompts sometimes aggressive attempts by promoters to convert ordinary income into capital gains. In the late 1970s and early 1980s, individuals entered into tax-driven transactions involving fine art, low-income housing, and breeding cattle. Congress, fed up with abuses, shut down the tax-driven operations, throwing out the legitimate (low-income housing) along with the illegitimate (cattle breeding). Be wary of noneconomic, tax-driven schemes.*

Taxable investors face an ever-changing landscape of laws and regulations regarding tax-advantaged investing. Keeping current on the general nature and specific character of available opportunities pays significant dividends in the form of enhanced after-tax returns. Rational market participants take maximum advantage of tax-advantaged investing.

Investors managing assets in tax-deferred accounts need not worry about the character of income or its realization. Dividends, interest, and short-term and long-term gains and losses all accrue in the accounts with taxes deferred until withdrawal. Tax-deductible contributions to accounts end up being treated as ordinary income upon withdrawal. Taxable contributions to accounts create a basis that allows tax-free distribution of that basis upon withdrawal. Managing tax-deferred assets poses relatively few tax-related questions.

In sharp contrast, investors holding assets in taxable accounts face a complicated set of tax-related issues. Does a high-turnover strategy with the attendant high level of realized gains produce sufficiently high after-tax returns to justify pursuing the portfolio management technique? Should taxable bonds with a high-current-income component be held in a tax-deferred account? Should tax-exempt bonds be held in a taxable account, freeing the tax-advantaged account capacity for aggressive active management strategies? The answers to these questions and others regarding tax planning lie in the character of the assets, the nature of the investment strategies—particularly as regards asset turnover—and the tax structure faced by the investor.

Dividends, Interest, and Capital Gains

Dividends from stocks and taxable interest from bonds produce current cash flow for investors. While investors benefit from receipt of cold, hard cash, the tax man takes his due. Taxable recipients of divi-

---

*For example, see *Grodt & McKay Realty, Inc. v. Commissioner of Internal Revenue* for a U.S. Tax Court case involving breeding cattle.

dends and taxable interest income cannot escape or defer the tax bill on current income.

Tax-exempt bonds provide investors with the opportunity to earn interest income free from federal tax consequences.* The relationship between taxable and tax-exempt bond yields on otherwise comparable securities provides specific information on the value of tax deferral. A comparison of the taxable/tax-exempt yield differential and the value of tax deferral for other asset classes help to determine the appropriate location of assets in taxable and tax-deferred accounts.

Taxable investors prefer low-dividend or no-dividend equity securities, since dividends tend to be more heavily taxed than capital gains and dividends cannot be deferred. In the 1990s, corporate managers, recognizing what has long been reality, responded by reducing dividend payouts and using the cash flow to buy back shares. By diverting excess corporate cash from dividends to share repurchases, corporate managers facilitate taxable investor substitution of capital gains for current income.

Tax consequences of gains and losses arise only when an investor closes a position. The fact that unrealized gains incur no tax provides powerful incentives for investors to hold winning positions, deferring the tax liability to some future date. The fact that unrealized losses harbor no tax consequence provides strong motivation for investors to dispose of losing trades, allowing current use of the loss or banking it for future use. Tax-sensitive investors show a bias toward low turnover of holdings with gains and high turnover of holdings with losses.

Realized losses not only offer opportunities to reduce taxable income, they also provide flexibility to portfolio managers. Losses allow investors to sell positions with gains without creating tax liability. Care must be taken, however, not to squander valuable losses (that can be carried forward to future tax years) in chimerical pursuit of securities with superior return prospects. In any event, issues surrounding payment of capital gains taxes play a larger role in portfolio management than do issues regarding utilization of capital losses. Because the equity markets tend to produce positive results over long periods of

---

*See Chapter 4, *Non-Core Asset Classes* for a discussion of tax-exempt bonds.

time, investors should expect to deal predominantly with taxes on gains, not benefits from losses.

Unfortunately for investors, tax treatment of investment income adds enormous complexity to the portfolio management process. On top of the intrinsic difficulty in understanding the existing tax code, investors operate in a constantly changing framework. Rational investors respond to the complex, ever-changing tax environment by taking care to minimize the tax burden carried by the investment portfolio. Taxes impair wealth accumulation.

CHAPTER SUMMARY

Investors generally fail to follow the most basic investment precepts. Instead of concentrating on the central issue of creating sensible long-term asset-allocation targets, investors too frequently focus on the unproductive diversions of security selection and market timing. Instead of constructing equity-oriented, well diversified, tax-sensitive portfolios, investors too frequently choose to mimic the conventional, poorly structured consensus. Disappointing results represent the nearly inevitable consequence of ignoring fundamental investment principles.

A thorough understanding of a rational approach to markets forms an important precondition for investment success. Real conviction proves necessary to stick with an out-of-favor strategy in the face of apparently poor results and obvious public skepticism. Investors ultimately reap rewards only if they maintain positions in the face of market woes. Individuals who prove unable to withstand the inevitable market traumas frequently end up whipsawed, abandoning sensible strategies just as the out-of-favor moves into the limelight.

The history of capital markets provides important support for the notions of owning equities and of creating diversified portfolios. Over reasonably long periods of time, stocks trump bonds and stocks trump cash, hands down. Close examination of asset-class returns produces evidence that supports the value of diversification. The volatility of risky asset classes occasionally proves too great for investors to stomach, arguing for moderation in exposure to any individual class of securities. Equity orientation and diversification make sense.

Taxes matter. Since payments to the tax man represent a direct diminution of investor assets, careful investors structure portfolios to avoid or defer as much tax as possible. Tax consequences impinge on both asset-allocation and portfolio-management decisions.

The articulation of portfolio targets constitutes the most powerful determinant of investment outcomes. Casual allocation decisions, honored in the breach and casually reversed, hold the potential to cause great harm to investor portfolios. Thoughtful policy targets, carefully implemented and steadfastly maintained, create the foundation for investment success.

Part One

ASSET ALLOCATION

Introduction

Sensible investors build portfolios starting with an asset allocation that rests on the bedrock of diversification, equity orientation, and tax sensitivity. The building blocks for the portfolio consist of core asset classes that rely on market-based returns to contribute basic, category-specific characteristics to the portfolio.

Six asset classes provide exposure to well-defined investment attributes. Investors expect equity-like returns from domestic equities, foreign developed market equities, and emerging market equities. Conventional domestic fixed-income and inflation-indexed securities provide diversification, albeit at the cost of expected returns that fall below those anticipated from equity investments. Exposure to real estate contributes diversification to the portfolio with lower opportunity costs than fixed-income investments.

In the portfolio construction process, diversification requires that individual asset-class allocations rise to a level sufficient to have an impact on the portfolio, with each asset-class accounting for at least 5 to 10 percent of assets. Diversification further requires that no individual asset class dominate the portfolio, with each asset class amounting to no more than 25 to 30 percent of assets.

The principle of equity orientation induces investors to place the bulk of the portfolio in higher-expected-return asset classes. Domestic equities, foreign equities, and real estate deserve large allocations, allowing the equity-oriented asset classes to drive long-term returns. Domestic bonds and inflation-indexed bonds receive low allocations, allowing the fixed-income-oriented asset classes to provide diversification without excessive opportunity cost.

Table I.1 Well-Diversified, Equity-Oriented Portfolios Provide a Framework for Investment Success

Asset Class	Policy Target
Domestic equity	30%
Foreign developed equity	15%
Emerging market equity	5%
Real estate	20%
U.S. Treasury bonds	15%
U.S. Treasury Inflation-Protected Securities	15%

A generic portfolio based on fundamental investment principles provides a starting point for a discussion of portfolio construction. Table I.1 contains an outline of a well-diversified, equity-oriented portfolio. Fully 70 percent of assets promise equity-like returns, meeting the requirement of equity orientation. Asset-class weights range from 5 to 30 percent of assets, meeting the requirement of diversification. A portfolio with assets allocated according to fundamental investment principles establishes a strong starting point for individual investment programs.

Ultimately, successful portfolios reflect the specific preferences and risk tolerances of individual investors. Understanding the quantitative and qualitative characteristics of asset-class exposure creates a basis for determining which asset classes to include and in which proportions to invest. Chapter 2, *Core Asset Classes,* offers a primer on those asset classes likely to contribute to investor goals. Chapter 3, *Portfolio Construction,* outlines a methodology that blends science and art in combining the core asset classes to produce a portfolio. Chapter 4, *Non-Core Asset Classes,* describes the shortcomings of those asset classes less likely to satisfy investor needs.

2
Core Asset Classes

Defining asset classes combines art and science in an attempt to group like with like, seeking as an end result a relatively homogeneous collection of investment opportunities. The successful definition of an asset class produces a combination of securities that collectively provide a reasonably well-defined contribution to an investor's portfolio.

Core asset classes share a number of critical characteristics. First, core asset classes contribute basic, valuable, differentiable characteristics to an investment portfolio. Second, core holdings rely fundamentally on market-generated returns, not on active management of portfolios. Third, core asset classes derive from broad, deep, investable markets.

The basic, valuable, differentiable characteristics contributed by core asset classes range from provision of substantial expected returns to correlation with inflation to protection against financial crises. Careful investors define asset-class exposures narrowly enough to ensure that the investment vehicle accomplishes its expected task, but broadly enough to encompass a critical mass of assets.

Core asset classes rely fundamentally on market-generated returns, because investors require reasonable certainty that the various portfolio constituents will fulfill their appointed missions. When markets fail to derive returns, investors seek superior active managers to do the job. In those cases where management proves essential to the success of a particular asset class, the investor relies on ability or good fortune in security selection to produce results. If an active manager exhibits poor skill or experiences bad luck, the investor suffers as the asset class fails to achieve its goals. Satisfying investment objectives proves too important to rely on serendipity or the supposed expertise of market players. Core asset classes, therefore, depend fundamentally on market-driven returns.

Finally, core holdings trade in broad, deep, investable markets. Market breadth promises an extensive array of choices. Market depth implies a substantial volume of offerings for individual positions. Market investability assures access by investors to investment opportunities. The basic building blocks for investor portfolios come from well-established, enduring marketplaces, not from trendy concoctions promoted by Wall Street financial engineers.

Core asset classes encompass stocks, bonds, and real estate. Asset classes that investors employ to drive portfolio returns include domestic equities, foreign developed market equities, and emerging market equities. Asset classes that investors use to create diversification include U.S. Treasury bonds, which promise protection from financial catastrophe, and U.S. Treasury Inflation-Protected Securities, which provide ironclad assurance against inflation-induced asset erosion. Finally, asset-class exposure to equity real estate produces a hybrid of equity-like and bond-like attributes, generating inflation protection at a lower opportunity cost than other alternatives. Core asset classes provide the tools required by investors to create a well-diversified portfolio tailored to fit investor-specific requirements.

Descriptions of the core asset classes help investors understand the role that various investment vehicles play in a portfolio context. By assessing an asset class's expected returns and risks, likely response to inflation, and anticipated interaction with other asset classes, investors develop the knowledge required for investment success. A description of issues surrounding alignment of interests between issuers of securities and owners of securities illustrates the potential pitfalls and possible benefits of participating in certain asset categories.

Core asset classes provide a range of investment vehicles sufficient to construct a well-diversified, cost-effective portfolio. By combining the basic building blocks in a sensible manner, investors create portfolios likely to meet broad investments objectives.

DOMESTIC EQUITY

Investment in domestic equities represents ownership of a piece of corporate America. Holdings of U.S. stocks constitute the core of most institutional and individual portfolios, causing Wall Street's ups and downs to drive investment results for many investors. While a large number of market participants rely far too heavily on marketable equities, U.S. stocks deserve a prominent position in investment portfolios.

Domestic stocks play a central role in investment portfolios for good theoretical and practical reasons. The expected return characteristics of equity instruments match nicely the needs of investors to generate substantial portfolio growth over a number of years. To the extent that history provides a guide, the long-term returns for stocks encourage investors to own stocks. Jeremy Siegel's two hundred years of data show U.S. stocks earning 8.3 percent per annum, while Roger Ibbotson's seventy-eight years of data show stocks earning 10.4 percent per annum. No other asset class possesses such an impressive record of long-term performance.

The long-term historical success of equity-dominated portfolios matches the expectations formed from fundamental financial principles. Equity investments promise higher returns than bond investments, although the prospect of higher returns sometimes remains unfulfilled. Not surprisingly, the historical record of generally strong equity market returns contains several extended periods that remind investors of the downside of equity ownership. In the corporate capital structure, equity represents a residual interest that possesses value only after accounting for all other claims against the company. The higher risk of equity positions leads rational investors to demand higher expected returns.

Stocks exhibit a number of attractive characteristics that stimulate investor interest. The interests of shareholders and corporate managements tend to be aligned, allowing outside owners of shares some measure of comfort that corporate actions will benefit both shareholders and management. Stocks generally provide protection against unexpected increases in inflation, although the protection proves notoriously unreliable in the short run. Finally, stocks trade in broad, deep, liquid markets, affording investors access to an impressive range of opportunities. Equity investments deserve a thorough discussion, since in many respects they represent the standard against which market observers evaluate all other investment alternatives.

Equity Risk Premium

The equity risk premium, defined as the incremental return to equity holders for accepting risk above the level inherent in bond investments, represents one of the investment world's most critically important variables. Like all forward-looking metrics, the expected risk premium stands shrouded in the uncertainties of the future. To obtain clues about what tomorrow may have in store, thoughtful investors examine the characteristics of the past.

Yale School of Management professor Roger Ibbotson produces a widely used set of capital market statistics that reflect a seventy-eight-year stock-and-bond return differential of 5.0 percent per annum.[1] Wharton professor Jeremy Siegel's two hundred years of data show a risk premium of 3.4 percent per annum.[2] Regardless of the precise number, historical risk premiums indicate that equity owners enjoyed a substantial return advantage over bondholders.*

The size of the risk premium proves critically important in the asset-allocation decision. While history provides a guide, careful investors interpret past results with care. Work on survivorship bias by Phillipe Jorion and William Goetzmann demonstrates the unusual nature of the U.S. equity market experience. The authors examine the experience of thirty-nine markets over a seventy-five-year period, noting that "major disruptions have afflicted nearly all of the markets in our sample, with the exception of a few such as the United States."[3]

The more or less uninterrupted operation of the U.S. stock market in the nineteenth and twentieth centuries contributed to superior results. Jorion and Goetzmann find that the U.S. market produced 4.3 percent annualized real capital appreciation from 1921 to 1996. In contrast, the other countries, many of which experienced economic and military trauma, posted a median real appreciation of only 0.8 percent per year. Thoughtful market observers place the exceptional

---

*See pages 15–17 for Ibbotson's and Siegel's stock and bond return data.

experience of the U.S. equity markets in a broader, less compelling context.

Even if investors accept the U.S. market history as definitive, reasons exist to doubt the value of the past as a guide to the future. Consider stock market performance over the past two hundred years. The returns consist of a combination of dividends, inflation, real growth in dividends, and rising valuation levels. According to an April 2003 study by Robert Arnott, aptly titled "Dividends and the Three Dwarfs," dividends provide the greatest portion of long-term equity returns. Of the Arnott study's two-hundred-year 7.9 percent annualized total return from equities, fully 5.0 percentage points come from dividends. Inflation accounts for 1.4 percentage points, real dividend growth accounts for 0.8 percentage points, and rising valuation accounts for 0.6 percentage points. Arnott points out that the overwhelming importance of dividends to historical returns "is wildly at odds with conventional wisdom, which suggests that . . . stocks provide growth first and income second."[4]

Arnott uses his historical observations to draw some inferences for the future. He concludes, with dividend yields below 2.0 percent (in April 2003), that unless real growth in dividends accelerates or equity market valuations rise, investors face a future far different and far less remunerative than the past. Noting that real dividends showed no growth from 1965 to 2002, Arnott holds out little hope of dividend increases driving future equity returns. The alternative of relying on increases in valuations assigned to corporate earnings for future equity market growth serves as a thin reed upon which to build a portfolio.

Simple extrapolation of past returns into the future assumes implicitly that past valuation changes will persist in the future. In the specific case of the U.S. stock market, expectations that history provides a guide to the future suggest that dividends will grow at unprecedented rates or that ever-higher valuations will be assigned to corporate earnings. Investors relying on such forecasts depend not only on the fundamental earning power of corporations, but also on the stock market's continued willingness to increase the price paid for corporate profits.

As illogical as it seems, one popular bull market tome published in 1999 espoused the view that equity valuation would continue to increase unabated, arguing for a zero equity risk premium. Advancing the notion that over long periods of time equities always outperform bonds, in *Dow 36,000: The New Strategy for Profiting from the Coming Rise in the Stock Market,* James Glassman and Kevin Hassett conclude that equities exhibit no more risk than bonds.[5] The authors ignore the intrinsic differences between stocks and bonds that clearly point to greater risk in stocks. The authors fail to consider experiences outside of the United States where equity markets have on occasion disappeared, leading to questions about the inevitability of superior results from long-term equity investment. Perhaps most important, the authors overestimate the number of investors that operate with twenty- or thirty-year time horizons and underestimate the number of investors that fail to stay the course when equity markets falter.

Finance theory and capital markets history provide analytical and practical underpinnings for the notion of a risk premium. Without expectations of superior returns for risky assets, the financial world would be turned on its head. In the absence of higher expected returns for fundamentally riskier stocks, market participants would shun equities. For example, in a world where bonds and stocks share identical expected returns, rational investors would opt for the equal-expected-return, lower-risk bonds. No investor would hold equal-expected-return, higher-risk stocks. The risk premium must exist for capital markets to function effectively.

While an expected risk premium proves necessary for well-functioning markets, Jorion and Goetzmann highlight the influence of survivorship bias on perceptions of the magnitude of the risk premium. Arnott's deconstruction of equity returns and analysis of historical trends suggest a diminished prospective return advantage for stocks over bonds. Regardless of the future of the risk premium, sensible investors prepare for a future that differs from the past, with diversification representing the most powerful protection against errors in forecasts of expected asset-class attributes.

Stock Prices and Inflation

Stocks tend to provide long-term protection against generalized price inflation. A simple, yet elegant, means of understanding stock prices developed by Nobel laureate James Tobin compares the replacement cost of corporate assets to the market value of those assets. In equilibrium, Tobin argued, the ratio of replacement cost to market value, which he named "q," should equal one. If replacement cost exceeds market value, economic actors find it cheaper to buy assets on the stock exchange than in the real economy. Conversely, if market value exceeds replacement cost, economic actors generate profits by building companies and floating shares on the stock exchange. Clearly, in rational markets, the value of corporate assets on a stock exchange should equal the real-world replacement cost of those selfsame assets.

To the extent that general price inflation increases the replacement cost of corporate assets, that inflation should be reflected in increasing stock prices. If inflation did not result in higher equity prices, the newly inflated replacement cost of assets would exceed market value, allowing investors to purchase companies on the stock exchange at below intrinsic value. Until and unless stock prices reflect price inflation, publicly traded companies represent bargain basement merchandise.

In spite of the clear theoretical link between stock prices and inflation, the stock market presents a mixed record on incorporating inflation into equity prices. The 1970s provide a dramatic example of equity market failure to reflect rising price levels in stock prices. In 1973 and 1974, inflation eroded purchasing power by 37 percent and stock prices decreased by a total of 22 percent, hitting equity investors with a double whammy that caused losses of 51 percent in inflation-adjusted terms. Clearly, with stock prices decreasing and inflation increasing, stock prices failed to reflect price inflation in the short run.

Jeremy Siegel observes that stock prices "provide excellent long-run hedges against inflation" and weak short-term protection against rising prices.[6] Presumably, the positive long-term relationship between inflation and stock prices stems from rational behavior, as market participants weigh the costs of acquiring assets in the real economy against the costs of acquiring similar assets on the financial exchanges. Possibly, the negative short-term relationship between inflation and stock prices results from irrational behavior, as investors respond to unanticipated inflation by increasing the discount rate applied to future cash flows, without adjusting those future flows for the increase in inflation. While capital markets history supports Siegel's observation, the difference in short-run and long-run responses by equity prices to inflation creates a paradox. Because the long run consists of a series of short runs, no theory explains both the poor short-term record and the strong long-term record of stock price protection against price increases. In any event, investors seeking shelter from inflation need to look beyond holdings of marketable equities.

Alignment of Interests

Stocks exhibit a number of characteristics that tend to serve investor goals. The general alignment of interests between corporate managers and shareholders bodes well for stock investors. In most instances, company executives benefit from enhancing shareholder value, serving the financial aspirations of management and investor alike. For example, corporate managers often share in gains associated with greater corporate profitability, indirectly through increased compensation and directly through increased values for personal shareholdings.

Unfortunately, the separation of ownership (by shareholders) and control (by management) in publicly traded companies introduces agency problems that occur when managements (the agents) benefit at shareholders' (the principals') expense. The most common wedge between interests of shareholders and management stems from compensation arrangements for management. High levels of salary and benefits accrue to management regardless of the level of underlying company achievement. Because larger companies tend to provide larger compensation packages than smaller enterprises, corporate managers may pursue corporate growth simply to achieve higher levels of personal earnings regardless of the impact of corporate size on enterprise profitability.

Management may divert funds to purposes that satisfy personal preferences at the expense of corporate performance. Company art collections, business jets, lavish offices, and corporate apartments frequently confer benefits on senior managers at the expense of legitimate company goals. Investors cringe upon reading stories regarding WorldCom chief executive Bernard Ebbers's receipt of more than $400 million of personal loans from the company and Tyco chief executive Dennis Kozlowski's alleged diversion of $600 million of company assets for personal purposes, including the purchase of a $6,000 shower curtain. Outsized financial and nonfinancial rewards for management, whether legitimate or otherwise, come directly from the pockets of company shareholders.

Yet the most troubling scandal lies not with the chief executives who have faced indictments, but with those who feathered their beds while following the rules. Former General Electric chief executive Jack Welch brought shame on himself and his company with a retirement package filled with personal perquisites. Beginning with lifetime use of a $15 million apartment bought by General Electric, the list includes access to the company's Boeing 737 jets, corporate helicopters, and a car and driver for him and his wife. No doubt worried that the hundreds of millions of dollars paid to Mr. Welch during his tenure at General Electric proved inadequate to support his retirement, the company provided "wine, flowers, cook, housekeeper and other amenities," including "tickets at top sporting events and the opera," to cater to the former chief executive's needs.[7] Even the reliably business-friendly editorial pages of the *Wall Street Journal* characterized Mr. Welch's retirement package "the playthings of corporate opulence."[8]

The compensation excess exemplified by Ebbers, Kozlowski, and Welch represents the tip of the iceberg. The deeper problem, as described by William McDonough, president of the Federal Reserve Bank of New York, in a September 2002 speech, is that rapid increases in chief executive compensation in the past two decades represent "terribly bad social policy and perhaps even bad morals." McDonough suggested that corporate boards "should simply reach the conclusion that corporate pay is excessive and adjust it to more reasonable and justifiable levels."[9]

The all too frequent breakdown in alignment of interests between shareholders and management highlights the risks involved in individual security selection, arguing for broadly based, diversified approaches to portfolio management. By holding portfolios with relatively few securities, casual investors face the risk of owning the few bad apples that taint the character of the entire barrel. In the context of the all-inclusive market portfolio, the good overwhelms the bad, allowing investors to obtain the expected benefits from equity market exposure.

Corporate Philanthropy

Corporate philanthropic contributions frequently fall in the gray area between actions driven to satisfy the personal desires of senior corporate executives and decisions made to support the legitimate business objectives of corporations. Conclusions regarding corporate giving suffer from lack of information, because disclosure of businesses' support of charities depends on the whims of the donors and the recipients.

Citibank, "one of the few companies that does disclose its philanthropic contributions in detail" according to the *New York Times,* provides a case study of the relationship between the chief executive's wishes and the company's actions.[10] Sanford "Sandy" Weill, the hard-charging leader of Citigroup, and his wife Joan cut high-profile figures in philanthropic circles. Known as generous donors to Cornell University, Carnegie Hall, and Alvin Ailey American Dance Theater, the Weills open their checkbooks and take out their pens. Cornell University boasts a Joan and Sanford I. Weill Medical College (where Sandy Weill serves as chairman), a Joan and Sanford I. Weill Cornell Medical College in Qatar, and a Joan and Sanford I. Weill Graduate School of Medical Sciences. Sandy Weill played a major role in the rehabilitation of one of Carnegie Hall's main performance venues, now named the Weill Recital Hall. Joan Weill, who serves as chair of the board of directors of Alvin Ailey, gave $15 million for the dance troupe's building, named the Joan Weill Center for Dance. By any standards, the Weills' philanthropy impresses.

Citigroup's corporate contributions dovetail perfectly with the Weills' philanthropic interests. According to the *New York Times,* from 1998 to 2001 "the biggest contributions made by Citigroup over the last four years were to the three institutions most identified with the Weills: Cornell, Carnegie Hall and Alvin Ailey." The *Times* noted that the Citigroup Foundation, chaired by Sandy Weill, also provided millions of dollars of support to each of the Weills' favored charities.[11]

While Citigroup's corporate support of the Weill's philanthropic interests raises a difficult-to-answer question about personal gain versus corporate responsibility, Citigroup's corporate gift to a nursery school run by the 92nd Street Y prompts no such difficult questions. Sandy Weill brazenly deployed Citigroup's assets to provide difficult-to-justify favors to an employee.

In 1999, Sandy Weill wanted Jack Grubman, a research analyst at Citigroup's Salomon Smith Barney subsidiary, to take a "fresh look" at his "hold" rating on AT&T stock. A more enthusiastic assessment of AT&T by Grubman would increase the likelihood of garnering investment banking business from AT&T and might improve the probability of enlisting AT&T chief executive and Citigroup board member Michael Armstrong's support in Weill's boardroom power struggle with Citigroup co-chief executive John Reed. Although throughout his years as a securities analyst Jack Grubman's assessment of AT&T consistently lacked enthusiasm, he saw an opportunity to trade a rating upgrade for help with his twins' education. In a memo to Sandy Weill entitled "AT&T and the 92nd Street Y," Grubman complained about the nursery school admissions process, famously noting that "it's statistically easier to get into the Harvard freshman class than it is to get into preschool at the 92nd Street Y." Sandy Weill responded, calling the school on behalf of Grubman's children and causing Citigroup to make a $1 million gift to the 92nd Street Y.[12] The Grubman twins gained admission to nursery school. AT&T received a research rating upgrade. Investors paid the price.

Stock Options

In the use of stock options to reward corporate management, another subtle disconnect arises between the interests of management and shareholders. Options-based compensation schemes work effectively when company share prices increase, as both management and shareholders gain. The alignment of interests breaks down when share prices decrease, as management loses only the opportunity to benefit from stock prices increases. In fact, management frequently fails to suffer at all, as corporate boards often reset option prices to reflect the newly diminished stock price. In sharp contrast to management's loss of a mere opportunity, when share prices decrease, shareholders lose cold, hard cash. Options-based compensation schemes represent a no-lose game for management of publicly traded companies.

Microsoft provides a textbook example of using option grants to insulate employees from share price declines. In April 2000, chief executive Steve Ballmer faced a problem of low morale among employees concerned about the consequences of the Justice Department's antitrust activity and a four-month, 44 percent stock price decline. To boost spirits, Ballmer awarded more than 34,000 Microsoft employees stock options priced at the then current stock price. The chief executive wrote in an email to employees that "we know stock options are an important part of our compensation." Even while asserting that preexisting options "will have value long run," Ballmer expressed his hope that "these new grants will let people see returns much sooner."[13] By setting the option strike price near the stock's fifty-two-week low, the company effectively insulated employees from the dramatic decline in Microsoft's shares. The company provided no such succor to shareholders.

In response to the all-too-numerous abuses of trust in the late 1990s, many corporations began to review options-based compensation. In a particularly notable move, in July 2003, Microsoft announced plans to eliminate its options program and substitute a program of restricted stock awards. Unlike the asymmetric option payoff, restricted stock produces a congruence of outcomes in which management and shareholders profit and suffer together. Ballmer remarked, "whether it's dividend policy or how much risk to take, it's always good to have the employees thinking as much like the shareholders as possible."[14] If substantial numbers of corporations follow Microsoft's lead, corporate management will likely better serve shareholder interests in the future.

In spite of a general alignment of interests between shareholders and company managers, too many abuses exist. Whether in the direct form of inflated salaries or the indirect form of unreasonable corporate perquisites, excessive executive compensation lines the pockets of corporate managers at the expense of shareholders. Sometimes, as in the case of options-based compensation, a subtle disconnect exists between management and shareholders. One sure way to reduce the conflict between the owners of shares and the managers of companies involves ownership of stock by corporate management. Savvy investors frequently seek companies with high levels of insider ownership.

Market Characteristics

At December 31, 2003, the U.S. stock market boasted assets in excess of $13.1 trillion, representing the largest liquid capital market in the world. More than 5,244 securities constituted the market, as defined by the (misnamed) Wilshire 5000. The enormous size of the U.S. stock market prompts many participants to divide the whole into any number of parts. Typical categories include size of market capitalization (small, medium, and large), character of security (growth or value), and nature of business (utility, technology, and health care, for example). In aggregate, the companies reported a dividend yield of 1.5 percent, a price-earnings ratio* of 25.5, and a price-book ratio† of 3.1.[15]

Summary

U.S. domestic equities represent the asset of choice for many long-term investors. Finance theory predicts and practical experience demonstrates that stocks provide superior returns over reasonably long holding periods. The general alignment of interests between shareholders and management tends to serve both the goals of outside owners of companies and the aspirations of inside managers. Holdings of equities provide protection against inflation in the intermediate and long run. Attractive characteristics of equity holdings argue for a significant role in most portfolios.

Yet investors must guard against relying on equities to exhibit their general characteristics in any specific time frame or allowing equities to account for too large a portion of the target portfolio. History may overstate the attractiveness of U.S. stocks. Returns of bonds and cash may exceed returns of stocks for years on end. For example, from the market peak in October 1929, it took stock investors fully twenty-one years and three months to match returns generated by bond investors.[16] Alignment of interests between shareholders and management breaks down with distressing frequency. Stock prices often fail to reflect underlying price inflation, at times for extended periods.

The best protection for investors against the shortcomings of equity investments lies in owning an all-inclusive, market-like portfolio of equity securities in the context of a well-diversified collection of as-

---

*A price-earnings ratio measures valuation by comparing a company's stock price per share to its earnings per share.
†A price-book ratio measures valuation by comparing a company's stock price per share to its book value (assets minus liabilities) per share.

set classes. Although equity markets do not always deliver handsome returns in a steady, stable, inflation-hedging fashion and corporate managements sometimes fail to serve shareholder interests, equity investments remain a central part of thoughtfully assembled, long-term-oriented investment portfolios.

U.S. TREASURY BONDS

Purchasers of U.S. Treasury bonds own a portion of the public debt of the United States government. Holdings of government bonds play a prominent role in fixed-income portfolios, reflecting the attractive investment characteristics of full-faith-and-credit obligations of the government and the significant volume of debt securities issued by the government.

Because U.S. Treasury bonds enjoy the full-faith-and-credit backing of the U.S. government, bondholders face no risk of default. Holders of government debt sleep secure in the knowledge that interest and principal payments will be made in a timely manner. Lack of default risk does not, however, liberate bondholders from exposure to price fluctuations. When interest rates rise, bond prices fall, as purchasers of existing assets need an adjustment to reflect the now-higher rates available on newly issued debt. When interest rates fall, bonds prices rise, as sellers of existing assets require greater compensation for their now-more-attractive fixed stream of future payments. Of all risky investments, investors expect the lowest returns from U.S. Treasury bonds, due to the high degree of security intrinsic in obligations of the U.S. government.

Interest Rate Risk

Bonds confuse investors. The inverse relationship between interest rates and bond prices (rates up, prices down, and vice versa) proves central to understanding the role of fixed income in an investment portfolio. Yet, investor surveys show that a large majority of individual investors fail to grasp even the most basic elements of bond math. Even highly respected market observers sometimes get it wrong. An article in the *New York Times* business section ironically entitled "Better Understanding of Bonds" asserted that "duration* and bond prices move in lockstep with interest rates. A bond with a duration of seven years would gain 7 percent of its price when interest rates moved up one percentage point. The same bond would lose 7 percent when rates moved down that amount."[17] Of course, the *Times* described the relationship between prices and yields in perfectly perverse prose. Increases in interest rates cause price declines, not price increases. If a highly regarded, financially sophisticated *New York Times* business reporter cannot get it right, what chance does an ordinary investor have?

In the realm of U.S. Treasury bond investing, risk relates primarily to time horizon. An investor with a six-month time horizon finds six-month Treasury bills riskless, as no doubt exists about the timely payment of the face value of the bill at maturity. That same six-month-time-horizon investor finds ten-year Treasury notes quite risky. As interest rates change, the value of the note might vary materially, even over a six-month holding period. An increase in rates leaves the investor with a loss, while a decline in rates provides the investor with an unexpected windfall.

Similarly, an investor with a ten-year time horizon faces significant risk with six-month Treasury bill investments. The six-month bills must be rolled over nineteen times to generate a ten-year holding period return. At the outset, the investor knows the rate only on the first six-month bill. The nineteen future rollover rates hold considerable uncertainty for the investor. Unless investors match holding period with maturity, price and rate changes may cause portfolio values to diverge from expected levels.

Diversifying Power

U.S. Treasury bonds provide a unique form of diversification for investor portfolios, protecting against financial crisis and economic distress. In the stock market collapse of October 1987, when the U.S. stock market plummeted more than 20 percent in a single day, investors sought the safe haven of U.S. Treasury obligations. Even as

---

*Duration measures the price sensitivity of a bond to interest rates. Duration provides a better measure of a bond's life than maturity, because duration incorporates a bond's coupon payments and adjusts for the timing of cash flows.

stock prices fell off a cliff, Treasury bonds staged an impressive rally. Similarly, in the economic distress surrounding the confluence of the 1998 Asian, Russian, and American capital markets crises, investors engaged in a "flight to quality," favoring the security of U.S. Treasury obligations. In times of crisis, government bonds provide the greatest degree of protection to investor portfolios.

The protection to portfolio values provided by government bonds comes at a high price. Expected returns for fixed-income instruments fall short of expected returns for equity-oriented investments. Some investors attempt to mitigate the opportunity costs of owning government bonds by holding higher-yielding corporate paper. Unfortunately, non-governmental bonds exhibit characteristics such as credit risk, illiquidity, and optionality that reduce effectiveness as a hedge against financial distress. The purity of noncallable, long-term, default-free Treasury bonds provides the most powerful diversification to investor portfolios.

At December 31, 2003, roughly 34 percent of U.S. government bond issues represented debt issued by non-Treasury entities, including a number of Government Sponsored Enterprises (GSEs). (The three largest non-Treasury obligors include: the Government National Mortgage Association, known as "Ginnie Mae," which enjoys the full faith and credit backing of the U.S. Treasury; the Federal National Mortgage Corporation, known as "Freddie Mac," which does not enjoy full faith and credit backing; and the Federal National Mortgage Association, known as "Fannie Mae," which also does not enjoy full faith and credit backing.) Many market participants treat debt issued by GSEs as close substitutes for U.S. Treasury obligations. In fact, many GSEs operate in a nether land between the certainty of government guarantees and the uncertainty of corporate promises to pay. While chances of default by GSEs seem quite low to most market observers, many GSE obligations contain options that may disadvantage bondholders.

Investors seeking the purity of U.S. Treasury debt face a surprisingly daunting task. Many government bond mutual funds hold large quantities of GSE debt, as fund managers pursue the time-honored investment practice of hoping to get something for nothing in the form of incremental yield on GSE paper (the something) without exposing the portfolio to additional risk (the nothing). The twin possibilities of credit deterioration of the GSEs and exercise of options by the GSEs carry the potential to harm bondholder interests. Investors seeking pure fixed-income exposure avoid GSE debt and opt for U.S. Treasury bonds, the full-faith-and-credit obligations of the U.S. government.

Bond Prices and Inflation

To add a further measure of complexity to the world of bond invest-ing, investors in traditional U.S. Treasury bonds deal with information only on nominal returns. In some instances, investors care primarily about nominal returns. For example, if a debtor desires to pay off a fixed obligation, the debtor requires only the amount of the debt, noth-ing more and nothing less. Nominally denominated investments, like Treasury bonds, match nominal liabilities nicely. If, on the other hand, a retiree hopes to maintain a certain standard of living, the retiree needs funds sufficient to keep pace with changes induced by inflation. Inflation-sensitive investments, unlike Treasury bonds, fulfill infla-tion-sensitive requirements. For holders of traditional Treasury debt securities, changes in inflation rates influence after-inflation returns in unpredictable ways, leading to potential variation between antici-pated and actual outcomes.

Investors price fixed-income instruments to generate positive in-flation-adjusted rates of return. When the inflation rates experienced by investors more or less match the expectations formed at the begin-ning of the holding period, bondholders receive the anticipated after-inflation return. When inflation rates exceed expectations, the unanticipated inflation erodes the purchasing power of the promised stream of fixed payments, causing investors to receive disappointing after-inflation returns. When inflation rates fall short of expectations, the lower rate of general price inflation provides investors with a pur-chasing power boost. Deviations between inflationary expectations and actual experience contain the potential to cause powerful changes in real returns for fixed-income investors.

When inflationary expectations fail to match actual experience, bonds tend to behave differently from other financial assets. Unantici-pated inflation crushes bonds, while ultimately benefiting equities. Unanticipated deflation boosts bonds, while undermining stocks. Bonds provide the greatest diversification relative to equities in cases where actual inflation differs dramatically from expected levels.

Alignment of Interests

The interests of Treasury bond investors and the U.S. government prove to be better aligned than the interests of corporate bond investors and corporate issuers. The government sees little reason to disfavor bondholders. In essence, action taken to reduce the value of government bonds represents a transfer from bondholders to non-bondholders. In fact, if all debt were held domestically, advantages or disadvantages accruing to the government from changes in bond values would balance equal and offsetting disadvantages or advantages accruing to bondholders, leading to transfer from one group of citizens (taxpayers or bondholders) to another group of citizens (bondholders or taxpayers). Moreover, were the government to disadvantage bond investors, future access to credit markets might be impaired. Worry over misalignment of interests causes little lost sleep for owners of Treasury bonds.

Investors in Treasury bonds generally perceive the government as a neutral player in the debt management process. Unlike corporate debtholders that sit squarely across the table from the issuers of corporate obligations, government bondholders expect fair treatment. Consider the fact that from 1975 to 1984, the U.S. Treasury offered a dozen issues of thirty-year bonds that contained call provisions for the final five years of the issues' life. A call provision allows the debt issuer to redeem a debt issue at a fixed price. Economically motivated issuers exercise call provisions only when the fixed-call price stands below the value of the bond calculated in absence of a call provision. Exercise of a call provision eliminates the high-coupon debt, benefiting the issuer and hurting the investor.

Because of the special nature of the government's role in debt markets, bond market participants debated whether the government would employ the call option only for debt management purposes or only for economic refundings. If the government used the call option only for debt management, then bondholders faced an idiosyncratic risk as likely to provide a benefit as a cost. If the government used the call option only for economic refundings, then bondholders faced a risk of economic loss.

Government bondholders received the answer to the question of how the Treasury would behave on January 14, 2000, when the Treasury "announced the call for redemption at par on May 15, 2000 of the 8-1/4% Treasury Bonds of 2000–05."[18] The government responded to economic incentives, calling high-interest debt to reduce financing charges.

In later refundings, the U.S. Treasury explicitly cited an economic motivation for calling bonds. In the unimaginatively titled January 15, 2004 *Public Debt News* release, "Treasury Calls 9-1/8 Percent Bonds of 2004–09," the government noted that "these bonds are being called to reduce the cost of debt financing. The 9.125 percent interest rate is significantly above the current cost of securing financing for the five years remaining to their maturity. In current market conditions, Treasury estimates that interest savings from the call and refinancing will be about $544 million."[19] In other words, the ability to refinance the 9-percent-plus-coupon bonds at an interest cost of between 3 percent and 4 percent resulted in substantial interest savings for the government.

Even though the government acted in an economic fashion by exercising the call provision on the 9.125 Treasury bonds of 2004–09, the fact that investors debated whether the government would exercise the call provision to generate interest savings signifies the unusual relationship between the government and its creditors. In fact, the program of callable Treasury issuance lasted a mere ten years and involved a relatively small portion of overall government bond issuance. Moreover, the call provisions affected only the last five years of the thirty-year bond's life, in contrast to the much more aggressive call provisions typically included in issues of long-term corporate debt. Perhaps the U.S. Treasury stopped selling callable bonds to improve the character of securities offered to government bond market participants. In any event, of all debt issuers, the government promotes the greatest alignment of interests with its creditors.

Market Characteristics

At December 31, 2003, U.S. government bonds totaled $2.8 trillion, of which $1.8 trillion represented full-faith-and-credit obligations of the U.S. Treasury and $1.0 trillion represented debt of government sponsored enterprises. U.S. Treasury bonds trade in the deepest, most efficient market in the world.

The universe of Treasury bonds sported a yield to maturity* of 3.4 percent at year-end 2003 with an average maturity of 7.5 years and a duration of 5.2 years. Agency issues promised a yield of 3.4 percent with a 6.2-year average maturity and 4.3-year duration.

Summary

U.S. Treasury bonds provide a unique form of portfolio diversification, serving as a hedge against financial accidents and unanticipated deflation. No other asset type comes close to matching the diversifying power created by long-term, noncallable, default-free, full-faith-and-credit obligations of the U.S. government.

Investors pay a price for the diversifying power of Treasury bonds. The ironclad security of Treasury debt causes investors to expect (and deserve) low returns relative to those expected from riskier assets. While holders of long-term Treasury bonds stand to benefit from declining price inflation, in an environment of unanticipated inflation Treasury bondholders lose. The Treasury bonds' modest expected returns and adverse reaction to inflation argue for modest allocations to the asset class by long-term investors.

INFLATION-LINKED BONDS

In January 1997, the U.S. Treasury began issuing Treasury Inflation-Indexed Securities, a.k.a. Treasury Inflation-Protected Securities (TIPS), creating an important new tool for U.S.-dollar-based investors. TIPS protect investors from increases in the general level of prices by adjusting the principal amount of the security for inflation. Since the fixed coupon rate on TIPS applies to the inflation-adjusted principal of the bonds, both interest and principal payments reflect changes in inflation rates.

At maturity, TIPS investors may receive a bonus, as the bonds pay the greater of the inflation-adjusted principal or the original face

---

*Yield to maturity represents the rate of return anticipated by holding a bond to its maturity date.

value. In a deflationary world, investors benefit from the payment of the nondiscounted par amount of the bonds. In an environment of general price inflation, the right to receive par for the TIPS at maturity carries the greatest value at the time of issuance. In concert with price increases, the indexed value of the bond's principal increases, creating a surplus over the par value of the bond. Were deflationary conditions to develop, the accumulated surplus would need to deplete before the par protection kicked in. Investors wishing to enjoy the maximum protection of the par "put" constantly roll holdings of TIPS into the most recently issued securities.

Just as standard U.S. Treasury bonds provide a riskless instrument for investors wishing to generate certain nominal returns, TIPS provide a riskless instrument for investors wishing to generate certain real returns. Based on commonality of issuer, default-free status, and structural similarities in payment of interest and principal, many market observers group standard U.S. Treasury bonds with TIPS. In fact, when the U.S. Treasury began issuing TIPS, Lehman Brothers, architect of the most widely used debt market indices, placed TIPS in a cohort that included regular-issue Treasury bonds.

The error of grouping regular Treasuries with TIPS lies in the fundamentally different response of the two types of bonds to unanticipated changes in the price level. Unanticipated inflation harms regular bonds by reducing the purchasing power of the fixed stream of payments. In contrast, unanticipated inflation flows through in the form of higher returns to holders of TIPS as payments adjust for increases in the price level. Unexpected deflation helps regular bonds by increasing the purchasing power of the fixed stream of payments. In contrast, unexpected deflation reduces the stream of periodic interest payments to holders of TIPS, even though deflation fails to reduce the final principal payment. TIPS, far from belonging with standard bonds, deserve a category of their own.

A comparison of a traditional U.S. Treasury bond and a TIPS illustrates critical differences in the two securities. Consider the U.S. Treasury 5.5 percent due February 15, 2008, and the U.S. Treasury Inflation-Indexed Security 3.625 percent due January 15, 2008. At year-end 2003, the straight bond and the inflation-protected bond boasted yields to maturity of 2.8 percent and 0.9 percent, respectively. Because the bonds share identical credit characteristics and nearly identical maturity dates, the difference in yields stems solely from differing payment characteristics. The 1.9 percent difference between the straight bond yield and the inflation-protected bond yield represents the market's best estimate of inflation over the bonds' term. If inflation exceeds 1.9 percent, the TIPS holder wins. If inflation falls short of 1.9 percent, the straight bond owner wins.

Some foreign governments issue inflation-protected securities. As with standard bond issues, U.S.-domiciled investors approach non–U.S. Treasury debt with caution. The United Kingdom, Canada, Australia, France, and Sweden boast substantial programs of inflation-indexed bond issuance. Because foreign government bonds generally make payments in the currency of the realm, U.S. investors face foreign exchange risk. The combination of future foreign inflation rates that will likely differ from U.S. inflation rates and an unknown future foreign exchange translation serve to render non–U.S. government inflation-indexed bonds useless as a hedge against U.S. inflation.

U.S. corporate issuance of inflation-protected securities poses a different set of issues. As is the case with straight corporate debt, inflation-indexed corporate securities generally suffer from credit risk, illiquidity, and unattractive call provisions. In addition, investors might consider the implications of holding corporate inflation-protected securities in a high-inflation environment. Just when the protection against price increases proves most valuable, the ability of a corporation to make good on its promises to pay might prove least likely.

TIPS Prices and Inflation

TIPS produce the perfect hedge against inflation, because the bond-payment mechanism dictates direct correspondence with changes in inflation rates. The combination of the default-free character of full-faith-and-credit obligations of the U.S. government and the mathematically certain protection against inflation provides investors with a powerful portfolio tool.

Alignment of Interests

TIPS share with standard-issue Treasury offerings a balance in alignment of interests between creditor and debtor. Unlike private borrow-lender relationships, in which the borrower seeks gains at the lender's expense, the government attempts to fashion a fair deal for citizens on both sides of the borrowing transaction.

In promoting TIPS, the Department of the Treasury highlights advantages to both the creditor and the debtor. From the creditor's perspective, TIPS "provide a distinctive contribution to any diversified portfolio." From the debtor's perspective, TIPS "allow Treasury to broaden its investor base and diversify its funding risks."[20] The even-handed approach to debtor and creditor separates the U.S. government from profit-seeking private-sector borrowers.

Market Characteristics

At December 31, 2003, outstanding issues of U.S. Treasury Inflation-Protected Securities amounted to only $201 billion. Introduced by the U.S. Treasury in January 1997, the program provides a valuable, diversifying alternative for investors. At year-end 2003, TIPS promised a nominal yield of 3.4 percent and a real (after inflation) yield of 1.7 percent with an average maturity of 11.7 years and a duration of 5.9 years.

Summary

Although TIPS amount to little more than 10 percent of the value of standard Treasury bonds, inflation-sensitive TIPS constitute a compelling addition to the tool set available to investors. Bolstered by the default-free, full-faith-and-credit backing of the U.S. government, TIPS serve as a benchmark against which to measure other inflation-sensitive investments.

FOREIGN DEVELOPED EQUITY

Investments in developed economy equity markets can be expected to provide the same returns as U.S. equity investments. Yet overseas investments exhibit two critical differentiating characteristics relative to domestic holdings. First, markets outside of the United States respond in different fashion to different economic forces, causing returns to behave differently from one region of the world to the next. Second, investment in non-U.S. markets exposes investors to foreign currency fluctuations, adding another variable to the investment equation.

Developed economy equity markets share similar levels of expected return. Comparability in economic infrastructure, commonality in drivers of economic performance, and secular liberalization in flows of labor, goods, and services across national boundaries combine to cause investors to expect similar long-run results from investments in developed equity markets. Although investor enthusiasm for individual countries waxes and wanes along with strong or weak recent market performance, over reasonably long periods of time, investors might expect the developed markets in North America, Europe, and Asia to produce roughly comparable returns.

In fact, in the thirty-four years since the 1970 inception of the Morgan Stanley Capital International (MSCI) Europe, Australasia, and Far East (EAFE) Index that tracks non-U.S. equity market performance, EAFE countries generated 10.0 percent per annum returns relative to 11.3 percent per annum returns for the U.S.-dominated S&P 500 Index. While the domestic and international results fall in the same neighborhood, the U.S. enjoys a visible margin of superiority. Because such market performance comparisons exhibit a high degree of sensitivity to beginning and ending dates, the most reasonable conclusion holds that historical evidence fails to counter the operating assumption of approximate equivalence between expected returns for domestic and international equities.

The lack of correlation between foreign markets and the U.S. market provides a valuable diversification opportunity for investors. Some observers speculate that the process of global economic integration has caused world equity markets to behave increasingly one like the other, leading to less prospective diversification. As evidence of increasing correlation between markets, diversification skeptics point to the behavior of equity markets in the Crash of 1987 and in the financial dislocations during the crisis of 1998. In both instances, stock markets worldwide exhibited similar, extraordinary declines. Yet market declines in 1987 and 1998 constituted short-term events in which market players expressed extreme preferences for liquidity and quality. After brief periods during which many developed equity markets moved in concert, individual country markets reverted to fluctuation in response to country-specific drivers of local market performance.

Consider the relative returns of equity markets in the United

States and Japan. In the 1980s, Japan dominated all other world stock markets, returning 28.4 percent per annum versus 16.5 percent per annum for other non-U.S. markets and 17.4 percent per annum for the U.S. equity markets. Near the end of the extraordinary bull run in Japanese stocks, Japan boasted the largest market capitalization in the world, surpassing even the massive U.S. market in size.

In the 1990s, Japan's fortunes reversed. During the last decade of the twentieth century, Japan's economy collapsed, contributing to a market decline of 0.9 percent per annum for the decade. In contrast, other non-U.S. markets returned 13.5 percent per annum and the United States market produced an astonishing 18.2 percent per annum. As Japan's stock market declined, the country lost its dominant equity market position, falling so far behind the United States that at one point Japan's equity market capitalization amounted to less than one-fifth of the U.S. market's capitalization. Clearly, investments in individual equity markets behave differently, generating returns that differ one from the other, thereby providing diversification to portfolio holdings.

Investors tend to seek diversification when the core portfolio asset disappoints, either in absolute or in relative terms. For instance, in January 1993, after an extended period of poor relative foreign equity market performance, foreign market exposure accounted for only 5 percent of the aggregate of mutual-fund equity holdings. In 1993 and 1994 foreign developed stock markets reversed the trend, outpacing the U.S. market by an aggregate of 29 percent. Mutual-fund investors, attracted by strong relative performance in October 1994, boosted foreign holdings to an all-time high of 14 percent of equities, more than tripling the allocation in less than two years. As might be expected from performance-chasing activity, the timing of the diversification move proved costly. For four successive years, domestic markets again outperformed foreign markets, with foreign investors dropping an aggregate of 84 percentage points of performance relative to domestic investors. As of January 1999, holders of mutual funds, far less enamored of the now-lagging overseas markets, reduced foreign equity positions by more than 40 percent, leaving foreign mutual-fund exposure at 8 percent of equity investments.[21]

Strong relative performance of foreign equities caused mutual-fund owners to dramatically increase non-U.S. equity holdings, with investors frequently citing diversification as the rationale for boosting foreign allocations. Disappointing performance from the diversifying asset caused investors to reduce allocations at an inopportune time. Sensible investors pursue diversification as a policy to reduce risk, not as a tactic to chase performance. By following a disciplined policy of maintaining a well-diversified set of portfolio exposures, regardless of market zigs and zags, investors establish the conditions for long-run success. In fact, when taking market conditions into account, investors increase the odds of success by diversifying into asset classes after they suffer poor performance. In any case, foreign equities provide an important tool for reducing portfolio risk without sacrificing expected returns.

Investors in foreign equities assume foreign exchange risk as an unavoidable part of overseas equity exposure. Realistic investors expect foreign currency translation to neither add to nor subtract from investment results. Even though much ink spills and many trees fall as market prognosticators fill reams of pages in attempts to divine the future of foreign exchange rates, no one really knows where currencies will go. Sensible investors avoid speculating on currencies.

Some observers suggest that holders of foreign equities should routinely hedge foreign exchange exposure. Unfortunately, hedges prove difficult to fashion as foreign equity managers face uncertain holding periods and unknowable future position sizes, creating issues regarding the appropriate term and magnitude of the hedge. As a result, foreign equity investors necessarily assume at least some foreign exchange risk along with commitments to the asset class.

Fortunately, finance theorists conclude that some measure of foreign exchange exposure adds to portfolio diversification. Unless foreign currency positions constitute more than roughly one-quarter of portfolio assets, currency exposure serves to reduce overall portfolio risk. Beyond a quarter of portfolio assets, the currency exposure constitutes a source of unwanted risk.

Foreign Equity Prices and Inflation

Investors in domestic equities face an inflationary paradox: stocks appear to provide good long-term protection against inflation, while they seem to offer poor short-term correlation with price increases. Foreign stock investors encounter no such conundrum. The tenuous link between domestic inflation and dollar-denominated returns of foreign stocks renders foreign equities useless as a hedge against inflation.

Alignment of Interests

As a first approximation, alignment of interests between U.S. investors and foreign corporations resembles the alignment to the relationship between U.S. investors and U.S. corporations. Generally speaking, both domestically and overseas, equity investors expect corporate management to look after shareholder interests.

Even though the corporate scandals at Enron and WorldCom, among others, highlighted the shortcomings of American corporate governance, the fact remains that in the United States a strong coincidence of interest exists between shareholders and management. As a broad generalization, elsewhere in the world corporate managements focus less single-mindedly on profit generation. In some countries, cultural norms lead to greater concern for the needs of other stakeholders, including workers, lenders, and the broader community. In other countries, poor governance structures allow controlling shareholders to divert resources from minority shareholders. While a lesser coincidence of interests between overseas managements and their shareholders constitutes a disadvantage to owners of foreign shares, the advantages of increasing the investment opportunity set argue for inclusion of non-U.S. securities in individual investor portfolios.

Market Characteristics

At December 31, 2003, developed foreign markets totaled $13.9 trillion, as measured by Morgan Stanley Capital International. The sum of the twenty-two countries included by MSCI in the non-U.S. developed world roughly matched the market capitalization of the U.S. market, which stood at $13.1 trillion as of year-end 2003. In spite of more than a decade of miserable returns, Japan led the non-U.S. world with $3.2 trillion in assets. Other large markets include the United Kingdom ($2.4 trillion), France ($1.4 trillion), and Germany ($1.1 trillion). Europe accounted for 62 percent of the non-U.S. world, Asia for 27 percent, Canada for 6 percent and Australia/New Zealand for 4 percent.

Overall, foreign developed equity markets sported a dividend yield of 2.4 percent, a price-earnings ratio of 23.5, and a price-book ratio of 2.0. Regional variations matter. Europe yielded 2.8 percent at year-end 2003 relative to 1.0 percent for Japan, while European securities posted a price-earnings ratio of 20.3 and a price-book ratio of 2.1 relative to respective ratios of 66.0 and 1.7 for Japan.

Summary

Since expected returns from non-U.S. markets roughly approximate expected returns from U.S. markets, investors establish positions in foreign developed equity markets primarily to provide portfolio diversification. The most important source of diversification stems from the fact that forces driving returns in equity markets outside of the United States differ from forces driving returns in the United States. Foreign currency exposure adds a further measure of diversification to investor portfolios.

Sensible investors invest in foreign equity markets through thick and thin, regardless of recent past performance. All too often, market players seek the "diversification" promised by foreign stocks following a period of strong relative foreign market returns. When the "diversifying" strategies fail to produce returns superior to domestic market results, investors abandon the disappointing "diversifying" assets. Performance-chasing players use international equities to whipsaw portfolios, locking in losses and damaging returns.

EMERGING MARKETS EQUITY

Investing in emerging markets represents a high-risk, high-expected-return segment of the marketable equities universe. Defined as a group of countries with economies in an intermediate stage of development, neither undeveloped nor developed, emerging markets present a formidable array of fundamental risks for investors. On a macro level, investors concern themselves with the development of the overall economy and the securities markets' infrastructure. On a micro level, investors worry about quality of management and profit orientation of nascent enterprises.

Economic history contains many examples of emerging markets that became submerged. In an article dramatically entitled "Survival," Stephen Brown, William Goetzmann, and Stephen Ross identify thirty-six stock exchanges operating at the beginning of the twentieth century. Of the thirty-six, "more than half suffered at least one major hiatus in trading . . . usually due to nationalizations or war." More distressingly to investors who believe in the inevitability of progress, of the thirty-six markets that operated in 1900, fully fifteen remain classified as emerging markets more than 100 years later. One market, located in Serbia's Belgrade, fails even to make the twenty-first-century list of emerging markets. The authors dryly note that "in fact, the very term 'emerging markets' admits the possibility that these markets might fail."[22]

In recent years, investors enjoyed the opportunity to invest in an ever-expanding set of developing markets. Morgan Stanley Capital International, the leading constructor of non-U.S. market indices, began tracking emerging markets in 1988 with an index of eight countries ranging from Mexico to Jordan to Thailand. Five years later, the population exploded to nineteen with notable additions including India, Korea, and Portugal. By 1998, the total reached twenty-eight as South Africa, Russia, and a number of central European countries joined MSCI's coverage universe.

On occasion, countries move out of the emerging world to the developed world. In 1997, Portugal made the leap, as did Greece in 2001. As emerging economies make progress, more countries will advance to the ranks of the developed world.

Market observers frequently confuse strong economic growth with strong equity market prospects. Consider the extreme case of a command economy with resource allocation rules that operate without the benefit of securities markets. Clearly, economic growth occurs without any impact on stock prices, as equity securities do not exist. In the less extreme case of market-oriented economies with poor resource allocation, providers of equity capital might receive consistently poor returns. Corporate revenues may accrue disproportionately to corporate management (through salaries) or government entities (through taxes), leaving inadequate recompense for capital. Ownership of public securities in China's hugely inefficient state-owned enterprises provide a case in point. In well-functioning economies, prices and returns adjust to reflect financial market conditions. Not all emerging market economies function well. Profitable equity market investments require profitable enterprises, for investors ultimately share in corporate earnings. Therein lies the primary microeconomic risk for emerging market investors. In emerging markets, as elsewhere, economic growth may not translate into stock market success.

Development of market infrastructure in emerging economies proceeds in fits and starts as legislators, regulators, and corporate managements begin to learn the rules of the game. Investors accustomed to the protections afforded in the United States find most emerging markets quite inhospitable. Quality of securities legislation ranges from poor to good, enforcement of regulations varies from inadequate to adequate, and fidelity of managements to shareholders interests falls all over the lot. *Caveat emptor.*

Government policies sometimes interfere with investor interests, occasionally in dramatic fashion. In 1998, during the Asian crisis, Malaysia restricted the convertibility of the ringgit, effectively prohibiting foreign investors from repatriating funds. Because of bad behavior regarding capital controls, MSCI removed Malaysia from one of the firm's emerging-market indices. Not until Malaysia removed capital controls in late 1999 did the country reestablish its credentials as a full-fledged member of the MSCI world.

In emerging markets corporate actions resemble, at times, the Wild West. One market observer suggested that equity investors put money in Russian enterprises where management attempts grand theft and avoid commitments to companies where management engages in petty larceny. The rationale for the superficially contradictory advice lay in the notion that managements that saw value in their enterprises attempted to steal the entire entity, while managements that saw little value in their enterprises simply sought to pilfer small pieces.

Alignment of Interests

The inferior alignment of interests facing investors in emerging markets represents one of the critical risk factors that cause investors to demand higher rates of return for emerging-markets equity investments. Since investors operate in an environment with less-evolved frameworks for the definition and resolution of legal and regulatory issues, the resulting uncertainty forces sensible investors to seek premium returns.

Governments of emerging markets occasionally drive wedges between the interests of shareholders and managements. Controls on the ownership and voting rights of local shares sometimes lead to the creation of two classes of share owners, with attendant problems for the second-class foreign investor. Capital controls, although infrequently imposed, interfere with the ability of foreign investors to transfer funds freely. Government regulation in the emerging markets contains the potential to harm the interests of foreign investors.

In other instances, corporate managements fail to act in shareholder interests. A particularly prevalent problem in many Asian countries involves family-controlled companies satisfying family desires at the expense of external minority-shareholder wishes. An absence of transparency compounds the problem as outside investors often lack the information required to identify and address insider-dealing issues.

As emerging markets mature and as global capital markets liberalize, structural problems with misalignment of interests become less severe. Nonetheless, rational investors require a substantial return premium to expose assets to companies that operate in the less-than-ideal legal and regulatory framework of emerging markets.

Market Characteristics

At December 31, 2003, equities in emerging markets totaled $2.8 trillion according to MSCI. Ranging from Taiwan ($364 billion) and Korea ($294 billion), which by market capitalization would rank in the middle of the developed market cohort, to the much smaller markets of Venezuela ($4 billion) and Sri Lanka ($3 billion), the emerging markets universe encompasses a broad range of countries. Asia accounts for 54 percent of emerging market equity assets, Latin America for 19 percent, Africa and the Middle East for 18 percent, and Europe for 9 percent.

Emerging market valuations trumped those of the United States at year-end 2003 (at least for investors seeking value). Dividend yields amounted to 2.3 percent relative to 1.5 percent for the U.S. Price-earnings ratios stood at 15.0 and price-book ratios at 1.9, representing substantial discounts to U.S. market levels.

Summary

Investors in emerging markets equities require substantial expected returns to compensate for the high level of fundamental investment risk. During the period for which good data exist, investors received scant compensation for risks incurred. From 1985, when the World Bank's International Finance Corporation began measuring emerging markets equity returns, to December 2003, emerging markets equities produced 9.8 percent per annum returns (as measured by the IFC Global Composite) relative to 13.3 percent for the S&P 500 and 11.0 percent for EAFE. The deficit relative to developed market returns indicates that emerging market investors accepted higher fundamental risks than developed market investors without earning excess returns. Investors in emerging markets hope the future treats them better than the past.

Because of macroeconomic and microeconomic concerns, emerging markets equities promise high expected returns with commensurately high levels of risk. A modest allocation to emerging markets stocks contains the potential to enhance the risk and return characteristics of most investment portfolios.

REAL ESTATE

Investments in real estate expose investors to the benefits and risks of owning commercial office properties, apartment complexes, industrial warehouse facilities, and retail establishments. High-quality real estate holdings produce significant levels of current cash flow generated by long-term, in-place lease arrangements with tenants. Sustained levels of high cash flow lead to stability in valuation, as a substantial portion of asset value stems from relatively predictable cash flows. In contrast, as leases approach expiration, owners face releasing risk, causing investors to face near-term variability in residual value. In the extreme case of properties without tenants, real estate takes on a speculative aura, as valuation depends entirely on prospective leasing activity.

Real estate assets combine characteristics of fixed income and equity. Fixed-income attributes stem from the contractual obligation of tenants to make regular payments as specified in the lease contract between tenant and landlord. Properties encumbered by long-term lease obligations exhibit predominantly bond-like qualities. Equity attributes stem from the residual value associated with leases expected to be executed for currently vacant space or for anticipated future vacancies. Properties without tenants or with tenants on short leases exhibit predominantly equity-like qualities.

Archetypal real estate investments consist of well-located, well-leased, high-quality properties that allow investors to anticipate regular receipt of rental income from leased space and to expect income within a reasonable time frame from vacant space. Real estate with a significant operating component fails to meet the set of core investment criteria, as the operational attributes largely determine the investment outcome, creating an equity-like investment play. Investment in raw land, ground-up development activity, and hotel operations fall outside of the definition of core real estate, primarily because these investments rely substantially on operating expertise to produce cash flows.

Risk and Return Characteristics

Real estate returns and risks fall between those of bonds and equities. With bond-like rental streams and equity-like residual values, investors expect real estate to produce results somewhere between the results expected from the bond market and those from the stock market. Ibbotson Associates data for the past seventy-eight years indicate that stocks returned 10.4 percent annually and government bonds 5.4 percent. Splitting the difference suggests that real estate investors might realistically expect returns in the neighborhood of 2.5 percent per annum above bonds.

Shorter-term data on market returns confirm the notion that real estate sits between stocks and bonds in risk and return characteristics. Returns covering the quarter century from 1978 to 2003 for an index of marketable real estate securities stand at 12.0 percent per annum, poised between the 13.5 percent per annum return for the S&P 500 and the 8.7 percent per annum return for intermediate-term U.S. Treasury bonds.[23] Capital markets history confirms expectations regarding relative returns for real estate.

Valuation of real estate poses less of a challenge than does valuation of many other risky assets. Consider the fact that, with markets in equilibrium, replacement cost for existing assets constitutes an important determinant of market value. In fact, the real estate market provides a powerful example of the efficacy of Tobin's "q," the ratio between market value and replacement cost of an asset. If the market value of a particular real estate asset exceeds replacement cost, nearby real estate development of a similar product type makes economic sense. Clearly, under such circumstances, the income yield expressed as a percentage of cost of a newly constructed building would exceed the income yield on the more highly valued existing asset, creating incentives to build new, high-yielding buildings. Conversely, if replacement cost exceeds market value, real estate development makes no economic sense. In such a situation, the income yield on cost falls short of the income yield on less highly valued existing assets. Instead of building new buildings, rational market participants buy existing properties, thereby driving market values toward replacement cost.

Tobin's "q" proves particularly useful in the real estate market, because replacement cost constitutes a readily determinable, easily observable variable. While in the stock market Tobin's "q" produces insight into valuation of individual companies, broad market sectors, and even the entire equity market, the challenges of determining replacement cost of today's complex, far-flung corporate entities proves daunting. In contrast, assessing the cost of producing a suburban retail mall or a downtown office building proves far more manageable. In fact, many knowledgeable investors assess an asset's cost of replication and then use discount to replacement cost as an important investment criterion when making real estate acquisitions.

Public versus Private Holdings

Real estate investments hold the unusual distinction of offering large numbers of investment vehicles in both publicly traded and privately held categories. The distinction between public and private positions in real estate lies in form, not substance. Both public and private holdings of real estate assets expose investors to the benefits and perils of property positions.

Many investors in real estate benefit from an unusual investment vehicle, the real estate investment trust, or REIT. A REIT, unlike a typical corporate entity, pays no income taxes as long as the REIT distributes at least 90 percent of its taxable income and generates at least 75 percent of that income from rents, mortgages, and sales of property.[24] REITs serve as a pass-through structure in which income passes through the security, without being taxed, to the security holders who take responsibility for the tax liability, if any. REITs exist in both publicly traded and privately held forms.

Even though both publicly traded and privately held real estate vehicles expose investors to real estate assets, public-market securities frequently trade at prices that deviate from fair value. Green Street Advisors, a highly regarded research firm that concentrates on publicly traded real estate securities, routinely examines discrepancies between market price and fair value. The results give short-term investors pause. At one point in 1990, by Green Street's estimate, real estate securities traded at more than a 36 percent discount to fair value. By 1993, the stock market reversed itself, valuing real-estate-related holdings at a 28 percent premium to fair value. The yin and yang continued. In late 1994, the discount reached nine percent, while in 1997, stock market investors paid more than a 33 percent premium to fair value. In the late 1990s, a poor market for real estate securities (that coincided with a wonderful market for most other securities) brought valuations to a deficit of more than 20 percent, a level reached in early 2000. As the non–real estate portion of the market entered bear territory, real estate securities took on bull characteristics, leading to a greater than 22 percent premium to fair value in early 2004. The wide swings between price and fair value in the public securities arena led to low correlation between returns of publicly traded and privately held real estate assets.[25]

Discrepancies between price and fair value disturb short-term players, because any premium paid on purchases and any deficit incurred on sales loom large in damaging holding-period returns. Longer-term investors face fewer issues regarding differences between price and fair value, because over longer investment horizons, the short-term noise in the price/fair-value relationship makes less difference. Careful investors employ dollar-cost averaging to enter and exit markets that deviate measurably from fair value.

Consider the returns of publicly traded and privately held real estate assets from 1978 to 2003. Marketable real estate securities, as measured by the National Association of Real Estate Investment Trusts (NAREIT) All REIT Index, produced a 12.0 percent per annum return for the period. Privately held real estate assets, as measured by the National Council of Real Estate Investment Fiduciaries (NCREIF) National Property Index (NPI), generated 9.3 percent per annum returns. Since the private assets in the NPI employ no leverage, on a risk-adjusted basis the returns occupy the same neighborhood as the reasonably leveraged REIT returns. In any event, both real estate results exceeded the intermediate-term U.S. Treasury bond returns of 8.7 percent per annum and fell short of the stock market returns, as measured by the S&P 500 Index, of 13.5 percent per annum. Even though day in and day out private and public real estate holdings exhibit low correlation, over longer periods of time private and public holdings produce similar results, consistent with capital market expectations.

Although exceptions exist, for individual investors, publicly traded real estate securities generally provide reasonably low-cost exposure to relatively high-quality pools of real estate assets. Unfortunately, with few exceptions, privately offered retail real estate partnerships provide exposure to real estate at such obscenely high cost that the individual investor stands no chance of earning fair returns.

Wells Private REIT

Wells Capital manages one of the largest private real estate investment programs for individual investors. In December 2003, the firm numbered its investors at more than 117,000 and valued its portfolio of managed assets at $4.7 billion, even while embarking on an effort to raise a further $7.8 billion for new investment.[26] The terms of Wells Capital's private real estate investment trust (REIT) offering guarantee riches for the firm and its brokerage network, while at the same time guaranteeing poor results for the firm's individual investors.

The problems begin with the fundraising process. In a July 26, 2002, offering, Wells Investment Services sought to raise $3 billion for a REIT to invest in high-quality, well-leased office and industrial properties. Despite a program to invest in a relatively uncomplicated segment of the real estate market, Wells Capital established a three-tiered fee schedule that demonstrated greed run amok. Category one fees deal with the organization and offering stage of the investment, category two fees deal with acquisition and development activities, and category three fees deal with asset management and dispositions.

The most generous characterizations of Wells's offering fees range from obscene to despicable. Selling commissions of 7.0 percent of gross offering proceeds, dealer manager fees of 2.5 percent of gross proceeds, and organization and offering expenses of 3.0 percent of gross proceeds combine to consume up to 12.5 percent of investor funds. Before one dollar of investor capital finances a real estate purchase, Wells Investment Securities and Wells Capital consume as much as $375 million of the $3 billion offering.

Wells relies on an aggressive set of incentives to sell its REIT. A significant portion of underwriting fees goes to broker dealers that push the Wells product. Money flows liberally to the internal sales force. After the first month in which Wells raised $100 million, managers handed out crisp $100 bills to employees. To celebrate the first $200 million month, neat stacks of two hundred single dollar bills made the rounds. But Wells employed more than the Benjamins and the Georges. As if financial rewards provided inadequate motivation for the sales force, Wells Investment Services threw lavish parties, supplying food, travel, and entertainment for the brokers and the brokers' guests. So-called "educational and due diligence conferences" in Scottsdale, Arizona, and Amelia Island, Florida, featured sock hops and beach bashes. For the less socially inclined, Wells offered free golf. One dinner at a Civil War fort included "costumed Civil War heroes, fireworks, fife and drum players, sky divers and a cannon reenactment." Regulatory authorities determined the conferences constituted "lavish affairs" that violated National Association of Securities Dealers rules.[27] The NASD censured Wells Investment Securities corporately and Leo Wells personally. Unfortunately for investors, fundraising continued unabated.

Once the investor's sadly depleted contribution stands ready to invest in real estate, Wells Capital moves to the acquisition and development stage fees, taking another bite of the apple. Acquisition and advisory fees "for the review and evaluation of potential real property acquisitions" amount to 3.0 percent of offering proceeds, or another $90 million.[28] Reimbursement for acquisition expenses (as if a 3.0 percent acquisition fee were inadequate) add an additional 0.5 percent, bringing the total to $105 million. Before reaching the final fee category, Wells Capital and its affiliates consume 16.0 percent of investor capital, leaving only 84.0 percent of contributions remaining. Of the $3 billion offering, fully $480 million of investor funds fail to make the trip from investors' accounts to real property investment.

Once Wells purchases property, the fee bonanza continues, as Wells Management charges property management and leasing fees of up to 4.5 percent of gross revenues. In addition, the firm may earn a separate fee for leasing activity at newly constructed properties. Of course, property sales require further feeding at the fee trough, with up to 3.0 percent of the contract sales price accruing to Wells Capital. Finally, upon ultimate exit of the portfolio, through private sale or public listing, Wells Capital receives a 10 percent profit participation after satisfying a rate of return hurdle requirement.

The operational stage fees seem high in light of the relatively simple nature of the assets that Wells acquires. The firm purchases "high-grade commercial office and industrial buildings," focusing on "properties that are less than five years old, the space in which has been leased or pre-leased to one or more large corporate tenants who satisfy our standards of creditworthiness."[29] Moreover, Wells tends to purchase assets with long lease terms. In the July 2002 prospectus, the rent roll showed more than 84 percent of leases expiring in 2008 and beyond. What could be simpler than managing recently constructed commercial properties with high-quality tenants on long-term leases? Do Wells Management's day-to-day asset management responsibilities justify the fees?

The Wells REIT prospectus helpfully points out that the firm targets properties with "triple net" leases where the landlord receives rent net of taxes, current expenses, and capital changes. In other words, the tenant bears responsibility for paying all costs of tenancy, leaving the landlord with few obligations other than cashing a check. Some industry participants call the Wells 4.5 percent property management and leasing fee "a total ripoff." Wells Management rolls up the score, while the investors have yet to take the field.

Apparently the cornucopia of fees fails to provide sufficient largess for the employees, fund directors, and broker dealers that produce and distribute this disservice to investors. On top of underwriting, acquisition, management, and disposition fees, Wells Capital provides additional inducements in the form of options and warrants. These derivative securities, if exercised, dilute investor holdings. The broker dealers lead the derivative dilution parade with a call on 2.0 percent of the offering, or 6 million shares. Employees enjoy access to 750,000 "authorized and reserved" shares. Independent directors bring up the rear with 600,000 shares subject to warrants and options. Wells Real Estate takes a slice at every turn. The investor dies a death of a thousand cuts.

The fees hit investors before investment, upon acquisition, during the holding period, and at exit. Lest confusion reign regarding the beneficiary of the staggering load of fees, the prospectus contains an illuminating chart showing Leo F. Wells as 100 percent owner of Wells Real Estate Funds, which in turn owns 100 percent of Wells Management, 100 percent of Wells Investment Securities, and 100 percent of Wells Capital.[30] The cozy structure contains a staggering assortment of conflicts of interest.

Conflicts begin with the offering of shares. The prospectus constructively notes that "since Wells Investment Securities . . . is an affiliate of Wells Capital, you will not have the benefit of an independent due diligence review and investigation of the type normally performed by an unaffiliated, independent underwriter in connection with the securities offerings."[31] At its best, Wall Street due diligence gives an investor comfort that a security offering's underwriter confirmed the completeness and accuracy of the offering document. Due diligence performed by an independent entity on an arms-length basis benefits investors. Due diligence performed by an affiliated person who looks in a mirror and admires the image benefits no one. The lack of independent due diligence begins to explain the egregious offering terms.

Conflicts continue with acquisition, management, and sale of properties. Wells Capital receives fees for transactions involving the purchase and sale of properties "regardless of the quality of the property acquired" and Wells Management receives fees "regardless of the quality of . . . the services provided." The prospectus clearly states that "every transaction with Wells Capital or its affiliates is subject to an inherent conflict of interest."[32] Wells Capital's and Wells Management's desire for high fees conflicts head on with the investors' desire for a fair deal. According to the prospectus, high fees trump the fair deal.

A high level of insider ownership might mitigate concerns regarding the staggering conflicts that abound in management of the Wells Real Estate Investment Trust. If the company's leaders own substantial amounts of stock, they tend to act in the interest of shareholders, simply because they too are shareholders. According to the stock ownership table on page 53 of the July 26, 2002 prospectus, Leo F. Wells III, president of Wells REIT, president of Wells Management Company, and president of Wells Investment Securities, owned a grand total of 698 shares valued at $6,980. Of Leo Wells's untold millions of personal profits, next to nothing found its way into the real estate investment vehicle that he so aggressively promoted.

Even though the Wells Investment Securities prospectus for the Wells Real Estate Investment Trust provides frank disclosure of numerous fundamental, irreconcilable conflicts of interest, the offering document's description of the use of proceeds appears disingenuous at best. Stating that "we intend to invest a minimum of 84% of the proceeds from this offering to acquire real estate properties, and the remaining proceeds will be used to pay fees and expenses," the document avers that " . . . these fees and expenses will not reduce your invested capital. Your invested capital amount will remain $10 per share and your dividend yield will be based on your $10 per share investment."[33] By underplaying the unjustifiably large gap between an investor's gross payment and the net share price, Wells Investment Securities misleads all but the most careful prospectus readers. Perhaps investors should pay closer attention to the boldface-type warning on the cover of the prospectus: "Neither the Securities and Exchange Commission, the Attorney General of the State of New York nor any other state securities regulator has approved or disapproved of these securities or determined if this prospectus is truthful or complete. It is a criminal offense if someone tells you otherwise."[34]

If the Wells REIT were a bit player in the real estate market, observers might conclude "little harm, minor foul." In fact, in 2003 the Wells REIT purchased $2.6 billion of real estate, more than any other investor in the property markets. If the Wells REIT were a lone bad apple, observers might conclude that the exception proves the rule. In fact, in the fee department, the Inland Western Retail REIT managed to outdo Wells, earning a gold medal by charging up-front fees of 16.5 percent (relative to Wells' 16.0 percent).[35] Even though the Inland REIT won the up-front fee derby, in 2003 it garnered only a silver medal in the acquisitions category, buying $2.5 billion of properties and losing to Wells by a scant $100 million.[36] The fee-heavy private REITs play a dominant role in the real estate world.

The voracious private REITs satisfy their appetites by paying top dollar. Wells bids so aggressively on properties that other potential acquirers simply walk away once they become aware that Wells wants a property. No rational buyer can compete with the Wells acquisition machine's willingness to overpay for product. As a consequence, investors suffer the double indignity of high fees and poor investment prospects. The leading actor on the commercial real estate stage struck a powerful villain's pose.

TIAA Private Real Estate Account

Contrast Wells Capital's private REIT with the private real estate investment vehicle offered by the Teachers Insurance and Annuity Association of America, better known as TIAA. With $3.7 billion in assets in the Real Estate Account on December 31, 2002, TIAA qualifies as a major force in providing direct real estate ownership to individuals. TIAA's real estate portfolio pursues an investment strategy roughly similar to the Wells REIT's, while offering superior diversification, greater liquidity, far lower fees, and vastly reduced conflicts of interest.[37]

TIAA invests in office, industrial, residential, and retail property. Instead of pursuing the low-management-intensive office assets typically held by Wells, TIAA purchases a much larger variety of assets, providing a better balanced portfolio for the investor. The TIAA Real Estate Account provides daily liquidity in stark contrast to the Wells REIT's highly restrictive share redemption program and ultimate dependence on a possible public offering or future disposition of assets.

Most important of all, TIAA wins hands down in the fee department. TIAA's direct investors entirely avoid Wells REIT's outrageous organization and offering stage fees. One hundred cents of every TIAA-investor dollar goes toward the real estate investment program. In contrast to Wells REIT's 3.5 percent acquisition and development stage fees, in mid 2004 TIAA charged only 0.6 percent for investment management, administration, and other fees. The Wells REIT and TIAA treat property management and leasing quite differently. Wells engages a wholly owned affiliate to conduct day-to-day operations, creating a substantial conflict of interest. TIAA engages local real estate management companies to provide property services, negotiating fair contracts in a competitive environment. The process virtually ensures that TIAA receives superior service at lower cost. TIAA charges no disposition fees and receives no profit participations. Finally, TIAA does not dilute investor interests with issuance of warrants or options. Unlike the Wells REIT deal structure, TIAA's investors receive a fair shot.

Publicly Traded Real Estate Securities

The light shines brighter in the world of publicly traded securities than it does in the murky world of privately offered partnerships. Since the investor ultimately obtains exposure to the real estate that underlies either the publicly traded or the privately held securities, investors must identify compelling reasons to forego the greater transparency and superior liquidity of public securities.

Market-mimicking index management represents the starting point for investors who wish to gain exposure to real estate securities. The passive approach to portfolio construction assures that investors realize market-like returns, eliminating the slippage (positive or negative) that comes with active management. Yet, even in the relatively constrained world of indexing, managers differ substantially, one from another.

As the preeminent practitioner of indexing for individual investors, Vanguard stands atop the industry in terms of excellence in tracking a wide variety of markets. Along with its market-replicating record of low-tracking-error products comes a well-deserved reputation for low fees. Like all of Vanguard's index products, the Vanguard REIT Index Fund provides high-quality, low-cost exposure to its target market.

The Vanguard REIT Index Fund imposes no sales charges, no pur-chase fees, and no distribution fees. To discourage market timing, Van-guard imposes a 1.0 percent redemption fee, paid to the fund, on shares held for less than one year. Annual fund operating expenses for 2003 amounted to 0.25 percent for management fees and 0.02 percent for other expenses. Total charges of 0.27 percent represent bare bones charges for high-quality execution of a sensible investment program.[38]

Not all firms provide Vanguard's low-cost, high-quality service. The Wells Family of Real Estate Funds, under the guidance of Leo F. Wells III, offers three classes of shares in the Wells S&P REIT Index Fund. The breadth of charges for the Wells Class A, Class B, and Class C shares defies credulity. Wells investors face the choice of simple, up-front sales charges or more complicated, contingent-deferred sales charges. Ongoing fees include management fees, distribution fees, and other expenses.[39]

Investors in the Wells S&P REIT Index Fund pay either a lot up front and too much later or nothing up front and way too much later. For instance, the Class A shares, with a maximum 4.0 percent load, charge continuing fees of 1.38 percent per annum. Class B shares, with a maximum deferred sales charge of 5.0 percent, charge continuing fees of 2.17 percent per annum.

The fees paid to Wells appear all the more outrageous when con-sidering that Wells Asset Management, which receives a 0.5 percent management fee, does not even manage the assets. Wells subcontracts the work to Rydex Global Advisors for a fee ranging from 0.1 percent to 0.2 percent of assets, depending on portfolio size. Wells raises the concept of getting something for nothing to a high art form.

Compare the expense burden of hypothetical $10,000 REIT index fund investments with Wells and Vanguard. After three years, Wells Class A investors shell out $819, Class B investors pay $979, and Class C investors cough up $685. In sharp contrast, Vanguard REIT investors pay only $87 in total fees. In the three-year period somewhere be-tween 6.9 percent and 9.8 percent of the Wells investors' funds go to fees. The comparable burden for the Vanguard investor amounts to less than 0.9 percent.

The Wells family of real estate funds places an insurmountable fee burden on investors hoping to replicate the returns of the S&P REIT In-dex. Leo F. Wells III and his cronies managed to produce a marketable security alternative nearly as hostile to investor interests as the infamous Wells private REIT. Careful investors must do far more than respond to financial advisory blandishments if they hope to succeed.

Real Estate Prices and Inflation

The strong relationship between replacement cost and market value leads to one of real estate's most attractive investment attributes, a high correlation with inflation. Since the labor and materials used to build real estate assets rise in cost along with inflation, the replacement cost of real estate tracks inflation closely. Yet even though replacement cost responds to changes in the general price level, the nature of an asset's lease structure influences the rate of response of changes in market value to inflationary pressures. For example, a property subject to long-term, fixed-rate leases shows little near-term correlation to inflation. Only as the expiration of the lease term nears will the impact of inflation influence asset valuation. Alternatively, properties with shorter-term leases exhibit much greater inflation sensitivity. Moreover, some leases explicitly allow landlords to pass through inflationary increases in expenses or, in the case of retail properties, contractually entitle landlords to receive a percentage of sales. Such inflation-responsive lease structures cause asset values to increase with inflation.

The importance of replacement cost both in valuation analysis and in inflation sensitivity relies on markets reflecting reasonable equilibrium between supply and demand. In cases where supply of real estate space fails to match demand, prices respond to the disequilibrium, not to the expected relationship with replacement cost or with inflation. In the late 1980s, investor enthusiasm for owning commercial real estate and federal tax incentives for developing properties combined to create a vast oversupply of commercial office buildings. The excesses in the real estate market contributed to the savings and loan crisis, as many thrifts suffered from the burden of underperforming or nonperforming real estate loans. High-quality, albeit poorly leased, properties traded at steep discounts to replacement cost. Prices responded to the disconnect between supply and demand, failing to track inflation. Unless markets reflect reasonable equilibrium, investors face difficulties in assessing the response of real estate prices to inflation. Yet, when markets exhibit equilibrium, sensitivity to changes in the general price level represents a particularly attractive characteristic of real estate.

Alignment of Interests

In the realm of publicly traded REITs, investors face the same set of questions about alignment of interests that apply to other publicly traded equities. Just as in the broader universe of marketable stocks, interests of shareholders and managements generally coincide.

In the world of private real estate vehicles, investors face an extraordinary range of investment structures. TIAA's private real estate fund furnishes investors with a nearly unimaginable fair deal. Wells Capital's private REIT defines the opposite end of the continuum, with deal terms that virtually ensure failure for investors. Unless investors identify an unusually equitable private deal structure, gaining real estate exposure through public securities makes the most sense.

Market Characteristics

Real estate investors face significant investment opportunities in both public and private markets. At December 31, 2003, the National Association of Real Estate Investment Trusts tracked a universe of real estate securities that totaled $230.2 billion. The REIT population posted a dividend yield of 5.7 percent and traded at a 17.5 percent premium over fair value.

At December 31, 2003, the NCREIF National Property Index included unleveraged real estate assets valued at an aggregate of $132.4 billion. The privately held real estate cohort paid a dividend yield of 8.0 percent, representing a premium over the ten-year U.S. Treasury yield of 3.8 percent.

Summary

In terms of risk and return, real estate falls between higher-risk equity and lower-risk debt. The hybrid nature of the expected investment characteristics matches the hybrid nature of the fundamental traits of real estate investments. With its inflation-sensitive nature, real estate provides powerful diversification to investor portfolios.

Real estate investors enjoy the opportunity to choose between publicly traded and privately held investment vehicles. While sensible alternatives exist in both public and private forms, careful investors pay close attention to fee arrangements and measure the options against the baseline of passively managed, publicly traded REIT funds.

CHAPTER SUMMARY

Investors find all of the tools necessary to build a well-diversified, equity-oriented portfolio with the core asset classes of domestic equities, foreign developed market equities, emerging market equities, U.S. Treasury bonds, U.S. Treasury Inflation-Protected Securities, and real estate. Domestic and foreign equities drive portfolio returns, along with an assist from real estate. Conventional and inflation-linked bonds provide diversifying power, with real estate again playing a supporting role. By combining the core asset classes in a well-diversified portfolio and adopting broadly based, index-like approaches to holding core asset-class positions, investors build a strong foundation for investment success.

In the course of providing basic, valuable, differentiable characteristics to investor portfolios, core asset classes rely on market-generated returns. By investing in asset classes in which market forces drive returns, investors achieve a high level of confidence that the various asset classes will produce the expected long-term results. By avoiding asset classes that rely on superior active management to generate returns, investors dramatically reduce the risk of slippage between hoped-for asset-class performance and actual results.

Core asset classes trade in broad, deep, investable markets, ensuring reasonable levels of commitment by a range of the Wall Street firms. The resulting competition leads to greater market transparency and efficiency, increasing the likelihood that investors transact on fair terms.

After identifying a critical mass of core asset classes, investors place them in a portfolio framework designed to satisfy financial goals. By combining assets in a manner that produces a low-risk, high-expected return portfolio, investors create the opportunity to achieve investment success.

3

Portfolio Construction

Construction of a financial-asset portfolio involves full measures of science and art. The science encompasses the application of basic investment principles to the problem of combining core asset classes in an efficient, cost-effective manner. The art concerns the use of common-sense judgment in the challenge of incorporating individual characteristics into the asset-allocation process. Devoting significant time and energy to the science and art of designing long-term portfolio targets increases the likelihood that investors will develop the conviction necessary to maintain a steady long-term course amid the turbulent crosscurrents endemic to security markets.

Diversification and equity orientation represent important objective principles for long-term investors. Diversification provides the free lunch of improved return and risk characteristics, while equity orientation promises the possibility of greater wealth accumulation.

Personal preferences play a critical subjective role in portfolio decision making. Unless an investor embraces wholeheartedly a particular portfolio structure, failure awaits. Lightly held positions invite casual reversal, exposing vacillating investors to the costly consequences of market whipsaw. By adopting asset-allocation targets that dovetail with personal risk tolerances, investors vastly increase the odds of investment success.

Individual circumstances introduce important considerations to the portfolio structuring process. Nonfinancial assets, such as homes and privately held businesses, influence an investor's desired portfolio composition. Financial liabilities, such as mortgages and personal loans, factor into investor decisions regarding asset allocation, particularly with respect to holdings of fixed income. Sensible investors consider financial asset allocations in a context that encompasses the broadest possible picture of individual assets and liabilities.

Unusual personal expertise holds the potential for individuals to generate superior returns by applying their skills in market-beating active management. If investors truly possess a demonstrable edge in selecting superior investments, then the arena to which investors bring special skills deserves a greater share of portfolio assets. Unfortunately, genuine investment skill proves so rare a commodity among individual investors that the incidence of extraordinary-expertise-justified overexposure to an asset class approaches zero.

Time horizon constitutes one of the most influential variables in structuring investment portfolios. Investors who need monies to satisfy short-term obligations require certainty of value and immediacy of liquidity, causing them to own high-quality money-market instruments. Investors who hold funds in excess of short-term needs enjoy the opportunity to accept variability of value and greater illiquidity, allowing them to own high-returning, equity-oriented instruments.

Fortunately, investors solve the time horizon problem most effectively without changing the character of the optimal, well-diversified, long-term, equity-oriented portfolio. Investors with long time horizons predominantly own the long-term portfolio. As the time horizon shortens, investors reduce long-term portfolio holdings in favor of cash positions. Investors with short time horizons own predominantly money-market instruments. Investors address changes in time horizon by altering the mix between the risky, long-term portfolio and the riskless, money-market portfolio.

The heart of the investment process lies in producing a coherent set of portfolio targets that reflect the science of applying basic investment principles and incorporate the art of meeting investor needs and preferences. Thoughtfully constructed, individually chosen asset-allocation targets provide the strongest foundation upon which to build a successful investment program.

THE SCIENCE OF PORTFOLIO STRUCTURE

Basic financial principles require that long-term investment portfolios exhibit diversification and equity orientation. Diversification demands that each asset class receive a weighting large enough to matter, but small enough not to matter too much. Equity orientation requires that high-expected-return asset classes dominate the portfolio.

Begin the portfolio structuring process by considering the issue of diversification, using the six core asset classes. The necessity that each asset class matter indicates a minimum of a 5 or 10 percent allocation. The requirement that no asset class matter too much dictates a maximum of a 25 or 30 percent allocation. The basic math of diversification imposes structural parameters on the portfolio construction process.

Investors achieve equity orientation by investing a preponderance of assets in the high-expected-return asset classes of domestic equity, foreign developed equity, emerging market equity, and real estate. The return-generating power of equity positions drives the results of long-term investment portfolios.

Investors give up expected return to defend portfolios against unanticipated inflationary or deflationary economic conditions. U.S. Treasury Inflation-Protected Securities protect against inflation with certainty, while real estate holdings guard against inflation with reasonable assurance. In the long run (in which, as John Maynard Keynes famously and correctly said, "we are all dead"[1]) domestic equities add to the inflation-hedging characteristics of a portfolio, but in the short run domestic equities prove notoriously unreliable as inflation hedges.

Investors insulate portfolios from deflationary conditions and from financial crises by holding long-term, noncallable, full-faith-and-credit obligations of the U.S. government. While standard U.S. Treasury bonds provide the most powerful deflation hedge, the return of principal guaranteed by U.S. TIPS affords investors a measure of deflation protection. Financial market crises often lead to extreme investor preference for safe investments. During flight-to-quality episodes, U.S. Treasury securities benefit from demand by fearful investors, leading government bonds to appreciate while nearly all other security types suffer.

Any number of portfolio allocations satisfy the mathematical and functional requirements of diversification and equity orientation. Table 3.1 contains an asset-class combination that serves as a reference portfolio for investors to consider. The portfolio passes the test of equity orientation with 70 percent of assets in the high-expected-return vehicles of domestic equity, nondomestic equity, and real estate. The reference portfolio meets the statistical requirement for diversification, with individual asset-class exposures ranging from a minimum of 5 percent of assets to a maximum of 30 percent of assets.

Table 3.1 Well-Diversified, Equity-Oriented Portfolios Provide a Framework for Investment Success

Asset Class	Policy Target
Domestic equity	30%
Foreign developed equity	15%
Emerging market equity	5%
Real estate	20%
U.S. Treasury bonds	15%
U.S. Treasury Inflation-Protected Securities	15%

Moving from the realm of numerical diversification to the arena of functional diversification, with 15 percent of assets in TIPS and 20 percent of assets in real estate, the reference portfolio provides significant inflation protection. With 30 percent of assets in U.S. government obligations, the portfolio exhibits a substantial commitment to the highest-quality securities, affording investors security in times of financial crisis. With 15 percent of assets in standard U.S. Treasury bonds (and a further 15 percent in guaranteed-return-of-nominal-principal U.S. TIPS), the portfolio gives investors protection against deflationary conditions. The reference portfolio meets the requirements of equity orientation, mathematical diversification, and functional diversification.

THE ART OF PERSONALIZATION

Personal preferences, circumstances, and abilities affect portfolio construction in a profound manner. Rational investors allow risk preferences to influence portfolio choices, increasing the likelihood of maintaining asset allocations through the inevitable rough patches and ultimately benefiting from expected portfolio risk and return characteristics. Personal circumstances cause nonfinancial assets and all manner of liabilities to affect portfolio holdings, ensuring consideration of the broadest range of factors in making portfolio decisions. Personal abilities play an occasional role in portfolio decisions, allowing the rare investor with investment-specific expertise to exploit an edge in structuring portfolios.

Personal preferences play a pivotal role in developing effective, long-lasting portfolio structures. Unless investors adopt firmly held convictions regarding the efficacy of target portfolios, nearly certain disappointment results. Confidence stems from deep understanding, developed by matching fundamental acceptance of basic investment principles with clear knowledge of individual risk preferences.

Personal preferences influence asset allocation in important ways. Investors who desire more certain protection from inflation increase the U.S. Treasury TIPS allocation. Investors who require greater protection against financial crises expand U.S. Treasury bond exposure. Investors who lack confidence in emerging markets avoid emerging markets investments. Sensible portfolios reflect individual preferences.

Incorporating personal preferences in portfolio decisions guards investors from counterproductive actions to adverse developments after the fact by limiting exposure to poorly loved asset classes before the fact. The emerging markets skeptic may reluctantly accept an allocation to emerging markets equities, having read that well-diversified portfolios invariably incorporate exposure to developing economies. At the first sign of trouble, manifested by declining prices for emerging markets securities, the reluctant investor reverts to form, overreacts to the risks of exposure to less-developed economies and immediately eliminates the position. Lack of conviction and absence of comfort cause investors to buy high and sell low, damaging portfolio returns.

Personal circumstances affect portfolio allocations. Sensible investors consider the size and character of nonfinancial asset exposure when making financial asset-allocation decisions. Nonfinancial assets and financial assets often respond similarly to forces that influence asset values. In cases where an individual possesses nonfinancial assets that share characteristics with financial assets, the rational asset allocator reduces exposure to the financial asset to avoid excessive exposure to the common risk factor.

Personal residences and privately held businesses constitute important nonfinancial assets on many personal balance sheets. Homeownership insulates individuals from changes in the cost of renting a place to live. Since inflation-sensitive habitation costs constitute a significant portion of most household budgets, homeownership reduces the need for inflation-hedging assets in investor portfolios. If an individual owns a small business, the equity-oriented nature of the private holding argues for a lower equity position in the investor's financial holdings. Investors benefit from taking the broadest view of their financial circumstances.

Financial and nonfinancial liabilities further influence portfolio decisions. Home mortgages and personal loans comprise the largest components of most individual financial liabilities. From a portfolio perspective, liabilities act like negative assets. In other words, borrowing by an individual offsets lending (ownership of bond or money-market funds) by that individual. In fact, wealth-maximizing individuals compare the after-tax costs of debt with the after-tax returns from bonds, liquidating bond positions to pay off loans when the costs of debt exceed the returns from bonds. Rational investors consider liability positions when making asset allocations.

Truly extraordinary expertise deserves consideration in portfolio decision making. If investors possess genuine market-beating skills, the ability to generate superior returns increases the attractiveness of the particular investment medium. The incremental returns produced by successful active management argue for a larger target allocation to the asset class in which investors exhibit unusual prowess.

Special investment skill constitutes an extremely rare commodity. The sad history of the mutual-fund industry provides a case in point. Thousands upon thousands of professionally managed funds routinely fall short of producing even market-matching results. If highly compensated, specially trained, handsomely supported investment professionals fail, what leads part-time, financially untutored, resource-deficient individuals to believe they can succeed?

The unrealistic belief in success emanates from a failure by individuals to recognize their investment limitations. Yale economist Robert Shiller observes that "a pervasive human tendency towards overconfidence" causes investors "to express overly strong opinions and rush to summary judgments."[2] Overconfidence contributes to a litany of investor errors, including inadequate diversification, overzealous security selection, and counterproductive market timing. In the overwhelming number of cases, misplaced confidence in forecasts of return prospects for broad asset classes and individual securities causes investors to misallocate assets and actively trade securities, thereby incurring higher costs, producing greater risks, and generating lower returns. In a nearly inconsequential number of instances, genuine investor skill creates risk-adjusted excess returns.

Forward-thinking investors consider anticipated changes in financial circumstances when making asset-allocation choices. For example, an individual who reasonably expects to inherit a portfolio dominated by equity securities correctly biases the existing portfolio allocations toward other assets, recognizing the implicit exposure to the equities contained in the inheritance. Anticipated receipt of a fixed amount from life insurance proceeds represents a virtual fixed-income asset, suggesting a diminished role for bonds in an investor's portfolio. Even though the future stands clouded in uncertainty, investors make better choices when considering expected changes in their financial condition.

Mindfulness of personal preferences, personal circumstances, and personal skills leads to better decisions regarding allocation of financial assets. Adjustment of portfolio allocations for personal preferences leads to greater likelihood of maintaining asset-class exposures through thick and thin. Consideration of personal circumstances produces financial asset exposures that complement an investor's overall asset and liability profile. Realistic assessment of personal investment skills generally causes investors to take a basic, no-frills approach to portfolio construction. A custom-tailored portfolio promises greater customer satisfaction than the one-size-fits-all alternative.

TIME HORIZON

Successful investors pay careful attention to time horizons in constructing investment programs. The period that investors intend to hold portfolios and the horizon over which they judge investment results play a critical role in determining the degree of risk appropriate for a portfolio and in assessing the likelihood of successful implementation of investment strategies. Time horizon influences particularly the asset-allocation decision.

Asset allocation depends on the time of forecasted use for the invested funds. For example, college savings programs differ markedly depending on the age of the prospective student. Viewed in isolation, a two-year-old ought to have a high-risk, high-expected-return portfolio, while a high school senior ought to own low-volatility, highly liquid assets. With a long time horizon, the young child can take substantial degrees of investment risk, opening up the possibility for significant long-term gains. In contrast, the teenager needs to have "cash in the bank" to provide reasonable certainty of meeting imminent tuition payments.

Asset allocators often deal with goals less clearly defined than saving to finance a child's education or investing to accumulate the down payment for a home. For example, retirees may wish to balance the need for a reasonably stable near-term flow of funds to facilitate current purchases with the desire for a nicely growing base of assets to underwrite future consumption. Moreover, most investors seek to satisfy a multitude of goals with invested funds. Young people may simultaneously save to buy a home, to send children to school, and to provide for retirement. To accommodate multiple goals, investors specify a hoped-for schedule of future financial flows, thereby defining the relevant investment horizon. By aggregating various needs and desires, a full picture of the investor's time horizon emerges.

The appropriate degree of investment risk depends on the time available until funds are needed. For periods of one to two years or less, investors ought to favor bank deposits, money-market funds or short-term bond funds. By avoiding material credit risk and searching for low management expenses, investors solve the simple problem of short-term investing.

For terms of eight to ten years or more, investors face much more interesting, more daunting, and potentially more rewarding investment alternatives. An equity-oriented, diversified asset allocation provides the most likely framework for longer-term success. By accepting the greater fundamental and financial risks inherent in portfolios of risky assets, investors with longer investment horizons enjoy the opportunity to generate higher returns.

Those investors with intermediate horizons, say between two and eight years, ought to combine risky long-term assets with less risky short-term investments. The investor with a long-term horizon begins with a portfolio composed entirely of risky assets. Then, as the investor's investment horizon contracts, the investor moves assets from high-risk to low-risk positions. Ultimately, when one or two years remain before expenditure of the funds, the portfolio consists entirely of low-risk positions. The nature of the risky portfolio need not change, only the proportion committed to risky assets.

Sensible investors take great care to minimize the tax bill associated with moving assets from the high-risk, long-term portfolio to the low-risk, short-term portfolio. Although the tax code introduces many complexities to investment decision making, as a starting point consider moving taxable long-term assets to the low-risk portfolio, thereby allowing tax-deferred holdings to continue to receive shelter from taxes. Wealth-maximizing investors study the ever-changing tax consequences of generating liquidity from various investment accounts, attempting to reduce current and future tax liabilities to an absolute minimum.

Finance theory supports the commonsense approach of using combinations of a risky portfolio and riskless assets to control overall risk exposure. Consider the expected investment risk and return space depicted in Figure 3.1. The concave line represents the efficient frontier, a set of risky investment portfolios that produce the highest return for a given risk level and that exhibit the lowest risk level for a given return. The straight line represents the capital market line, a series of combinations of the riskless asset (point E) and the risky portfolio (point A). Sensible investors operate along the capital market line.

A long-term investor might reasonably hold the diversified portfolio of risky assets shown as point A in Figure 3.1. As the investor's time horizon moves from ten years to eight years, the investor sells 25 percent of the risky portfolio, placing the proceeds in cash. When the investment horizon becomes six years, another quarter of the risky portfolio moves to cash. At four years, holdings consist of 75 percent cash and 25 percent risky assets. Finally, with a two-year investment horizon, the short-term investor holds 100 percent of assets in cash. Note that as the investment horizon shortens, the risk profile of the investor's holdings decreases. Observe that the character of the risky portfolio remains constant. Only the mix of risky and riskless assets changes. Finance theory provides an elegant solution to the problems of dealing with shortening time horizons.

Figure 3.1 Investors Reduce Risk as Time Horizon Shortens

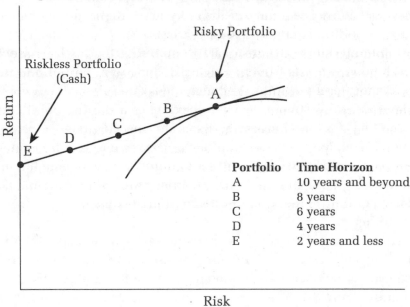

Portfolio	Time Horizon
A	10 years and beyond
B	8 years
C	6 years
D	4 years
E	2 years and less

Obviously, the pattern of risk-altering portfolio changes outlined above represents only an illustrative example. Personal preferences and individual risk tolerances militate against a standardized approach to any aspect of asset allocation. Nonetheless, regardless of investor-specific nuances, investment time horizon plays an important role in asset-allocation decisions.

CHAPTER SUMMARY

Effective investors combine science and art in constructing investment portfolios likely to satisfy long-term aspirations. Objective factors include following the principles of diversification and equity orientation. Diversification imposes a mathematical requirement of not too big and not too small, as well as a functional requirement of protection against unanticipated changes in economic conditions. Equity orientation demands that a solid majority of assets produce high levels of expected returns. Subjective considerations include tailoring the portfolio to personal circumstances, individual preferences, and investor skills. Fashioning a portfolio of risky assets that comports with investor traits proves indispensable to investment success.

As time horizons shorten, investors enjoy the opportunity to maintain the composition of the risky portfolio, lowering the level of risk in overall holdings by substituting riskless cash positions for portions of the risky asset portfolio. By increasing cash positions, investors reduce risk and increase liquidity, allowing the satisfaction of near-term consumption requirements.

Asset allocation represents the most powerful implement in a rational investor's toolbox. By using the basic principles of diversification and equity orientation to build a foundation that accommodates individual characteristics and risk preferences, investors establish a framework that promises superior investment outcomes.

4
Non-Core Asset Classes

Non-core asset classes fail to meet at least one of the three criteria that define core asset classes: contribution of a basic, valuable, differentiable characteristic to a portfolio; fundamental reliance on markets, not on active management, to generate returns; and representation in a broad, deep investable market. Discussion of investment vehicles that fail one of the first two criteria assists investors in avoiding positions that may harm portfolio results. Investors pursuing strategies that fail the third criterion (that is, by investing in narrow, shallow, uninvestable niches) deserve their fate.

Fixed-income alternatives dominate the population of well-defined markets that serve no valuable portfolio role. While default-free, noncallable, full-faith-and-credit obligations of the U.S. government play a basic, valuable, differentiable role in investor portfolios, investment-grade corporate bonds, high-yield bonds, foreign bonds, and asset-backed securities contain unattractive characteristics that argue against inclusion in well-constructed portfolios. Understanding the shortcomings of particular fixed-income investment alternatives, particularly in regard to how those alternatives relate to the objectives of the fixed-income asset class, helps investors in making well-informed portfolio decisions.

Those asset classes that require superior active management results to produce acceptable risk-adjusted returns belong only in the portfolios of the handful of investors with the resources and fortitude to pursue and maintain a high-quality active investment management program. Understanding the difficulty of identifying superior hedge-fund, venture-capital, and leveraged-buyout investments leads to the conclusion that hurdles for casual investors stand insurmountably high. Even many well-equipped investors fail to clear the hurdles necessary to achieve consistent success in producing market-beating active management results. When operating in arenas that depend fundamentally on active management for success, ill-informed manager selection poses grave risks to portfolio assets.

The superficially appealing strategy of engaging external expertise to select alternative investment managers, perhaps through a fund of funds or perhaps through a paid advisor, fails to withstand close scrutiny. Unfortunately, the supposedly expert intermediary interposes a filter between the investor and the investment activity. If the investor fails to understand the investment strategy pursued by the ultimate trigger puller, then the investor finds no sensible grounds upon which to evaluate the success or failure of either the intermediary or the investment program. Ultimately, successful investors must understand directly the investment choices contained in portfolio allocations.

Non-core asset classes command a sizable portion of the pool of investment alternatives and, perhaps, an even more sizable portion of investment-related media coverage. Casual investors all too frequently allocate monies to a broad range of vehicles, regardless of the investment merits of the underlying securities or strategies. Trendy investors often pursue the cocktail-party-chatter benefits of commitments to the promise, seldom fulfilled, of actively managed alternatives. Sensible investors avoid non-core asset classes.

DOMESTIC CORPORATE BONDS

Owners of corporate bonds hold a piece of a loan to the corporation that issued the bonds to borrow the money. In a company's capital structure, debt obligations rank higher than equity interests, causing a company's bonds to exhibit less fundamental risk than a company's equity. Because bonds carry less risk than equities, fixed-income investors expect lower returns than do equity investors. Unfortunately for investors, corporate bonds contain a variety of unattractive characteristics, including credit risk, illiquidity, and callability. Even if corporate bond investors receive fair compensation for these unattractive characteristics, astute investors recognize that the credit risk and callability of corporate obligations undermine the fundamental diversifying power expected from fixed-income holdings.

Credit Risk

Credit risk stems from the possibility that a corporation will not meet the obligation to make full and timely payments on its debt. Rating agencies, such as Standard & Poor's and Moody's Investors Service, publish ratings for bond issues, purporting to grade the likelihood that an issue will produce as promised. The most important factors in assessing a bond issuer's ability to pay lie in the size of the equity cushion supporting the debt and the amount of cash flow servicing the debt. investment-grade ratings, assigned to the most creditworthy borrowers, range from triple A (the highest) to triple B. High-yield or "junk" bonds carry ratings of double B and below. Lower-rated bonds embody greater credit risk and exhibit more equity-like characteristics.

Moody's describes triple-A rated bonds as being "of the best quality" and carrying "the smallest degree of investment risk," with interest payments "protected" and principal "secure." Double-A bonds exhibit "high quality by all standards," while single-A bonds "possess many favorable investment attributes." The bottom category of investment-grade obligations (triple-B) manifests adequate security "for the present," but "lacks outstanding investment characteristics."[1] Despite the shades of gray introduced by the description of the triple-B rating category, Moody's paints a bright picture for investment-grade debt obligations.

Unfortunately, from a corporate debt investor's perspective, triple-A rated bonds can only decline in credit quality. Sometimes, bondholders experience a downward drift in quality to less exalted, albeit still investment-grade ratings. At other times, bondholders face a lengthy, Chinese-water-torture deterioration in credit that results in exile to the "fallen angel" realm of the junk bond world. On occasion, triple-A rated obligations maintain their standing. In no case, however, do triple-A bonds receive upgrades.

IBM illustrates the problem confronting purchasers of corporate debt. The company issued no long-term debt until the late 1970s, as prior to that time IBM consistently generated excess cash. Anticipating a need for external finance, the company came to market in the fall of 1979 with a $1 billion issue, at the time the largest-ever corporate borrowing. IBM obtained a triple-A rating and extremely aggressive pricing on the issue, which resulted in an inconsequential yield spread over U.S. Treasuries and (from an investor's perspective) underpriced call and sinking fund options. Bond investors spoke of the "scarcity value" of IBM paper, allowing the company to borrow below U.S. Treasury rates on an option-adjusted basis. From a credit perspective, IBM debt had nowhere to go but down. Fourteen years later, IBM's senior paper carried a rating of single A, failing to justify both the rating agencies' initial assessment of IBM's credit and the investors' early enthusiasm for IBM's bonds.

Bond investors had no opportunity to lend to the fast-growing, cash-generative IBM of the 1960s and 1970s. Instead, bond investors faced the option of providing funds to the 1980s and 1990s IBM that needed enormous sums of cash. As IBM's business matured and external financing requirements increased, the quality of the company's credit standing eroded.

Contrast the slow erosion of IBM's credit to instances in which corporate credit quality declines dramatically. In early April 2002, WorldCom's senior debt boasted a single-A rating from Moody's, placing the fixed-income obligations of the telecommunications company firmly in the investment-grade camp. On April 23, Moody's downgraded WorldCom to triple B, one notch above junk status, as the company struggled with lower demand from business customers and concerns regarding accounting issues. A little more than two weeks later, following chief executive Bernard Ebbers's resignation, on May 9 Moody's chopped WorldCom's rating to double-B, junk-level status. According to Bloomberg, the firm thereby achieved the dubious distinction of becoming the "biggest debtor to ever be cut to junk." [2]

To the dismay of WorldCom's creditors, the rapid-fire descent continued. On June 20, Moody's assigned a rating of single B to WorldCom's senior debt, citing deferral of interest payments on certain of the company's obligations. One week later, Moody's dropped WorldCom's rating to single C, characterized by the rating agency as "speculative in a high degree." In the middle of the following month, on July 15, the company defaulted on $23 billion worth of bonds. Finally, on

July 21, WorldCom filed for the largest bankruptcy in history, listing in its court filing assets in excess of $100 billion.

WorldCom's transformation from a single-A credit, possessing "adequate factors giving security to interest and principal," to a company in bankruptcy spanned less than three months. Most holders of bonds watched helplessly as the train wreck of WorldCom's bankruptcy demolished billions of dollars of value in what Moody's described as a "record-breaking default."[3]

During the final stage of the firm's death spiral, the WorldCom senior 6.75 percent notes of May 2008 fell from a price of 82.34 in the week before the Moody's downgrade to a price of 12.50 after the firm's bankruptcy. Owners of equity fared worse. From the week before the downgrade to the date of the bankruptcy, the stock price collapsed from $5.98 per share to 14 cents per share. Measured from the respective peaks, equity investors took by far the rougher ride. The World-Com senior notes traded as high as 104.07 on January 8, 2002, resulting in an 88.0 percent loss to the bankruptcy declaration. Stock-holders saw a price of $61.99 on June 21, 1999, creating a high-water mark that allowed investors to lose 99.8 percent to the date of the corporate demise.

Clearly, on a security-specific basis, WorldCom's collapse hurt equity holders more than it hurt debt holders, consistent with the notion that equity carries more risk than bonds. Yet, ironically, equity owners likely found it easier to recover from the WorldCom debacle than bondholders. The key to this apparent contradiction lies in the superior ability of a portfolio of equities to absorb the impact of single-security-induced adversity. Because individual stocks contain the potential to double, triple, quadruple, or more, a portfolio of equities holds any number of positions that could more than offset one particular loser. In contrast, high-quality bonds provide little opportunity for substantial appreciation. The left tail of the negatively skewed distribution of outcomes hurts bond investors in dramatic fashion.

The deterioration in IBM's ability to pay over more than two decades and the much more compressed collapse of WorldCom's credit standing mirrored a broader trend in the corporate debt markets. In recent times, corporate debt downgrades far outnumbered upgrades, forcing bond investors to manage against substantial headwinds. For the two decades ending June 30, 2003, Moody's Investors Service downgraded 5,955 debt issues while upgrading 3,412. In the last decade alone, $4.5 trillion of debt deteriorated in quality relative to the $3.4 trillion of debt that improved.[4]

The across-the-board decline in credit standards stems in part from the past two decades' relentless increase in leverage in corporate America. On June 30, 1983, the debt-equity ratio of S&P 500 companies stood at 0.46, signaling that the constituent companies of the S&P 500 carried 46 cents of debt for every dollar of equity. As leverage increased in popularity, on June 30, 1993, the ratio reached .94. By June 30, 2003, the S&P 500 posted a debt-equity ratio of 1.37, indicating that debt levels exceeded the equity base by nearly 40 percent. As the level of corporate borrowings increased, the security of corporate lenders decreased.

Countering the impact of higher-leverage ratios, the two-decade decline in interest rates made debt more affordable. As ten-year U.S. Treasury yields moved from 10.9 percent in June 1983 to 6.0 percent in June 1993 to 3.3 percent in June 2003, the burden imposed by debt service obligations diminished markedly. Consider the ratio between the cash flow available to service debt and a firm's interest expense. At June 30, 1983, the constituent companies of the S&P 500 boasted $3.90 of cash flow for every $1.00 of interest expense. A decade later, the cash flow coverage ratio stood at an identical 3.90, indicating that the positive impact of lower interest rates offset the negative impact of higher leverage. By June 30, 2003, the ratio increased to $6.25 of cash flow per $1.00 of interest expense, representing a dramatic improvement. Obviously, as cash flows increased relative to fixed charges, the security of the bondholders increased commensurately.

Balance sheets and income statements tell different stories. Debt-equity ratios increased markedly over the past two decades, signaling deterioration in corporate credit. Cash-flow-coverage ratios improved significantly over the same twenty years, suggesting an improvement in corporate financial health. The question remains unanswered as to why during this period rating agency downgrades far outnumber upgrades.

The particular nature of companies that issue corporate debt may contribute to the surplus of downgrades over upgrades. The universe of corporate debt issuers consists of generally mature companies. Relatively young, faster-growing companies tend to be underrepresented in the ranks of corporate bond issuers, in many cases because they have no need for external financing. Bond investors cannot purchase debt of Microsoft, because the company sees no need to tap the debt markets for funds. Bond investors can purchase debt of Ford Motor Company, because the firm requires enormous amounts of external finance. If the group of corporate debt issuers excludes fast-growing, cash-generative companies and includes more-mature, cash-consuming companies, perhaps bond investors should expect to see more credit deterioration than credit improvement. Regardless of the cause, if history provides a guide to the future, bond investors can expect more bad news than good on credit conditions.

Liquidity

Liquidity of corporate bond issues pales in comparison to the liquidity of U.S. Treasuries, which trade in the deepest, most liquid market in the world. Most corporate issues tend to trade infrequently, as many holders buy bonds at the initial offering and sock them away, pursuing buy-and-hold strategies.

Yet bond investors value liquidity highly. Compare U.S. Treasury issues and Private Export Funding Corporation (PEFCO) bonds. Even though both bonds enjoy full-faith-and-credit backing of the U.S. government, the less liquid PEFCO bonds trade at prices that produce yields of as much as 0.6 percent per annum higher than comparable-maturity Treasuries. The difference in yield stems entirely from the value that the market places on liquidity. Liquidity of most corporate bonds tends to stand closer to the PEFCOs than to the Treasuries, illustrating the significant yield premium that corporate bond issuers pay to compensate investors for lack of liquidity.

Highly liquid markets allow market players to pursue trading-intensive investment strategies. In contrast, long-term investors happily accept illiquidity in exchange for enhanced returns. While liquidity provides little value to long-term investors, holders of corporate bonds might wonder if yield spreads over comparable Treasury issues provide adequate compensation for the combination of credit risk, illiquidity, and call risk.

Callability

Callability poses a particularly vexing problem for corporate bond investors. Corporations frequently issue bonds with a call provision, allowing the issuer to redeem (or call) the bonds after a certain date at a fixed price. If interest rates decline, companies call existing bonds that bear higher-than-market rates, refunding the issue at lower rates and generating debt service savings.

The holder of corporate bonds faces a "heads you win, tails I lose" situation. If rates decline, the investor loses the now high-coupon bond through a call at a fixed price. If rates rise, the investor holds a now low-coupon bond that shows mark-to-market losses. The lack of parallelism in a callable corporate bond's response to rising and falling rates favors the corporate issuer over the bond investor.

The asymmetry implicit in the corporate bond call provision prompts questions regarding relative market power and sophistication. Why do many bonds incorporate call provisions? Why do put provisions appear rarely?* Surely, if interest rate increases prompt bond price decreases, investors would like to put the now underwater bonds to corporate issuers at a fixed price. The answer to the asymmetry no doubt lies in the superior sophistication of issuers of debt relative to the limited market savvy of purchasers of debt.

In point of fact, fixed-income markets attract analysts several notches below the quality and sophistication of equity analysts, even though the complexity of the task facing the fixed-income analyst arguably exceeds the difficulty of the equity analyst's job. Corporate bond investors need familiarity not only with the complexities of fixed-income markets, but also with the full range of issues involved in equity valuation. Since understanding the cushion provided by a company's equity proves essential in evaluating a corporation's ability to service debt, bond analysts require a full assessment of a company's stock price. Ironically, because financial rewards for successful equity analysis far outstrip the rewards for successful fixed-income analysis,

---

*A put option allows the put holder to sell a security at a fixed price during a specified period of time. If a bond issue contained a put option, the purchaser would enjoy the right to sell the bond (or put the bond) to the issuer at a fixed price during the period of time specified in the bond indenture.

the talent gravitates to the easier job of simply analyzing equity securities.

Negatively Skewed Distribution of Outcomes

Atop the peril facing investors in the corporate bond market stands a further handicap. The expected distribution of corporate bond returns exhibits a negative skew. The best outcome for holding bonds to maturity consists of receiving regular payments of interest and return of principal. The worst outcome represents default without recovery. The asymmetry of limited upside and unlimited downside produces a distribution of outcomes that contains a disadvantageous bias for investors.

Shorter holding periods manifest the same distributional problem. Return of principal at maturity (or prematurely upon corporate exercise of a call provision) limits appreciation potential. The nearer the date of expected repayment, the greater the dampening effect. In the case of credit deterioration, bondholders experience no such dampening effect. When corporate prospects deteriorate, bond prices decline as purchasers require greater returns for the now-riskier issue. In a worst-case default scenario, bond investors face a total wipeout. Both when holding bonds to maturity and for shorter terms, bond investors deal with a decidedly unattractive, limited-upside, unlimited-downside, negatively skewed distribution of returns.

Investors prefer positively skewed distributions by a wide margin. Active equity investors prize positions with limited downside, perhaps supported by readily ascertained asset values, and substantial potential upside, perhaps driven by anticipated operational improvements. Under such circumstances, investors see a high likelihood of preserving capital with a considerable possibility of significant gains. Positively skewed distributions of expected investment results definitively trump negatively skewed distributions, creating yet another hurdle for fixed-income investors.

Alignment of Interests

Interests of stockholders and bondholders diverge dramatically. Equity owners benefit by reducing the value of debt obligations. Equity owners suffer as the cost of debt finance increases. To the extent that corporate management serves shareholder interests, bondholders beware.

Consider the enterprise value of a corporate entity. Analysts assess company values either by evaluating the left side or the right side of the balance sheet. The left side of the balance sheet contains difficult-to-value physical assets. What price reflects the fair market value of the various and sundry facilities owned by Ford Motor Company? What value accrues to Ford from its world famous trademark? Even the most diligent analysts recoil at the thought of conducting the asset-by-asset inventory required to value the left side of a company's balance sheet.

The right side of the balance sheet contains easier-to-value liabilities. Summing the market value of a company's debt and the market value of a company's equity produces the enterprise value of a corporation. The enterprise value reflects the price an investor would pay to buy the entire company. If all equity were purchased at the market price and all debt and other liabilities were purchased at market prices, the purchaser would own the entire corporation (debt free!).

From this description of a firm's debt and equity positions follows the fundamental corporate finance principle that a firm's value stands independent of a firm's capital structure. Because an investor holds the power to undo what a firm has done with its capital structure, or to do what a firm has not done with its capital structure, the enterprise value of a company must be independent of its financing. For example, an investor might undo a firm's leverage by purchasing that firm's bonds, thereby negating the effect of corporate leverage. Conversely, an investor might create a leveraged position in a firm by borrowing to buy the firm's stock, thereby creating leverage where none existed. Since investors can destroy or create leverage independent of a company's actions, the enterprise value must be independent of the company's capital structure.*

The description of enterprise value highlights the clear, direct trade-off between the interests of stockholders and bondholders. The

---

*If corporations enjoy superior access to debt financing, either because of creditworthiness or tax advantages, then the value of the corporation may be enhanced by increasing balance sheet leverage.

value of the enterprise lies in the sum of the value of the debt and the value of the equity. To the extent that owners of a company reduce the value of the bondholders' position, the equity owners benefit. Stockholders gain by imposing losses on bondholders.

Because corporate management's interests generally align with equity investors, bondholders find themselves sitting across the table from corporate management. Recognizing the vulnerability created by relying on corporate management to protect lender interests, bond investors employ complicated contracts, called indentures, that seek to cause corporate issuers of debt to serve bondholder needs. Unfortunately for bondholders, contracts generally prove insufficient to influence corporate behavior in the desired manner, particularly when the hoped for actions run against the economic interests of management.

At times, the transfer of wealth from bondholders to stockholders occurs in dramatic fashion. When companies engage in leveraged-buyout or leveraged-recapitalization transactions, the debt levels of the corporations increase substantially. The increase in debt heightens the risk for existing lenders, leading directly to a decrease in the value of existing debt positions. KKR's 1989 RJR Nabisco buyout exemplifies the pain suffered by bondholders when debt levels balloon. During the bidding war for RJR, as the price for the company increased to ever-more-absurd levels, so did the prospective debt burden. Before the buyout, RJR Nabisco's liabilities amounted to something less than $12 billion. Post-buyout fixed obligations exceeded a staggering $35 billion. As a direct result of the dramatic change in capital structure, pre-buyout bondholders lost an estimated $1 billion of value while equity owners enjoyed a $10 billion windfall. The bondholder losses went directly into the equity owners' pockets.

In other situations, management employs more subtle methods to disadvantage bondholders. Simply by seeking to borrow at the lowest possible costs and on the most flexible terms, management acts to lessen the position of bondholders. Aside from working to achieve low borrowing rates, bond issuers might include favorably priced call options or attractively structured sinking fund provisions in bonds. Upon exercise of a call option, bondholders suffer and equity owners gain. Companies may negotiate indenture terms that grant wide operating latitude for management, including the flexibility to take actions that impair bondholders' interests.

The ultimate check on management's actions to disadvantage bondholders comes from a desire to retain access to the debt financing markets. Repeated, egregious actions that hurt bondholders may lead to a temporary hiatus in a company's ability to borrow on favorable terms. Yet the transactions most likely to raise bondholders' ire, buyouts and leveraged recapitalizations, occur infrequently, allowing the market's memory to fade before a company needs to reenter the market. More subtle actions taken by management to pick bondholders' pockets seldom receive much notice. By taking a seat across the table from corporate management, bondholders expose their position to potential impairment.

Market Characteristics

At December 31, 2003, the market value of investment-grade corporate bonds totaled $1.8 trillion. Yield to maturity stood at 4.5 percent, with the proviso that future changes in credit quality contain the possibility of increasing or decreasing the forecasted yield. Average maturity and duration stood at 9.7 years and 5.9 years, respectively.[5]

Summary

Many investors purchase corporate bonds, hoping to get something for nothing by earning an incremental yield over that available from U.S. Treasury bonds. If investors received a sufficient premium above the default-free U.S. Treasury rate to compensate for credit risk, illiquidity, and callability, then corporate bonds might earn a place in investor portfolios. Unfortunately, under normal circumstances investors receive scant compensation for the disadvantageous traits of corporate debt. At the end of the day, excess returns prove illusory as credit risk, illiquidity, and optionality work against the holder of corporate obligations, providing less than nothing to the corporate bond investor.

Corporate bond investors find the deck stacked against them as corporate management's interests align much more closely with equity investors' aspirations than with bond investors' goals. A further handicap to bond investors lies in the negative skew of the potential distribution of outcomes, limiting the upside potential without dampening the downside possibility.

Provision of a safe haven justifies inclusion of fixed income in well-diversified portfolios. Unfortunately, in times of duress, credit risk and optionality serve to undermine the ability of corporate bonds to protect portfolios from the influences of financial crisis or deflation. In troubled economic times, a corporation's ability to meet contractual obligations diminishes, causing bond prices to decline. In declining-rate environments, caused by flight to quality or by deflation, bond call provisions increase in value, heightening the probability that companies call high-coupon debt securities away from bondholders. Sensible investors avoid corporate debt, because credit risk and callability undermine the ability of fixed-income holdings to provide portfolio protection in times of financial or economic disruption.

Historical returns confirm that investors received insufficient compensation for the array of risks inherent in corporate debt. For the ten years ending December 31, 2003, Lehman Brothers reported annualized returns of 6.7 percent for U.S. Treasury bonds and 7.4 percent for investment-grade corporate bonds. While index-specific differences in market characteristics and period-specific influences on market returns cause the comparison to fall short of a perfect apples-to-apples standard, the 0.7 percent per annum difference between Treasury and corporate returns fails to compensate corporate bond investors for default risk, illiquidity, and optionality. U.S. government bonds provide a superior alternative.

HIGH-YIELD BONDS

High-yield bonds consist of corporate debt obligations that fail to meet blue chip standards, falling in rating categories below investment grade. The highest category of junk bonds carries a double-B rating, described by Moody's as having "speculative elements," leading to a future that "cannot be considered as well assured." Moving down the ratings rungs, single-B bonds "lack characteristics of the desirable investment," triple-C bonds "are of poor standing," double-C bonds "are speculative in high degree," and the lowest class of bonds (single-C) have "extremely poor prospects of ever attaining any real investment standing."[6]

High-yield bonds suffer from a concentrated version of the unattractive traits of high-grade corporate debt. Credit risk in the junk-bond market far exceeds risk levels in the investment-grade market. Illiquidity abounds, with the lowest-rated credits trading by appointment only. Callability poses the familiar "heads you win, tails I lose" proposition for owners of junk bonds, with an added twist.

Holders of both investment-grade and junk bonds face callability concerns in declining-rate environments. Lower rates prompt refunding calls in which the issuer pays a fixed price to the bondholders and reissues debt at lower cost. Holders of high-quality paper and junk bonds face interest-rate-induced refunding risks of similar nature.

Above and beyond the possibility that junk bondholders lose bonds in a declining-rate environment, callability potentially thwarts the junk bondholder's ability to benefit from an improving credit. One of the goals of junk-bond purchasers involves identifying companies that face a brighter future, leading to greater ability to service debt, improved marks from the rating agencies, and higher prices in the market. Fixed-price call options serve to limit the ability of junk-bond investors to benefit from improving credit fundamentals, marking yet another means by which equity holders benefit at the expense of bondholders.

Packaging Corporation of America

Consider the fate of investors in Packaging Corporation of America (PCA) 9.625 percent Series B Senior Subordinated Notes of April 1, 2009. Issued by a highly leveraged manufacturer of containerboard and corrugated cartons, at the initial offering in April 1999 the bonds carried a coupon rate approximately 500 basis points above comparable maturity Treasury notes and boasted a rating at the bottom of the single-B category. According to Moody's Investors Service, the single B-rating indicated that "assurance of interest and principal payments or of maintenance of other terms in the contract over any long period of time may be small."[7] Purchasers of the bonds no doubt hoped for a better future, one in which the likelihood of maintenance of contract terms might be larger rather than smaller. Perhaps investors foresaw a future characterized by an improvement in corporate fundamentals, a bull market in bonds, or both.

The PCA 9.625s of April 2009 provided more than $530 million of proceeds to help finance a leveraged buyout of Tenneco's packaging business by Madison Dearborn, a private-equity firm. The single-B rating flowed naturally from the highly leveraged nature of the buyout transaction. At the time of the bond issuance in the second quarter of 1999, PCA carried net debt of $1.6 billion, representing a borrowing level equal to 4.9 times the company's equity base.

In January 2000, PCA floated equity shares in an initial public offering conducted near the peak of a two-decade-long bull market. Underwritten by Goldman Sachs, the 46.25 million shares, offered at $12 each, raised a total of $555 million in proceeds for the company. As for the bondholders, the 9.625s of April 2009 retained a single-B rating and a price near par.

Shortly after the company's IPO, the hoped-for improvement in PCA's credit picture began. Second quarter 2000 net debt declined to $1.3 billion, improving the debt-equity ratio to 2.2. In April 2000, Moody's increased the company's senior subordinated note rating from single B3, the lowest rung of the single-B category, to single B2, the middle-rung rating. More good news followed in September 2000, when Moody's boosted the rating of the PCA 9.625s of April 2009 to B1, the top of the single-B category. In a mere eighteen months, the quality of the senior subordinated securities showed significant improvement.

Positive momentum in PCA's financial situation continued. By the third quarter of 2001, the company paid down enough debt to bring outstanding borrowings to $751 million, resulting in a debt-equity ratio of 1.1. Moody's Investors Service recognized the improvement by assigning a mid-range double-B rating to PCA's senior subordinated debt, moving investors from the "small assurance" of single-B paper to the far-more-exalted "uncertainty of position" of double-B obligations.

By the second quarter of 2003, bondholders faced far better circumstances than they confronted in January 2000. Over that period, net debt declined from $1,292 million to $607 million. The debt-equity ratio decreased from 2.4 to 0.9. Credit fundamentals moved dramatically in favor of PCA's junk-bond investors.

Not only did the PCA 9.625s of 2009 benefit from the company's ability to pay down debt, thereby improving the credit standing of the remaining obligations, but the bonds also profited from a dramatic decline in interest rates. In January 2000, ten-year U.S. Treasury rates stood at 6.7 percent. By June 2003, ten-year Treasury yields halved, promising investors only 3.3 percent. The powerful bond market rally and the dramatic credit improvement combined to move the price of the PCA 9.625s of 2009 from approximately par in early 2000 to around 108 in June 2003.

Unfortunately for bondholders, call provisions of the PCA 9.625s of April 2009 dampened the security's appreciation potential. On April 1, 2004, the company enjoyed the right to purchase the outstanding bonds at a fixed price of 104.81. Because of improved credit standing and lower interest rates, PCA would almost certainly exercise its right to call the bonds and refinance at lower rates. Investors evaluating the bonds in mid-2003 knew they would almost certainly lose the bonds at a price of 104.81 on April Fool's Day in 2004, placing a limit on the amount they would reasonably pay for the securities.

In fact, holders of the PCA 9.625s of April 2009 did not need to wait until April 2004 to relinquish their bonds. On June 23, 2003, the company announced a tender offer for the securities at a price of 110.24, representing somewhat more than a two-point premium to the pre-tender market price. The company opted to pay 110.24 for the bonds on July 21, 2003, instead of waiting to pay 104.81 on April 1, 2004, because the combination of the firm's improved credit condition and the market's decreased interest rates made it too expensive for PCA to leave the bonds outstanding. The tender proved successful, as holders of 99.3 percent of the notes surrendered their bonds to the company.

PCA issued new bonds to refund the PCA 9.625s of April 2009, paying much lower rates of 4.5 percent on the five-year tranche and 5.9 percent on the ten-year tranche. The dramatically reduced coupons saved PCA tens of millions of dollars of interest expense over the remaining term of the original financing. Both of the new refinancing bond issues eschewed fixed-price call provisions, as the junk-bond investors firmly demanded that the company close the barn door after the stalls had emptied.

From an investor's perspective, accepting the company's tender maximized returns. Based on the bond's coupon, the tender price, and the call price, if investors held the securities until the call date, they faced an expected return of only 60 to 65 basis points over comparable-maturity Treasuries. Rational holders of the PCA 9.625s of 2009 had no choice but to tender their holdings.

The call provision proved costly to PCA's senior subordinated bondholders. In June 2003, the bonds traded in a close range, from a low of 108.2 to a high of 108.6, averaging approximately 108.4. Based on lower interest rates and PCA's improved credit standing, had the PCA 9.625s of 2009 not had a call provision, the price would have been in excess of 125. The company's fixed-price call option dramatically reduced the potential for junk bondholder gains.

In spite of the dampening effect of the PCA 9.625s' call provision, bondholders received handsome holding-period returns. Buoyed by improving credit fundamentals and declining interest rates, the junk-bond investors garnered a return of 49.2 percent from January 28, 2000, the date of the company's IPO, to July 21, 2003, the date of the completion of the tender offer. Junk-bond investors could not hope for better circumstances or better results.

How did the PCA junk bond returns compare to results from closely related alternative investments? Strikingly, a comparable-maturity U.S. Treasury note produced a holding period return of 45.8 percent, as the noncallable nature of the government issue allowed investors to benefit fully from the bond market rally. The 3.4 percent holding period increment, realized by PCA bondholders over the three and one-half years, represents scant compensation for accepting a high degree of credit risk. U.S. Treasuries produced risk-adjusted returns significantly higher than those realized by holders of the PCA 9.625s.

Holders of PCA stock faced a tough set of circumstances. In contrast to the strong market enjoyed by bondholders, equity owners faced a dismal market environment. From the date of PCA's IPO, which took place near the peak of one of the greatest stock market bubbles ever, to the bond-tender offer date, the S&P 500 declined a cumulative 24.3 percent. Bucking a decidedly adverse market trend, PCA's equity rose from the initial offering price of $12.00 in January 2000 to $18.05 on July 21, 2003, representing a holding-period gain of 50.4 percent. Even in the worst of worlds for equity holders and the best of worlds for bondholders, the equity owners of PCA eked out a victory.

Upon reflection, the superior returns garnered by PCA's equity holders might be expected. Improving credit fundamentals for junk bond positions necessarily correspond to an increase in the equity cushion supporting the company's fixed liabilities. An increase in the stock price enhances the underlying support for the firm's debt burden. Since improving credit fundamentals frequently go hand in hand with rallying stock prices, investors face better odds by owning unlimited-upside stocks as opposed to constrained-potential bonds.

In the case of deteriorating credit fundamentals, junk-bond investors attain little or no edge relative to equity investors. Recall that the PCA 9.625s of April 2009 entered the markets in 1999 at the bottom of the single-B rating category, precariously positioned with a "small assurance of maintenance of contract terms." Credit deterioration would likely damage the investments of bondholders and stockholders alike.

Junk-bond investors cannot win. When fundamentals improve, stock returns dominate bond returns. When rates decline, noncallable bonds provide superior risk-adjusted returns. When fundamentals deteriorate, junk-bond investors fall along with equity investors. Well-informed investors avoid the no-win consequences of high-yield fixed-income investing.

Alignment of Interests

Junk-bond owners face misalignment of interest problems even more severe than those faced by investment-grade bondholders. In the case of fallen-angel junk issues that began life as high-quality bonds and suffered a fall from grace, declines in credit quality correspond to reductions in equity values. In distressed situations, corporate managements usually work hard to prevent further erosion in the company's equity base. Tools available to management include revenue enhancement and cost reduction. Obviously, reducing interest expense and otherwise decreasing the value of debt obligations represents one important means by which management can improve the equity position. Holders of fallen angels find their interests at odds with the interests of corporate management.

In the case of new-issue junk bonds, particularly those employed to finance leveraged-buyout deals or leveraged-recapitalization transactions, bondholders confront even more highly motivated, adversar-

ial management groups. Sophisticated, equity-oriented financial engineers bring numerous tools to bear on the problem of increasing equity values substantially and rapidly. As the financial operators work
to minimize the cost of debt, the bondholders realize the mirror image
of cost minimization in the form of return diminution.

Market Characteristics

At December 31, 2003, the market value of high-yield corporate bonds
totaled $550 billion. Yield to maturity amounted to 7.9 percent, with
the market showing an average maturity of 8.2 years and an average
duration of 4.8 years.

Summary

Junk-bond investors face a concentrated combination of the factors
that make high-grade corporate bonds a poor choice for investors.
Magnified credit risk, greater illiquidity, and more valuable call options pose a triple threat to bondholders seeking high risk-adjusted returns. The relatively high cost of junk-bond financing provides
incentives to stock-price-driven corporate managements to diminish
the value of the bond positions in order to enhance the standing of
share owners.

As protection against financial accidents or deflationary periods,
junk bonds prove even less useful than investment-grade bonds. The
factors that promise incremental yield—credit risk, illiquidity, and
callability—work against junk-bond owners in times of crisis, undermining the ability of junk bonds to provide portfolio protection.

The recent historical experience of junk-bond investors confirms
the inadvisability of owning debt positions in highly leveraged corporations. For the ten years ending December 31, 2003, Lehman Brothers
U.S. Corporate High-Yield Index produced annualized returns of 5.9
percent relative to 6.7 percent for U.S. Treasuries and 7.4 percent for
investment-grade corporates. While structural differences in the indices
(most notably differences in duration) make the comparison less than
perfect, the fact that junk-bond investors took greater risk for less return comes through loud and clear.

TAX-EXEMPT BONDS

Qualifying governmental entities enjoy the ability to issue tax-exempt bonds that allow bondholders to earn interest that incurs no federal tax liability. Certain issues permit eligible residents to receive exemption from state and local taxes as well. For example, bonds floated by New York City provide a triple tax exemption to New York City residents, freeing holders from paying income taxes levied by the City of New York, the State of New York, and the U.S. government. Connecticut residents who own City of New York obligations obtain only a federal tax exemption. Market participants sometimes refer to tax-exempt bonds as municipal bonds, even though the range of issuers extends far beyond the ranks of America's municipalities.

From a superficial perspective, tax-exempt bonds appear to offer investors the opportunity to place fixed-income assets in taxable accounts (where their special tax characteristics lessen or eliminate tax consequences), freeing capacity in tax-deferred accounts for higher-tax-burdened assets. Regrettably, the problems of credit risk and callability lessen the appeal of tax-exempt bonds to investors.

The tax-exempt debt market shares with the corporate debt market an imbalance of power between issuers and purchasers of debt. When more-sophisticated borrowers deal with less-sophisticated lenders, the outcome favors the borrowers. Wall Street bankers, eager to support the winning side, fashion deals to benefit the stronger player. Borrowers issue debt at interest rate levels that provide inadequate recompense for the risk that the borrower fails to make timely and complete payments of interest and principal. Borrowers issue debt with inexpensive call provisions that create the opportunity for repurchasing and refunding issues at lower interest rates. Lenders benefit from no symmetric provision that protects them in the case of higher interest rates. In structuring deal terms, Wall Street gains the opportunity to satisfy the debt-issuing party, leading to an anticipated stream of new business opportunities.

A large number of individual investors buy and sell tax-exempt bonds directly. Because the secondary market for tax-exempt bonds suffers from an extraordinary lack of transparency, the Wall Street dealing community enjoys a dramatically unfair edge in the trading of tax-exempt debt. Careful investors in tax-exempt securities weigh the substantial one-time costs of direct trades against the material ongoing costs of mutual-fund investments, attempting to choose the lesser of the two evils.

Pre-Tax and After-Tax Yields

Market mechanisms cause after-tax yields for taxable and tax-exempt bonds to move toward rough equality. When markets operate efficiently, the highest marginal tax rate plays a powerful role in defining the difference between taxable and tax-exempt yields.

The equilibrating mechanism generally works most effectively for short-term debt maturities, because less uncertainty exists regarding the immediate future. Consider three-month interest rates in early September 2004. As shown in Table 4.1, investors could earn 1.9 percent on a taxable basis by holding high-quality corporate paper or 1.2 percent on a tax-exempt basis by holding high-quality general obligation bonds. Note that an investor who owns taxable short-term paper (and pays taxes at the highest marginal rate of 35 percent) earns 1.2 percent on an after-tax basis.* The equality of the taxable investor's after-tax yield of 1.2 percent and the tax-exempt investor's yield of 1.2 percent indicates that in this case, the short-term money markets work well.

Table 4.1 Longer-Term Tax-Exempt Investors Earn Premium Rates of Return (Percent)

Term to Maturity	Taxable Yield	Equivalent Tax-Exempt Yield	Tax-Exempt Yield	Actual Tax-Exempt Advantage
3 months	1.9	1.2	1.2	0.0
1 year	2.5	1.6	1.5	−0.1
5 years	3.8	2.5	2.7	0.2
10 years	4.7	3.1	3.6	0.6
30 years	5.5	3.6	4.6	1.1

Source: Bloomberg, *6 September 2004.*
Notes: Taxable yields reflect trading levels for triple-A rated industrial company securities. Equivalent tax-exempt yields reflect a marginal tax rate of 35 percent applied to the taxable yields. Tax-exempt yields reflect trading levels for triple-A rated general obligation securities.

---

*Multiply the taxable interest rate of 1.9 percent times 1.0 minus the tax rate (1.0 − 0.35) to realize 1.2 percent on an after-tax basis.

For longer maturities, the equilibrating mechanism works less well. Note that thirty-year tax-exempt yields exceed after-tax taxable yields by a full percentage point. A variety of factors complicate the relationship between taxable and tax-exempt yields, including credit concerns and liquidity issues. Even though Table 4.1 shows yield levels for triple-A rated securities, whether tax-exempt or taxable, the market may differentiate between the default probability of a triple-A rated municipal bond and a triple-A rated corporate bond. The market almost certainly recognizes that tax-exempt bonds trade in terribly illiquid markets, causing investors to demand higher yields to compensate for lower liquidity. Differences in default risk and tradability mask the hoped-for apples-to-apples comparison between long-term taxable and tax-exempt yields.

Perhaps the most important question for longer-maturity tax-exempt bonds concerns the uncertainty regarding future tax rates and the longevity of the tax exemption. If tax rates change, the value of the tax exemption for municipal bonds changes too. A reduction in tax rates reduces the value of the tax exemption and vice versa. If Congress limits or eliminates the tax exemption, the values of municipal bonds would decline. Legislative uncertainty contributes to higher-than-expected long-term tax-exempt yields.

Proving that generalizations invite exceptions, sometimes market forces fail to work on the short end of the yield curve. Consider yields for Vanguard's money-market offerings. In September 2004, the tax-exempt money fund yield matched the taxable fund yield. A top-marginal-bracket taxpayer benefited to the tune of 0.4 percent on an after-tax basis by choosing the tax-exempt fund. The early-September yields represented more than a passing opportunity. For the year prior to August 31, 2004, Vanguard's tax-exempt fund produced a yield of 0.9 percent, materially higher than the taxable fund's yield of 0.8 percent. Of course, the investor earns the higher tax-exempt yield before considering the advantages of tax exemption! On rare occasions, markets confound proponents of the efficient market hypothesis, providing opportunities for easy money.

Since after-tax returns for taxable and tax-exempt bonds tend to fall in the same neighborhood, the primary benefit to owning tax-exempt debt lies in freeing capacity in an investor's tax-deferred accounts for non-fixed-income assets. While investors gain clear

**Table 4.2 Vanguard's Taxable Money-Market
Investors Miss an Opportunity**

Fund	Status	Yield as of September 3, 2004 (Percent)	One-Year Return Through August 31, 2004 (Percent)
Vanguard Prime Money Market Fund	Taxable	1.2	0.8
Vanguard Tax-Exempt Money Market Fund	Tax-exempt	1.2	0.9

Source: Vanguard.

short-term economic benefits from employing tax-deferred accounts for non-fixed-income assets, the short-run gains come at the expense of long-run portfolio characteristics. Investors who substitute tax-exempt debt for core holdings of Treasury bonds dilute the value of fixed income's diversifying power by introducing call risk and credit risk to the bond portfolio.

Call Options

Unsophisticated purchasers of municipal bonds demand too little in terms of yield premium to compensate for the value of fixed-price call options. While comprehensive data on call options do not exist, a snapshot of the pricing of call features available to a triple-A rated tax-exempt issuer illustrates the disadvantages that municipal bond investors face.

In late July 2004, triple-A rated, thirty-year, tax-exempt, non-callable borrowing costs totaled 4.8 percent. With noncallable bonds, issuers accept the responsibility to pay the stated interest rate year in and year out for thirty years, regardless of the future course of interest rates. If the issuer were to incorporate the ability to call the bonds at par after five years, the borrowing costs increase to 5.0 percent. The cost of the call provision amounts to the 0.2 percent differential between the noncallable yield and the callable yield. By paying a fifth-of-a-percent yield premium, the bond issuer acquires the right to repurchase the bonds at a fixed price, allowing for profitable refunding transactions in the event that interest rates decline.

While the call option cost of 0.2 percent in yield terms seems like small potatoes, over the thirty-year life of a bond the tiny tubers add up. Converting the yield differential to a dollar-price difference leads to the conclusion that the market values the call option at 3.6 percent of the bond's offering price.

A variety of models provide methods to value call options. Unlike many academic constructs that contain little real-world insight, option-pricing models play an important day-to-day role in securities markets. Market markers and market players rely on option-pricing models to determine fair value for option-related positions, employing model-derived fair-value calculations in making purchase and sale decisions.

A comparison of the estimated cost of the call option to the theoretical value of the option indicates that the borrower benefits at the lender's expense. The value of the five-year par call option as calculated by Bloomberg clocks in at 5.0 percent of the offering price, representing a 1.4 percent premium over the issuer's estimated cost. In other words, according to Bloomberg, the bondholder subsidizes the bond issuer by an amount equal to 1.4 percent of the bond's price. An alternate model, developed by Lehman Brothers, places the value of the five-year par call at 6.3 percent, implying a 2.7 percent premium over the borrower's cost. As outlined in Table 4.3, for both five-year and ten-year par calls, the value of the option exceeds the issuer's cost by material amounts. The difference between the theoretical value and the market value (issuer's cost) represents a clear boon to bond issuers.

An examination of option values at one point in time provides limited evidence of option mispricing. Yet, the valuation discrepancy proves consistent with the imbalance in power between the sellers of securities and the buyers of securities. Investors in municipal bonds lose in the call pricing contest.

Trading Costs

The problems with municipal bond investments intensify when individual investors attempt to execute direct purchases and sales of tax-exempt debt issues. Individuals directly own approximately one-third of the $1.9 trillion in municipal bonds outstanding, suggesting that

**Table 4.3 Market Value of Municipal Bond Call Options
Fall Short of Theoretical Values**

Hypothetical Triple-A Rated 30-Year Bonds (Percent)

Non-Call Term	Market Value	Black-Derman-Toy Value	Lehman Brothers Value
5 years	3.6	5.0	6.3
10 years	2.2	3.9	4.3

Notes: Data provided by Lehman Brothers. Black-Derman-Toy model calculation made using Bloomberg software. Lehman Brothers' valuation stems from the firm's proprietary valuation model. Data as of July 2004.

market structure issues affect a large number of players.[8] Recognizing the potential for abuse of individual investor interests, the U.S. government created a regulatory framework for the tax-exempt bond market.

The Municipal Securities Rulemaking Board (MSRB), authorized by an act of Congress in 1975 "to protect investors and the public interest," oversees the issuance and trading of municipal bonds.[9] Ironically, the MSRB superintends a dealer-friendly, investor-hostile arena. The source of the pro–Wall Street bias becomes clear when evaluating the membership of the MSRB. According to the *Wall Street Journal,* in early 2004, ten of the fifteen members worked for banks or brokerage firms. With the fox in charge of the chicken coop, little wonder that municipal bond investors operate in the dark.

Asymmetric access to information constitutes one of the most significant problems in the tax-exempt bond arena. Main Street's individual investors operate with a severe informational disadvantage relative to Wall Street's institutional players. Up until the end of 2004, investors received data on bond trades with a one-day lag.[10] The lack of real-time publicly available information hurt smaller market participants, as the dealing community enjoyed information about the here and now, while small transactors knew only the there and then.

Poor market transparency results in higher costs for investors and higher profits for dealers. A study by two SEC economists concludes that "the individual investors trading tax-advantaged municipal bonds pay an 'effective spread' of two percent of the securities' price."[11] The authors note that the municipal bond spread exceeds the average spread for stock market trades, a startling result, since riskier equity assets should cost more to trade than less risky bond positions. In a damning indictment of municipal dealers' greed, smaller trades cost proportionally more than larger trades, turning the expected relationship between size and cost on its head. In a disarmingly simple conclusion, the authors state "we attribute these results to the general lack of price transparency in the bond markets. Large institutional traders generally have a good sense of the values of municipal bonds, whereas small traders do not."[12] Municipal bond market makers prey on the small investor's vulnerability. Sensible investors avoid dealing with Wall Street sharks.

Alignment of Interests

Tax-exempt bond investors face the same set of misaligned interests that bedevil all non-Treasury bondholders. Aggressively priced debt issues that benefit the borrowers fail to compensate the lenders. Wall Street sharpies exploit Main Street marks both on initial offerings and during subsequent trading. Careful investors approach municipal bonds with great caution.

Market Characteristics

At December 31, 2003, the market value of municipal bonds totaled $923 billion. Yield to maturity amounted to 4.1 percent, with the market exhibiting an average maturity of 13.8 years and an average duration of 8.1 years.

Summary

Tax-exempt securities exhibit a powerful attraction for taxable investors based on the valuable feature that exempts interest income from federal and, in some cases, state taxes. Issues related to tax-rate uncertainty, credit risk, call optionality, and trading costs combine to diminish in dramatic fashion the utility of tax-exempt bonds.

For shorter-term maturities, the negative factors cause investors far less concern. In the case of a tax-exempt money-market fund, the near-dated maturity of the underlying securities obviates concerns regarding tax regime changes and mitigates concerns regarding credit risk.

Money-market instruments carry no call options and trade in relatively efficient transparent markets. Short-term tax-exempt money-market funds deserve serious consideration.

As term to maturity increases, the troubling aspects of tax-exempt debt increase in lock step. Changes in marginal tax rates and changes in credit quality possess the power to alter the value, positively or negatively, of longer-term tax-exempt bonds. Call options and opaque trading regimes generally serve to diminish expected returns. Investors in longer-term tax-exempt securities gain a valuable tax advantage at the expense of the certain portfolio protection benefits of non-callable default-free U.S. Treasury securities.

ASSET-BACKED SECURITIES

Asset-backed securities consist of fixed-income instruments that rely on a broad range of underlying assets (the backing in asset-backed) to provide cash flows and security for payments to bondholders. While the most commonly used asset in asset-backed securities consists of home mortgages, bankers employ assets ranging from credit card receivables to commercial lease payments to automobile finance obligations as collateral for asset-backed deals.

Asset-backed transactions share a high degree of sophisticated financial structuring. Driven by a security issuer's desire to remove assets from the balance sheet and obtain low costs for the financing, the asset-backed security purchaser sits across the table from a formidable adversary.

In the case of mortgage-backed securities—financial instruments that pass through mortgage payments from homeowners to security holders—investors face an unappealing set of responses to changes in interest rates. If interest rates decline, homeowners enjoy the opportunity to prepay and refinance the mortgage. Just as discharging a high-rate mortgage favors the borrower, it hurts the holder of a mortgage-backed security by extinguishing an attractive stream of high interest payments. Similarly, if rates rise, homeowners tend to pay only the minimum required principal and interest payment. Holders of mortgage-backed paper lose high-return assets in a low-rate environment and retain low-return assets in a high-rate environment.

In exchange for accepting a security that shortens when investors prefer lengthening and lengthens when investors prefer shortening, holders of mortgage-backed securities receive a premium rate of return. Whether the premium constitutes fair compensation for the complex options embedded in mortgage securities poses an extremely difficult question. Wall Street's version of rocket scientists employ complicated computer models in a quest to determine the fair value of mortgage-backed securities. Sometimes the models work, sometimes not. If financial engineers face challenges in getting the option pricing right, what chance do individual investors have?

Optionality proves even more difficult to assess than credit risk. In the case of fixed-income instruments with credit risk, sensible investors look at bond yields with skepticism, knowing that part of the return may be lost to corporate downgrades or defaults. In the case of fixed-income instruments with high degrees of optionality, everyday investors hold no clue as to the appropriate amount by which to discount stated yields to adjust for the possible costs of the options. In fact, many professionals fail to understand the difficult dynamics of fixed-income options.

Piper Capital's Worth Bruntjen

In a celebrated case of the early 1990s, Worth Bruntjen, a fixed-income specialist at Piper Capital in Minneapolis, built an enormous reputation as a manager of mortgage-backed securities portfolios. Based on stellar results in the early years of the decade, Bruntjen attracted significant amounts of capital from retail and institutional investors alike.

Bruntjen managed the Piper Jaffray American Government Securities Fund (AGF), one of a group of mortgage-bond investment vehicles for retail investors. Driven by a powerful bull market in bonds and a portfolio highly sensitive to interest rates, for the five years ending December 31, 1993, the fund returned 19.3 percent per annum, representing a substantial increment over the 11.2 percent annual return of the Salomon Brothers Mortgage Index. Bruntjen's top-of-the-charts returns prompted Morningstar to name this "visionary and guiding force" runner-up in its portfolio-manager-of-the-year competition.[13]

Public records indicate that Bruntjen counted the State of Florida among his institutional separate account clients. In fact, Florida pursued a perverse investment strategy with its conservative operating funds, taking assets from poorly performing managers and adding assets to market-beating accounts. As a result of Bruntjen's stellar results, by January 1994, the State of Florida's account with Bruntjen totaled in excess of $430 million, more than double that of the nearest competitor.[14]

Bruntjen explained his strategy: "We buy government-agency paper that has a higher interest rate than the thirty-year bond, but has an average life of only three to five years."[15] The fund manager's "paper" included mortgages and mortgage derivatives with a bull market bias. Nonetheless, Bruntjen's something-for-nothing explanation of his investment approach found a receptive audience. Funds under Bruntjen's management rose rapidly until early 1994.

Unfortunately for fixed-income investors, the fall of 1993 marked a high point of the bond market rally, with ten-year U.S. Treasury yields reaching a twenty-six-year low of 5.3 percent. Within a few short months, by May 1994, a wrenching decline in bond prices drove yields to 7.4 percent. The *Wall Street Journal* described the spring meltdown: "The bloodbath in mortgage derivatives is claiming new casualties as investors and dealers continue to rush for the exits, feeding a vicious cycle of falling prices and evaporating demand."[16] The bear market that rocked bond portfolios laid waste Bruntjen's approach.

During calendar year 1994, AGF's individual investors experienced investment losses of nearly 29 percent. In contrast, the Salomon Brothers Mortgage Index posted a modest 1.4 percent loss. Between January and September, the State of Florida incurred investment losses of $90 million, an entirely unacceptable result for supposedly conservatively invested operating funds. Frustrated by the dismal returns, Florida announced that it would pull nearly $120 million from Bruntjen's account. Retail and institutional investors suffered side by side.

The bond market carnage turned Bruntjen's strategy on its head. When rates rose, the mortgage specialist's use of "significant investments in volatile derivatives like inverse floating-rate bonds and principal-only strips" caused his funds to behave like long-term, thirty-year bonds, not like the shorter-term bonds he cited in his strategy description.[17] Heightened sensitivity to interest rates in a rising rate environment doomed Bruntjen's investors.

Worth Bruntjen, Morningstar's "visionary," failed to understand the risks of his strategy as did Bruntjen's superiors at Piper Capital. Supposedly sophisticated institutional investors at the State of Florida failed to understand the risks of his strategy. Mutual-fund consulting firm Morningstar failed to understand the risks of his strategy. The complexity inherent in understanding and evaluating mortgage-related securities argues for avoiding exposure to the potentially harmful options imbedded in mortgage instruments.

From a broader portfolio perspective, the optionality in mortgage-backed securities works against investors who wish to use the bonds to hedge against deflation or financial distress. The prepayment option held by the homeowner works like a call option on a corporate bond. If rates fall, prompted by deflationary forces or financial distress, the holder of mortgage-backed securities may lose the investment, along with protection against the circumstances that caused exercise of the call to prove profitable for the borrower.

Alignment of Interests

Holders of asset-backed securities sit across the table from some of the marketable securities world's most sophisticated financial engineers. At best, asset-backed security investors buying newly minted securities should anticipate low returns from the issuer's use of a complex structure to further the corporate objective of generating low-cost debt. At worst, the complexity of asset-backed securities leads to an opacity that prevents investors from understanding the intrinsic character of investment positions. In extreme situations, the Rube Goldberg nature of asset-backed security arrangements contributes to the potential for serious damage to investor portfolios.

Market Characteristics

At December 31, 2003, the market value of asset-backed securities totaled $138 billion. Yield to maturity amounted to 3.2 percent, with the market exhibiting an average maturity of 3.1 years and an average duration of 2.7 years.[18]

Summary

Asset-backed securities involve a high degree of financial engineering. As a general rule of thumb, the more complexity that exists in a Wall Street creation, the faster and farther investors should run. At times, the creators and issuers of complex securities fail to understand how the securities might behave under various circumstances. What chance does the nonprofessional investor have?

Many mortgage-backed securities enjoy the support of government-sponsored enterprises (GSE), causing investors to assume that the securities carry low levels of risk. Investor assumptions may prove false on two counts. First, the credit risk may ultimately prove greater than market participants assume. Second, the GSE-induced investor complacency may mask significant risk of exposure to hard-to-understand options. Investors beware.

Just as with other forms of fixed income, the issuer of asset-backed securities seeks cheap financing. Cheap financing for issuers translates into low returns for investors. Combine low expected returns with high complexity and investor interests suffer.

As with many other segments of the fixed-income markets, investors in asset-backed securities appear not to have reaped rewards for accepting credit and call risk. For the ten years ending December 31, 2003, the Lehman Brothers Asset-Backed Security Index returned 7.2 percent per annum, falling short of the Lehman Brothers U.S. Treasury Index return of 7.5 percent per annum. Like other comparisons of bond index returns, the numbers do not account for differences in index composition. Nonetheless, over the past decade asset-backed bond investors appear to have fallen short in the quest to generate risk-adjusted excess returns.

FOREIGN BONDS

By asset size, foreign-currency-denominated bonds represent a formidable market, falling just short of the aggregate market value of U.S.-dollar-denominated debt. Yet, in spite of the market's size, foreign bonds offer little of value to U.S. investors.

Consider bonds of similar maturity and similar credit quality, with one denominated in U.S. dollars and the other denominated in foreign currency. Because monetary conditions differ from country to country, the two bonds would likely promise different interest rates. An investor might expect that different interest rates and different economic conditions in different countries would lead to different investment results. If, however, the investor hedges each of the foreign bond's cash flows by selling sufficient foreign currency in the forward markets to match the anticipated receipt of interest and principal payments, then the U.S. dollar cash flows of the dollar-denominated bond match exactly the U.S. dollar cash flows of the foreign-currency-denominated bond hedged into U.S. dollars. In other words, an unhedged foreign currency bond consists of a U.S. dollar bond plus some foreign exchange exposure.

Foreign currencies, in and of themselves, provide no expected return. Some market players, as part of so-called macro strategies, speculate on the direction of foreign exchange rates. Foreign bond mutual funds provide a vehicle through which investment managers sometimes take speculative positions. Top-down bets on currencies fail to generate a reliable source of excess returns, because the factors influencing economic conditions, in general, and interest rates, in particular, prove far too complex to predict with consistency. Sensible investors avoid currency speculation.

In a portfolio context, foreign exchange exposure may produce the benefit of additional diversification. Even with no expected return, the lack of full correlation between currency movements and other asset-class fluctuations reduces portfolio risk. However, investors should obtain foreign exchange exposure not through foreign bond positions, but in connection with an asset class expected to produce superior returns, namely foreign equities.

Since foreign currency positions, per se, promise a zero expected return, investors in foreign bonds expect returns similar to returns from U.S. dollar bonds. Yet, unhedged foreign bonds fail to provide the same protection against financial crisis or deflation enjoyed by holders of U.S. Treasury securities. In the event of a market trauma, U.S. investors have no idea what impact foreign exchange rates will have on the value of foreign bond positions. The unknown influence of foreign currency translation forces investors hoping to benefit from fixed income's special diversifying characteristics to avoid unhedged foreign bond exposure.

Alignment of Interests

Holders of domestic Treasury bonds expect fair treatment from their government. Unlike the inherently adversarial relationship between corporate issuers and corporate creditors, governments find no reason to disadvantage their citizens. If investors purchase foreign-currency-denominated bond issues held largely by citizens of the country of issue, those investors may well benefit from a reasonable alignment of interests.

In those circumstances, however, where a foreign government debt issue resides primarily in the hands of external owners, the alignment of interests breaks down. In fact, if political considerations trump contractual obligations, external holders of government paper may suffer worse consequences than owners of troubled corporate debt. When international politics enter the picture, foreign bondholders suffer.

Market Characteristics

At December 31, 2003, foreign-currency-denominated bonds totaled a substantial $9.1 trillion, of which $6.1 trillion represented issuance by foreign governments and $1.3 trillion represented investment-grade issues of corporations. Foreign-currency-denominated, high-yield corporate issues totaled a paltry $74 billion, reflecting the market's relative immaturity.

Yield to maturity for foreign-currency-denominated government paper amounted to 2.5 percent, with an average maturity of 7.3 years and duration of 5.6 years. Foreign-currency-denominated investment-grade corporate bonds promised yields of 3.5 percent with average maturity of 6.0 years and duration of 3.8 years.

Summary

Foreign-currency-denominated bonds share domestic bonds' burden of low expected returns without the benefit of domestic fixed income's special diversifying power. Fully hedged foreign bonds mimic U.S. bonds (with the disadvantage of added complexity and costs stemming from the hedging process). Unhedged foreign bonds supply investors with U.S. dollar bond exposure, plus (perhaps unwanted) foreign exchange exposure. Foreign-currency-denominated bonds play no role in well-constructed investment portfolios.

HEDGE FUNDS

Hedge funds encompass a range of investment approaches so broad as to preclude classification in a single homogeneous class. With categories ranging from event driven to relative value to macro strategies to fixed-income arbitrage, the hedge fund investor faces a lengthy menu of distinct options from which to choose. In spite of significant differences in management strategy, hedge funds generally share a common legal structure (limited partnership), a comparable fee structure (base management fee plus profits interest), and an overwhelming dependence on active management.

In the case of investment approaches designed to avoid correlation with returns of traditional marketable equities and bonds, investors depend solely on active management skill to generate investment returns. Such absolute return strategies attempt to produce positive returns regardless of the state of the markets. Without market exposure, in the absence of skill, investors earn only a money-market rate of return. Clearly, investors paying high management fees and substantial profits interests expect much more than a money-market return. Absolute return hedge fund investing only makes sense if the investor identifies managers with superior active management skill.

In contrast, investors in traditional marketable asset classes expect returns to derive fundamentally from the underlying asset class, modified in the case of actively managed accounts by the increment or decrement provided by security-selection decisions. For instance, in the case of domestic marketable equities, even in the absence of manager skill, simple market exposure causes investors to expect returns more or less commensurate with the broad market. No such prevailing force drives returns in absolute return investing.

To achieve success in the hedge fund world, investors must identify active managers with sufficient skill to overcome the typically rich fee arrangements commanded by fund managers. In traditional asset classes, both finance theory and real-world experience teach that the majority of actively managed assets fail to exceed market returns. On average, investors lose by the amount of transactions costs incurred and management fees paid. While the multiplicity of strategies employed by hedge fund managers prevents the straightforward application of the negative-sum, closed-system model that describes active management of traditional marketable securities, the fact remains that managers avoiding market exposure deserve money-market returns in the absence of superior investment choices. In the hedge fund world, as in the whole of the money management industry, consistent, superior active management constitutes a rare commodity. Assuming that active managers of hedge funds achieve success levels similar to active managers of traditional marketable securities, investors in hedge funds face dramatically higher levels of prospective failure due to the materially higher levels of fees.

Survivorship Bias

Statistics on past performance of hedge funds fail to provide much insight into the character of this relatively new segment of the investment world. Survivorship bias represents a pervasive problem for gatherers of historical return data. The fact that poorly performing firms fail at higher rates than well-performing firms causes data on manager returns to overstate past results, since compilations of data at any point in time from the current group of managers frequently lack complete performance numbers from firms that failed in the past. In the well-established, comprehensively documented world of traditional marketable securities, survivorship bias presents a significant, albeit quantifiable problem. In the less-well-established, less comprehensively documented arena of hedge fund investing, survivorship bias creates a much more substantial informational challenge.

Even in those instances in which database managers attempt to include results from failed firms, the history of returns often lacks completeness. Because most compilers of data rely on self-reporting of results by hedge funds, the integrity of the data depends on the fidelity of the hedge funds. As struggling hedge funds fight to stay in business, reporting of results to third-party database providers takes a back seat to the day-to-day challenges of crisis management.

Consider the record of Long Term Capital Management (LTCM), the infamous hedge fund that nearly brought down the world's financial system. According to the *New York Times,* the database of Tremont

Capital Management, a leading purveyor of hedge fund data, contains LTCM's performance only through October 1997, nearly a year prior to the firm's collapse.

Inception-to-date-of-reporting-cessation performance (March 1994 through October 1997) for LTCM stood at 32.4 percent per year net to investors, representing an impressive return on a large amount of capital. Obviously, Long Term Capital's early record inflated the hedge fund industry's aggregate results. From the point in October 1997 that Long Term Capital stopped reporting results to the point of the firm's October 1998 demise, returns (if they can be called returns) amounted to -91.8 percent. The staggering loss appears nowhere in Tremont's treasure trove of data.

The yawning chasm between Tremont's reported account of 32.4 percent per annum and LTCM's actual record of −27.0 percent per annum produces a staggering gap between perception and reality. The statistical omission of the implosion of LTCM inflates history in a manner that fundamentally misleads investors regarding the true character of hedge fund investing.

Statistical descriptions of hedge fund returns suffer from a type of inclusion bias related to, but distinct from, survivorship bias. As hedge funds became popular in the 1990s, only those funds with successful track records rose above the fray, attracting attention from market observers and money from investors. Funds with mediocre records languished in obscurity. Funds with strong returns garnered assets and acclaim, entering the consultants' manager universes and generating a substantial positive spin on the reported returns. In some instances, the keepers of the numbers added the past results of newly found strong performers to the ranks of the reporting managers, providing yet another unrepresentative boost to past performance data. Public reports of hedge fund performance systematically overstate the realities of the hedge fund marketplace.

The stellar, well-publicized records of early hedge fund winners caused many investors to conclude that hedge funds routinely delivered 20 percent per annum returns. That conclusion came from casual reference to high-profile successes and superficial analysis of poorly constructed databases, not careful consideration of hard-to-gather comprehensive data.

Disciplined Long/Short Investing

Hedge fund managers who attempt to produce truly independent returns generally articulate reasonably modest goals. Consider a fund manager with a portfolio consisting of equal measures of long positions and short positions. From a market perspective, the longs offset the shorts. In a rising market, losses from the shorts offset gains from the longs. In a falling market, losses from the longs offset gains from the shorts. Balanced long/short investing takes the market out of the equation.

Security selection represents the primary source of return for disciplined long/short investors. To the extent that managers identify undervalued long positions and select overvalued short positions, the portfolio stands to benefit from twice the security-selection power available to long-only managers.

A secondary source of returns for long/short managers comes from the rebate earned from establishing short positions. Short sales generate cash proceeds that earn close to a money-market rate of interest. While the short rebate adds to the return of the long/short investor, a short rebate proves insufficient in and of itself to justify pursuing a long/short investment strategy. If an investor wishes to earn a money-market return, buying a money-market fund provides a more direct, less costly, and less risky route to generating cash returns.

Suppose long/short fund managers exhibit security-selection skill consistent with top-quartile, long-only domestic equity managers. For the ten years ending December 31, 2003, one widely used universe of active managers showed top-quartile returns of 2.3 percent per annum above the market.* If a long/short manager produces top-quartile results on each of the long and short sides of the portfolio, security selection generates a return of 4.6 percent. The expected magnitude of gains available from astute security selection falls far short of double digits.

Adding a short-term interest rate (reflecting the short rebate) to the value added from security selection produces the gross return for long/short investing. Over the ten years ending December 31, 2003,

---

*Russell/Mellon Analytical Services produces the manager data used in this section. The Russell 3000 provides the passive benchmark employed to measure relative performance.

short-term interest rates averaged 4.1 percent per annum. Combining the top-quartile security-selection return of 4.6 percent with the money-market return yields a total return of 8.7 percent, before fees.

Fees create a substantial burden for hedge fund investors. A management fee of 1 percent and a profits interest of 20 percent combine to subtract 2.5 percent from the gross return, leaving a net return of 6.2 percent for the investor.* Even with substantial active management success (as defined by top-quartile results), net returns to long/short hedge fund investors show only a modest increment over money-market rates.

In cases where long/short managers exhibit mediocre stock picking skill, results disappoint. Consider the results of the median equity manager. For the ten years ending December 31, 2003, the median active domestic equity manager produced gross returns of 1.2 percent per annum above the market return. Doubling the median active management return produces a 2.4 percent return for security selection. Incorporating the cash return of 4.1 percent generates a gross return of 6.5 percent. The fee burden shaves the net return to 4.4 percent, a result disturbingly close to the return of simply holding cash!

Finally, contemplate the poor position of an underperforming manager. Over the ten years ending December 31, 2003, third-quartile active managers matched the market before fees. With no active management return, long/short investors simply earn the cash yield of 4.1 percent. Fees take the gross result to a 2.5 percent net result, bringing the misery of below-cash returns to investors suffering the consequences of poor active management.

Even though average and below-average investment results sting investors, the investment manager makes out nicely in all cases. Regardless of performance, the manager collects a 1 percent fee, representing more-or-less standard compensation for traditional long-only money management. Including the asset-based fee, the first-quartile manager earns 2.5 percent, a hefty load on a single-digit return. Total fees for median stock-picking skill amount to 2.1 percent. Even in instances where net returns to investors fail to reach the returns avail-

---

*Begin with a gross return of 8.7 percent. Subtract the 1.0 percent management fee, leaving an 7.7 percent return. Take a 20 percent profits interest (0.2 x 7.7 = 1.5) from the remaining return, producing a 6.2 percent net result.

able on cash, the manager profits handsomely. Fees for third-quartile performers total 1.6 percent, adding the injury of excessive fees to the insult of poor performance.

The example of balanced long/short equity management provides a powerful illustration of the central role that active management plays in absolute return investing. In fact, in the absence of superior active results, investors face certain disappointment. Long/short equity managers must consistently produce better than top-quartile returns to justify the fee structure accepted by hedge fund investors. Unfortunately, the resources required to identify and engage high-quality investment managers far exceed the resources available to the typical individual investor. The high degree of dependence on active management and the expensive nature of fee arrangements combine to argue against incorporating long/short investment strategies in most investor portfolios.

Hedge Funds with Market-Related Risk

The story for hedge funds that pursue strategies other than disciplined long/short investing proves more complicated. To evaluate the rest of the hedge fund universe, consider two categories of funds—those that avoid market-related risk and those that accept market-related risk. In cases where funds steer clear of market risk, investors deserve to earn only money-market levels of return. The argument that supports a cash-like return as a base for investors that do not accept market risk depends on the line of reasoning underpinning the analysis of long/short manager returns: those hedge fund strategies that do not expose assets to systematic market risk depend solely on strong active results to achieve gross results in excess of cash returns.

A substantial number of hedge fund strategies consistently expose assets to various types of systematic risk. Perhaps the worst example of regular exposure to market forces lies in the long-only manager who simply establishes a private partnership, calls it a hedge fund, and charges a 20 percent profits interest. In such cases, the manager receives 20 percent of the market's return, an egregiously high fee for a factor over which the manager exerts no control.

Fair fee structures reward managers for adding value by manipulating variables under the manager's control. In the case of a fully invested, long-only domestic equity fund, a manager might be reasonably rewarded with 20 percent of the incremental return over an appropriate market benchmark, such as the S&P 500 for a large-capitalization domestic-equity manager or EAFE for a foreign-stock specialist. In the case of a disciplined long/short equity fund, the manager might receive 20 percent of the incremental return over a short-term money-market rate. In those cases where managers receive a portion of gains over and above a fair benchmark, the managers receive a reward for adding value. Unfortunately, hedge fund structures almost universally pay managers a share of the profits after returning capital, representing a zero percent rate of return hurdle. Without a market-sensitive hurdle rate, managers receive a percentage of the gains generated by market exposure. The substantial toll imposed by typical hedge fund fee structures rules out pursuing market-sensitive hedge fund investing.

Evaluating the returns of market-sensitive hedge funds poses nearly insurmountable problems, challenging to even the most sophisticated of investors. Separating the impact of the wind at the back (or the wind in the face) contributed by market forces from the influence of the skill (or lack thereof) exhibited in security selection proves incredibly difficult, particularly in instances where the manager frequently adjusts market exposure. Regardless of the insight garnered by investors investigating market-sensitive hedge funds, the investment manager with an industry-standard deal structure receives a share of the returns generated by market action, representing unreasonable compensation for gains over which the manager exercises no control.

Alignment of Interests

The profits interest typically paid by investors in hedge fund structures creates an option for managers that threatens investor interests. In the event of hedge fund gains, the manager shares in a substantial portion of profits. In the event of hedge fund losses, the investor bears the burden alone. The asymmetry of the profits-interest structure clearly favors the fund manager.

Significant co-investment on the part of the manager works to reduce, if not eliminate, the dysfunction of the incentive-compensation option. In the case where the hedge fund experiences good performance, the manager reaps rewards both from the co-investment and from the profits interest. In the case where the fund loses money, the manager's co-investment causes a sharing of the investor's pain. A meaningful side-by-side commitment of investment manager capital substantially reduces the misalignment of manager and investor interests.

Market Characteristics

At December 31, 2003, the hedge fund industry contained an estimated 6,000 firms, controlling more than $800 billion in equity capital.[19] Moreover, because many hedge funds employ significant leverage, their actual buying power exceeds their equity capital. Note that of all the asset classes, hedge funds do not represent an independent set of securities. Hedge funds employ securities from other asset classes, most notably marketable equities and bonds.

Summary

Hedge funds appeal to investors who believe that providing funds to superior managers operating with few constraints will lead to impressive investment results regardless of the upswings and downswings of traditional marketable securities. Indeed, the experience of a number of sophisticated institutional investors indicates that some hedge fund strategies produce high, uncorrelated returns with low risk, adding an extremely valuable diversifying stream of returns to investor portfolios. Of course, successful investors in hedge funds devote an extraordinary amount of resources to identifying, engaging, and managing high-quality managers.

On top of the enormous difficulties of identifying a group of genuinely skilled investment managers and overcoming the obstacle of extremely rich fee arrangements, investors confront a fundamental misalignment of interests created by the option-like payoff embedded in most hedge fund fee arrangements. Investors find coincidence of interests only in those situations where the hedge fund manager invests substantial personal assets side-by-side with investor monies.

Casual approaches to hedge fund selection lead to almost certain disappointment. Hedge fund investing belongs in the domain of sophisticated investors who commit significant resources to the manager evaluation process. While the promise of hedge funds proves attractive to many market participants, those investors who fail to identify truly superior active managers face a dismal reality. In the absence of superior security-selection, investment strategies that avoid market exposure deliver money-market-like expected returns. The hefty fee arrangements typical of hedge funds erode the already low cash-like return to an unacceptable level, especially after adjusting for risk. Investors in hedge funds find generating risk-adjusted excess returns nearly an impossible task.

LEVERAGED BUYOUTS

Leveraged-buyout transactions involve private ownership of mature corporate entities that have greater-than-usual levels of debt on their balance sheets. The high levels of leverage produce a correspondingly high degree of variability in outcomes, both good and bad. Leveraged-buyout investments, in the absence of value-adding activities by the transaction sponsor, simply increase the risk profile of the company.

The increase in risk generally comes at a high price. Buyout partnerships charge substantial management fees (often ranging between 1.5 percent and 2.5 percent of committed funds), a significant profits interest (usually 20 percent), and a variety of transactions and monitoring fees. The general partners of many buyout funds suggest that they engage in more than simple financial engineering, arguing that they bring special value-creation skills to the table. While the value added by operationally oriented buyout partnerships may, in certain instances, overcome the burden imposed by the typical buyout fund's generous fee structure, in aggregate, buyout investments fail to match public market alternatives. After adjusting for the higher level of risk and the greater degree of illiquidity in buyout transactions, publicly traded equity securities gain a clear advantage.

Active Management and Buyout Funds

In the private equity world, active management success goes hand-in-glove with investment success. In asset classes such as domestic equities and fixed income, which contain passive investment alternatives, investors can buy the market. By owning a marketable-security index fund, investors reap market returns in a cost-efficient, reliable manner. In the inefficient private equity world, investors cannot buy the market, as no investable index exists. Even if a leveraged-buyout index existed, based on past performance, index-like results would fail to satisfy investor desires for superior risk-adjusted returns. In fact, only top-quartile or top-decile funds produce returns sufficient to compensate for private equity's greater illiquidity and higher risk. In the absence of truly superior fund selection skills (or extraordinary luck), investors should stay far, far away from private equity investments.

The history of the buyout industry proves the point. For the twenty years ending June 30, 2003, a group of 304 buyout funds tracked by investment consultant Cambridge Associates produced a pooled mean return of 11.5 percent.[20] Over the same period the S&P 500 returned 12.2 percent. Buyout investors incurred greater risk and paid higher fees to achieve inferior results, which hardly represents a description of investment success.

Investors in buyout partnerships received miserable risk-adjusted returns over the past two decades. Since the only material differences between privately owned buyouts and publicly traded companies lie in the nature of ownership (private vs. public) and character of capital structure (highly leveraged vs. less highly leveraged), comparing buyout returns to public market returns makes sense as a starting point. But, because the riskier, more leveraged buyout positions ought to generate higher returns, sensible investors recoil at the buyout industry's deficit relative to public market alternatives. On a risk-adjusted basis, marketable equities win in a landslide.

A Yale Investments Office study provides insight into the additional return required to compensate for the risk in leveraged buyout transactions. Examination of 542 buyout deals initiated and concluded between 1987 and 1998 showed gross returns of 48 percent per annum, significantly above the 17 percent return that would have resulted from comparably timed and comparably sized investments in the S&P 500.* On the surface, buyouts beat stocks by a wide margin.

---

*The sample for the buyout study contains extraordinary survivorship bias. The data employed came from offering memoranda provided to the Yale Investments Office by firms hoping to attract Yale as an investor. Needless to say, only firms with successful track records came calling on the university, hoping to attract funds.

Adjustment for management fees and general partners' profit participation brings the estimated buyout result to 36 percent per year, still comfortably ahead of the marketable security alternative.

Because buyout transactions by their very nature involve higher-than-market levels of leverage, the basic buyout-fund-to-marketable-security comparison fails the apples-to-apples standard. To produce a fair comparison, consider the impact of applying leverage to the hypothetical public market investments. Comparably timed, comparably sized, and comparably leveraged investments in the S&P 500 produced an astonishing 86 percent annual return. The risk-adjusted marketable security result exceeded the buyout result by 50 percentage points per year.

In recent years, buyout firms tended to employ lower levels of leverage, so if the exercise were repeated, and if the buyout funds maintained their historical performance records, the gap between the adjusted marketable equity returns and the buyout returns might narrow. Nevertheless, buyout investments must produce substantial returns above and beyond stock market returns to justify the commitment.

Some part of the failure of buyout managers to produce risk-adjusted returns stems from an inappropriate fee structure. Buyout investors generally pay 20 percent of profits to the investment firm's partners. Because the incentive compensation fails to consider the investor's cost of capital, buyout partnerships capture 20 percent of returns generated by the favorable wind at the long-term equity investor's back. Of course, in the case of transactions that employ greater-than-market levels of leverage, the investor's cost of capital increases along with the degree of leverage. Pure financial engineering represents a commodity, easily available to marketable securities investors through margin accounts and futures markets. Buyout managers deserve scant incremental compensation for adding debt to corporate balance sheets. By paying buyout partnership sponsors 20 percent of all gains, the fund investors compensate the fund manager with a significant portion of leveraged market gains over which the fund manager exercises no control and for which the fund manager deserves no credit. The large majority of buyout funds fail to add sufficient value to overcome a grossly unreasonable fee structure.

Another part of the industry-wide problem of poor returns relates to misalignment of incentives in large funds. Buyout firms generally begin with modest amounts of assets under management, totaling in the tens of millions or hundreds of millions of dollars. Management fees cover overhead, and incentive fees reward superior performance. Successful buyout funds almost invariably increase fund size, for example, moving from $250 million for Fund I to $500 million for Fund II to $1 billion for Fund III to $2 billion for Fund IV and ever more for funds of increasing numerals. As fund size increases, management fees as a percentage of assets remain relatively constant, resulting in a dramatic increase in the dollar value of fee income. The change in compensation structure alters general partner motivation.

The partners of newer, smaller funds focus exclusively on generating investment returns. Since modest levels of fees cover reasonable operating expenses, strong investment returns define the only path to wealth. Not only do superior returns lead to large profits interests, strong results allow the general partners to raise subsequent, ever larger funds.

Eventually, as fund size increases, fee income becomes an increasingly significant profit center. As fee income grows, general partner behavior changes, focusing on protecting the firm's franchise and maintaining the annuity-like character of the stream of fees. Larger buyout funds pursue less-risky deals, employing lower levels of leverage. The big partnerships devote more time to cultivating and nourishing limited partner relationships, the source of the funds (and fees). Less time remains for investment activity. Returns suffer.

Past return data provide dramatic support for the notion that larger funds produce inferior results. For the twenty years ending June 30, 2003, Cambridge Associates data show that buyout funds with more than $1 billion of committed capital produced returns of 6.0 percent per year, falling short of the overall buyout industry return of 11.5 percent per year and the S&P 500 return of 12.2 percent per year. In contrast, funds under $1 billion returned 17.8 percent per year, a dramatically superior result.[21]

Casual observers might draw the superficial conclusion that the key to success in buyout investing involves concentrating on smaller buyout funds. While smaller funds undoubtedly offer greater alignment of interests between the general partners and the passive providers of funds, a policy of simply choosing to invest in smaller funds may not lead to satisfactory results.

First, after adjusting the returns of smaller buyout funds to account for higher levels of risk, excess returns may disappear. Smaller buyout funds invest in smaller companies, which necessarily carry higher levels of operational risk. Adding greater operational risk to higher financial risk creates a substantial risk-adjusted hurdle for the small-company buyout investor. Investors must receive material compensation for the heightened risk and additional illiquidity in small-company buyout investing.

Second, an investor backing smaller buyout funds solely based on historical performance makes the mistake of investing while looking through the rearview mirror. Superior absolute, if not risk-adjusted, returns attract flows of capital. As market participants conclude that small buyouts outperform large buyouts, the market responds by creating large numbers of partnerships devoted to pursuing middle-market buyout transactions. Any excess returns that may have existed will be threatened by the influx of new capital and new participants. Be wary of the market's ability to eliminate sources of superior returns.

Alignment of Interests

Investors in buyout funds benefit from structural forces that serve to align the interests of corporate management and providers of capital. High degrees of balance sheet leverage force company managers to manage assets efficiently, with energies focused on generating cash flows to satisfy debt service obligations. The lure of shareholder-unfriendly corporate perquisites pales in comparison to the specter of default and the grail of profit participation. Buyout transactions serve to align interests of managers and investors.

Unfortunately, investors in buyout partnerships face the set of issues that confront investors in any scheme where the sponsor receives a profits interest. Profit-sharing arrangements create options that may lead to behavior that benefits the fund operator and disadvantages the provider of funds. To offset the optionality of the profits interest, substantial levels of co-investment by the sponsor of the buyout partnership create a symmetry regarding gains and losses that goes a long way toward keeping interests aligned.

Excessive management fees, a particularly acute problem for larger buyout funds, drive a wedge between the interests of the general partners and those of the limited partners. Deal fees, which many funds charge upon successful consummation of a transaction, represent an egregious means by which fund managers enrich themselves at the expense of their capital-contributing partners. The rationale for deal fees mystifies thoughtful investors. If management fees cover reasonable firm overhead, and profits interests provide attractive incentive compensation, what role do transactions fees play? In fact, buyout funds, particularly large funds that produce fees of hundreds of millions of dollars, represent an unfortunate example of misalignment of interests between fund managers and investors.

Market Characteristics

At December 31, 2003, the U.S. leveraged-buyout industry controlled approximately $230 billion in capital, of which approximately 60 percent was invested in companies, with the remainder committed by investors, but undrawn. More than four hundred buyout partnerships were active in the U.S. at the end of 2003.[22]

Summary

Buyout funds constitute a poor investment for casual investors. The underlying company investments in buyout funds differ from their public market counterparts only in degree of balance sheet risk and in degree of liquidity. The higher debt and the lower liquidity of buyout deals demand higher compensation in the form of superior returns to investors. Unfortunately for private equity investors, in recent decades buyout funds delivered lower returns than comparable marketable securities positions, even before adjusting for risk.

Fees create a hurdle that proves extremely difficult for buyout investors to clear. Aside from substantial year-to-year management fees, buyout funds command a significant share of deal profits, usually equal to one-fifth of the total. On top of the management fee and incentive compensation, buyout managers typically charge deal fees. The cornucopia of compensation ensures a feast for the buyout manager, while the buyout investor hopes at best for a hearty serving of leftovers.

As with other forms of investment that depend on superior active management, sensible investors look at buyout partnerships with a high degree of skepticism. Unless investors command the resources necessary to identify top-quartile or even top-decile managers, results almost certainly fail to compensate for the degree of risk incurred.

VENTURE CAPITAL

Venture capital partnerships provide financing and company building skills to start-up operations, working to develop companies into substantial, profitable enterprises. Providers of funds to venture capital partnerships respond to multiple sources of attraction, including supporting an important driver of the capitalist system, savoring the glitz surrounding the celebrity of the venture capital industry, and garnering a share of the gains generated by entrepreneurial investment activity.

Part of the attraction of venture capital investing lies in the option-like character of individual investments. Downside losses cannot exceed the amount invested. Upside gains can multiply the original stake manyfold. The combination of limited downside and substantial upside produces an investor-friendly, positively skewed distribution of outcomes.

Unfortunately for investors, the promise of venture capital exceeds the reality. Over reasonably long periods of time, aggregate venture returns more or less match marketable equity returns, indicating that providers of capital failed to receive compensation for the substantial risks inherent in startup investing.

Aside from the dismal picture provided by historical experience, all but the most long-standing investors in venture partnerships face a problem in adverse selection. The highest-quality, top-tier venture firms generally refuse to accept new investors and ration capacity even among existing providers of funds. Venture firms willing and able to accept money from new sources may represent relatively unattractive, second-tier investment opportunities.

Prior to the technology bubble of the late 1990s, investors in venture partnerships received returns inadequate to compensate for the risks incurred. For a few glorious years, the Internet mania allowed venture investors to share in a staggering flood of riches. Yet, the bubble-induced enthusiasm for private technology investing produced an unanticipated problem for venture investors. Indiscriminate demand allowed the managing partners of venture funds to increase the flow of management fees and take a greater share of profits. After the post-bubble collapse in technology asset valuations, venture capital partnerships maintained their newly fashioned investor-unfriendly terms, creating an even higher hurdle for partnership investing success.

Although investing in venture capital partnerships promises participation in the substance and glamour of backing start-up enterprises, investors providing capital to the venture industry receive returns inadequate to compensate for the high degree of risk. Only if investors generate top-quartile, or even top-decile results do returns suffice to compensate for the risks incurred.

The Glamorous Appeal of Venture Capital

In September 1995, Pierre Omidyar, a French-born Iranian immigrant, started an online auction site, ostensibly to help his girlfriend sell her collection of Pez dispensers. Even though by late 1996 the business expanded nicely and produced solid profits, the company's founder decided to seek outside assistance. Two years after the humble beginnings of the company now named eBay, Omidyar invited venture capital provider Benchmark Capital to make an investment and join the board. The recently formed Silicon Valley venture firm made a $6.7 million investment in Omidyar's eBay, valuing the company at $20 million.

After Benchmark's investment, eBay's growth continued apace, fueled by the engagement of a new management team headed by the impressive Meg Whitman. The company soon proved ready for prime time, as the September 1998 launch of eBay's initial public offering powered the company's valuation to $700 million. The IPO pricing proved fleeting, as investor interest drove the first day's price from the offering level of $18 per share to $47 per share, representing the "fifth-highest first-day gain in the market's history."[23] At the close of trading on September 23, 1998, the market valued eBay at more than $2 billion. Benchmark's $6.7 million investment exploded to more than $400 million, a breathtaking sixty-fold increase in a little more than a year.

The eBay rocketship had barely begun its journey. In April 1999, with the stock trading at $175 per share, the company's market value totaled in excess of $21 billion. Looking to lock in a portion of the firm's extraordinary gains, Benchmark Capital distributed a portion of its position to the firm's limited partners. With Benchmark's $6.7 million investment worth $6.7 billion, the investment multiple of 1,000 times qualified eBay as "the Valley's best-performing venture investment ever." [24]

Far from a flash in the pan, eBay continued to mature, becoming a standard-bearer among Internet companies. On July 22, 2002, boasting a market capitalization of $15.7 billion, eBay joined the ranks of the S&P 500, taking the 104th place, just ahead of the venerable BB&T Corporation, a North Carolina–based financial services concern with a storied past that dated to the Civil War. On the last day of trading in December 2003, eBay's valuation reached an all-time high of more than $41 billion, representing more than a 2,000 multiple of the valuation assigned to the firm by Benchmark Capital's original investment.

Everyone made money. Pierre Omidyar, eBay's founder, created wealth beyond imagination. Meg Whitman, along with the rest of eBay's management and employees, received a huge payday. Venture capitalists and their financial backers posted staggering investment gains. Even public shareholders generated significant holding-period returns. Venture capital ruled.

Although eBay stands apart from the venture capital world's other successes, companies such as Cisco, Genentech, Amazon.com, Starbucks, and Intel produced enormous gains for entrepreneurs and investors alike. Even startups that ultimately failed, such as @home and Excite.com, provided opportunities for financial backers to profit as company valuations soared to multibillion-dollar levels, before plummeting back to earth.

The Harsh Reality of Venture Capital Performance

Unfortunately for investors, gains from high-profile venture-backed successes prove insufficient to produce acceptable returns on an industry-wide basis. Over long periods of time, venture investors receive no more than market-like returns with demonstrably higher levels of risk. The promise of venture capital fails to deliver.

Venture capital returns prove disappointing to investors, even when measured at the peak of one of the greatest speculative manias. Venture Economics, in its authoritative *2001 Investment Benchmarks Report,* stated that a sample of nearly 950 venture capital funds produced a 19.6 percent rate of return for the twenty-year period ending December 31, 2000. In absolute terms, the nearly 20 percent per year over twenty years appears handsome indeed.

Consider, however, if instead of making venture capital investments, investors made equivalent investments, in timing and in size, in the S&P 500. The marketable security result of 20.2 percent per annum outpaces the composite venture capital return. Investors in plain old large-capitalization common stocks enjoyed higher returns with lower risks.

Apologists for the venture capital industry might wish to examine a shorter time frame, allowing the concentrated impact of the bubble to exercise greater influence over the results. Trailing ten-year numbers for the Venture Economics sample clock in at 29.4 percent per annum, compared to 23.0 percent per annum for the common stock equivalent. Perhaps the 6.4 percentage points of incremental returns provide adequate recompense for the extraordinary risk of investing in start-up enterprises. Even so, the incremental return exists solely because of the technology bubble.

Examine the trailing ten-year results for a period ending in the pre-bubble year of 1996. The Venture Economics sample of nearly six hundred funds produced a trailing ten-year return of 15.2 percent per annum, relative to a public market equivalent of 14.9 percent per annum. The decade ending December 31, 1996, represents a much more reasonable assessment of venture capital's relative return-generating power than does the decade ending December 31, 2000. Of all of the investment arenas influenced by the extraordinary speculative excess of the late 1990s, venture capital stands atop the list of the most heavily affected. If aggregate venture returns simply match public market results, venture investors fail miserably on a risk-adjusted basis.

Aside from the intuitive conclusion that investors in privately held start-up companies face materially higher risk than investors in publicly traded large-capitalization corporations, more rigorous definition of the risk differential proves difficult. Suffice it to say that venture investors must achieve top-quartile or top-decile results to begin to argue that they achieved superior risk-adjusted returns.

Franchise Firms

Atop the hierarchy of venture capital partnerships stand a relatively small number of venture firms that occupy an extraordinary position. This group of eight or ten firms enjoys a substantial edge over less exalted practitioners. Top-tier venture capitalists benefit from extraordinary deal flow, a stronger negotiating position, and superior access to capital markets. In short, participants in the venture capital process, from the entrepreneur to the investment banker, prefer dealing with this small set of "franchise firms."

In no other area of the capital markets does the identity of the source of funds matter in the way that it does in the venture capital world. Consider the bond markets. Do the issuers of government or corporate debt care about the identity of the bondholders? Consider the equity markets. Do the managements of publicly traded companies care about the identity of the stockholders? While in certain unusual circumstances, such as in a contested change in corporate control, issuers of securities may care about the identity of their holders, generally the name, rank, and serial number of security owners prove of little interest to security issuers. Consider the real-assets markets. Do managers of office buildings, operators of oil wells, or caretakers of timberlands care about the identity of the owners? Overwhelmingly, the source of funds for investment purchases matters little or nothing to the individuals responsible for managing assets.

In contrast, managers of venture-capital-backed enterprises care enormously about the source of funds. A disproportionate share of entrepreneurs seeking start-up financing seek out venture firms with strong franchises, in the belief that funding from a top-tier firm increases the odds of ultimate success. General partners of franchise venture firms constitute a truly extraordinary group, bringing exceptional judgment and unequaled company-building skills to the board table. Start-up firms benefit from the franchise venture capitalists' accumulated wisdom, well-established connections, and hard-won investment insights. Thoughtful entrepreneurs often willingly and knowingly accept a discounted valuation to cement a deal with a venture capitalist of choice. The reputation of the venture capital elite creates a virtuous circle in which investment success begets investment success.

Recent entrants to the arena of venture investing, as well as longer-term players with run-of-the-mill portfolios, face a challenge unique to the venture industry. All of the top-tier venture capital partnerships limit assets under management, and none of the top-tier partnerships currently accepts new investors. Consequently, outsiders remain outside, limiting the available set of choices for new entrants and investors hoping to upgrade portfolios.

New participants in the venture market must consider the return prospects of venture firms available for new-money investment. Obviously, industry-wide returns suffer with the removal of a number of relatively long-standing, relatively large, relatively high-performing funds. Since the available opportunity set for the overwhelmingly large proportion of investors excludes the top-tier venture firms, return expectations require a commensurate downward adjustment. In the context of an industry that historically produced returns similar to marketable equity returns, even a moderate downward adjustment spells trouble. The inability to access the venture elite drives the final nail in the coffin of prospective venture-investor aspirations.

Alignment of Interests

Venture funds share with buyout funds and hedge funds the incentive compensation scheme that creates option-like payoffs for the general partner. A high level of co-investment by the general partner represents a sure way to align investor interests, creating a salutary symmetry in general partners' attitudes toward gains and losses. Unfortunately, in the broader venture world, significant general partner co-investment represents the exception, not the rule. Interestingly, however, a fair number of the venture capital elite invest substantial amounts of personal funds side by side with their limited partners.

Investment success allows fund sponsors to move the terms of trade in the general partners' favor. The technology bubble of the late 1990s provides a case in point. Inspired by enormous investor demand, venture firms raised bubble-era funds in the neighborhood of ten times the size of funds raised only a decade earlier, moving from a typical 1990-vintage fund size of $100 million to $150 million to a 2000-vintage fund size of $1 billion to $1.5 billion. Along with the increase in fund size came an increase in fee income that far outpaced the growth in the size of the professional staff. The dramatic rise in asset-based income moved fees from a means to cover overhead to a way to generate income.

More distressing to limited partners, venture partnerships used the huge increase in investor interest in all things technological to extract a greater share of fund profits. Prior to the technology mania, venture firms operated in a well-defined hierarchy that gave most firms a 20 percent share of profits, a handful of demonstrably superior firms a 25 percent share of profits, and Kleiner Perkins Caufield & Byers—the dean of the industry—a 30 percent share of profits. Elite firms double-dipped by creating larger profits and keeping a greater share.

During the Internet bubble, greed prevailed. Seemingly limitless demand for venture capital investments allowed the rank and file to move from 20 percent to 25 percent profits interests and the superior firms to move from 25 percent to 30 percent profits interests. In an extraordinary act of selflessness and generosity, Kleiner Perkins, which could have moved its share of profits to 40 percent or even 50 percent, kept its profit share at 30 percent. The general partners of Kleiner Perkins, while acutely aware of their market power, no doubt decided to leave the firm's profit share at 30 percent to benefit the institutional missions of the firm's endowment and foundation investors.

Faced with an opportunity to skew deal terms in the general partners' favor, venture capitalists reacted with aplomb, in spite of the industry's mediocre record of adding value. In the aftermath of the bubble, a number of firms reduced fund sizes to more rational levels, reducing the negative impact of excessive fees, but instances of funds reducing the profits interest have yet to come to light. In spite of dismal post-mania venture investment performance, the ratchet in profits interest appears to work in one direction only.

Market Characteristics

At December 31, 2003, the U.S. venture capital industry controlled approximately $135 billion in capital, of which approximately 50 percent was invested in companies, with the remainder committed by investors but undrawn. More than 1,300 venture partnerships were active in the United States at the end of 2003.[25]

Summary

Venture capital investments appeal to a wide range of market participants, motivated by the prospects of participating in a fundamental driver of the capitalist system, reveling in the glamour of high-profile start-up success and benefiting from outsized investment returns. As illustrated by the case of eBay, venture investing sometimes produces truly breathtaking results.

Unfortunately, eBay's corporate achievements and stock market success stand far apart from the usual venture investment results. In aggregate, venture investors fare about as well as their marketable equity counterparts. After adjustment for risk, the overwhelming majority of venture capital fails to produce acceptable risk-adjusted returns.

The new entrant to the world of private entrepreneurial finance faces an obstacle quite apart from the barriers hampering investment success in other asset classes. The top-tier venture partnerships, essentially closed to new money, enjoy superior access to deals, entrepreneurs, and capital markets. Exclusion from the venture capital elite disadvantages all but the most long-standing, most successful limited partners.

Suppliers of funds to the venture capital industry generally realize poor risk-adjusted returns. Sensible individual investors look elsewhere for investment performance.

CHAPTER SUMMARY

Non-core asset classes provide investors with a broad range of superficially appealing but ultimately performance-damaging investment alternatives. A host of fixed-income markets fall short of the diversifying power inherent in default-free, full-faith-and-credit obligations of the U.S. government. Factors including credit risk, call options, illiquidity, and foreign exchange exposure limit the attractiveness of investment-grade corporate bonds, high-yield bonds, foreign bonds, and asset-backed securities. Other investment choices depend fundamentally on active management to produce returns. Hedge funds, leveraged-buyout partnerships and venture-capital participations prove successful only when managed by extraordinarily talented (or unusually lucky) individuals. Because of the enormous difficulty in identifying and engaging superior active managers, prudent investors avoid asset classes that derive returns primarily from market-beating strategies.

Non-core asset classes command a significant portion of the investment spectrum. Brokers aggressively market fixed-income funds that produce higher fees than mundane government bond vehicles. Talking heads prattle about the attractions of alternative asset classes. Wall Street pushes vehicles that allow investors to access inefficient markets. Investors require unusual self-confidence to ignore the widely hyped non-core investments and to embrace the quietly effective core investments.

Part Two

MARKET TIMING

Introduction

Market timing represents a short-term bet against well-articulated long-term asset-allocation targets. Market timers hope to underweight prospectively poorly performing asset classes and overweight prospectively strongly performing asset classes, employing tactical moves to enhance portfolio returns.

Active market timers usually fail. Market timing requires taking relatively few, generally undiversifiable positions. Timing decisions involve the large questions of asset-class valuation, forcing short-term asset allocators to develop views on an impossibly broad range of factors. Even if the market timer overcomes the odds by making a correct call, notoriously fickle markets may fail to resolve valuation discrepancies in the short run. Serious investors avoid entering the market-timing morass.

Although only sparse evidence exists regarding market-timing activity, institutional investors, who generally operate in a well-defined investment environment, appear to relegate market timing to an inconsequential role. Individual investors, who operate in a much less well-defined context, often fail even to articulate portfolio asset-allocation targets. Without clearly specified targets, the notion of market timing loses definition.

Some evidence points to individual investor acceptance of a passive form of market timing that allows asset allocations to drift with the ebb and flow of markets. More worrying, a fair number of individual investors engage in counterproductive performance chasing that results in buying high and selling low. Buying yesterday's winners and selling yesterday's losers inevitably hurts tomorrow's performance.

Avoiding bull market purchases and forsaking bear market sales constitute first steps in sensible implementation of a reasonable investment program. Chapter 5, *Chasing Performance,* describes some of the environmental factors that encourage investors to behave in a consensus-oriented, albeit ultimately counterproductive, fashion. Supremely rational investors take the further step of acting against the consensus, rebalancing to long-term portfolio targets by buying the out-of-favor and selling the in-vogue. Chapter 6, *Rebalancing,* makes the case for fidelity to policy asset-allocation targets, while providing evidence that few investors appear to pursue rebalancing activity.

5
Chasing Performance

In choosing superior active managers, the most sophisticated market participants base investment decisions on fundamental factors such as the quality and integrity displayed by management, the investment philosophy espoused by the firm, and the thoroughness and discipline shown in decision making by the principals. Yet even savvy investors frequently seek the comfort of owning funds that exhibit market-beating historical performance. After satisfying all the sensible criteria for manager selection, most investors then place too much emphasis on seeing strong performance numbers for the recent past.

Less sophisticated investors forego the necessarily complex and time-consuming consideration of underlying portfolio characteristics and investment management style, preferring to focus only on historical performance. By chasing funds distinguished only by strong performance and avoiding well-managed funds that produced several years of weak results, investors position themselves for future disappointment.

In an environment dominated by managers with skills insufficient to overcome the powerful forces of market efficiency, randomness plays a significant role in separating the winners from the losers. Ignoring for the moment the high costs of playing the active management game, after the contest closes, one-half of assets under management ought to beat the market and one-half ought to fall short. Because bets against particular stocks by particular managers offset exactly the bets for those same stocks by other active managers, final results fall neatly into either a winning column or a losing column. In fact, the amount by which the winners win equals precisely the amount by which the losers lose. The basic task for investors becomes distinguishing between those mutual-fund managers who were lucky and those managers who were skillful.

Because favorable investment results all too often depend on having a strong tailwind, and unfavorable returns stem from facing a stiff headwind, the contemporaneous investment climate often overwhelms manager ability as a factor in determining results. By examining only the tea leaves of past performance, investors may pursue poor fund managers in a hot market segment and ignore skillful managers in an out-of-favor arena. Seasoned investors enhance the chances for long-term success by identifying a truly talented manager and providing funds when the manager's portfolio suffers from a temporary, market-induced setback. Conversely, mutual-fund investors magnify the far too common experience of investment failure by chasing returns of hot, lucky managers, investing near the peak and suffering from poor relative (and, perhaps, absolute) performance.

Regression to the mean, one of the most powerful influences in the world of finance, explains the tendency for reversal of fortune. Hot stocks and hot funds attract interest from the investment community. Investors, fund managers, research analysts, investment bankers, financial journalists, and television pundits direct time, energy, and attention to the flavor of the month. Profits and reputations stem from flashy, momentum-driven success. As prices rise, increases in price attract more money, causing further increases in price.

The self-reinforcing process allows short-term speculators to profit temporarily from trend following. Trend followers, also known as momentum players, ignore fundamentals to focus purely on security appreciation. As the wave of speculative money enters the market, prices respond by increasing, attracting yet another wave of funds. Speculators garner easy gains.

As ever more money crowds into the rapidly appreciating sector, the resulting price increases sow the seeds of the trend's eventual demise. Enlargement of the supply of overpriced securities and exhaustion of the supply of trend-following speculators combine to write the epitaph of the speculative bubble. An important part of the story relates to increases in the supply of securities. Actions by companies in response to excessive stock price appreciation tend to limit extraordinary share price gains. Corporate treasurers enhance the financial value of business enterprises by issuing shares when shares trade above the fair value of corporate assets. As a speculative spree takes stock prices above rational levels, sensible corporate treasurers issue new shares. From a market perspective, the increased supply of securities created by corporate sales of shares satisfies demand that otherwise might have fueled further price increases.

As strong stock prices cause the market value of companies to exceed replacement cost of assets, investment bankers encourage floatation of securities for new companies operating in the same industry. Seeing that the stock market places a higher value on corporate assets than the cost of those selfsame assets, entrepreneurs happily work with Wall Street to create new enterprises. Again, the appearance of close substitutes for the hot stocks siphons money otherwise destined for the original securities, dampening future return prospects for the sector as a whole.

The problem with trend following lies in the fact that it works only as long as it works. When inexorable market forces ultimately reverse a trend, speculators rush for the exits, leaving all but the most nimble with disappointing results. Because momentum investors play a game without the benefit of solid fundamental research, the trend followers have nothing at their disposal to identify the all-important inflection point that separates rising from falling prices.

MUTUAL-FUND FLOWS IN THE INTERNET BUBBLE

The Internet bubble provides an example of the roller-coaster ride of initial gains and subsequent losses created by investors who chase performance. In retrospect, little, if any, of the stock market activity surrounding Internet companies resulted from fundamental assessment of business prospects. In fact, the game had everything to do with price momentum fueled by naïve market participants and cynical Wall Street bankers.

The initial public offering of Netscape marked the beginning of the Internet mania. As the company's public market debut approached, Wall Street's price talk steadily advanced, as did the number of shares on offer. On August 8, 1995, the fortunate participants in the five-million-share IPO paid $28 per share, roughly double the upper end of the range of the underwriter's initial indications. Netscape's shares opened at \$71 before closing the day at \$58.25. Wall Street firms made handsome fees, insiders held shares valued by the public market at hundreds of millions of dollars, and investors tasted easy money. Thus began the bubble.

By the beginning of 1997, technology stocks captured the imagination of large numbers of market players, attracting media attention and investor dollars. An examination of what proved to be the top-performing funds in the bubble period provides insight into investor behavior. Net gains and losses, calculated by assessing returns on money flows into the hot performers during the manic run-up in prices, tell a little-known tale about the consequences of chasing performance. Unfortunately, the story concludes with withdrawals from the frigid funds during the dramatic collapse of the valuation bubble, illustrating the wealth-destroying impact of trend following.

Using annual information on mutual-fund asset levels and quarterly data on performance, the three-year periods on either side of December 31, 1999, provide a symmetric look at the rise and fall of technology stocks. Winners for the three years ending December 31, 1999 produced absolutely dazzling records. Led by 119.4 percent per annum returns for the Kinetics Internet fund, the list includes offerings by the obscure—Munder NetNet and WWW Internet Fund—and by the well known—Morgan Stanley Institutional Technology and Credit Suisse Global Technology. As shown in Table 5.1, all of the top ten funds generated eye-popping appreciation. Even mutual-fund giant Fidelity's Select Technology Fund, bringing up the bottom of the top ten, produced 64.6 percent annual returns over the three-year period, enough to multiply an initial investor's stake nearly 4.5 times.

The tech fund group made a middling start in 1997 with an average performance ranking that stood right in the middle of the pack of nearly nine thousand mutual funds in Morningstar's 1997 databank. The fund leaders ramped up performance in 1998 and 1999, dominating the performance charts with an average ranking in the top two percent of funds in 1998 and an average ranking in the top one percent of funds in 1999. Of course, based on top-of-the-charts performance, for the full three-year period the group ranks in the top percentile.

Three years later the list changed dramatically. All of the 1999 winners dropped to the bottom quartile of the performance universe,

**Table 5.1 Top Ten Performing Mutual Funds
Take Investors on a Roller Coaster Ride**

Fund	Annualized Return (Percent)			Return Multiple		
	1997–1999	2000–2002	1997–2002	1997–1999	2000–2002	1997–2002
Kinetics Internet	119.4	−30.5	23.5	10.56	0.34	3.55
Munder NetNet	92.3	−49.1	−1.1	7.11	0.13	0.94
Pimco RCM Global Technology	79.6	−32.3	10.3	5.79	0.31	1.80
Credit Suisse Global Technology	78.3	−35.4	7.3	5.67	0.27	1.53
Morgan Stanley Technology	76.6	−40.5	2.5	5.50	0.21	1.16
Amerindo Technology	74.1	−50.7	−7.4	5.28	0.12	0.63
Pimco PEA Innovation	66.5	−43.2	−2.8	4.61	0.18	0.85
WWW Internet	66.1	−52.8	−11.4	4.58	0.11	0.48
PBHG Technology & Communications	64.8	−50.4	−9.6	4.48	0.12	0.55
Fidelity Select Technology	64.6	−34.1	4.2	4.46	0.29	1.28
Arithmetic Average	78.2	−41.9	1.5	5.80	0.21	1.27

Notes: The arithmetic average of the annualized returns and the arithmetic average of the return multiples do not correspond to one another. For example, the average return of 1.5 percent per annum for the period 1997–2002 clearly does not correspond to the six-year multiple of a 1.27 times return. In contrast, percentage returns and return multiples for individual funds do correspond to each other.

as the wind at the back of technology stocks shifted to become a gale force storm in the face. In 2000, the average rank of the formerly hot funds dropped to the decidedly chilly 96th percentile. The following year provided little respite as the funds posted an average ranking in the 94th percentile. Finally, for good measure, at year-end 2002 the average ranking fell in the 95th percentile. Three years of disaster followed three years of bliss.

Investors fortunate enough to select a technology fund at the outset of 1997 initially experienced nothing short of thrilling returns. The average multiple return of the top ten tech funds for the three years ending December 31, 1999, stood at a lofty 5.8 times the original investment, a compound annual return in excess of 78 percent.

The following three years produced an unfortunate mirror image. Investors holding those once top-performing technology funds for the three years ending December 31, 2002, lost 79 percent of their initial stake and realized an average annual return of -42 percent. The full six-year period from January 1, 1997 to December 31, 2002, showed an average compound annual return of 1.5 percent.

If the end of the story were that investors took a terribly risky ride to generate a barely visible single-digit annual return, observers might conclude "no harm, no foul." But an examination of investor inflows and outflows over the period paints a different picture.*

Consider cash flows to the top-performing Kinetics Internet Fund. At the outset of 1997, the fund boasted approximately $100,000 under management. Modest returns of 13 percent during the year did little to draw capital. Incipient Internet fever contributed to spectacular 1998 returns of 196 percent, attracting investor contributions that caused assets to grow to more than $22 million. Intensifying enthusiasm for technology stocks, along with stupendous 1999 results of 216 percent, stimulated staggering cash flows to the Kinetics Internet Fund, multiplying assets under management more than fiftyfold to $1.2 billion at December 31, 1999. Performance-chasing behavior exposed the maximum amount of assets to the maximum level of risk.

The storyline proved parallel for the other funds. Because investors operate with cloudy crystal balls, what later became the top-performing technology funds reported a total of only $1.3 billion of assets under management at the beginning of 1997. Even as the technology boom began to catch the attention of market players, assets in the top ten tech funds grew only slightly to $1.5 billion at the end of the year. The average 1998 return of 81 percent accounted for the bulk of the increase in assets during that year as the total reached $2.5 billion. Not until the very end of the mania did investor behavior show a

---

*See Appendix 1 for a discussion of measuring investment gains and losses.

dramatic change. To cap off the bubble, 1999's return of 182 percent attracted a torrent of investor funds, causing the ten leading tech funds to reach a stunning $20.6 billion at the end of 1999.

In the early years of the run-up, investment performance explained the overwhelming portion of increases in funds under management. As shown in Table 5.2, of the 1997 increase in assets under management of $114 million, 84 percent came from investment gains. Of the 1998 increase of $1.1 billion, 89 percent came from investment gains. Only in 1999 do investor contributions begin to add materially to the assets, amounting to 43 percent of the total, as the enthusiasm of the investing public fueled the more than eightfold increase in assets during the year.

The tale of the next three years brought tears to those who came late to the party. The year 2000 saw the peak of the market in March, marking the start of the disaster for technology investors. Investment performance turned sharply negative, with the average –41 percent return wiping out an estimated $11.5 billion of investor funds, more than offsetting all of the gains of the previous three years. Remarkably, investors—conditioned to buy the dips—continued to contribute cash to the technology funds, pouring $6.3 billion into the teeth of the collapse.

Table 5.2 Investors Chase Performance in the Technology Bubble

Cash Flows and Investment Performance of the Top Ten Technology Funds
(Millions of Dollars)

Calendar Year	Average Returns (Percent)	Beginning Assets (A)	Investor Flows (B)	Investment Performance (C)	Ending Assets (A+B+C)
1997	14.4	1,343	18	96	1,457
1998	81.0	1,457	116	954	2,527
1999	182.3	2,527	7,740	10,284	20,552
2000	–40.8	20,552	6,263	–11,497	15,318
2001	–40.6	15,318	–1,134	–6,378	7,805
2002	42.0	7,805	–669	–3,330	3,807
Average		1,343	12,334	–9,870	3,807

Notes: Data are for the top ten performing technology mutual funds, as defined by trailing three-year performance on December 31, 1999. Appendix 1 describes the calculation of investor contributions and investment performance.

In 2001, a different picture developed. Tired of seemingly relentless stock price declines, investors began to withdraw assets from
funds. While miserable performance accounted for $6.4 billion of the
$7.5 billion decline in assets under management, investor with-
drawals totaled $1.1 billion, or 15 percent of the decrease.

The final scene of the debacle took place in 2002 as investors withdrew $669 million from funds and poor investment performance sub-
tracted another $3.3 billion. With only $3.8 billion under management,
the top ten tech funds amounted to less than 15 percent of the peak
size of $26.6 billion, registered in the spring of 2000.

Investor flows to and from top-performing technology funds point
to a pattern of untimely late arrival followed by an equally poorly
timed late departure. Investors began with $1.3 billion invested at Jan-
uary 1, 1997, and made net investments of funds totaling $12.3 billion
over the six-year period, amounting to a total commitment of $13.7
billion. Net investment losses consumed $9.9 billion of investor capi-
tal, or more than 72 percent of investor contributions. Top ten tech investors experienced wealth destruction on a massive scale.

The pain inflicted on investors by the first hot, then cold technology funds went beyond the incredibly poor investment performance.
Fund managers churned portfolio holdings, triggering the realization
of significant amounts of capital gains. In aggregate, gains distributions for the top ten tech funds totaled $3.3 billion over the six-year
period, forcing investors to pay untold amounts of taxes. On top of the
indignity of investment losses, many investors suffered further as they
paid their due to Uncle Sam.

The gains distributions fall mostly in 1999 and 2000, during the
height of the technology stock bull market. Not surprisingly, capital
gains largely evaporated in 2001 and disappeared in 2002. Yet, even
though technology fund portfolios suffered substantial declines after
the bubble burst, not one of the funds declared a distribution of capital losses. An asymmetry in the tax law governing mutual funds
works to the clear detriment of fund investors. Gains realized by mutual-fund portfolio managers must be distributed to shareholders,
triggering potential tax liabilities. In contrast, losses realized by fund
managers may be used only to offset current or future gains and cannot be distributed to shareholders. Asymmetric tax treatment of gains
and losses hurts investors by forcing the immediate recognition of

capital gains and deferring or eliminating the opportunity to use capital losses.

Investors examining published returns for the top-performing tech funds would see an average return of 1.5 percent per year over the six years from 1997 to 2002. The superficial look at time-linked results masks serious investor losses. Because performance-chasing players bought high and sold low, an estimated 72 percent of contributed assets disappeared in the post-bubble break. Overly active fund management exposed a further 24 percent of investor contributions to potential tax liability. The technology bubble proved injurious to investor health.

Presumably the best-performing funds attracted the hottest money, leading to the largest losses. Would the story be different for the ten largest (as opposed to the ten best-performing) technology funds? At the beginning of 1997, none of the funds destined to generate the best performance numbers appeared on the top ten list by size. The largest funds, with $15.9 billion under management at the start of the period, produced three-year bull market returns averaging 47 percent per year. In a now-familiar mirror image, the funds proceeded to give it back with a three-year bear market performance of –33 percent per year. Over the six-year period, performance averaged 0.1 percent per year.

Cash flow analysis again produces a depressing depiction of wealth destruction. Investor capital contributions of $29.3 billion generated cumulative losses of $11.4 billion, or 39 percent of funds contributed. While the ten largest tech funds failed to destroy as much value through miserable investment performance as did the ten hottest performers, the larger funds presented investors with more sizable tax bills. Capital gains distributions amounted to fully 73 percent of investor contributions over the six-year period.

The ten largest tech funds began the manic phase of the bull market with a longer history than the ten best-performing funds. As a consequence of operating for a number of years in a strong environment for equities, the large tech funds possessed a significant embedded potential tax liability. When 1997 began, the ten largest funds contained unrealized gains of $3.2 billion, representing more than 20 percent of assets under management. Investors purchasing shares in the ten largest tech funds bought into a tax position that clearly dampened future wealth creation prospects.

The storyline for the ten best-performing tech funds contains differences only in degree. In spite of the fact that the hot-performing crowd included three funds with no embedded gains, because they started operations in late 1996, the undistributed profits still totaled $190 million, or more than 14 percent of assets.

Nearly all investors who bought technology-oriented mutual funds in the late 1990s acquired hidden tax liabilities that caused future pain. Fund managers proceeded to realize the embedded profits and other subsequent gains in the frenzied trading typical of the mutual-fund industry. Even though the degree of investment loss experienced by large fund investors failed to match the pain felt by the hot money crowd, the greater tax burden borne by large fund investors served to even the distribution of pain.

Table 5.3 Technology Funds Destroy Investor Wealth
1997 to 2002

	Investor Contributions (Millions of Dollars)	Investment Losses (Millions of Dollars)	Percentage Loss	Gains Distributions (Millions of Dollars)	Percentage of Contributions
Top ten funds by performance (as of December 31, 1999)	13,677	9,870	72	3,331	24
Top ten funds by size (as of December 31, 1996)	29,287	11,383	39	21,339	73

Note: Gains distributions in the first third of the year are applied to previous year-end shares outstanding; gains distributions in the middle third of the year are applied to the average of previous year-end and current year-end shares outstanding; and gains distributions in the final third of the year are applied to current year-end shares outstanding.

In the mutual-fund world, yesterday's winners tend to transmute into tomorrow's losers. While a superficial examination of time-linked returns of technology fund performance indicates that the collapse of the bubble simply reversed earlier gains, a close look at investor cash flows shows a far different outcome. From start to finish, by chasing yesterday's hot prospect and shunning today's also-ran, investors lost billions of dollars in technology mutual funds. Buying high and selling low provides a poor formula for investment success.

MERRILL LYNCH INTERNET STRATEGIES FUND

The collective saga of performance-chasing behavior contains a multitude of individual tales, told investor by investor, company by company, and fund by fund. One of the most dramatic disasters of the technology bubble emanated from the bowels of Merrill Lynch, the largest broker of securities to middle-class America.

After watching from the sidelines as other investment banks generated staggering returns from technology-related securities activity, in February 1999 Merrill Lynch decided to enter the fray by hiring high-profile Internet analyst Henry Blodget. Blodget had hoped for a career as a writer but that "lasted only until I couldn't finish my first short story." He came to Merrill Lynch from CIBC/Oppenheimer, where he had made an extraordinary, self-fulfilling call on Amazon.com.[1] Blodget explained his $400 per share forecast for Amazon.com: "I was trying to say, 'Stop asking me the price target. There's plenty of upside.' But it was like I threw gasoline on a bonfire."[2] Three weeks after Blodget articulated the self-admitted "outlandish" price target, Amazon.com blew through the $400 price level.[3]

Blodget's approach to security analysis followed new era standards. According to Blodget, "sometimes it's helpful not to look at valuations too closely. Just blur your eye and say 'I see a big future for these stocks.'"[4] With a talking head to compete for air time on CNBC, Merrill Lynch—purveyor of stocks to the masses—ramped up tech stock activity.

According to the *Wall Street Journal,* Merrill Lynch's asset management arm "came to the Internet party late," as the firm's conservative leadership had initially treated the technology phenomenon as a passing fancy.[5] In fact, Merrill Lynch suffered the embarrassment of experiencing net outflows of $1.2 billion in January 2000 from the firm's value-oriented stock and bond mutual funds, an almost inconceivable failure at the peak of the bull market frenzy.[6] By ignoring the speculative hype, the brokerage firm created enormous internal pressures. Merrill Lynch's army of brokers—at odds with the conservative leadership—demanded that the firm produce a high-octane Internet fund. At the peak of the market, senior management capitulated to the brokers' demands.

In March 2000, Merrill Lynch offered shares in Merrill Lynch Internet Strategies Fund, an investment vehicle that sought "long term growth of capital through investment primarily in equity securities of issues that the Investment Advisor believes will use the Internet as a component of their business strategies." While the ridiculously broad investment mandate rules out few companies, the fund's focus on the extraordinarily risky arena of pure Internet plays came through loud and clear to prospective investors. To assist technology neophytes, the offering documents helpfully defined terms such as Internet, World Wide Web, and Intranet, as well as basic financial terms such as Shareholder Fees, Annual Fund Operating Expenses, Management Fees, Distribution Fees, and Service (Account Maintenance) Fees.

Hoping to launch the fund in the securities world's equivalent of Internet time, Merrill Lynch attempted to complete the offering process in two weeks instead of the usual five.[7] The abbreviated process did nothing to lessen the splash surrounding the fund's debut. An early March meeting, broadcast to Merrill Lynch's more than 14,000 brokers, featured best-selling author Michael Lewis, Merrill Lynch's own Henry Blodget, and the firm's global asset management head, Jeffrey Peak. Fund manager Paul Meeks reportedly grabbed a microphone at the San Francisco event and boomed, "Let's get ready to ruuuumble!"[8] The *New York Times* commented that "the fanfare showed what a departure the new fund is for Merrill Lynch, whose fund managers are still working to shed their reputation as diehard value investors."[9]

Merrill Lynch offered investors four classes of shares representing four different fee schemes. The various classes allowed investors to pay more now or pay more later, all the while paying an awful lot year in and year out. In fact, using a reasonable set of assumptions, the prospectus showed a three-year fee burden ranging from 7.7 percent of assets to 10.4 percent of assets, an extraordinary price to pay for garden-variety mutual-fund management.[10]

The combination of the flashy launch of the Merrill Lynch Internet Strategies Fund, the generous fee incentives for the firm's brokers, and the public's insatiable appetite for tech-related stocks led to enormous demand for the offering. On March 22, 2000, the fund commenced operations with more than $1 billion under management. The enormous size of the offering generated up-front fees for Merrill Lynch of tens of millions of dollars along with the promise of substantial recurring fee revenues.

Fund management fees turned out to represent the least of investor worries. Almost perfectly coincident with the inception of the Internet Strategies Fund operations, the technology stock bubble burst. Even with the benefit of excess holdings of cash—a natural consequence of a fund start-up—the Internet fund registered miserable performance.

After little more than a year of operations, at March 31, 2001, losses for the Internet fund amounted to 76 percent of assets, without including the impact of sales charges. The up-front sales loads, which ranged up to a maximum of 5.25 percent, added the insult of egregious fees to the injury of poor performance.

Aside from the horrific absolute return numbers, investors suffered from poor relative performance. The Internet Strategies Fund managed to underperform the NASDAQ by 14 percentage points and Merrill Lynch's own custom technology benchmark by nine percentage points.

After reviewing the debacle of the first year, the board of directors decided on April 30, 2001, to end the fund's existence, approving a plan to merge the Internet Strategies Fund into Merrill Lynch's own, less poorly performing Global Technology Fund. Reasons cited by the board to justify the merger included economies of scale, greater flexibility in portfolio management, and increased diversification. Motivations that the board neglected to mention included retention of assets under the Merrill Lynch umbrella, continuation of the stream of fees for the firm, and elimination of the colossally embarrassing track record of the Internet Strategies Fund.

On October 5, 2001, the Internet Strategies Fund ceased to exist. From the much-hyped beginning in the spring of 2000 to the quiet demise in the fall of 2001, investors incurred losses of 81 percent, representing nearly $900 million. For the disservice provided to investors, Merrill Lynch collected fees of approximately $45 million.

Unfortunately for investors, the economies of scale and greater flexibility of the Global Technology Fund did nothing to improve investor results. From the date of the merger until the end of 2002, investors suffered additional losses of 32 percent, bringing the inception-to-date returns for steadfast investors to a truly miserable minus 87 percent.

Merrill Lynch's untimely offering of a mutual fund specializing in Internet-related securities provides a cautionary tale for investors. The very nature of speculative excess demands that the greatest amounts of investor dollars be exposed to the market at the absolute top in valuations. Of course, peak prices result from formerly skeptical participants throwing in the towel and joining the party. Conservative Merrill Lynch fit the bill as the ultimate capitulator. In the words of a prominent Silicon Valley venture capitalist, "Merrill Lynch appears as a wanton, fair weather carpetbagger that invariably opens a new office here just before some trend peaks and then scuttles out of town as fast as their little bikes can carry them." Sensible investors avoid the speculative opportunity of the moment, whether promoted by a high-flying fringe operator or middle-of-the-road companies like Merrill Lynch.

MUTUAL-FUND ADVERTISEMENTS

Investors face a barrage of forces pushing the flavor of the month. During bull markets, television and radio pundits fill the airwaves with soundbites extolling the virtues of equity investing. Newspaper stories profile the heroes of the rapidly rising stock market. Measured views receive little notice, except as occasional fodder for the favored, bullish commentators. Skeptics face outright scorn.

Mutual-fund advertisements add to the bull market cacophony. Every quarter the *Wall Street Journal* publishes a special section devoted to fund-related articles, performance statistics, and advertisements. An examination of changes in the content of the *Wall Street Journal's Mutual Funds Quarterly Review* over the course of the boom and the bust provides insight into some of the subtle forces shaping the environment that influences investor decisions.

As stock prices hit the peak, advertising hype reached a coincident apex. Consider ads appearing in issues of the *Wall Street Journal* published in the first week of March 2000. Opposite a full-page picture of a bull, Merrill Lynch touted ways to speculate on Internet-related securities. Alliance Capital suggested, "See why we're the professional's choice." Dresdner RCM urged, "Get in on the ground floor of the Technology Revolution." An evocative Van Kampen advertisement employed a historical metaphor in pushing the firm's growth equity funds: "Long ago people navigated by the stars. Some still do." American Century, in promoting a passel of aggressive equity funds, simply said, "Smile if you own one. Call if you don't."

Two years later, long after investors' smiles faded from memory, the tone of advertising changed markedly. Lord Abbett, under the banner "Steady," rather redundantly advocates a "disciplined process of evaluation and discipline." TIAA-CREF, in asking the non-question, "The cure for a shaky market?" prescribes "A solid foundation." The products featured in advertisements have changed, too. The aggressive growth equity funds give way to municipal bond funds, guaranteed annuities, and government fixed-income funds.

To the extent that mutual-fund advertising influences investor choice, the bull-market message proves ill-timed. At the very peak in stock valuations, purveyors of funds push the most aggressive equity funds. Even if fund companies fail to sell the specific funds highlighted in advertising campaigns, page after page of bull market exhortations create a backdrop of frenzied sentiment. Just when leaning against the wind would prove particularly profitable, investors receive encouragement to place more and more assets into the heart of a windstorm.

A systematic look at the *Wall Street Journal's Mutual Funds Quarterly Review* shows a pattern of poorly timed advice from the mutual-fund industry. Not surprisingly, as the bull market swelled, so did the size of the *Journal's* special mutual-fund section. From thirty-eight pages in the first quarter of 1997, the *Mutual Funds Quarterly Review* grew to between forty-six and forty-eight pages in the first quarters of 1998, 1999, and 2000. After the bursting of the bubble, as stock prices declined so did the *Mutual Funds Quarterly Review,* falling to forty pages in early 2001, thirty-six pages in 2002, and thirty-four in 2003.

As stock prices waxed and waned, the character of the *Mutual Funds Quarterly Review* moved with the markets. The percentage of space devoted to mutual-fund advertisements, after ranging from 40 to 45 percent of total pages during the bull market, fell precipitously along with stock prices, amounting to 29 percent of space in 2001, 22 percent in 2002, and 16 percent in 2003. The volume reached a crescendo at the most inopportune time for investment, softening considerably as the stock market moved towards more attractive levels.

Along with changes in the level of mutual-fund promotion came changes in the composition of the messages. In those advertisements highlighting specific classes of assets, stock fund advertising gained share as stock prices rose. In early 1997, stocks accounted for 86 percent of asset-class-specific advertising in the *Wall Street Journal's Mutual Funds Quarterly Review*, leaving a scant 14 percent for bonds. From 86 percent in 1997's *Mutual Funds Quarterly Review*, stocks moved to 92 percent of 1998's and 97 percent of 1999's, before capturing a perfect 100 percent at the peak of the bubble in early 2000. Not one single mutual-fund advertisement mentioned bond fund investment opportunities in the April 2000 *Mutual Funds Quarterly Review*.

Table 5.4　Fund Companies Push Stocks at the Top:
Advertisements in the Wall Street Journal's
Quarterly Mutual Fund Review

	1997	1998	1999	2000	2001	2002	2003
Number of pages	38	48	46	48	40	36	34
Percentage of space devoted to ads	45	44	43	40	29	22	16
Stock ads as percent of security-specific' ads	86	92	97	100	79	79	50
Image ads as percentage of total ads	42	36	26	34	25	61	64
Performance ads as percentage of total ads	44	44	61	56	28	26	36

Source: Data are from the first quarter's Wall Street Journal Mutual Funds Quarterly Review, *published in the first week of April in each year.*

As stock performance withered and bond performance grew, mutual-fund companies prepared to whipsaw clients. In 2001 and 2002, stock fund ads declined to 79 percent of asset-class-specific advertising, subsequently dwindling to 50 percent in 2003. With stocks becoming cheaper and bonds becoming more expensive, instead of urging investors to stay the course, the mutual-fund industry's rearview mirror focused increasingly on the fixed-income markets.

While mutual-fund companies generally push products by describing past performance, in ebullient markets recent results take center stage. More than one-half of mutual-fund advertising in the torrid environment of 1999 and 2000 cited performance statistics. In the far cooler investment world of 2001 and 2002, less than 30 percent of advertising mentioned past investment results.

Along with the bear market's deemphasis of performance came a concomitant increase in image advertising. In early 2002 and early 2003, when investors had little about which to feel good, fund companies devoted more than 60 percent of advertising space to corporate puffery. Consider the April 2003 offering from Oppenheimer Funds:

> What can an investor believe in today? These are times that can try an investor's patience and conviction. And many people are desperately searching for some certainty in an uncertain world. We don't have all the answers. Nobody does. But we do have a set of beliefs that have withstood the test of time and continue to guide us today. We think they're worth sharing. We believe in America. In the strength of our people, our institutions and the American idea. We believe in history. The wars, recessions, and bear markets in the last 100 years have ultimately been followed by recovery and growth. And we believe in the fundamental principles of investing: long-term goals, diversification and professional advice. Simple ideas, based on essential truths. To us they're something to hold on to, in the worst or best of times.[11]

Of course, in the bull market of April 1999, Oppenheimer's full page ad promoted its Main Street Growth and Income Fund with a picture of a boxing glove belting the S&P 500. Without winning funds to tout, Oppenheimer pulled its punches, opting for vague, feel-good generalities.

Every aspect of the *Wall Street Journal's Mutual Funds Quarterly Review* pushes the investing public in the wrong direction. The weight of the message increases as the attractiveness of the opportunity decreases. The focus on stocks peaks as stock prices peak. When bonds might prove most useful to investor portfolios, nary an advertisement mentions fixed income. The perversity of the mutual-fund industry's advertising rates a perfect ten.

SCHWAB'S BULL MARKET ADVICE

In April 2000, Charles Schwab employed a particularly lavish advertising spread to promote the Mutual Fund OneSource Select List funds available at Schwab's Mutual Fund Marketplace. The advertisement's protagonists included Leilani, a winsome client, and Paul, a handsome Schwab investment specialist. For page after page in the *Wall Street Journal,* Leilani gushed that the discount broker "makes it easy for me to feel in control of my investments," "put together a mutual-fund portfolio that fits my needs," and "helped me figure out . . . the smartest approach for me." Scattered across eight pages, the promotion concluded, "Schwab helped Leilani feel confident about investing. We can help you too."[12]

Fourteen funds, listed in the advertisement and in Table 5.5, presumably constituted the set of "top performing mutual funds" selected for Leilani's "moderate portfolio." The fund names, designed to appeal to impressionable investors, included an Enterprise Fund, an Emerging Leaders Fund, a Young Investor Fund, and a Millennium Fund. The fund management companies responsible for managing the assets constituted a "Who's Who" of the mutual-fund industry, with entries from American Century, Dreyfus, Warburg Pincus, Scudder, and Federated.

The fourteen funds boasted impressive past performance. Strong's Enterprise Fund led the pack with a trailing one-year return of 178.9 percent, barely nosing out the Berger Information Technology Fund result of 173.5 percent. Bringing up the rear echelon, the Marisco Focus Fund return of 38.2 percent escaped the shame of last place by exceeding the 32.8 percent return of the Liberty Young Investor Fund.

Each of the profiled funds produced past performance that exceeded the market's return of 17.8 percent, as measured by the S&P 500. In fact, the average return of 97.5 percent posted by the group defeated the market by an impressive margin of nearly 80 percentage points. Had Paul advised Leilani to invest in this group of funds in early 1999, she would have done exceedingly well.

Unfortunately for winsome Leilani, handsome Paul's unshrinking advice came too late. In the year following Schwab's advertisement, each of the fourteen funds posted significant losses, ranging from the relatively modest loss of 15.8 percent realized by investors in the Dreyfus Emerging Leaders Fund to the much more substantial decline of 63.6 percent visited upon the holders of the Berger Information Technology Fund. In fact, the decline of each fund, save for the Dreyfus entry, exceeded the decline of the broad market. The average loss for the funds amounted to 41.3 percent, substantially in excess of the S&P 500's loss of 21.7 percent.

Table 5.5 Leilani's Moderate Portfolio Posts Immoderate Results

Mutual Fund	Sector	Prior Year's Performance to March 31, 2000 (Percent)	Subsequent Year's Performance From March 31, 2000 (Percent)
American Century International	Foreign stock	69.7	−32.8
Marisco Focus Fund	Large-cap growth	38.2	−33.3
Invesco Growth and Income Fund	Large-cap growth	42.7	−43.5
Dreyfus Emerging Leaders Fund	Small-cap growth	54.0	−15.8
Safeco Northwest Fund	Mid-cap blend	69.2	−35.4
Montgomery Global Long-Short Fund	International	125.7	−41.6
Loomis-Sayles International Equity Fund	Foreign stock	104.4	−42.1
Strong Enterprise Fund	Mid-cap growth	178.9	−51.3
Berger Information Technology Fund	Specialty	173.5	−63.6
Credit Suisse Global Telecommunications Fund	Specialty	138.3	−54.9
Scudder International Fund	Foreign stock	51.6	−31.2
Federated International Small Company Fund	Foreign stock	123.4	−48.3
Liberty Young Investor	Large-cap growth	32.8	−28.8
Neuberger Berman Millennium Fund	Mid-cap growth	161.9	−55.9
Arithmetic average of Leilani's portfolio		97.5	−41.3
S&P 500		17.8	−21.7

Sources: Morningstar; adapted from Charles Schwab advertisements, Wall Street Journal, *10 April 2000.*

Leilani's feeling of confidence and intelligence must have proved short-lived. When Paul offered her the opportunity to "choose among many top performing mutual funds" his firm made the all-too-typical mistake of emphasizing past results.[13] Instead of applying analytical and judgment tools to identify potential future winners, Schwab took the easy path of simply touting past success. Consequently, the investment opportunities presented by Schwab damaged investor portfolios in dramatic fashion.

The greater-than-market losses suffered by the highlighted funds suggest that Schwab's earnest investment specialist failed to construct a moderate portfolio. Based on the firm's classification of three funds as low risk, three funds as moderate risk, and two funds as high risk (with six funds in an undefined risk category), the combination of funds should have produced overall returns with middle-of-the-road volatility, as the three low-risk funds served to dampen the variability of the two high-risk entries. In fact, only the Dreyfus Emerging Leaders Fund performed as promised, posting lower-than-market losses. The other thirteen funds showed greater-than-market risk with losses far in excess of the market's, indicating serious flaws in Schwab's fund-risk-assessment scheme. Apparently, Schwab recognized its error, eventually losing confidence in the funds highlighted in the April 2000 advertising spectacular. An April 2003 examination of the firm's Mutual Fund OneSource Select List failed to turn up even a single survivor from the list so prominently displayed three years earlier in the *Wall Street Journal.*

A glance at the management style of the U.S. equity funds confirms Schwab's bull market bias. Five of the eight U.S. funds sported a growth orientation, while one specialized in technology. Only two of the eight funds fell into the blend classification. Not one fund employed the value management style. Schwab put a tiger in the tank of Leilani's moderate portfolio, utterly neglecting to mitigate an overwhelming reliance on ever-expanding stock market valuations.

Leilani obtained little benefit from engaging multiple U.S. equity fund managers, as several of the growth funds in her portfolio proved quite similar. The three large-capitalization growth funds (Marisco Focus Fund, Invesco Growth and Income Fund, and Liberty Young Investor Fund) and the specialty technology fund (Berger Information Technology Fund) shared a number of top-ten holdings, led by three funds reporting positions in Cisco Systems and followed by two funds holding shares in each of Microsoft, Oracle, EMC, Veritas Software, and The Home Depot. The domestic-oriented small- and mid-capitalization funds contained further duplicative positions in Microsoft, Intel, and Applied Micro Circuits. The common underlying holdings of the various recommended funds resulted in little more than unnecessary complexity and unhelpful redundancy.

An examination of the top-ten holdings of the large-capitalization foreign stock funds (American Century International Growth Fund, Loomis-Sayles International Fund, and Scudder International Fund) shows the same lack of diversification as do the large-capitalization domestic holdings. Bubble-era darlings, Vodaphone and Nokia, nabbed a spot among the largest positions in each of the funds, while Nortel, Ericsson, Samsung, Siemens, and Vivendi ranked in the top ten holdings of two of the three funds.

The specialty communications fund amplified the exposure to the foreign stock fund favorites. The Credit Suisse Global Telecommunications Fund's top-ten holdings in Vodaphone and Ericsson added to already sizable positions in her foreign funds, while ownership of NTT Mobile duplicated a top holding of the Scudder International Fund. (For good measure, the U.S. domestic Invesco Growth and Income Fund contained a position in Nokia, bringing to four the number of funds with top-ten positions in Nokia and matching Vodaphone's total.) A simple examination of significant portfolio holdings calls into serious question the rationale behind choosing this particular set of foreign mutual funds. Not surprisingly, the large-capitalization international stock funds—with their similar portfolios—deflated side-by-side-by-side, losing air in the collapse of the bubble.

Aside from problems with risk assessment and redundant style, Schwab failed to diversify adequately by asset type. On what should be a positive note, the firm spotlights five non-U.S. equity funds, investments that might provide a source of uncorrelated returns. Alas, not only did Paul fail to identify a group of foreign funds different enough one from the other to justify inclusion in Leilani's portfolio, he failed to find foreign funds substantially different from her domestic holdings. The growth-oriented domestic portfolios derived performance from the likes of Cisco Systems, Microsoft, and Oracle. By combining hot stocks in the United States with the European bull market darlings Vodaphone, Nokia, and Ericsson, Leilani realized essentially no diversification of risk.

In the year following Leilani's *Wall Street Journal* debut, declines in domestic securities, Cisco (79.6 percent), Microsoft (48.6 percent), and Oracle (61.7 percent), appeared distressingly similar to the decreases posted by the foreign stocks Vodaphone (44.4 percent), Nokia (50.3 percent), and Ericsson (70.0 percent). Commonality of investment style caused the high flyers to crash together, undermining the potential of the foreign funds to diversify Leilani's portfolio.

From a broader perspective, Paul failed Leilani on an even greater scale. By creating a portfolio entirely of equity funds, Schwab's investment specialist neglected to recommend investing in a well-diversified selection of asset types. The advertisement ignores diversifying assets such as fixed-income holdings, real estate investment trusts, inflation-indexed securities, and emerging markets equities. No portfolio, especially one characterized as moderate risk, should hold only growth-oriented equities.

The wrongs visited on Leilani by Paul span a continuum from fund specific to portfolio wide. Beginning with a flawed assessment of individual fund risk characteristics, Paul chose inappropriate building blocks for Leilani's holdings. Next, the shared growth characteristics of her funds, both domestic and foreign, caused the building blocks to be too similar to prove effective in the diversification process. Finally, by paying essentially no attention to asset-class diversification, Paul created a structure unable to withstand a range of market forces.

Schwab failed to provide the tools necessary to build an effective portfolio for Leilani. Far from "taking a load off her mind,"[14] the firm took a load from her pocketbook. The Select List of recommended funds exhibited neither the breadth of choice nor the risk profile appropriate for the client, resulting in a clear failure to address the client's investment objectives.

In a peculiar footnote to the story of Schwab's April 2000 top-of-the-market enthusiasm, by mid-2003 the firm changed its approach to separating investors from their dollars. Pat, a smiling, bespectacled, fifty-something Charles Schwab investor, replaced winsome Leilani. Paul, the handsome Schwab investment specialist, disappeared completely, perhaps having lost his job in one of the firm's several staffing reduction exercises.

A June 6, 2003, advertisement in the *Wall Street Journal* states that "At Charles Schwab, we can help you put together a well-balanced portfolio by going beyond equities to include fixed income."[15] Why did the firm change its tune? Could Schwab be cognizant of the fact that from March 2000 to May 2003, bond market returns bested stock market returns by a whopping 68.7 percentage points, as bonds generated a result of positive 36.0 percent while stocks produced a return of negative 32.7 percent? Could Schwab be aware that in 2002, investors withdrew more than $27 billion from equity mutual funds and contributed more than $140 billion to bond mutual funds? Did Schwab want its share of the action?

Somewhat disingenuously, Schwab asserts that its "advice is driven by your needs, not commissions."[16] Far from providing a public service, the brokerage firm profits handsomely from its mutual-fund marketplace. Schwab likes to characterize its Mutual Fund OneSource as commission free. A June 2003 *Forbes* article notes "that's true, in the sense that someone getting the Janus Twenty fund via Schwab bears the same 0.83% annual expense ratio as someone buying directly from Janus. But Schwab extracts undisclosed fees from the fund vendors for acting as middleman, and these fees necessarily put upward pressure on fund expense ratios."[17] A May 5, 2003, *Wall Street Journal* article estimates Schwab's fees at 0.40 percent of assets and $20 per year for each fund account.

Schwab's fee arrangements serve to restrict investor choice. Consider the consequences of the firm's early 2003 increase in charges to all but the very largest mutual-fund complexes. The increase in fees drove one of the country's finest mutual-fund managers—Southeastern Asset Management—to leave Schwab's system. Southeastern characterized Schwab's fee increase as "duplicative and excessive."[18] By eliminating one of the few superior active managers from its list of offerings, Schwab put its interest in profits far ahead of its clients' needs.

Schwab's advice to comely Leilani and rotund Pat simply encourages readers to allocate assets in security types that have done well. The performance of growth-oriented stock funds bedazzled investors prior to Schwab's April 2000 spread featuring Leilani. The performance of bonds, both in absolute terms and relative to stocks, provided a lonesome bright spot for investors in the period before Schwab's June 2003 advertisement introducing Pat. The brokerage's rearview-mirror orientation further comes through in the boast that it offers "most 4 and 5-star Morningstar-rated bond funds,"[19] touting a rating system that utilizes only backward-looking analysis. By emphasizing asset types and mutual funds that have done well, Schwab encourages investors to buy high and sell low, providing a poor recipe for wealth accumulation.

PERFORMANCE PRESENTATION

Mutual-fund companies employ a variety of subterfuges to mask poor performance, ranging from the extreme of merging poorly performing funds out of existence to more subtle manipulative techniques. When large mutual-fund complexes highlight a handful of funds, the firms invariably choose the best-performing, leaving the poor-performing nowhere to be seen. If a fund boasts an excellent five-year record and a mediocre ten-year record, the company trumpets the strong numbers in dramatic advertising campaigns and buries the weak in the small type of the offering prospectus. Selective presentation of data enhances the superficial appeal of mutual-fund offerings, providing an unrealistic picture to the unsophisticated investor.

Janus uses its mythic two-faced icon to project an image of omniscience to the investing public. With a collection of aggressive growth mutual funds, Janus could do no wrong in the go-go years of the 1990s. Driven by holdings in Cisco, Microsoft, and Nokia, the firm's performance bested the market averages by substantial margins year after year. Stellar investment results attracted substantial capital inflows, causing assets under management at the firm to grow from $31 billion at year-end 1995 to $250 billion at year-end 1999. Press reports indicate that Janus controlled in excess of $300 billion of funds at the peak in early 2000.

Notwithstanding Janus's two faces, evidently the firm could see only bull market gains. As the stock market began to collapse in early 2000, Janus's concentrated positions in large-capitalization growth stocks and significant exposures to corporate frauds proved perilous to investors. Market-induced losses in Sun Microsystems and General Electric compounded the damage of malfeasance-generated declines in Tyco and Enron, harming Janus both in terms of position-specific losses and in terms of corporate pride. In a now familiar story, poor performance and investor withdrawals caused assets under management to decline from more than $300 billion at the peak to $122 billion at the end of 2002.

In the Janus Institutional Year-End Report for 1999, the firm provided a wide range of performance numbers, highlighting the rolling three-year returns gross of fees. For instance, the firm's top-performing Aggressive Growth Fund posted extraordinary results of 54.5 percent per annum for the three-year period ending December 31, 1999.

In spite of a dismal 2000, which saw a decline of 24.6 percent for Janus's Aggressive Growth Fund, trailing three-year numbers remained in positive territory. Investors took comfort in Janus's report of three years of 28.7 percent per annum results.

As Janus's troubles extended into 2001, the Aggressive Growth Fund lost 29.0 percent, far in excess of the market drop of 11.9 percent as measured by the S&P 500. For the first time in the history of the fund, trailing three-year returns turned negative, with a result of −1.7 percent per year. The modestly negative three-year return took its customary place in the Institutional Year-End Report for 2001.

As the bear market approached its third anniversary, Janus's miserable performance continued. In 2002, the Aggressive Growth Fund lost a further 26.8 percent, again exceeding the S&P 500's loss, which amounted to 22.1 percent. Trailing three-year returns came in at a truly pathetic -26.8 percent per year. (Losses of 26.8 percent per year for the three years turn one dollar into 29 cents.)

Faced with dismal results, the firm identified a creative means to address the problem of three years of terrible numbers. In the space customarily devoted to reporting three-year results, the 2002 report suddenly switched to highlighting trailing five-year numbers. The Aggressive Growth Fund's five-year performance of 2.1 percent per year showed far better than the three-year bear market result of −26.8 percent per annum.

Recognizing that investors tend to chase good performance and flee poor performance, Janus faced a quandary regarding presentation of unimpressive bear market numbers. By moving from an emphasis on three-year numbers to five-year numbers, the firm substituted positive returns for negative and good relative results for poor. But, by selling five-year performance, Janus obfuscated rather than illuminated. Instead of presenting a consistent set of data for investors, the firm chose to spin the numbers, hoping to hide miserable performance.

MORNINGSTAR RATINGS

Most investors have scant access to truly unbiased, objective invest-ment advice. Brokers push high-commission products. Investment companies tout trendy mutual-fund offerings. Even the most ethical purveyors of financial products sometimes confuse the best route for the client with the most profitable path for the service provider. The all-too-prevalent charlatans never suffer from confusion about which road to take.

Amidst the conflict-ridden wasteland stands the apparently inde-pendent Morningstar. Beginning in 1985, the Chicago-based consult-ing firm proffered a five-tier rating scheme for four broad categories of assets—domestic equities, foreign equities, taxable bonds, and munic-ipal bonds. The firm awarded stars to funds, with one star going to the lowest rank and five going to the highest.

Over the years, the number of asset categories grew and the method of determining rankings changed, but the five-star classifica-tion structure remained constant. In 1996, Morningstar expanded the rated asset classes from the original four to forty-four, adding distinc-tions for size (small-capitalization, mid-capitalization, and large-capitalization securities), style (value and growth), sector (technology and natural resources), geography (Europe, Japan, and Latin America), and security type (convertible, international, and high-yield bond). In July 2002, the firm further expanded the number of categories to forty-eight and refined the calculations that produced the fund ratings. In May 2003, Morningstar added eleven more categories to the mix, bringing the total to fifty-nine.

Investors pay attention to Morningstar ratings. Between 1999 and 2003, four-star and five-star funds garnered an average of 106 percent of net cash flows to mutual funds. Given that an average of 44 percent of net cash flows went to unranked funds, simple math leads to the conclusion that top-rated and unrated funds captured 150 percent of net cash flows. Three-star, two-star, and one-star funds suffered net withdrawals amounting to an aggregate of 50 percent of net flows.[20]

The consistency of Morningstar's impact suggests slavish adher-ence by starstruck investors to the Morningstar rating system. As shown in Table 5.6, investors added massive quantities of funds to the two starriest categories, while subtracting significant amounts of

**Table 5.6 Morningstar's Four-Star and Five-Star Funds
Dominate Mutual-Fund Flows**

Net Flows by Ranking (Billions of Dollars)

Stars	1999	2000	2001	2002	2003	5-Year Average
0	50	134	97	74	58	83
1	−25	−8	−13	−16	−13	−15
2	−30	−32	−36	−40	−37	−35
3	−46	−95	−34	−45	−1	−44
4	11	55	27	43	85	44
5	281	158	86	115	129	154
Total	241	211	127	130	223	186

Source: Financial Research Corporation.
Note: Funds with zero stars do not have Morningstar ratings because they have been in existence for less than three years.

funds from the three least highly rated cohorts. Strikingly, for every year from 1999 to 2003, four-star and five-star funds experienced inflows while one-star, two-star, and three-star funds experienced outflows. In an expression of hope over experience, investors ploughed vast quantities of money into funds that possess no stars, thereby acquiring exposure to funds that lack even a three-year history of producing returns. Morningstar's influence on investor cashflows boosts the prospects for four-star and five-star winners, diminishing the future for less starry losers.

Apparently, the power of Morningstar's rating system stems from the investing public's search for any source of guidance in making investment decisions. Unfortunately, investors find no useful assistance from Morningstar, as the firm's rating system proves hopelessly naïve. Historical performance numbers, tempered by a measure of risk, provide the grist for assigning stars. The firm originally defined risk as "underperformance relative to a . . . 90-day Treasury bill." According to Morningstar, "if a fund's return exceeded this benchmark each month, the fund was deemed riskless."[21] Even the most unseasoned students of finance would balk at calling any equity-oriented fund riskless. Morningstar's obviously flawed system fails by focusing only on the past, by considering only quantitative measures, and by using a fundamentally compromised measure of risk.

Consider the Morningstar ratings for technology funds in the bubble era. In 1997, tech funds received an average rating of 2.1 stars, indicating a ranking barely above the bottom third of funds. Certainly, an investor using ratings to screen mutual funds would not have found the low ratings attractive. In 1999, following superb performance by technology shares, the funds leapt to an average rating of 4.7 stars, placing the group close to the top of the heap. In fact, 90 percent of rated tech funds had five stars at the end of 1999.[22] The stellar rankings attracted investor capital to the severely overpriced shares. In 2001, after the beginning of the collapse, the average rating for technology funds dropped to 2.4 stars, putting the group once again well below average.[23] In ranking technology mutual funds, Morningstar's record proved perfectly perverse.

Exhibiting remarkable candor, Morningstar noted that ". . . funds with highly variable returns are likely to produce losses, even if they're currently enjoying a run of success. Internet funds provide a perfect example. Because they outperformed the Treasury bill for many successive months they exhibited little downward risk in 1999; but they suffered huge losses in subsequent years."[24] Morningstar recognized that its system produced terribly faulty guidance for investors wishing to buy low and sell high.

In July 2002, Morningstar made two changes in its system to address the problem highlighted by the tech fund miseries. First, it started publishing ratings only for its narrow fund categories, eliminating the possibility that hot performers will dominate a broad category (because broad category ratings ceased to exist). Under the new scheme, five-star technology funds will be limited to 10 percent of the Specialty Technology subset of the mutual-fund universe and five-star real estate funds will be limited to 10 percent of the Specialty Real Estate subset. Of course, assigning ratings to nearly sixty niches reduces dramatically the value of the rating to a general purpose user of the system. Second, Morningstar changed the calculation of the risk factor, using "variation in the fund's performance, with more emphasis on downward variation." While the new risk metric likely represents an improvement over the naïve calculation used during the firm's first seventeen years, the improved version cannot be assessed, because Morningstar considers the risk penalty calculation "proprietary."

Because Morningstar fails to realize that information on past performance provides precious little advantage in the hunt for superior future performance, the firm's regular attempts to tweak its ratings system hold no promise for success. Constant culling of subgroups of niche funds from the larger population of investment management offerings represents an exercise in futility. A new group of fringe funds inevitably rises to the top of the newly created·subgroup, forcing yet another purge to rid the star system of its unwanted, unexpectedly strong performers. By looking only at the historical numbers, the star system identifies what worked in the past, not what might work in the future. In a market that enjoys sustained rushes of enthusiasm and suffers long-lasting bouts of despair, Morningstar's backward-looking performance measurement metrics prove useless to forward-looking investors.

Morningstar does provide at least one service to investors. By calculating returns net of front-end loads and other fees, the ratings tend to favor efficiently run, shareholder-friendly, no-load or low-load funds. By drawing attention to the importance of costs, even if indirectly, Morningstar helps its customers. Unfortunately, the service of promoting today's low-cost funds fails to offset the disservice of recommending yesterday's winners.

The highly touted Morningstar rating system reinforces the investing public's unfortunate tendency to focus on past performance. Purely statistical, backward-looking calculations provide no help in identifying superior managers. Yet Morningstar's four-star and five-star ratings do much to attract investor money to the anointed funds. Starry ratings poured fuel on the fire of the stock market inferno of the late 1990s and failed to insulate investors from the chill of the subsequent decline. Sensible investors avoid Morningstar's useless rating scheme.

CHAPTER SUMMARY

Environmental influences almost invariably point investors down the path to investment failure. Advertisements flog stocks at equity market peaks, with nary a mention of diversifying fixed-income assets. After stocks suffer bear-market losses, the media tout the beneficial effects of owning bonds as an important part of a well-balanced portfolio. The overwhelming bulk of messages to investors suggest owning yesterday's darling and avoiding yesterday's goat.

Even highly respected market observers focus far too much on past investment results. Morningstar's vaunted five-star rating system rests on the precarious foundation of historical performance numbers. Yet the assignment of a four-star or five-star rating to a mutual fund carries enormous influence on flows of investor funds. Just as in *The Wizard of Oz*, a pathetic little man stands behind the curtain.

Chasing performance produces disastrous results for investors. During the six-year period centered around the March 2000 peak of the Internet bubble, samples of large and successful technology mutual funds produced essentially no investment returns. Astonishing bubble era returns disappeared completely in the post-bubble collapse.

The simple time-linked returns do not tell the entire story. Because investors poured money into tech funds at the peak of the market, on a dollar-weighted basis staggering amounts of money disappeared. When adding tax bills for capital gains distributions to losses from poorly timed investments, investors in tech funds experienced truly disastrous results.

Sensible investors avoid fads, behaving in a disciplined, independent fashion. Discipline starts with careful articulation of reasonable portfolio targets and follows with close adherence to the chosen portfolio. Fidelity to asset-allocation targets requires regular purchase of the out-of-favor and sale of the in-favor, demanding that investors exhibit out-of-the-mainstream, contrarian behavior.

6
Rebalancing

Rebalancing involves taking action to ensure that the current portfolio characteristics match as closely as is practicable the targeted portfolio allocations. As market forces cause various assets to rise or fall in value, proportions of portfolios allocated to the various assets rise and fall concurrently. To maintain desired allocations, investors sell assets that appreciate in relative terms and buy assets that depreciate in relative terms. Unless investors engage in systematic rebalancing of portfolios, the risk and return profile of the actual portfolio invariably differs from the risk and return profile of the desired portfolio.

Rebalancing requires behavior at odds with traditional thinking. Under normal market conditions, systematic rebalancers trim winners and bolster losers, moves that go against the conventional grain. Under extreme market conditions, rebalancers face a test of their mettle. Dramatic bear markets signal the need for significant purchases of losers, while extraordinary bull markets call for substantial sales of winners. When markets make radical moves, investors demonstrate either the courage or the cowardice of their convictions.

When making incremental commitments or withdrawals of funds, sensible investors consider the asset-allocation implications. Allocating new funds to underweight asset classes provides a means by which the portfolio moves closer to target, without creating tax consequences. Similarly, withdrawing funds from overweight asset classes moves portfolios closer to target. However, in the case of withdrawals investors need to consider the tax implications of transactions. In fact, overweight classes frequently contain appreciated securities that may incur tax liabilities upon sale, giving investors pause.

Taxpaying investors use a variety of methods to avoid generating taxable gains in the rebalancing process. Careful investors direct fresh flows of funds to underweight asset classes, causing the actual portfolio allocations to move closer to targeted levels. Depending on the circumstances, losses generated from security sales may provide an offset to gains realized elsewhere, thereby enabling tax-free rebalancing. Alternatively, investors might employ tax-deferred accounts to conduct rebalancing activity, eliminating concerns about incurring current tax liabilities in the portfolio adjustment process. Tax sensitivity plays an important role in rebalancing.

In spite of the importance of rebalancing in maintaining appropriate asset-allocation targets, few investors pursue the practice systematically. A recent study of investors in funds managed by TIAA-CREF suggests substantial indifference to portfolio allocations on the part of the firm's college and university staff participants. The lack of rebalancing activity seems particularly surprising given the character of the investor base. If a well-educated, sophisticated group of investors fails to engage in systematic portfolio rebalancing, the larger population of investors most likely exhibits even more extreme inattention to portfolio allocations.

THE PSYCHOLOGY OF REBALANCING

Contrarian behavior lies at the heart of most successful investment strategies. Unfortunately for investors, human nature craves the positive reinforcement that comes from running with the crowd. The conventional attitude comes through loud and clear in the words of *Cabaret*'s Sally Bowles: "Everybody loves a winner, so nobody loved me." Contrarian investment behavior requires shunning the loved and embracing the unloved. Most people do the opposite.

In fact, the world of commerce (as opposed to the world of investment) generally rewards following the trend. Feeding winning strategies and killing losing gambits leads to commercial success. Executives who hypercharge winners produce attractive results. Managers who starve losers conserve scarce resources. In the Darwinian world of business, success breeds success.

In the world of investment, failure sows the seeds of future success. The attractively priced, out-of-favor strategy frequently provides much better prospective returns than the highly valued, of-the-moment alternative. The discount applied to unloved assets enhances expected returns, even as the premium assigned to favored assets reduces anticipated results.

Most investors find mainstream positions comfortable, in part because of the feeling of safety in numbers. The attitudes and activities of the majority create the consensus. By definition, only a minority of investors find themselves in the uncomfortable position of operating outside of the mainstream. Once a majority of players adopts a heretofore contrarian position, the minority view becomes the widely held perspective. Only an unusual few consistently take positions truly at odds with conventional wisdom.

Initiating and maintaining out-of-the-mainstream positions requires great conviction and substantial fortitude. Friends and acquaintances describe fundamentally different investment programs. The media push a dramatically divergent world view. Brokers urge the sale of yesterday's losers and the purchase of today's hot prospects. Advertisements proclaim a new paradigm. In the face of a seemingly overwhelming consensus, successful contrarian investors turn a deaf ear to the blandishments of the multitudes.

Establishing a contrarian position constitutes only half of the battle. Failure awaits the contrarian investor who loses nerve. Suppose an investor initially avoids the flavor of the month. Months become quarters and quarters become years. Ultimately, the weak-kneed contrarian capitulates, buying into the new-era reasoning. Of course, the buy-in comes just as the mania peaks, causing the realization of pain without the offset of gain. Taking a contrarian tack in the absence of the ability to persevere leads to poor results.

Rebalancing represents supremely rational behavior. Maintaining portfolio targets in the face of market moves dictates sale of strong relative performers and purchase of poor relative performers. Stated differently, disciplined rebalancers sell what's hot and buy what's not. Under normal circumstances, rebalancing asks for modest degrees of fortitude. When markets make extreme moves, rebalancing requires substantial amounts of courage.

INVESTOR BEHAVIOR AFTER THE CRASH OF 1987

Rebalancing portfolios proves most difficult when markets experience intense stress. Investors confront the opportunity and the peril associated with buying assets that have declined precipitously or selling assets that have risen abruptly. The opportunity comes from the ability to buy cheaply or sell dearly. The peril comes from the inability to remain steadfast as the cheap turns cheaper and the dear turns dearer.

The stock market crash of October 1987 serves as a textbook example of market stress. On October 19, 1987, the U.S. stock market, as measured by the S&P 500, declined by 23 percent. The unprecedented decline nearly defies probabilistic description. Based on historical daily volatility, the one-day collapse represented a 25-standard-deviation event. In layman's terms, a 25-standard-deviation event constitutes a near impossibility.*

The unprecedented worldwide equity market debacle shook the public's confidence in markets. Market pundits painted a gloomy picture, forecasting a dismal future for equity investments. Newspapers focused relentlessly on bad news. (The *New York Times* ran a regular feature with a graph of post–October 1987 stock prices superimposed on a graph of post–October 1929 stock prices.) Against a backdrop of almost universal bearishness, rebalancing investors needed to purchase equities to restore allocations to target levels. Needless to say, in the eyes of public opinion, rebalancing constituted rash, irrational behavior. Few investors demonstrated the fortitude needed to rebalance.

Data on mutual-fund allocations around the time of the 1987 crash provide some clues regarding individual investor behavior. Note that the aggregate allocations of mutual-fund assets fail to provide a complete picture of household balance sheets. Because individual investors hold assets other than mutual funds, changes in mutual-fund holdings may be offset or amplified by changes in other asset hold-

---

*In a normal distribution, a one-standard-deviation event occurs with a probability of one in three, a two-standard-deviation event occurs with a probability of one in twenty and a three-standard-deviation event occurs with a probability of one in a hundred. Based on a 250-business-day year, an eight-standard deviation event occurs once every three trillion years. Twenty-five-standard-deviation events should not happen.

ings. Nonetheless, in spite of the open nature of the mutual-fund system, moves in mutual-fund allocations carry important information about individual investor behavior.

Consider the allocation of mutual-fund assets at the end of September 1987, three short weeks prior to the crash in stock prices. Swelling investor enthusiasm for stocks caused holdings of equity mutual funds to reach a multiyear high of 28 percent of assets. Bonds, uninteresting in the context of a bull market for equities, stood at a twelve-month low of 30 percent of assets. Money-market funds, even more dramatically out of favor than bonds, accounted for only 37 percent of assets, down from levels in the 60 percent range only a few years earlier.

Table 6.1 Mutual-Fund Investors React Badly to the 1987 Stock Market Crash

Mutual-Fund Asset Allocations

	Equities	Bonds	Money Market	Other
September 1987 allocation	28.4%	30.4%	37.1%	4.1%
November 1987 allocation	21.9%	32.3%	42.1%	3.8%
Months to reach September 1987 share	50	18	57	

Source: Investment Company Institute.
Note: "Months to reach September 1987 share" reflects the amount of time that investors remained underallocated to equities and overallocated to bonds and money markets, measured relative to September 1987 allocation levels.

If investors pursued a disciplined rebalancing regimen, post-crash allocations would resemble pre-crash portfolios. Even the most cursory comparison of September 1987 and November 1987 allocations shows no evidence of rebalancing activity. Equity allocations dropped from 28 percent to 22 percent, representing a decline equal to almost one-quarter of the level two months earlier. Bond allocations, benefiting from a crash-induced rally, rose from 30 percent to 32 percent. Money-market funds, viewed as providing a safe haven, increased from 37 percent of mutual-fund assets to 42 percent. As outlined in Table 6.1, in two short months investors dramatically reduced equity allocations in favor of bond and money-market commitments.

The flow of money to and from mutual funds tells a similar tale. In July 1987, the bull market in equities marked its fifth anniversary, having posted a nearly four-fold total return during the five-year period. The strong market for stocks fanned the flames of investor greed, as shown in flow-of-funds data portrayed in Table 6.2. In the six months prior to the 1987 crash, investor avarice stimulated net flows of more than $17 billion to equity mutual funds, facilitated by net withdrawals of nearly $6 billion from bonds and more than $7 billion from money markets. After the crash, the picture changed. Greed turned to fear, prompting investors to yank more than $10 billion from equity funds and in excess of $3 billion from bond funds. The flight to safety benefited only money-market funds, which attracted slightly more than $29 billion. Investors bought high before the crash and sold low after the crash, following a recipe unlikely to produce satisfactory results. Evidence from both asset-allocation figures and flow-of-funds numbers shows that in the immediate aftermath of the crash, investors failed to rebalance. In fact, the data suggest that mutual-fund shareholders exacerbated the effect of the crash with bull market purchases and bear market sales.

Table 6.2 Investors Buy High and Sell Low Around 1987 Crash

(Millions of Dollars)

	Equities	Bonds	Money Markets
Flows six months before crash	17,274	−5,916	−7,269
Flows six months after crash	−10,379	−3,029	29,025

Source: Investment Company Institute.

The dramatic, fear-induced flight from risk prompted by the crash of October 1987 damaged portfolios for years to come. After the market collapse, investors only slowly reentered the stock market. Not until more than four years after the crash did the equity share of mutual-fund assets rise to the pre-crash level. Not until nearly five years later did money-market assets decline to the pre-crash level. Amid one of the greatest bull markets of all time, mutual-fund investors held cash-heavy, equity-light portfolios.

INVESTOR REACTION TO THE INTERNET BUBBLE

Investors receive similarly poor marks for their asset allocation of mutual funds during the inflation and deflation of the 1990s stock market bubble. Throughout the bull market, mutual-fund investors consistently increased stock holdings at the expense of bond and money-market allocations. Consider the period from 1993 to 2000. Investors registered equity-allocation readings in the 30 percent range in 1993 and 1994, in the 40 percent range from 1995 through 1997, in the 50 percent range in 1998 and 1999, and in excess of 60 percent at the market peak in 2000. A reduction in bond holdings served to complement the increase in equities, as fixed income moved from the 30 percent range in 1993, to the 20 percent range for 1994 and 1995, to the 10 percent range for 1996 through 1999, and bottoming at low double digits at the peak of the equity mania in March 2000. The decline in money-market holdings represented a muted version of the bond picture, as 1993's 30 percent-plus level slid to low-20-percent readings by the market top in the year 2000.

Between 1993 and 2000, mutual-fund equity holdings nearly doubled, while bonds and money markets collectively nearly halved. Investors embraced greater levels of risk during the late stages of the bull market in two ways. First, from a fundamental asset-allocation perspective, the increased marketable-equity orientation produced higher levels of risk. Second, from a valuation viewpoint, the increased prices of equity securities created heightened vulnerability at the security level. At the market peak in March 2000, investors exposed the maximum amount of assets to the maximum amount of risk.

As stock prices deflated after the market top, exposure to equities declined dramatically. From the 60 percent–plus peak in March 2000, the equity allocation dropped to just above 40 percent in March 2003. Bond holdings revived, climbing from 11 percent in March 2000 to 19 percent in March 2003. Money-market allocations jumped from 23 percent in March 2000 to 35 percent in March 2003, representing the highest level in more than a decade. In a perfectly perverse response to declining stock prices, investors held less of the now-more-attractively-priced equity assets. Figure 6.1 outlines the sad story.

Figure 6.1 Mutual-Fund Investors Get Played by the Bubble

Allocation of Mutual-Fund Assets

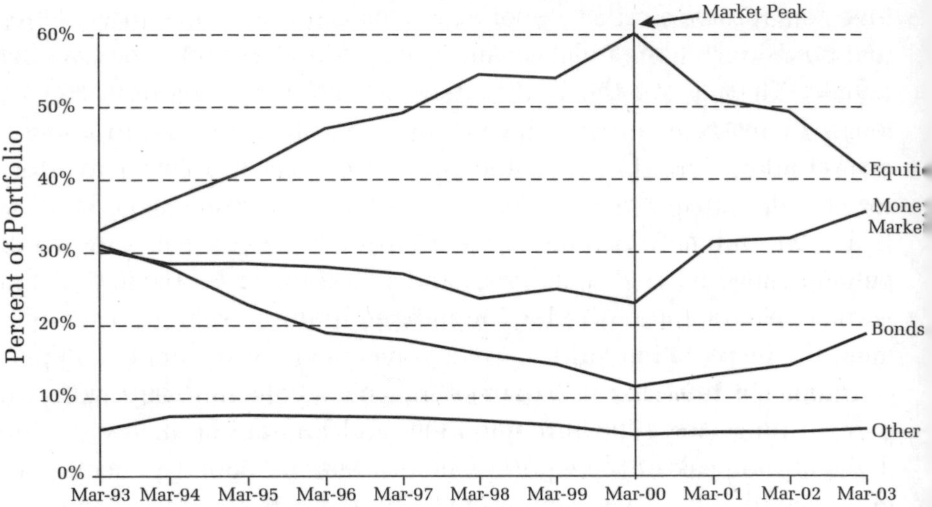

Source: Investment Company Institute.

Consider the composition of fund flows for the three-year periods on either side of the March 2000 peak in stock prices. First, note that mutual funds of all types experienced a decline in net inflows from $1.6 trillion in the three years prior to the market top to $1.1 trillion in the three years thereafter. Post-bubble, investors clearly showed less interest in holding mutual-fund shares. Second, notice that investor risk preferences exhibited a dramatic shift. In the final three bull-market years, as shown in Table 6.3, equity flows accounted for 46 percent of the total flows to mutual funds, while bonds amounted to 10 percent. In the following three bear-market years, equities and bonds changed places, with bonds accounting for 32 percent of flows and equities for 21 percent. Before the Internet bubble, mutual-fund investors aggressively bought high and after the bubble they dramatically tempered their purchases.

Mutual-fund cash contributions tell a similar tale. Investor response to the late 1990s mania played out over a longer time frame and in a more muted fashion than shareholder reaction to the crash of 1987. After a five-year-plus bull market, the dramatic October 1987 free-fall decline in prices elicited an immediate investor response, motivated by abject fear. In contrast, the attenuated post-2000 decline in prices followed a much more prolonged build-up in equity values during the 1980s and 1990s. The extraordinarily long-lived bull market created investor belief in the cult of equities. Investors learned that price increases invariably followed declines, rewarding a strategy of buying the dips. For a period after the March 2000 peak in prices, investors continued to pour money into the market, expecting short-term rewards from increasing equity exposure. Only after many months of disappointment did investors throw in the towel, signaled by significant net withdrawals from equity mutual funds in 2002. Whether abrupt as in 1987 or drawn out as in the early 2000s, investor response to bubbles and bursts harmed portfolio returns.

Table 6.3 Investors Fail to Rebalance During the Internet Bubble Asset Flows to Mutual Funds by Asset Class

(Dollars Figures in Millions, Percent of Total Flows)

	Equities	Bonds	Money Markets	Other	Total
Flows three years before March 31, 2000 market peak	729,158 45%	158,000 10%	695,080 43%	21,519 1%	1,603,756
Flows three years after March 31, 2000 market peak	225,859 21%	351,156 32%	484,380 44%	33,083 3%	1,094,479

Source: Investment Company Institute.

INDIVIDUAL INVESTOR INDIFFERENCE TO PORTFOLIO ALLOCATIONS

Because hard numbers on individual investor asset allocations prove difficult to unearth, little insight exists regarding individual rebalancing behavior. A 2001 study of 16,000 randomly selected participants in investment behemoth TIAA-CREF programs provides unusual clues regarding allocation and rebalancing strategies.[1] Authored by John Ameriks and Stephen Zeldes, the study uses a "unique panel data set" to follow participant asset-allocation decisions over a number of years. TIAA-CREF manages a pool of defined-contribution assets, largely for faculty members and administrators of educational institutions.

TIAA-CREF's investor base represents a highly educated, extremely well-informed population with a significant degree of financial sophistication. Yet few investors in the study made regular changes to portfolio allocations. In a ten-year period, 47 percent of individuals made no changes to the flows of contributions to the various asset alternatives. A further 21 percent made only one change. In other words, nearly seven of ten investors made minimal, if any, changes to their new money allocations over the decade.

The story proves similar for allocations of existing holdings. Approximately 73 percent of investors made no changes over the decade, while 14 percent made only one change. In other words, nearly nine of ten investors made minimal, if any, changes to their existing portfolio holdings.

Obviously, holdings at TIAA-CREF represent only a portion of an investor's portfolio. Rebalancing activity may occur outside the purview of the TIAA-CREF portfolios, invisible to the Ameriks and Zeldes study. Yet, the tax-deferred character of TIAA-CREF's asset

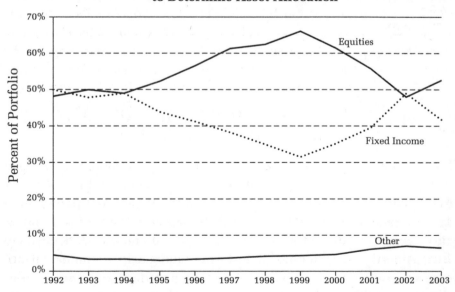

**Figure 6.2 Investors Allow the Market Roller Coaster
to Determine Asset Allocation**

Source: Martin L. Leibowitz and P. Brett Hammond, "The Changing Mosaic of Investment Patterns," Journal of Portfolio Management 30, no. 3 (Spring 2004).
Note: Data reflect allocations as of December 31.

base provides an ideal environment for rebalancing, suggesting that if participants rebalance, they would use their TIAA-CREF accounts. The Ameriks and Zeldes evidence leads to a strong suspicion that the overwhelming portion of participants do not rebalance.

The lack of rebalancing activity indicates that investors allow portfolios to drift with the whims of the market. Data from a paper by investment guru Marty Leibowitz and Brett Hammond, depicted in Figure 6.2, illustrate the ebb and flow of TIAA-CREF participant allocations.[2] The TIAA-CREF investors began with a roughly even split between fixed income and equities in the early 1990s. During the 1990s, the bull market in equities inexorably increased the share of stocks in participants' portfolios. By 1999, fixed income bottomed with a roughly 30 percent share of assets while equities peaked with a roughly 65 percent share. TIAA-CREF participants clearly allowed asset allocations to drift with the markets. As a result, equity exposure peaked along with the market, exposing investors to the greatest danger at the most vulnerable moment in time.

TIAA-CREF participants experienced significant pain as the bear market crushed equity positions. After the market peak, investors continued to allow markets to dictate allocations, as between 1999 and 2002 stock allocations moved from more than twice bonds back to the approximate equality witnessed in the early 1990s. Suggesting that TIAA-CREF participants learned little from the experience of the 1990s, during 2003 a resurgent stock market once again increased participant equity holdings, setting the stage for another leg of the roller coaster trip. Market forces provided a wild ride for TIAA-CREF participants.

RETURN AND RISK BENEFITS FROM REBALANCING

When markets exhibit excess volatility, rebalancing enhances portfolio returns. Excess volatility, a phenomenon described by Yale economist Robert Shiller, refers to a situation in which market prices fluctuate more than necessary to reflect changes in fundamental drivers of security values, such as corporate earnings and interest rates. Since stock prices tend to fluctuate around fair value, excess volatility allows systematic rebalancers to buy low (on relative declines) and sell high (on relative increases).

Consider TIAA-CREF participants' experience from year-end 1992 to year-end 2002. Allocations between fixed income and equity began the period roughly at parity, diverged during the equity bull market, and returned to rough parity at year-end 2002. To test the proposition that TIAA-CREF participants allowed market moves to dictate allocations, compare the actual participant stock and bond mixes for each year with the mixes that result from an unrebalanced portfolio. The unrebalanced portfolio starts at year-end 1992 with the same 49 percent equity and 51 percent fixed-income mix as the initial TIAA-CREF allocation. Throughout the ten-year study period, the unrebalanced portfolio operates on automatic pilot, with each asset class growing or declining by the class's respective performance. Table 6.4 shows that the actual TIAA-CREF allocations mirror the unrebalanced allocations. In three of the ten years, the portfolios match precisely; in three years, the portfolios differ by one percentage point; in three years, by two percentage points; and, in one year, by three percentage points. The strong correspondence between the TIAA-CREF participant allocations and the unrebalanced portfolio strongly suggests that TIAA-CREF participants fail to rebalance portfolios.

Suppose, instead of allowing markets to dictate allocations, participants decided to rebalance. Annual rebalancing to a 51 percent fixed income and 49 percent equity portfolio produces some interesting results. First, and most important, the rebalanced portfolio reduces the year-to-year variation in asset allocation, which dampens the variation in risk profile. Second, the rebalanced portfolio creates more wealth. Even though portfolio allocations for both market drifters and active rebalancers begin in December 1992 at roughly the same place and end in December 2002 at roughly the same place, the active rebalancers sell high and buy low, creating portfolios with lower risk and higher returns.

Obtaining the desired portfolio characteristics represents the most important consequence of rebalancing. In contrast to the wide valuation swings experienced by the unrebalanced portfolio, the rebalanced portfolio produced a much steadier pattern of results. As shown in Table 6.4, the hare-like unrebalanced portfolio peaked at a wealth multiple of 2.59 in 1999, at which time the tortoise-like rebalanced portfolio registered a wealth multiple of only 2.40. Lack of rebalancing led to a substantially higher risk profile. The unrebalanced portfolio's

70 percent equity allocation at year-end 1999 inflicted greater bear-market pain, as the wealth multiple dropped from 2.59 to 2.19 at year-end 2002. The rebalanced portfolio suffered far less damage, as the wealth multiple declined from the peak of 2.40 at year-end 1999 to 2.29 at year-end 2002.

Ultimately, the rebalanced portfolio produced both more stable and higher returns. At the end of the ten-year period, the rebalanced portfolio earned an 8.6 percent annual return, producing a 2.29 times wealth multiple. The unrebalanced portfolio generated an 8.2 percent annual return, creating a 2.19 times wealth multiple. The TIAA-CREF participant allocations yielded an 8.4 percent annual return, leading to a 2.23 times wealth multiple. Higher returns with lower risk dominates the alternative. Just as in Aesop's fables, the rebalancing tortoise beat the undisciplined hare.

The return benefit generated by rebalancing in an environment of excess security price volatility shows quite clearly in the circumstance where beginning and ending allocations of drifting and rebalanced portfolios match one another precisely. The TIAA-CREF example, with identical starting and finishing points, highlights both the risk-control benefits and incremental-return-generating ability of rebalancing activity.

In contrast to the TIAA-CREF example, unrebalanced portfolios frequently generate higher returns than rebalanced portfolios. Evaluate the portfolio implications of allowing asset allocation to drift with market forces by considering the circumstance in which high-expected-return asset classes actually produce high returns. As time passes, high-returning asset classes increase their share of assets in drifting portfolios, creating superior portfolio returns that generate greater wealth. When high-expected-return assets produce expected levels of return, unrebalanced portfolios realize superior results, albeit at the cost of a higher risk profile.

Accepting the varying level of risk associated with an unrebalanced portfolio represents a fundamentally irrational approach to portfolio management. If investors feel comfortable with the level of risk inherent in a portfolio with 68 percent in equities, as revealed by the 1999 TIAA-CREF participant asset allocation, then investors should have acquired that level of equity market exposure earlier and benefited from the higher returns from stocks. If investors had maintained the higher level of equity exposure and rebalanced throughout the period, they would have generated a wealth multiple of 2.33, even after suffering the unfortunate bear-market consequences. Allowing portfolio risk characteristics to drift with the waxing and waning of markets makes no sense. Investors who maintained a consistent risk profile profited from systematic sales of stocks from 1994 to 1999 at bull-market prices and benefited from disciplined purchases from 2000 to 2002 at bear-market valuations. Rational investors rebalance.

Table 6.4 Rebalancing Smoothes the Market Cycles

	TIAA-CREF Portfolio Allocations			Unrebalanced Portfolio Allocations			Rebalanced Portfolio Allocations		
Year	Equities	Fixed Income	Wealth Multiple	Equities	Fixed Income	Wealth Multiple	Equities	Fixed Income	Wealth Multiple
1992	49%	51%	1.00	49%	51%	1.00	49%	51%	1.00
1993	51%	49%	1.11	49%	51%	1.11	49%	51%	1.11
1994	50%	50%	1.09	50%	50%	1.09	49%	51%	1.09
1995	55%	45%	1.39	54%	46%	1.39	49%	51%	1.39
1996	58%	42%	1.57	58%	42%	1.57	49%	51%	1.55
1997	62%	38%	1.92	62%	38%	1.91	49%	51%	1.87
1998	64%	36%	2.27	65%	35%	2.26	49%	51%	2.18
1999	68%	32%	2.60	70%	30%	2.59	49%	51%	2.40
2000	64%	36%	2.52	65%	35%	2.50	49%	51%	2.44
2001	58%	42%	2.41	60%	40%	2.39	49%	51%	2.40
2002	49%	51%	2.23	52%	48%	2.19	49%	51%	2.29

Source: TIAA-CREF.
Note: Unrebalanced portfolio allocations and rebalanced portfolio allocations reflect the author's calculations.

Rebalancing activity mitigates the portfolio swings caused by fluctuations in the equity markets. As equities appreciate relative to bonds, diligent rebalancers sell stocks and buy bonds to restore allocations to target levels. Conversely, if bonds appreciate relative to stocks, rebalancers sell bonds and buy stocks. Throughout the 1990s bull market, rebalancing required sale of rapidly appreciating equities and purchase of less-rapidly appreciating bonds. Viewed from the 2000 top-of-the-market perspective, rebalancing dampened returns during the decade of the 1990s, as it systematically required sale of stocks.

Viewed from the 2002 post-bubble perspective, risk control proved profitable. As the bear market in equities relentlessly reduced values in stock portfolios, rebalanced portfolios performed far better than portfolios allowed to drift with the markets. Even though rebalancing sometimes appears costly in the short run, by maintaining asset-allocation targets investors expose themselves to the desired risk level and position themselves for long-run success.

REAL-TIME REBALANCING

Frequent rebalancing activity allows investors to maintain a consistent risk profile and to exploit return-generating opportunities created by excess security price volatility. Moreover, real-time rebalancing tends to cost less, as trades generally prove accommodating to the market. Frequent rebalancers buy in the face of immediate declines and sell in the face of immediate increases, in both cases supplying liquidity for traders pursuing the opposite, predominant tack. Although few investors commit the time and resources necessary to conduct real-time rebalancing, an examination of the benefits of intensive rebalancing provides a context for understanding the value of the strategy.

Consider Yale University's rebalancing activity. Yale possesses a number of advantages unavailable to most investors. The university's endowment enjoys tax-exempt status, allowing frequent trading without adverse tax consequences associated with realization of gains. A sophisticated team of investment professionals manages the funds on a day-to-day basis, providing the staff support needed for management-intensive activities. Yale's special tax status and dedicated investment staff permit the university to engage in real-time rebalancing activity.

Yale's trading activity during the fiscal year ending June 30, 2003, provides some insight into the potential magnitude of rebalancing profits. During the year, the U.S. equity market, as measured by the Wilshire 5000, produced a total return of 1.3 percent. Investors undertaking an annual review of portfolio allocations would likely do little to rebalance domestic equity holdings (unless returns of other asset classes caused the domestic equity allocation to change markedly). In fact, in Yale's case the overall portfolio return for the fiscal year amounted to 8.8 percent, implying reasonable stability in portfolio allocations and suggesting modest annual rebalancing requirements.

For Yale's fiscal 2003, the placid surface of the equity market concealed some powerful undercurrents. Early in the fiscal year, markets collapsed. In July, the Wilshire 5000 posted a peak-to-trough decline of more than 18 percent. The market subsequently rebounded, nearly regaining the July peak in late August with a greater than 19 percent return. From the August high the market once again fell, declining by more than 19 percent to what proved the fiscal-year low on October 9. The hidden currents continued to roil the markets with a 21 percent increase by November followed by a 14 percent decrease through March. A powerful surge lifted the market by nearly 27 percent to the fiscal-year high in mid June, from which the market drifted down to close the twelve-month period essentially where it started.

The stock market volatility provided numerous opportunities to execute rebalancing trades. Every substantial drop and every meaningful increase allowed investors to buy the dips and sell the peaks. During the university's fiscal 2003, rebalancing activity produced a host of profit-generating transactions.

As a matter of course, every trading day, Yale estimates the value of each of the components of the endowment. When marketable securities asset classes (domestic equity, foreign developed equity, emerging market equity, and fixed income) deviate from target allocation levels, the university's investments office takes steps to restore allocations to target levels. In fiscal year 2003, Yale executed approximately $3.8 billion in rebalancing trades, roughly evenly split between purchases and sales. Net profits from rebalancing amounted to approximately $26 million, representing a 1.6 percent incremental return on the $1.6 billion domestic equity portfolio.

Even though rebalancing profits represent a nice bonus for investors, the fundamental motivation for rebalancing concerns adherence to long-term policy targets. In the context of a carefully considered policy portfolio, rebalancing maintains the desired risk level. Generating profit while controlling risk represents an unbeatable combination.

Few institutions and even fewer individuals possess the resources to conduct daily rebalancing of investment portfolios. Yet, regardless of the frequency of rebalancing, fidelity to asset-allocation targets proves important as a means of risk control and valuable as a tool for return enhancement. Thoughtful investors employ rebalancing strategies to meet policy asset-allocation targets.

CHAPTER SUMMARY

Rebalancing to long-term policy targets plays a central role in the portfolio management process. Unless investors take action to boost underweight classes and to trim overweight classes, actual portfolio characteristics differ from target portfolio characteristics, exposing investors to an expected risk-and-return profile that deviates from the desired profile. Careful investors rebalance.

While rebalancing constitutes an important portfolio management tool, sensible investors pay close attention to the tax consequences of rebalancing trades. By employing tax-deferred accounts for trading activity or directing incremental flows of funds to underweight classes, investors achieve portfolio goals without incurring tax liabilities. In cases where adverse tax consequences accompany rebalancing trades, investors must weigh the certain tax costs against the uncertain portfolio benefits. Often, investors will choose to allow allocations to drift modestly from the target to avoid paying taxes on appreciated positions.

Rebalancing forces investors to act against the crowd. When an asset class performs relatively poorly, rebalancing requires compensating purchases. When an asset class performs relatively well, rebalancing requires compensating sales. Under normal market conditions, rebalancers occupy a mildly contrarian space, seen as slightly out of step with conventional wisdom.

In times of severe market stress, rebalancing takes on a decidedly dramatic cast. Market collapses require substantial purchases in an environment pervaded by bearish sentiment. Market bubbles require substantial sales in an environment suffused with bullish enthusiasm. Under extraordinary market conditions, rebalancers must demonstrate unusual determination and fortitude.

In spite of the central importance of rebalancing to effective portfolio management, investors appear largely indifferent to the process. Evidence indicates that, at best, investors allow portfolios to drift with the ebb and flow of the market, causing strong relative performance to increase allocations and weak relative performance to diminish holdings. At worst, investors behave in a perverse fashion, chasing strong performers and shunning weak performers. Buying high and selling low provides a poor recipe for investment success.

Even though the primary motivation for rebalancing concerns fidelity to the risk-and-return profile of long-term policy asset-allocation targets, in markets characterized by excess volatility rebalancing holds the potential to boost returns. When security prices fluctuate more than necessary to reflect changes in market fundamentals, investors enjoy the opportunity to buy low and sell high, enhancing overall portfolio results.

As part of a quarterly, semiannual, or annual portfolio review, sensible investors consider rebalancing requirements and opportunities. The requirements stem from market-induced changes in allocations. The opportunities arise from tax-loss creation, tax-deferred account trading, and cash-flow allocations. By using the available opportunities to move toward target allocations, investors position portfolios to satisfy long-term investment goals.

Part Three

SECURITY SELECTION

Introduction

Individual investors possess neither the time nor the resources to succeed in active management of marketable securities portfolios. Sophisticated institutional investors dominate the marketable security landscape, aggressively competing to unearth the rare security that promises risk-adjusted excess returns. Individuals who attempt to compete with resource-rich money management organizations simply provide fodder for large institutional cannon.

"If you can't beat 'em, join 'em" represents the conventional response to the recognition that individuals compete in a hopelessly skewed contest when participating in the game of individual security selection. Investors of modest means hope that mutual-fund investments level the playing field by providing fairly priced access to institutional-quality investment management services. Sadly, individual investor aspirations remain unfulfilled.

The mutual-fund industry consistently fails to meet the basic active management goal of providing market-beating returns. A well-constructed academic study conservatively puts the pre-tax failure rate at 78 percent to 95 percent for periods ranging from ten to twenty years. The same study places the after-tax failure rate at 86 percent to 96 percent.[1] The omission of the impact of vanished firms, also known as survivorship bias, colors the results with another shade of pessimism. Sales charges imposed by Wall Street further reduce the chances of success. Churning of mutual-fund holdings by investors adds an additional odds-lengthening factor to the equation. At the end of the day, as described in Chapter 7, *The Performance Deficit of Mutual Funds,* investors cannot win the active management game.

The failure of the mutual-fund industry to produce attractive investment results stems from the inherent conflict between behaving as a fiduciary and acting as a profit-maximizer. The contest between serving investor interests and making money never even makes the starting gate. Profits win in a runaway.

The crux of the conflict stems from divergence between the goals of the mutual-fund-investor principal and the mutual-fund-manager agent. Investors benefit from low fees, low taxes (related to low portfolio turnover), and fair, transparent arrangements. Managers profit from high fees, high portfolio turnover (related to high taxes), and inequitable, opaque arrangements.

Fees contribute substantially to the gap between investor aspirations and performance reality. The mutual-fund industry levies an assorted collection of charges, including up-front loads, contingent deferred sales loads, standard management fees, distribution and marketing assessments and incentive payments. The aggregate of the compensation paid to mutual-fund managers virtually guarantees that investors fail to achieve market-beating results.

Portfolio turnover constitutes a significant source of performance-reducing activity. Direct costs of turnover come from commissions paid and market impact incurred. Indirect costs of turnover relate to taxes paid on realized capital gains. In an industry dominated by taxable accounts, the indifference of portfolio managers to the tax consequences of high turnover of mutual-fund portfolios constitutes a little-noticed scandal.

Even index fund investors need to consider the implications of portfolio turnover. Sensibly constructed indices, such as the S&P 500 and the Wilshire 5000, exhibit low implementation costs and high tax efficiency. Poorly structured indices, such as the Russell 1000 and the Russell 2000, demonstrate high costs and low tax efficiency.

In 2002, median active management costs amounted to 2.35 percent of assets, comprised of 1.5 percent management fees and 0.85 percent transactions costs. The 2002 two–percent plus mutual-fund costs correspond closely to the twenty-year, two–percent plus annual performance deficit described in a thoughtfully executed academic study. Chapter 8, *Obvious Sources of Mutual-Fund Failure,* concludes that, in the highly efficient securities markets, mutual-fund managers lose by the amount that it costs to play the game.

Not all sources of mutual-fund failure stare investors in the face. A number of under-the-table practices serve to increase the take of the mutual-fund industry at the direct expense of investor interests.

Pay-to-play activity leads the parade of abusive tactics that fall outside the scope of the average investor's radar screen. In order to cement an unholy alliance, mutual-fund management companies make payments to financial services intermediaries with the explicit understanding that the payments purchase a preferred position among the intermediary's product offerings. As a result, the investor ends up owning funds that prove profitable for the broker as opposed to suitable for the individual.

Stale-price trading benefits the mutual-fund industry by attracting large sums from sophisticated, if morally challenged, players. The stale-price traders, a.k.a. market timers, enlist the cooperation of mutual-fund managers by bringing fee-generating assets to the table, fattening the bottom line of mutual-fund management companies. The market-timing players profit at the direct expense of small-time investors.

As the mutual-fund scandal unfolded in the early 2000s, industry spokesmen took great pains to portray the highly publicized problems as aberrant, arguing that the longer history of mutual-fund investing could be described as "scandal free." Nothing could be further from the truth. In fact, stale pricing plagued mutual funds from the very early days of the industry. A recurring cycle—problem recognition, delayed and ineffective regulatory response, industry adaptation—began in the 1920s and continues to this day. Regulatory authorities prove no match for profit-seeking charlatans.

Soft dollars, the slimy underbelly of the investment world, deserve a harsher name that reflects the odious nature of the kickbacks they describe. In their simplest form, soft-dollar trades involve paying higher-than-pure-execution commissions for security transactions, with the transactor receiving a soft-dollar credit that purchases investment-related goods and services. Originally designed as a means to circumvent the fixed-trading-commission regimes under which Wall Street operated until May Day 1975, soft dollars morphed into murky means of transferring costs from investment fund managers to clients. Ironically, instead of attacking soft dollars, the SEC created a safe harbor that protects investment firms pursuing this investor-hostile practice.

The mutual-fund industry engages in an invidious variety of non-transparent practices that limit investor choices and reduce investor returns. Chapter 9, *Hidden Causes of Poor Mutual-Fund Performance,* describes the profit-producing, investor-damaging activities of pay-to-play, stale-price market timing, and soft-dollar trading.

In spite of the enormously long odds that argue against active-management success, a handful of mutual-fund companies stand poised to produce market-beating returns. Devotion to investor interests, even at the expense of investment management profits, tops the list of required manager characteristics. In identifying first-class high-quality investment managers, qualitative traits prove far more important than quantitative attributes.

Choosing a manager who transcends the role of agent to behave as a principal represents the most fundamental requirement for winning the active-management game. Because a principal orientation demands that mutual-fund managers forsake profits to generate investment returns, relatively few qualify for consideration. In the profit-seeking investment management industry, fidelity to fiduciary responsibility constitutes a rare commodity.

Scarcely any individual investors command the resources and enjoy the access required to obtain the information necessary to make the critical judgments about the quality and character of the individuals responsible for mutual-fund portfolio management. Ironically, investors may identify an attractively positioned mutual fund only to find that, in an investor-friendly asset-limiting move, management closed the fund to new investors. Chapter 10, *Winning the Active Management Game,* describes the all-too-ephemeral odds of prevailing in market-beating fund-manager-selection activity.

Exchange-traded funds (ETFs)—open-end mutual funds that trade on stock exchanges—provide an attractive alternative for investors who desire to implement passively managed investment programs. ETFs promise real-time pricing and superior tax efficiency, but suffer from the necessity of dealing with the brokerage industry to make purchases and sales. Dominated by index-related products, the ETF market contains a far greater proportion of sensible vehicles than the traditional mutual-fund universe. As ETFs increase in popularity, Wall Street responds by creating more dysfunctional, high-fee offerings. Chapter 11, *The Exchange-Traded Fund Alternative,* depicts the ETF landscape, outlining the potential portfolio applications.

7

The Performance Deficit of Mutual Funds

Mutual funds play an important role as a vehicle for ever-increasing amounts of individual investor savings. In recent decades, the share of household assets invested in mutual funds moved from barely visible to quite substantial. In the critical role of providing retirement income, the shift from defined-benefit plans to defined-contribution plans forces individuals to take increased responsibility for retirement investment decisions, placing mutual funds in an ever-more-significant position in the investment world.

Conventional wisdom dictates that retail investors fare best by entrusting funds to the investment professionals who actively manage mutual funds, instead of trying to compete with far more sophisticated players in creating portfolios of individually selected securities. Proponents of mutual-fund investing hold that by pooling funds with like-minded investors, mutual-fund owners gain access to market-beating investment management that would otherwise be unavailable to small investors. The economies of scale gained by combining thousands of individual accounts benefit all participants.

Unfortunately, the conventional wisdom proves less than wise. Actively managed mutual funds consistently fail to produce superior returns. Pre-tax returns fall short of the market-mimicking, passively managed alternative by a substantial margin. Taxes cause actively managed portfolios to produce even more dismal shortfalls. When taking sales charges into consideration, the failure of actively managed mutual funds reaches staggering proportions. In the final analysis, the benefits of active management accrue only to the fund management companies, not to the investor. Asset managers profit, while investors lose.

GENERAL BACKGROUND

Mutual funds control a significant portion of U.S. financial assets. The Investment Company Institute, a trade organization for the mutual-fund industry, estimates that in 2003, mutual funds held about 22 percent of domestic equities, with pension funds, insurance companies, endowments, and households holding the remaining 78 percent. Equities dominated mutual-fund portfolios with a 50 percent share, followed by money-market funds (28 percent), bond funds (17 percent), and hybrid funds (6 percent). In total, 8,126 mutual funds contained 261 million accounts with assets valued at nearly $7.4 trillion.[1]

Active managers supervise the overwhelming portion of mutual-fund assets. At year-end 2003, Lipper classified more than 90 percent of mutual funds as engaged in market-beating efforts. A more restrictive definition that includes only passively managed, core-asset-class funds brings the active management total to in excess of 93 percent.

In the past decade, the proportion of passively managed funds increased substantially. In 1993, Lipper identified only 2.3 percent of funds as market-mimicking. The more restrictive, passively managed, core-asset-class definition captured only 1.6 percent of 1993's funds. In spite of significant growth in recent years, index funds account for a small fraction of the total, and investor-friendly index funds account for an even smaller fraction.

In 2003, 91 million individuals in 53 million households owned mutual funds, representing almost one-half of all households in the country. In contrast, only 25 percent of households owned mutual funds in 1990 and a mere 6 percent in 1980, indicating a significant broadening of the mutual-fund market in the past twenty-odd years.[2] The Investment Company Institute avers that the increasing popularity of mutual funds stems from "a combination of diversification, professional management, liquidity, convenience and . . . affordability."[3] Regardless of the reasons for the growth in mutual-fund assets, the dramatic increase in breadth of fund ownership contributed to a rise in the share of household financial assets held in mutual funds.

Figure 7.1 Core Index Funds Gain Share

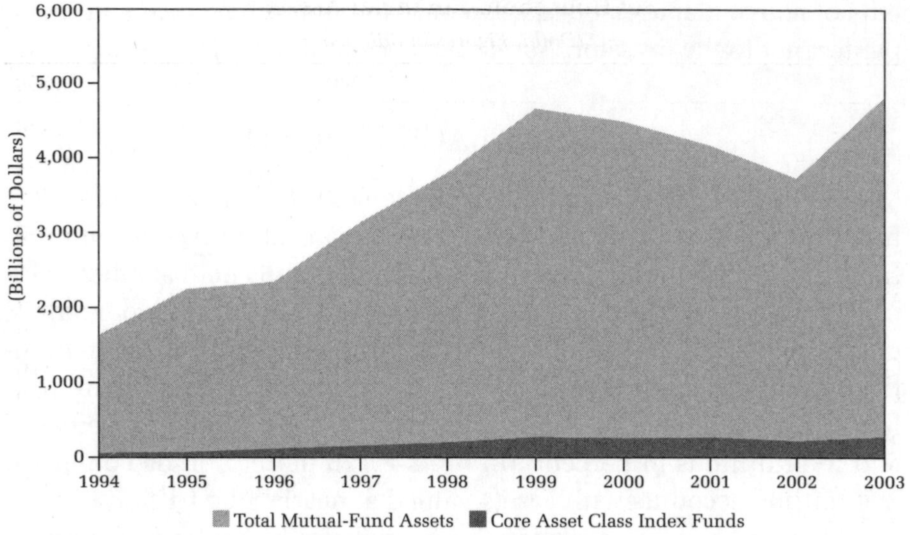

Source: Data from Lipper, Inc.

U.S. household financial assets experienced a more than fivefold increase during the two decades ending December 31, 2000, according to Federal Reserve Board Flow of Funds data. Mutual-fund holdings played an ever-increasing role in household balance sheets, moving from a barely visible 1.6 percent portion in 1980 to a much more substantial 11.8 percent share in 2000. In spite of the relative market share gains posted by the mutual-fund industry, direct holdings of stocks and bonds attracted far greater flows of funds (an increase of more than $8.6 trillion relative to an increase of $4.0 trillion for mutual funds) and commanded a far larger share of household assets (29.3 percent relative to 11.8 percent for mutual funds).

Retirement plans represent an important driver of mutual-fund industry growth. In 2003, mutual funds held 22.5 percent of the $12.0 trillion U.S. retirement asset market, with the remainder managed by pension funds, insurance companies, banks, and brokerage firms. The more than one-fifth share of retirement monies managed by mutual funds reflects the trend away from defined-benefit programs (traditional pension funds) to defined-contribution programs (401(k) and 403(b) accounts). Retirement assets account for about 36.4 percent, or $2.7 trillion, of mutual-fund assets.[4]

**Table 7.1 Mutual Funds Claim an Increasing Share
of Household Financial Assets**

(Dollar Figures in Billions)

	1980	1990	2000
Total financial assets	6,638	14,861	33,950
Deposits (minus money-market funds)	1,459	2,891	3,384
Percent of total financial assets	22.0	19.5	10.0
Bonds and equities	1,301	3,338	9,947
Percent of total financial assets	19.6	22.5	29.3
Mutual-fund and money-market fund shares	108	825	4,004
Percent of total financial assets	1.6	5.6	11.8
Other financial assets	3,771	7,808	16,616
Percent of total financial assets	56.8	52.5	48.9

Source: Federal Reserve.
*Note: "Other financial assets" consists of security credit, life insurance reserves, pension
fund reserves, investment in bank personal trusts, equity in noncorporate business, and
miscellaneous assets.*

In recent decades, employers increasingly offered defined-contribution retirement plans to employees instead of defined-benefit plans.
In a traditional defined benefit arrangement, employees receive
promises from their employer of regular pension payments upon retirement. Those promises enjoy the backing of the plan assets, the sponsoring entity (corporation, not-for-profit institution, or government),
and, in the nongovernmental world, the Pension Benefit Guaranty
Corporation (PBGC). Pension plan assets generally receive professional
management, helping to assure the security of America's workers.

In the event that dedicated pension assets prove insufficient to
meet defined pension obligations, both current and prospective pensioners look to the general credit of the sponsoring organization to fulfill the promises to pay. In the event that the sponsoring organization
fails, pension plan participants look to the Pension Benefit Guaranty
Corporation for satisfaction. Defined-benefit plans thus provide three
safety nets for plan participants in the form of a segregated pool of assets, the credit of the plan sponsor, and the PBGC.

The shift from defined-benefit plans to defined-contribution plans
carries enormous implications for the retirement security of American
workers. Driven in part by desire to avoid the uncertain future liabilities associated with defined-benefit plans, corporations increasingly

favor defined-contribution plans to provide for employee retirement needs. In a defined-contribution plan, the corporation and the employee contribute funds to an account, which must then be managed by the employee. Instead of looking forward to a promised benefit supported by a variety of safety nets, employees face a future determined by their usually ill-considered decisions regarding savings levels and their frequently ill-informed actions regarding investment alternatives. Regardless of the thoughtfulness of the decision-making process, the defined-contribution investor's retirement security waxes and wanes with the vagaries of the markets.

The shift from defined-benefit to defined-contribution plans occurred relatively quickly. In 1981, around 90 percent of wage and salary workers covered by pension plans enjoyed the security of a defined-benefit plan. By 2001, the percentage of workers with access to a defined-benefit plan dropped to just above 40 percent. In contrast, defined-contribution plan exposure grew from around 40 percent in 1981 to nearly 90 percent in 2001.[5] Clearly, the workers of America find their retirement destiny increasingly in their own hands.

Serious problems result from forcing individuals to accept responsibility for retirement saving, beginning with lack of full participation in defined-contribution plans. According to the 2001 Federal Reserve Survey of Consumer Finances, more than one of four eligible 401(k) plan candidates chose not to participate. Of those employees that do participate, less than 10 percent made the maximum contribution. When participants change jobs, a distressingly high percentage cash out their accumulated retirement plan assets. Without setting aside the seed corn to begin the asset accumulation process, employees face a bleak retirement harvest.

Once investors set aside a pool of funds to meet future needs, the challenge of investing those assets begins. The ever-increasing role of mutual funds in supplying investment management services to individuals deserves special scrutiny. In particular, as corporate and governmental decisions shift responsibility for retirement security from employers to employees, society's stake increases in seeing effective, ethical management of mutual-fund assets. Regardless of the ultimate purpose of an investor's nest egg, careful investors pay particular attention to the variety of conflicts that separate investor hopes from fund manager desires.

MUTUAL-FUND PERFORMANCE

Equity mutual-fund returns in recent decades provide a textbook example of the negative-sum game of active management. Recall that active managers as a group must underperform the market by a margin equal to the cost of trading (market impact and commissions) and the burden of fees. The theoretical possibility exists that mutual funds as a group might exhibit superior performance, with other market players producing shortfalls sufficient to counterbalance the superior mutual-fund results. Unfortunately for the mutual-fund investor, U.S. equity markets contain insufficient numbers of mullets for fund managers to exploit for active management gains. In fact, mutual-fund managers and other sophisticated market participants control such a large portion of the aggregate market capitalization that they dominate the trading of securities and the price-setting mechanism. Because well-informed institutions define the market, would-be market-beating investors as a group face the unwelcome prospect of losing to the market by the amount that it costs to play the active management game.

The lessons learned from careful examination of equity mutual-fund returns apply equally to other marketable securities. For example, active managers of foreign equity and fixed-income assets operate in the same negative-sum environment as do U.S. equity managers. While the magnitude of underperformance for different asset classes differs because of asset-class-specific factors, the historical fact and prospective expectation of disappointing active management results remain.

In a well-executed study, Robert Arnott, Andrew Berkin, and Jia Ye examine mutual-fund returns over the two decades ending in 1998. The results, summarized in Table 7.2, show that during the twenty years covered by analysis the average mutual fund underperformed the market (as measured by the Vanguard 500 Index Fund) by 2.1 percent per year. A fifteen-year deficit of 4.2 percent per annum and a ten-year deficit of 3.5 percent per annum prove even more disappointing and more damaging to investor hopes.[6]

The Arnott team's work provides a *prima facie* case for avoiding active mutual-fund management. Unlike many other studies, Arnott's work uses a result obtainable by investors as the benchmark for measuring success and failure of actively managed funds. Because the

Table 7.2 Mutual Funds Provide Miserable Results
Performance Relative to Vanguard 500 Index

Period	Pre-Tax Shortfall (Percent Per Annum)
10 years	3.5
15 years	4.2
20 years	2.1

Source: *Arnott et al.,* Journal of Portfolio Management *26, no. 4 (2000).*
Notes: *These returns do not reflect survivorship bias. Data reflect periods ending December 31, 1998.*

Vanguard 500 Index Fund returns include the effect of all fees and expenses, the results provide a fair standard by which to measure other fund results. In contrast, many return comparisons use theoretical benchmark calculations that ignore the real-world phenomena of management fees and transaction costs.

A significant portion of the twenty-year, 2.1 percent per year underperformance arises from the payment of management fees. The average equity mutual-fund fee amounted to 1.35 percent in 2000 relative to Vanguard's 500 Index Fund fee of less than 0.2 percent.[7] Presuming a relatively constant fee load over the past two decades, the fee differential explains more than one-half of the return shortfall. The remaining performance deficit stems from a combination of poor security selection, costs associated with the mindless trading conducted by managers in futile attempts to best the market, and various forms of chicanery visited upon the hapless mutual-fund investor.

For investors undaunted by the averages, Table 7.3 outlines the probability of picking a winner and the average margin of the victory. Only 22 percent of funds in the twenty-year sample manage to produce returns that exceed Vanguard's 500 Index Fund result. Even more discouraging for active managers may be the slim 1.4 percent per annum advantage garnered by the winners. The overwhelming majority (78 percent) of mutual funds lose ground to the market with losers losing by a greater margin (−2.6 percent per annum) than the margin (1.4 percent per annum) by which the winners win.

Fifteen-year results show a scant 5 percent probability of picking a winner, making active manager selection akin to backing a long shot at the race track. In a cruel twist of fate, for those skilled (or lucky) enough to identify a mutual-fund winner, the gain proves far more mediocre than the race track's long-shot payoff, as the average winnings amount to a scant 1.1 percent per year. Fully 95 percent of active investors lose to the passive alternative, dropping 3.8 percent per annum to the Vanguard 500 Index Fund results. Ten-year numbers tell a similar story, with poor odds of winning, small gains for the winners, and disproportionate penalties for the losers. Just as at the racetrack, the overwhelming number of players lose.

Table 7.3 Mutual-Fund Investors Face Poor Odds of Winning
Pre-Tax Results Relative to Vanguard 500 Index Fund (Percent)

Period	Odds of Winning	Average Margin of Victory	Average Margin of Defeat
10 years	14.0	1.9	−3.9
15 years	5.0	1.1	−3.8
20 years	22.0	1.4	−2.6

Source: Arnott et al., Journal of Portfolio Management 26, no. 4 (2000).
Notes: These returns reflect survivorship bias. Data reflect periods ending December 31, 1998.

TAXES AND FUND RETURNS

Taxable investors fare even worse at the heavy-handed trading of the mutual-fund managers. Rational tax-sensitive investors employ a high hurdle for portfolio transactions, recognizing the wealth-destroying impact of paying taxes on realized capital gains. Even though, as shown in Table 7.4, for the past two decades between two-thirds and three-quarters of mutual-fund assets sat in taxable accounts, mutual-fund advisors apparently ran the money as if it were not subject to tax. By churning portfolios, managers realize gains and force fund shareholders to pay taxes. In contrast, passively managed index funds exhibit reasonable tax efficiency. As a result, the after-tax shortfalls of actively managed funds exceed pre-tax performance deficits across the board.

As shown in Table 7.5, for the two decades ending December 31, 1998, the Arnott study observes a 2.8 percent per year after-tax deficit relative to the 2.1 percent per year pre-tax shortfall. Over fifteen years, mutual funds disappoint by a staggering after-tax margin of 5.1 percent per year, compared to the 4.2 percent pre-tax level. Ten-year results show pre-tax and after-tax deficiencies of 3.5 percent and 4.5 percent per year, respectively. Regardless of the measurement period, the mutual-fund industry ill serves its taxable investors.

Table 7.4 Most Mutual-Fund Assets Reside in Taxable Accounts

Year	Assets in Taxable Accounts (Percent)
1992	73
1997	65
2002	67

Source: Investment Company Institute.

Table 7.5 After-TaxMutual-Fund Returns Disappoint
Performance Relative to the Vanguard 500 Index Fund

Period	After-Tax Shortfall (Percent Per Annum)
10 years	4.5
15 years	5.1
20 years	2.8

Source: Arnott et al., Journal of Portfolio Management *26, no. 4 (2000).*
Notes: *These returns do not reflect survivorship bias. Data reflect periods ending December 31, 1998.*

To add insult to injury, the Vanguard 500 Index Fund results emanate from a portfolio that lays no claim to tax-sensitive investing. While the generally low turnover of the Vanguard 500 Index Fund portfolio leads to reasonably attractive tax characteristics, paying attention to tax issues could further improve the after-tax results. For example, taxable investors gain an edge by simply realizing losses when they reach a critical size and using the proceeds to purchase a close substitute for the loss-making security. While such a strategy falls outside the bounds of the rigid discipline of managing an index-tracking fund, employing a few tax-oriented trading rules in a basically passively managed portfolio holds the potential to improve after-tax returns.

In spite of its limitations as a tax-efficient investing vehicle, on an after-tax basis over the two decades of the Arnott study, the Vanguard

500 Index Fund bests the average mutual fund by 2.8 percent per year. Only 14 percent of funds, as shown in Table 7.6, post superior after-tax results, winning by an average margin of only 1.3 percent per year. Losers, much larger in number than winners, lose by a greater margin, posting a 3.2 percent per annum after-tax deficit.

The fifteen-year after-tax results provide the most powerful case against actively managed mutual funds. A minuscule 4 percent of funds produce market-beating after-tax results with a scant 0.6 percent margin of gain. The 96 percent of funds that fail to meet or beat the Vanguard 500 Index Fund lose by a wealth-destroying margin of 4.8 percent per annum. Arnott notes that "starting with an equal amount of money in 1984, fifteen years later an investor in the average losing fund would have roughly half the wealth that would have been amassed had the money been invested in the Vanguard 500 Index Fund."[8] Few winners win next to nothing. Lots of losers lose a bundle.

The management of taxable mutual-fund assets without considering the tax consequences of trading activity represents a highly visible, yet little considered scandal. A serious fiduciary with responsibility for taxable assets recognizes that only extraordinary circumstances justify deviation from a simple strategy of selling losers and holding winners. Investment maven Philip Fisher said of choosing an investment advisor: "If they take losses and small losses quickly and let their profits run, give them a gold star. If they take their profits quickly and let their losses run, don't go near them."[9] The mutual-fund industry, with an overwhelming preponderance of taxable assets, shows few signs of sensitivity to the tax consequences of trading activity and even fewer signs of fidelity to investor interests.

Table 7.6 Odds of Winning Decline After Considering Taxes
After-Tax Results Relative to the Vanguard 500 Index Fund (Percent)

Period	Odds of Winning	Average Margin of Victory	Average Margin of Defeat
10 years	9.0	1.8	−4.8
15 years	4.0	0.6	−4.8
20 years	14.0	1.3	−3.2

Source: Arnott et al., Journal of Portfolio Management 26, no. 4 (2000).
Notes: These returns reflect survivorship bias. Data reflect periods ending December 31, 1998.

CHAPTER SUMMARY

Mutual funds play an increasingly important role in the financial picture of ordinary Americans. As ever larger portions of household assets fall under the purview of mutual-fund managers, society acquires a more serious interest in the structure and results of the mutual-fund industry.

In the case of retirement assets, societal issues take center stage. As individuals find increasing levels of responsibility thrust upon them for accumulating and managing retirement assets, some important challenges arise. The issues range from improving levels of employee participation in defined-contribution programs to enhancing sophistication of employee investment management activities to providing robust sets of investment alternatives in defined-contribution plan menus. Evidence suggests that individuals face a high likelihood of disappointing retirement incomes, based on low savings rates, poor investment choices, and inferior portfolio execution.

Finance theory teaches that active management of marketable securities constitutes a negative-sum game, as the aggregate of active security-selection efforts must fall short of the passive alternative by the amount of the fees, commissions, and market impact that it costs to play the game. Well-constructed academic studies confirm the theoretical premise. Robert Arnott's 2000 examination of U.S. equity mutual-fund returns shows a twenty-year pre-tax deficit of 2.1 percent per year relative to the result achieved by investors in Vanguard's 500 Index Fund. Nearly 80 percent of actively managed funds failed to reach Vanguard's market-mimicking return. Well-informed tax-deferred investors reach an obvious conclusion: look no further than low-cost, passively managed index funds.

Since mutual-fund managers pay little or no attention to the tax consequences of their actions, after-tax results prove even more dismal for investors. Arnott shows a twenty-year after-tax shortfall of 2.8 percent per year relative to the Vanguard 500 Index Fund, which itself takes no account of tax considerations. More than 85 percent of mutual funds fail to meet the Vanguard 500 Index Fund after-tax return. The after-tax return deficit proves stunning both because of its size and because it describes the experience of the majority of mutual-fund investors. Sensible taxable investors reach an obvious conclusion: invest in low-turnover, passively managed index funds.

Even though Arnott's study describes a depressing landscape, the reality experienced by investors proves far worse. Arnott deals only with the indignities inflicted by the mutual-fund industry. His work ignores the damage wrought by the brokerage industry and by the investors themselves. Wall Street brokers extract front-end loads or impose deferred sales charges, thereby reducing realized returns to levels below those reported in the Arnott study. Many mutual-fund investors trade out of disappointing funds to buy into more promising alternatives, thereby producing adverse tax consequences above and beyond the tax burden imposed by the mutual-fund industry's too-frequent trading. Sales charges from buying funds and tax burdens from churning funds combine to reduce already poor investor returns. Owners of actively managed mutual funds almost invariably lose.

The overwhelming number of mutual-fund investors clearly suffer at the hands of the mutual-fund industry. Some of the causes—outrageous fees, excessive trading, and bloated assets—stand as obvious culprits in producing performance deficits. Other factors—unethical kickbacks and indefensible distribution practices—remain generally hidden from view. An examination of the sources of the mutual-fund industry's performance deficit serves to buttress the argument in favor of passive management.

8

Obvious Sources of Mutual-Fund Failure

Nearly all mutual-fund organizations face a fundamental conflict that prevents mutual funds from serving investor interests. On the one hand, mutual-fund managers take on fiduciary responsibility to provide high-quality investment management services to investors. On the other hand, the overwhelming number of mutual-fund organizations exist to generate profits, either for public shareholders, private owners, or corporate parents. Conflicts of interest abound. Investors desire low fees. Profit seekers demand high fees. Taxable investors prefer low-turnover investment strategies that defer taxable gains. Profit seekers revel in the money and influence that accompany high trading volume. Investors benefit from limits on assets under management. Profit seekers gather assets. Investors search for fair, transparent fee arrangements. Profit seekers thrive under complex, opaque transaction structures. In short, corporate profits come at the expense of serving investor interests.

The crux of the problem facing mutual-fund investors centers on differences between interests of mutual-fund-manager agents and mutual-fund-investor principals. Agency issues arise when fee-collecting asset managers profit at the expense of return-seeking investors. In simple terms, a principal owns assets and an agent extracts fees while purporting to work on the principal's behalf. Owners of assets invariably employ agents to assist in various aspects of investment management, including stockbrokers to execute trades, research analysts to advise on security selection, financial advisors to fashion investment programs, and mutual-fund companies to perform portfolio management.

Conflicts exist between the goals of principals and agents. Principals wish to pay fair, competitively determined fees for financial services. Agents prefer larger, less-transparent means of compensation. Sophisticated asset owners engage principal-oriented agents to reduce the impact of conflicts and increase the alignment of interests.

In the case of investment management fees, agent and principal objectives clearly diverge as high fees augment agents' incomes and deplete principals' assets. In the case of strong investment performance, agents' and principals' objectives appear to align as good return numbers produce assets for agents and provide results for principals. But this apparent alignment breaks down as the mutual-fund agent touts superior investment results to attract new investment flows. Because size constitutes the enemy of performance, fund inflows inevitably diminish future return prospects. The mutual-fund investor loses as the asset-gathering manager wins. Bloated portfolios and excessive fees represent the most visible ways in which mutual-fund-manager agents extract rents from mutual-fund-investor principals.

Agents take on the role of principal either by allowing the satisfaction of client interests to transcend the imperative of profit generation or by employing the technique of side-by-side investment to transform the fundamental character of the incentive structure. In the case of subordinating profit maximization to client outcomes, the agent pursues the unusual path of valuing client results more highly than personal profit. Unfortunately, few agents in the financial services profession reject the Economics 101 notion of profit-maximizing behavior. In the case of agent co-investment alongside the principals' assets, the agent becomes a principal. As the degree of co-investment increases, so does the principal orientation of the manager. Few agents possess the means (or the desire) to allow return generation to trump fee collection. Aside from the unusual circumstances in which agents exhibit principal-like behavior, investors face the challenge of dealing with an adversarial agent who profits at the investor's expense.

The market system imposes some unavoidable agency costs on investors as the price for services rendered. Even though mutual-fund fees reduce investor returns, at least a portion of such fees serve as a necessary means to compensate fund managers. While market forces of competition and economies of scale should serve to limit fees for basic financial services, mutual-fund complexes seemingly defy the laws of economics, managing year in and year out to extract excessive amounts of fee income at the expense of clients. Beyond the highly visible fees, investors contend with costs associated with growth in assets and turnover of portfolios. Sensible investors investigate the entire range of agency costs, seeking high-quality investment management at the lowest available price.

MUTUAL-FUND FEES

Mutual-fund investors pay a variety of fees for the privilege of purchasing mutual funds. On initial investment, investors frequently pay a load, or sales charge, to acquire shares. Loads range up to 8.5 percent, sometimes varying with the size of investment and length of holding period. Funds without sales charges carry the no-load designation. Regardless of whether an investor incurs an up-front load, mutual-fund owners invariably pay management fees to compensate investment advisors for investment management services. On top of the necessary management fees, many funds assess further charges, known as 12b-1 fees, to compensate fund advisors for marketing and distribution expenses. The aggregate burden of fees serves to reduce investor returns by a considerable margin. Careful investors scrutinize mutual-fund fee arrangements.

Sales Loads

A particularly clear example of the principal-agent conflict arises in the marketing and distribution of mutual funds. Mutual funds come in two basic varieties—load funds and no-load funds. Aside from the sales charge for load funds, no-load and load funds do not differ in any systematic way. In fact, a well-constructed study shows that load funds underperform their no-load cousins roughly by the amount of the (significant) additional fees.[1] Brokers clearly prefer the high up-front fees from selling load funds. Well-informed investors avoid lining brokers' pockets with unproductive fees and enjoy higher expected returns from buying no-load funds.

Sales loads create significant drag on investor returns. In 1979, prior to the introduction of 12b-1 annual marketing fees, the median sales load amounted to a staggering 8.5 percent of assets. By 1999, the median front-end load declined to a still substantial 4.75 percent. The reduction in front-end loads might lead mutual-fund industry observers to conclude that the shareholders' lot improved with the decline in up-front charges. Two countervailing influences negate that happy conclusion. First, to the extent that annual 12b-1 fees displace up-front charges, long-term investors end up worse off as the annual fees accumulate year in and year out, eventually imposing a larger burden than the egregious, but one-time-only, up-front fees. Second, since many mutual-fund companies adopted contingent deferred sales charges that short-holding-period shareholders pay upon exit from a fund, short-term investors get hit with an unwelcome departure fee. Mutual-fund companies that employ loads and marketing fees place a burden on short-term and long-term shareholders coming and going.

Matthew Morey, of the Lubin School of Business at Pace University, examined a broad group of load and no-load funds, concluding that no-load funds generate materially better returns. Morey's study, which examined returns of 635 funds from 1993 to 1997, describes in clinical terms the ugly load-fund landscape: "The average front-end load for the load group of funds was 5.14 percent with Equity-Income funds having the highest average load. The highest load was 8.5 percent while the lowest was 1.5 percent with [the] majority of load funds having loads between 4.50 and 6.49 percent." The sample included 334 no-load funds and 301 load funds.[2]

Unlike many previous studies of load and no-load fund results, Morey's work corrects for the mortality of poorly performing funds. When results disappoint, funds lose existing clients and fail to attract new customers. Mutual-fund companies eliminate the poor performers, either through liquidation or merger. Not surprisingly, in the more marketing-sensitive load-fund world, funds disappear at a higher rate than in the no-load-fund arena. During the course of Morey's study, 19 percent of load funds vanish as compared to 12 percent of no-load funds. By adjusting for so-called survivorship bias—the tendency for continuing funds to show results superior to those from discontinued funds—Morey's study reaches a conclusion supported by common sense. No-load funds outpace load funds by a margin of 11.8 percent per year to 10.5 percent per year. The underperformance of the load funds (1.3 percent per year) nearly matches the average up-front load amortized over a five-year holding period (1.0 percent per year). In other words, results from load and no-load funds mirror each other, but for the higher costs of the load funds.

Management Fees

While astute mutual-fund investors avoid loads, all holders of mutual funds pay management fees. In the asset categories that provide the basic building blocks for investor portfolios, Lipper data indicate that in 2003, dollar-weighted annual expenses ranged from 0.60 percent for money-market funds to 1.15 percent for world equity funds, with the all-important general equity funds registering a 0.91 percent expense ratio.*[3] Mutual-fund fees consume a hefty chunk of asset-class returns.

The Lipper fee data include charges for management fees, nonmanagement fees, and 12b-1 fees. In the case of general equity funds: management fees for "portfolio management and administration" account for 58 percent of the total; nonmanagement expenses for back-office functions such as "transfer agents, custodians, and legal" account for 20 percent of the total; and 12b-1 fees to "promote distribution" account for 21 percent of the total.

In the general equity category, Lipper reports that recent years saw fees range between 0.86 percent and 0.93 percent before settling at the current level of 0.91 percent. World equity fund fees consistently led the pack, fluctuating in a tight band between 1.12 percent and 1.15 percent. Money-market funds showed little change from 1999 to 2003, hovering around 0.60 percent of assets. Taxable fixed-income funds exhibited a declining ratio, moving from 0.81 percent to 0.75 percent.

---

*Core asset classes include domestic equities, foreign developed equities, emerging market equities, conventional fixed income, inflation-indexed bonds, and real estate. Lipper data aggregate foreign developed equities and emerging market equities, as well as conventional fixed-income and inflation-indexed bonds. Lipper does not report a separate category for marketable real estate securities. Money-market funds serve as virtually risk-free vehicles that allow investors to reduce exposure to the risky portfolio as time horizons shorten.

Table 8.1 Mutual-Fund Expense Ratios Show Stability

Dollar-Weighted Total Expense Ratio (Percent of Assets)

Year	General Equity	World Equity	Taxable Fixed Income	Money Market	Weighted Average Cost
1999	0.86	1.15	0.81	0.60	0.69
2000	0.89	1.12	0.78	0.60	0.71
2001	0.92	1.13	0.76	0.61	0.70
2002	0.93	1.15	0.75	0.60	0.67
2003	0.91	1.15	0.75	0.60	0.66

Source: Lipper, Inc. "Global Themes in the Mutual Fund Industry—2003."
Note: 2003 data reflect updates received after the publication of the initial report.

Lipper's fee data present a troubling and difficult-to-explain picture of the substantial fee burden imposed on mutual-fund investors.

Even though the dollar-weighted fund expense data show reasonably stable fees for the aggregate of mutual funds invested in core asset classes, examination of median expense ratios paints a different picture. Median levels of fees measure the charges imposed by the middle-of-the-pack fund, regardless of size. As shown in Table 8.2, median fees increased for all asset classes, including taxable fixed income. Unfortunately, the reconciliation between a stable aggregate fee burden and an increasing median fee level stems from a greater concentration of assets in larger funds that charge lower fees. The situation proves adverse to investors who play the beat-the-market game, because the larger funds carry the anchor of size to the active manage-

Table 8.2 Median Expenses Increase for Core Asset Classes

Median Expense Ratio (Percent of Assets)

Year	General Equity	World Equity	Taxable Fixed Income	Money Market
1999	1.32	1.75	0.93	0.67
2000	1.33	1.70	0.95	0.68
2001	1.36	1.75	0.97	0.70
2002	1.42	1.80	0.97	0.70
2003	1.45	1.80	1.00	0.70

Source: Lipper, Inc. "Global Themes in the Mutual Fund Industry—2003."
Note: 2003 data reflect updates received after the publication of the initial report.

ment race. The dollar-weighted and equal-weighted Lipper data indicate that in recent years, investors drank one of two poisons: the burden of higher fees or the drag of larger portfolios.

The excessive costs of active management become apparent when comparing the industry's average fee levels to Vanguard's passively managed alternatives. Vanguard's annual cost advantage ranges from 0.8 percent for the general equity and world equity categories to 0.6 percent for municipal bonds to 0.5 percent for taxable fixed income to 0.3 percent for money-market funds. Vanguard's Admiral shares, available to larger and more longstanding clients, show even more dramatic cost advantages. Lower fees produce a quantifiable advantage for investors.

Table 8.3 Vanguard Funds Provide Substantial Cost Savings
2003 Total Expense Ratios (Percent of Assets)

	General Equity	World Equity	Taxable Fixed Income	Money Market
Lipper	0.91	1.15	0.75	0.60
	Total Stock Market	Total International Stock Market	Total Bond Market	Prime Money Market
Vanguard Investor Shares	0.20	0.36	0.22	0.32
	Total Stock Market	Total International Stock Market	Total Bond Market	Prime Money Market
Vanguard Admiral Shares	0.15	0.36	0.15	0.14

Source: Lipper, Inc. "Global Themes in the Mutual Fund Industry—2003"; Vanguard.
Note: 2003 data reflect updates received after the publication of the initial report.

The old adage that "you get what you pay for" fails to apply to the mutual-fund world. According to a study conducted by Standard & Poor's, funds that charge lower fees consistently produce higher performance.[4] In an examination of more than 17,000 funds in the firm's database, researchers divided three size classifications of equity funds (small-cap, mid-cap, and large-cap) and three style classifications of equity funds (value, blend, and growth) into above-median-fee and below-median-fee groups, producing a matrix of eighteen categories. In eight of nine domestic-equity size and style categories, low-fee funds beat high-fee funds by material margins, ranging from ten-year annual advantages of 0.8 percent to 3.8 percent. Only in the case of mid-cap blend funds did high-fee management match low fee management. The S&P data demonstrate a powerful relationship between lower fees and higher performance.

Table 8.4 Low-Fee Fund Performance Advantage
Ten Years through May 31, 2004 (Percent)

	Above-Median-Fee-Fund Performance	Below-Median-Fee-Fund Performance	Low-Fee Fund Performance Advantage	Low-Fee Fund Expense Advantage
Large-cap growth	7.2	8.9	1.7	1.1
Large-cap blend	7.9	10.0	2.1	1.1
Large-cap value	9.2	10.5	1.3	0.9
Mid-cap growth	6.6	9.5	2.9	1.2
Mid-cap blend	12.1	12.1	0.0	1.0
Mid-cap value	11.0	12.2	1.2	0.9
Small-cap growth	6.5	10.3	3.8	1.0
Small-cap blend	10.7	11.5	0.8	1.1
Small-cap value	11.4	13.4	2.0	1.0

Source: Standard and Poor's, "S&P Research on Fees Show Cheaper Funds Continuing to Outperform Their More Expensive Peers." Press Release, 29 June 2004.

Fee differentials between the high-cost and low-cost groups of funds exhibit relatively tight distribution, ranging from 0.9 percent to 1.2 percent per year. Interestingly, in seven of nine categories, the low-fee-fund performance advantage exceeds the low-fee-fund expense advantage. In other words, superior performance of low-fee funds generally surpasses the magnitude of the cost edge enjoyed by low-fee funds. Perhaps the above-average greed exhibited by high-fee fund managers accompanies below-average competence.

Within the realm of active equity management, investors inhabit a perverse world where higher fees correspond to lower returns. In the broader universe that includes active and passive management, index funds exhibit a dramatic cost advantage over their actively managed counterparts. Well-informed investors recognize that fund fees matter.

Distribution Fees

In 1980, the Securities and Exchange Commission caused considerable damage to mutual-fund shareholder interests by permitting mutual funds to pay for marketing and distribution expenses directly
from fund assets. Under Rule 12b-1, mutual-fund companies charge
fund investors directly for promotional activities designed to increase assets under management. Consider the tradeoff between asset size and investment performance. Higher levels of assets allow
investment advisors to enjoy an enhanced stream of management
fees. Larger portfolios impede investment advisor efforts to manage
assets actively. The unfortunate shareholders subject to 12b-1 fees
face a double-barreled diminution of returns, brought on by the direct impact of the fees and the indirect effect of increasing portfolio
size.

Ironically, a December 2000 SEC study on mutual-fund fees and
expenses concluded that 12b-1 fees essentially represented a net
transfer from the fund shareholder to the fund management company.[5]
The Commission's report concluded that "funds with 12b-1 fees had
total expenses that were higher than those of other funds by an
amount equal to 93 percent of the maximum 12b-1 fee authorized by a
fund."* In other words, mutual-fund advisors who charge 12b-1 fees
take nearly the entire 12b-1 fee to the bank.

The SEC continues to allow 12b-1 fees, even while explicitly
recognizing the "inherent conflict of interest between the fund and its
investment adviser." The Commission identifies the conflict as origi-
nating "because the directors of the fund (who typically have initially
been selected by the adviser) approve the amount of the fees that the
fund will pay."[6] Without the blessing of the SEC, fund directors could
scarcely approve something as damaging to investors as 12b-1 fees.
The explicit regulatory approval of 12b-1 fees provides a safe harbor
for fund directors who wish to increase management company profits
at the direct and indirect expense of investor interests.

Even while working within an established management-company-

---

*Under NASD regulations investment advisors can charge 12b-1 fees of up to 1 percent of
assets.

friendly regulatory framework, fund directors engage in strange contortions to approve 12b-1 programs. According to the SEC, the fund's independent directors must conclude "that there is a reasonable likelihood that a [12b-1] plan will benefit the fund and its shareholders."[7] Under almost no circumstances do shareholders benefit from paying fees above and beyond the basic management fee in an effort to attract more assets to a fund.* Shame on the SEC for allowing 12b-1 fees, shame on the directors for approving them, and shame on the mutual funds for assessing them.

While charging mutual-fund shareholders for marketing activities proves difficult to justify as reasonable and fair under any circumstances, charging fund shareholders for marketing activities after marketing ceases proves impossible to defend. In an extraordinarily offensive maneuver, a number of mutual-fund companies continued to charge 12b-1 fees even after the management company closed funds to new investors. According to a December 2003 issue of the *Wall Street Journal,* more than one hundred mutual funds sponsored by some of the nation's best-known fund management organizations assessed marketing and distribution fees on closed funds.[8] Dreyfus, Lord Abbett, Putnam, and Eaton Vance led the ranks of firms that pursued this odious practice. Rule 12b-1 fees entered the picture with the wafer-thin rationale that the mutual-fund industry needed special assistance to gather assets to reach appropriate scale. No rationale supports the imposition of 12b-1 fees on funds that have closed.

The SEC took notice of the practice of charging marketing fees on closed funds, sending letters to "several companies seeking information."[9] Regardless of whether or not the SEC takes the further step of assessing fines and getting companies neither to admit nor to deny wrongdoing, common sense dictates that 12b-1 fees apply only to asset-gathering funds. In charging marketing fees on closed funds, fund management companies further insult the intelligence and deplete the wallets of their investors.

---

*Investors in a sub-scale fund with insufficient levels of assets under management would benefit from net inflows. This extraordinarily unusual circumstance certainly fails to justify widespread charging of 12b-1 fees by mutual funds that operate at or above a reasonable scale.

Rule 12b-1 fees, explicitly created to pay for marketing and distribution expenses, illustrate the principal-agent conflict in high relief. Marketing and distribution benefit only the fund management company. To the extent that marketing and distribution efforts succeed, assets under management increase, leading to higher fees for the fund manager. To the extent that size impedes performance, increases in assets lead to lower returns for fund shareholders. Mutual-fund investors pay the 12b-1 fees and suffer the consequences.

Incentive Fees

The principal-oriented fund manager focuses on producing high investment returns relative to the degree of risk assumed by the portfolio. After all, superior risk-adjusted returns represent the investment goal of mutual-fund investors and the fiduciary responsibility of mutual-fund managers. Yet standard asset-based fee structures produce incentives that cause the interests of fund investors and fund managers to diverge.

If a fund manager receives compensation only from asset-based fees, the manager's incentives point toward achieving scale and stability in the flow of fees. As assets under management grow, fee income to the mutual fund increases, providing incentives for the agent to grow the pool of assets. Unfortunately, as asset size increases, active portfolio management becomes increasingly difficult, reducing the likelihood of producing attractive returns for fund shareholders.

Portfolio managers realize that fund inflows follow strong performance and fund outflows follow poor results. Once managers accumulate a substantial pool of assets, behavior frequently changes in a not-so-subtle way. Risk-averse managers value retaining existing assets, leading to dampening of active management "bets" and more-market-like performance. By creating portfolios unlikely to deviate in material fashion from market results, mutual-fund managers ensure continued employment for themselves (and mediocre investment results for their shareholders). Differences between the goals of agents seeking stable, substantial flows of income and principals pursuing high risk-adjusted investment returns generally resolve in favor of the agent.

Certain performance-based fee schemes work to align the interests of fund managers and fund shareholders, encouraging fund managers to profit from performance excellence instead of asset gathering. Most incentive fee structures involve the combination of an asset-based fee and a performance-based fee. The asset-based fee covers reasonable overhead involved in running investment management operations. The performance-based fee rewards superior returns, defined by the amount by which the returns exceed an appropriate benchmark. For example, a large-capitalization equity fund manager might receive ten percent of the fund's gains in excess of the return on the S&P 500. In such a dual fee structure, the asset-based fee covers costs and provides a fair income, while the incentive fee rewards managers for producing superior investment returns.

The Numeric Investors SmallCap Value Fund employs a reasonably structured performance fee arrangement. In 2003, Numeric charged an overhead-related fee of 0.89 percent, consisting of a base management fee of 0.45 percent and other costs of 0.44 percent. In an investor-friendly move, the firm charged no 12b-1 fee. Numeric received a performance-related fee of 0.10 percent for each percentage point that the Numeric SmallCap Value Fund outperformed the Russell 2000 Value Index, up to a maximum of 0.90 percent for nine percentage points (or more) of outperformance.[10] The principals of Numeric give investors an extremely fair deal.

According to Morningstar, based on 2003 data, if Numeric's fund simply matches its benchmark, the total expense ratio amounts to less than two-thirds of the peer group average of 1.55 percent.[11] If the fund produces a stunning level of more than nine full percentage points of excess performance, the maximum total expense ratio slightly exceeds the peer group average. Numeric's incentive fee works, because it penalizes mediocrity and rewards excellence. Fortunately for Numeric and Numeric's investor base, the firm outperformed its benchmark by nearly 10 percent per year over the four-year-plus life of the fund. Numeric received fair compensation and investors paid a fair price for excellence.

Unfortunately, others in the mutual-fund industry employ incentive fees to double dip. Instead of lowering base fees and using incentive fees to drive pay for performance, some funds use incentive fees as a source of compensation above and beyond already outlandish asset-based fees. Consider the example of the Granum Value Fund. In

2003, Granum began with minimum fees of 1.83 percent, comprised of a 12b-1 fee of 0.75 percent, a base management fee of 0.50 percent, and other costs of 0.58 percent.[12] Earning a full incentive fee adds a further 1.5 percent to costs, bringing maximum total fees to 3.33 percent. Morningstar, in a masterful understatement, characterizes Granum's fees as ranging from "expensive to obscene." Granum Value Fund shareholders face a no-win situation. The 2003 minimum fee of 1.83 percent exceeds the Morningstar peer group average of 1.55 percent, guaranteeing that investors pay above-average fees regardless of performance. If Granum manages to earn an incentive fee, investors get taken to the cleaners.

Morningstar observes that the S&P 500 fails to meet the test of providing a fair benchmark for Granum's value-oriented style. While under all circumstances investors benefit from employing a sensible standard to assess manager performance, when calculating incentive compensation the selection of a fair benchmark rises to the level of an absolute necessity. In the absence of an appropriate measure for judging manager performance, managers may generate incentive fees simply from the lack of correlation between the measurement standard employed (in Granum's case, the mismatched S&P 500 Index) and the fair benchmark (in this case, the well-matched Russell 1000 Value Index).

The use of a fair benchmark assumes heightened importance when incentive fee arrangements fail to incorporate investor-friendly characteristics such as clawbacks and high-water marks. A clawback forces managers to disgorge past incentive fees when subsequent performance falls short of the benchmark. (In vivid imagery, taloned investors claw back previously paid fees.) In the absence of a clawback, investors face the ugly prospect of paying fees for performance that came and went. A high-water mark requires managers to fill performance deficits produced after having received incentive fees, prior to earning more incentive fees. In the absence of a high-water mark, investors face the unattractive possibility of paying fees on past gains without getting an offset for subsequent losses. Granum Value Fund investors benefit neither from a clawback nor from a high-water mark.

The use of a poorly structured incentive fee arrangement with an inappropriate benchmark enriched the management of the Granum Fund at the direct expense of investors. Consider the six-year period from the inception of the Granum incentive fee to October 31, 2003. As expected, the mismatched S&P 500 Index posted a lower correlation to the Granum Value Fund than did the better-matched Russell 1000 Value Index, with the S&P 500 showing a 76 percent correlation relative to the Russell 1000 Value correlation of 88 percent. Not surprisingly, the S&P 500 Index proved more volatile relative to the Granum Value Fund than the Russell 1000 Value Index, as evidenced by the 11.7 percent standard deviation of the return differential between the S&P 500 and the Granum Value Fund and the 10.1 percent standard deviation of the return differential between the Russell 1000 Value Index and the Granum Fund. The combination of the S&P 500's lower correlation and higher relative variability led to imposition of incentive fees based on the noise in the relationship between the returns of the Granum Value Fund and the returns of the S&P 500, not for truly superior performance.

Granum Value Fund's ill-served investors ultimately paid incentive fees for far-from-superior performance. For the six full years during which the fund operated with an incentive fee structure, investors received returns of 4.4 percent per annum. As shown in Table 8.5, the Granum Value Fund results fell short of the Russell 1000 Value Index returns by 1.1 percent annually, hardly representing an outcome worthy of exceptional reward. Yet, because the fund modestly outperformed the S&P 500, with sizeable year-to-year deviations from the S&P 500, Granum Capital Management levied a toll for supposedly superior results. In four of six years, Granum charged incentive fees ranging from 0.79 percent to 1.50 percent of assets, with two years maxing out at the 1.50 percent level. In large part as a result of the incentive fee arrangement, in Granum's 2002 fiscal year (ending October 31) investors staggered under a fee burden of 3.26 percent of assets. Few managers possess the ability to beat the market by a margin sufficient to justify fees of that level. Granum certainly does not. Granum did, however, manage to beat its investors by earning an indefensible performance fee without producing performance.

Granum's undeserved incentive fee payments resulted from the triple threat of no high-water mark, no appropriate benchmark, and no investor clawback. In the absence of a high-water mark, Granum faced no requirement to redress the relative performance deficits of 28.2 percent in 1998 and 10.0 percent in 1999. Instead of making amends, after dramatically underperforming the S&P 500, Granum wiped the slate clean, allowing the firm to extract an incentive fee in 2000, without filling the hole created by dismal returns for 1998 and 1999.

The use of a mismatched benchmark hurt investors in two ways. Over the six-year period, Granum posted positive results relative to the poorly matched S&P 500 Index and showed negative results relative to the better-matched Russell 1000 Value Index. Investors paid for illusory gains. The greater variability of Granum's returns vis-à-vis the S&P 500 compounded investor woes. Both the Granum Fund's 1998-to-1999 performance deficit and the Fund's 2000-to-2002 rebound proved to be much greater when compared to the S&P 500 than when measured against the Russell 1000 Value. The heightened volatility of relative performance caused investors to pay incentive fees on spurious gains.

Finally, the lack of a clawback cheated investors of the opportunity to mitigate the damage done by 2003's poor relative performance. Good relative performance benefits Granum and poor relative performance hurts only investors, creating a "heads I win, tails you lose" situation for the firm.

Table 8.5 Granum Value Fund Investors Face a Lose-Lose Situation

Period	Granum Value Fund	Performance Relative to S&P 500 Index	Performance Relative to Russell 1000 Value Index	Difference Between S&P 500 Index and Russell 1000 Value Index
1998	−6.2	−28.2	−21.0	−7.2
1999	15.7	−10.0	−0.8	−9.2
2000	16.3	10.2	10.8	−0.6
2001	−3.7	21.2	8.2	13.0
2002	−6.4	8.7	3.6	5.1
2003	13.8	−7.0	−9.1	2.1
Average	4.4	0.6	−1.1	1.7

Sources: Granum Value Fund, 1998 Annual Report: 11; Granum Value Fund, 2003 Annual Report: 14; Data from Bloomberg.
Note: Data are for periods ending October 31, corresponding to the Granum Value Fund's fiscal year.

Over the six years ending October 31, 2003, the Granum Value Fund took over $6 million in payments for nonexistent superior performance. Even though Granum's results failed to meet the returns of a fair benchmark, the fund managers extracted incentive fees of more than 5.0 percent of average assets over the six-year period. The scandalous incentive fees accompany the 4.5 percent of assets consumed by 12b-1 fees, the 3.0 percent of assets consumed by base management fees, and the 2.6 percent of assets consumed by other costs. Granum Capital Management extracted extraordinary fees from investors in exchange for far-from-extraordinary performance.

Even though fair incentive fees provide possible benefits to investors, the potential perversion of performance-based schemes by the mutual-fund industry forces investors to approach incentive arrangements with great skepticism. Consider the Granum Value deal. Without a fair benchmark, a clawback, and a high-water mark, success produces increased income and failure causes no countervailing deficit. The asymmetry in the payoff structure creates an option for the fund manager. The interests of the fund manager and investor correspond in the case of success, but fail to match in the case of failure. The option-like character of the incentive fee insulates fund managers from the agonies of defeat, while providing a share of the spoils of victory. All too often when investment results disappoint, the fund shareholder alone bears the brunt of the pain.*

Intermediaries

As a general rule, a greater number of parties involved in a transaction leads to a greater fee burden. Unfortunately, not only do a majority of investors employ intermediaries in purchasing mutual funds, but the use of intermediaries has grown in importance. In 1992, nearly a quarter of investors avoided the costs of intermediation by purchasing funds directly from mutual-fund management companies. By 2002, the number of self-reliant investors dropped to 12 percent of the total, indicating that increasing numbers of investors paid an extra something, receiving in exchange less than nothing.[13]

The brokerage industry accounts for the largest share of fund sales, posting a consistent market share of 62 percent in 1992 and 2002.

---

*The issues with incentive fees parallel the shortcomings in much-touted alignment of interests purported to be created between company shareholders and company managements by the issuance of stock options. In fact, corporate grants of options not only suffer from problems of asymmetry, but misalignment of interests frequently becomes magnified with repricing of options after declines in stock prices.

Here, investors face the greatest likelihood of disservice. Sales loads, marketing fees, and portfolio churn serve to enrich the broker and impoverish the client. The conflict of interest between agent and principal provides a powerful subtext that permeates the relationship between broker and client. The mind-numbing complexity of various share classes with bewildering combinations of up-front loads, contingent deferred sales charges, and 12b-1 fees produces a fee bonanza for the broker at the investor's expense. Sensible investors avoid the brokerage community, opting for the lower-cost, self-service alternative.

Fund sales through employer-sponsored retirement programs and mutual-fund supermarkets grew from 14 percent of the total in 1992 to 25 percent in 2002. Growth in tax-deferred accounts offered through employer-sponsored programs represents a net plus for investors, as investors increase exposure to an attractive investment vehicle. Growth in fund supermarkets represents a net negative, as the intermediary adds another layer of fees to an already fee-burdened system.

At first glance, in spite of increases in the number of intermediary-influenced investments, front-end loads appear to burden a smaller portion of fund purchases than in the past. To the investor's detriment, reality proves the old saw that appearances can be deceiving. According to a broad-based SEC study, in 1979, approximately 70 percent of mutual-fund assets were held in funds that charged up-front loads.[14] In a superficial improvement, by 1999 around 50 percent of assets were invested in funds that charged sales loads, a 12b-1 fee of more than a quarter of 1 percent, or both.[15] The missing link concerns the impact of deferred and contingent loads.

As the brokerage community encountered investor resistance to outrageous up-front loads, Wall Street's financial engineers substituted less-visible deferred charges that frequently escape investor notice.

Deferred charges kick in when an investor redeems a fund within a pre-specified period of time, typically amounting to as long as five or six years. Deferred charges protect the broker's position, guaranteeing either an ongoing management fee stream from a long-term investor or a one-time deferred-charge exit from a short-term player. Although no reliable data exist on the incidence and impact of deferred sales charges, since fickle fund investors turn over their holdings reasonably rapidly, deferred charges may have a material influence on returns.

In choosing among various broker-sponsored share classes, investors far too often face the option of a high up-front load or a low up-front load with deferred charges. Paying now or paying later, investors pay far too much for sales and distribution of mutual funds.

Economies of Scale

The intrinsic characteristics of the mutual-fund industry suggest that economies of scale should lead to lower fees as assets under management expand. In fact, history suggests that benefits of scale accrue only to fund management companies, leaving the investors' lot unchanged. To obtain a longer-term perspective on mutual-fund fees, consider the work of an SEC study that found little change in mutual-fund fees as a percentage of assets over two recent decades. As shown in Table 8.6, no-load fund annual charges registered an almost imperceptible decline, moving from 0.75 percent of assets in 1979 to 0.72 percent in 1999. Load funds imposed an annual burden of 1.50 percent on investors in 1979 as compared to a nearly indistinguishable 1.52 percent in 1999.*[16]

Table 8.6 Fees Remain Stable as Assets Rise

Year	Mutual-Fund Assets (Billions of Dollars)	No-Load Fund Fees (Percent)	Load Fund Fees (Percent)
1979	51.7	0.75	1.50
1999	4,457	0.72	1.52

Source: SEC, Report on Mutual Fund Fees and Expenses *(Washington, DC: GPO, 2000), 40–44.*
Note: The load-fund fee figures assume ten-year amortization of up-front loads.

Even though fee levels remained essentially unchanged over the two decades, load fund investors face a less transparent environment

---

*The load fund calculations assume ten-year amortization of the up-front load. Five-year amortization produces total costs of 2.28 percent in 1979 and 1.88 percent in 1999. The decline in loads from 1979 to 1999 reflects substitution of 12b-1 fees for a portion of the up-front sales load. Note that long-term holders suffer more from the imposition of recurring 12b-1 fees, as the fee stream never stops. Moreover, consider the fact that the analysis fails to incorporate contingent deferred sales charges. Contingent deferred sales charges, which did not exist in 1979, serve to increase the aggregate costs of 1999 funds.

today. As Wall Street brokers faced pressure from clients to reduce up-front loads, clever financial engineers came up with the idea of substituting a combination of contingent deferred sales charges and 12b-1 fees for a portion of the up-front load. If an investor redeems shares within a few years, a contingent sales charge kicks in and offsets a portion of the reduced up-front load. If an investor holds shares for a number of years, the 12b-1 fees accumulate and compensate for the forgone up-front charge. By reducing the egregious average 1979 load of 8.5 percent to a still-debilitating 1999 load of 4.75 percent and making up the difference with deferred charges and 12b-1 income, fund management companies fool load-fund investors into continuing to accept an unpalatable deal.

The shocking fact that fees as a percentage of assets remained stable over two decades as assets grew more than eighty-sixfold runs counter to the idea that managing mutual funds involves economies of scale. Clearly, investment management efforts, the most important (and most expensive) input into portfolio management, do not increase along with portfolio size. A portfolio manager can invest $5 billion nearly as easily as $1 billion and $20 billion nearly as easily as $10 billion. (Size may impair performance, but it imposes little logistical challenge.) As scale increases, fees as a percentage of assets ought to decline, allowing both fund manager and fund shareholder to benefit. In fact, fund shareholders saw no reduction in fee levels. The benefits from scale inured exclusively to mutual-fund management companies.

Hard evidence regarding economies of scale comes from those mutual-fund companies that hire external money managers to perform day-to-day portfolio management activities. The contractual relationship between the advisor (the mutual-fund company with its name on the door) and the subadvisor (the portfolio manager that actually does the work) frequently specifies break points in the fee schedule. The break points reflect the economic reality of the direct relationship between decreasing marginal costs and increasing portfolio size.

Consider the case of the Principal Partners LargeCap Value Fund, one of the family of mutual funds organized by Principal Life Insurance of Des Moines, Iowa. Principal Management Corporation, the manager of the LargeCap Value Fund, actually provides no investment management services, focusing instead on "clerical, recordkeeping and bookkeeping services." Responsibility for the day-in and day-out portfolio management rests with a subsidiary of Alliance Capital Management, Bernstein Investment Research and Management.[17]

The fee arrangement between Principal and Bernstein involves only a portion of Principal's take from its investors. For the year ended December 31, 2003, Principal's no-load Class B shares bore the burden of a 2.51 percent expense ratio, as detailed in Table 8.7. Investors paid a 12b-1 fee of 0.91 percent, other expenses of 0.85 percent and a management fee of 0.75 percent. Principal's fees all but guarantee that investors will fail to generate satisfactory returns.

The management fee arrangement between Principal and Bernstein provides clues to the economies of scale available in the money management industry. At asset levels below $10 million, of the 0.75 percent management fee, 0.60 percent goes to Bernstein and 0.15 percent goes to Principal. As assets under management increase, Bernstein's fee share decreases and Principal's fee share increases. At the final break point of $200 million in assets, of the scale-invariant 0.75 percent fee, Bernstein receives 0.20 percent and Principal receives 0.55 percent. The fee structure clearly illustrates scale economies in the investment management business. Bernstein, the party responsible for the heart of the portfolio management process, earns fees that diminish (with increases in assets under management) from 0.60 percent of assets to 0.20 percent of assets. Since Bernstein's work changes not at all as asset levels increase, the reduction in marginal charges makes sense.

It makes no sense that Principal's mutual-fund clients accrue no benefits from economies of scale. Total expenses incurred by investors remain at 2.51 percent regardless of portfolio size. As Bernstein's management fee declines, Principal's management fee increases. For assets above $200 million Principal adds a management fee of 0.55 percent to other fees of 1.76 percent, bringing the egregious total to 2.31 percent for Principal and 0.20 percent for Bernstein. In this topsy-turvy world, Principal earns a marginal management fee of 0.55 percent for performing back-office functions, while Bernstein earns a marginal management fee of 0.20 percent for making security-selection decisions. As scale increases, Bernstein earns less while Principal takes more.

Table 8.7 Principal Partners Large-Cap Value Fund

Fund Investors Fail to Benefit from Economies of Scale (Percent)

Assets (Millions of Dollars)	Management Fees			Other Fees		Total Expenses
	Bernstein	Principal	Total	12b-1 Fee	Other Expenses	
10	0.600	0.150	0.750	0.910	0.850	2.510
50	0.470	0.280	0.750	0.910	0.850	2.510
100	0.385	0.365	0.750	0.910	0.850	2.510
500	0.245	0.506	0.750	0.910	0.850	2.510
1,000	0.222	0.528	0.750	0.910	0.850	2.510
5,000	0.204	0.546	0.750	0.910	0.850	2.510

Source: Principal Mutual Funds, Statement of Additional Information, 1 March 2004: 44, 48. Notes: Fees reflect charges for Class B shares, which carry no sales charge. Deferred sales charges apply for holding periods of less than seven years. Figures represent charges for the year ending December 31, 2003.

Compare the Principal Partners LargeCap Value Fund with the Vanguard U.S. Value Fund.[18] The two funds share a large-capitalization, value-oriented investment strategy. Like Principal, Vanguard employs a subadvisor to manage the portfolio. Unlike Principal, Vanguard provides its investors with a fair fee structure. Vanguard's total charges amount to 0.63 percent for the year ended September 30, 2003, compared to Principal's total charges of 2.51 percent for the year ended December 31, 2003. Table 8.8 outlines Vanguard's charges, including the split between Vanguard and its subadvisor, Grantham Mayo van Otterloo (GMO). Note that Vanguard undercut Principal in every line item.

Similar to Principal's arrangement with Bernstein, Vanguard's arrangement with GMO reflects the scale economies of the investment management business. For asset levels in excess of $1 billion, GMO's incremental compensation declines by more than 20 percent. Unlike Principal's investors, Vanguard's investors benefit from any reduction in fees paid to its subadvisor GMO. Because Vanguard "provides services to its member funds on an 'at cost' basis, with no profit component," decreases in costs flow through to investors in the form of lower fees.[19]

In spite of fund-specific evidence that managers explicitly recognize economies of scale in managing investment portfolios, industry-

Table 8.8 Vanguard U.S. Value Fund Investors Receive a Fair Deal

(Percent)

Assets (Millions of Dollars)	Management Fees			Other Fees		Total Expenses
	GMO	Vanguard	Total	12b-1 Fee	Other Expenses	
10	0.225	0.385	0.610	0.000	0.020	0.630
50	0.225	0.385	0.610	0.000	0.020	0.630
100	0.225	0.385	0.610	0.000	0.020	0.630
500	0.225	0.385	0.610	0.000	0.020	0.630
1,000	0.225	0.385	0.610	0.000	0.020	0.630
5,000	0.185	0.385	0.570	0.000	0.020	0.590

Source: The Vanguard Group, Vanguard U.S. Value Fund Prospectus, 29 January 2004: 2, 7. Notes: Figures represent charges for the year ending September 30, 2003. As of September 30, 2003, the Vanguard U.S. Value Fund had approximately $474 million in net assets. Charges for asset levels in excess of $1 billion represent estimates. Management fees represent base fees, ignoring incentive fees that increase or decrease GMO's compensation by as much as 0.125 percent.

wide data show no decrease in fee burden as assets under management grow. The overwhelmingly likely explanation for this dichotomy suggests that benefits of scale accrue largely to fund-management-company profits with nothing left over for improving shareholder returns. Vanguard and GMO represent the exception; Principal and Bernstein, the rule.

Beyond the unmet expectation that increasing scale should lead to decreasing fees, other evidence points to mutual-fund company fee gouging. In a spring 2001 article, John Freeman and Stewart Brown demonstrate that mutual funds charge excessive advisory fees, using a variety of cleverly constructed tests. For example, the authors show that not-for-profit Vanguard, operating in its investor-oriented fiduciary capacity, manages to negotiate extremely competitive fees for external management of its actively managed funds. In 1999, Vanguard's fee arrangements, which frequently involve an incentive clause, amounted to approximately 25 percent of the "prevailing fund industry rate." Freeman and Brown cite evidence that mutual funds extract fees amounting to roughly twice the level of fees for comparable services provided to public pension plans. Presenting evidence in a variety of ways, including a particularly damning chart that shows specific money managers charging mutual-fund clients substantially more than pension fund clients, the authors conclude that "the chief reason for substantial advisory fee level differences between equity pension fund portfolio managers and equity mutual-fund portfolio managers is that advisory fees in the pension field are subject to a market place where arm's-length bargaining occurs."[20] Fund shareholders do not reap the benefits of a competitive marketplace.

Fees impose a substantial burden on mutual-fund returns. Performance maximizing investors make every effort to reduce the impact of fees. First, avoid paying something for nothing by rejecting funds with front-end loads and 12b-1 fees. Second, pay attention to the impact of management fees by opting for lower-cost alternatives. Finally, consider that index funds charge the lowest fees of all.

PORTFOLIO TURNOVER

In an industry characterized by a long litany of shockingly dysfunctional behaviors, the frenetic churning of mutual-fund portfolios stands near the top of the list. In 2002, the weighted-average turnover of equity mutual-fund portfolios registered at a staggering 67 percent, representing a level consistent with an average holding period for security positions of 1.5 years.*[21] Frequent trading of mutual-fund portfolios takes a toll on investors ranging from easy-to-measure commission costs to difficult-to-assess market impact costs to impossible-to-defend tax consequences. Rapid portfolio turnover proves inconsistent both with strategy for investment success and with fidelity to fiduciary responsibility.

Investors expose assets to higher-than-necessary turnover in both poorly constructed passive index funds and poorly conceived active management strategies. In the case of index funds, the solution lies in selecting an appropriately structured low-turnover index fund. In the case of active management strategies, the investor wishing to play the

---

*Turnover measures correspond to the investment horizon employed by a manager. A portfolio with 100 percent annual turnover implies an average one-year holding period for individual positions, since such a turnover level corresponds to the sale of each existing position and the purchase of a replacement position during a particular year. Fifty percent turnover relates to an average two-year holding period, while 10 percent turnover corresponds to a ten-year horizon.

beat-the-market game increases odds of success by selecting a deliberate, low-turnover approach to picking stocks.

Stock pickers hoping to beat the market quarter in and quarter out
accept a formidable challenge. In attempting to find securities with
both material mispricings and near-term triggers to move positions to
fair value, the money manager places substantial limits on the available choices. Operating with a longer investment horizon increases
the opportunity set of choices, dramatically improving the odds of
creating a winning portfolio.

Focusing on winning every quarter constrains the investor's opportunity set to companies with triggers to resolve mispricings within
days or months. Because security prices generally reflect important
relevant information, markets provide few opportunities to purchase
undervalued securities. Further limiting security-selection choices to
those expected to become fairly valued in the near term unreasonably
restricts portfolio choice.

High turnover produces obstacles to superior performance. Buys
and sells create market impact and generate commissions, draining
funds from an investor's account. Short-term ideas force investors to
operate on an investment treadmill. As one short-term mispricing resolves itself (either to the portfolio's benefit or detriment) it must be
replaced by another idea. Be wary of the costly, exhausting, high-
turnover approach to portfolio management.

Substantial amounts of money pursue short-term success. For example, mutual-fund managers face pressure to outperform the market
every month, every quarter, every year. Short-term winners garner attention as the *Wall Street Journal* highlights the hottest funds with
headlines like "Bad Market, Good Bet: Our One-Year Winner Draws a
Flush"[22] and "Second-Quarter Champions Focus on Small-Cap Stocks
and Distressed Companies."[23] Fund management companies boast of
strong recent performance in 72-point type plastered on full-page advertisements. Winning in the short run brings fame and riches to the
successful manager.

Unfortunately, short-term success often proves transitory. The successful position, soon sold because of the mispricing's near-term resolution, must be replaced by yet another new holding. In the crowded
market for short-term winners, managers face daunting obstacles.

By lengthening time horizons, managers face a much-expanded set of investment opportunities. Not only do longer-term investment possibilities enter the picture, but the competition to identify mispricings lessens as the short-term players disappear. With fewer players in the arena, the odds for success increase.

If extending investment time horizon produces clear benefits to investors, why do so few practice the art of long-term investing? Pressures to act in the short term frequently prove overwhelming. Talking heads on financial news programs provide channel surfers with minute-by-minute updates on market action. Screaming headlines exhort readers to chase a hot manager's performance. Wall Street research asks investors to focus on next quarter's earnings forecasts. Few market participants display the fortitude to ignore the cacophony.

Wall Street plays a particularly odious role in directing investor attention to fundamentally irrelevant short-term issues. Heavy trading of portfolios creates substantial revenue streams, so financial firms seek to create reasons for investors to buy and sell. Attention paid to quarterly earnings announcements represents a favorite method for Wall Street to benefit at the expense of Main Street.

In a well-functioning market, stock prices reflect the present value of all future dividend flows generated by a corporation. It follows that the future earning power of a company matters greatly in valuation. The next several months of earnings represent only one small piece of the future that determines a stock's value. In fact, results for the next five or ten years play the overwhelmingly important role in security valuation. Why then does Wall Street focus inordinate attention on next quarter's results?

Part of the answer lies in the difficulty in making long-term forecasts. As investors evaluate opportunities and challenges farther in the future, the crystal ball proves increasingly cloudy. Human nature causes analysts to seek the relative certainty of near-term forecasts, aided by guidance (wink wink) from corporate investor relations officials.

What motivates high turnover? The most constructive interpretation of fund manager behavior suggests that in seeking superior performance, managers actively attempt to buy low and sell high. If managers trade aggressively to produce performance, they choose to compete in a difficult contest. High turnover implies short holding periods, suggesting a limited investment horizon. True short-term price anomalies provide little grist for the investment management mill. Yet the possibility exists that high turnover stems from a well-meaning, albeit likely futile, quest to beat the market quarter in and quarter out.

Even if managers engage in high levels of short-term trading activity in an attempt to produce superior results, high pre-tax returns represent the best possible outcome. The burden imposed by taxes on realized gains makes high after-tax returns quite unlikely with a high-turnover investment strategy. Fund management companies seem genuinely indifferent to the tax consequences of investment activity, as mutual-fund advertisements almost always tout the funds' pre-tax returns, relegating after-tax performance to the funds' far-less-visible formal offering documents.

High-turnover strategies almost invariably cause taxable investors to fall short of the goal of earning satisfactory after-tax returns. Given the substantial portion of mutual-fund assets in taxable accounts, hyperkinetic managers fail to address the needs of the majority of their investors. Even when ascribing the most charitable interpretation of motives, high-turnover fund management misses the mark.

The least charitable interpretation of mutual-fund manager behavior involves trading to generate favors from the brokerage industry. High-volume traders currently choose between soft dollars and directed commissions, fancy names for kickbacks denominated in kind or in cash, respectively. Soft dollars and directed commissions benefit fund managers and hurt investors. Regardless of the future of soft dollars and directed commissions per se, mutual funds will always find ways to use investor assets to grease the palms of Wall Street distributors and vice versa. No amount of regulation can counter the fact that mutual-fund assets generate Wall Street commissions and Wall Street firms distribute mutual-fund products. Mutual funds win, Wall Street wins, and investors lose.

In contrast to the frenzy of high portfolio turnover, low portfolio turnover implies longer holding periods for securities and deferred realization of gains. Under some circumstances, low-turnover strategies represent a cynical ploy to protect the fund manager's income stream by pursuing a low-risk strategy. Many managers create portfolios that largely mimic the market, with a handful of small "bets" on securities expected to outperform in the near term. Such "closet-indexed" portfolios move the investor off the high-turnover treadmill as market-mimicking positions make up the bulk of the holdings. Unfortunately, actively managed market-like portfolios lose the opportunity to produce robust returns, as low-active-management risk and high-active-management fees virtually guarantee failure to achieve the market-beating goal of active management.

In other instances, low portfolio turnover represents a thoughtful attempt to generate superior results. A longer time horizon creates greater investment opportunities, allowing exploitation of inefficiencies unavailable to short-term players. Since truly mispriced assets represent a rare, difficult-to-identify commodity, long-term investors tend to create concentrated portfolios of the few good ideas that exist. Unfortunately, the long-term investor faces a difficult task, not only missing the excitement of the quick trigger, but also running the risk of interim setbacks. Potential loss of assets and termination of employment face the fund manager who pursues a deliberate approach to investing that fails to produce strong results in the short run. Yet the long-term investor stands most likely to serve investor interests, positioned to generate potentially attractive returns with superior tax characteristics.

Trading Costs

Trading costs represent a material part of active management's performance deficit. Costs of buying and selling securities include commissions paid to brokers for completing trades and the market impact created by executing trades. Commissions appear as a separate line item charge. Market impact consists of spreads earned by market makers and price movements required to accommodate transactions.

SEC-mandated disclosure of mutual-fund trading costs serves to confuse rather than to enlighten. Two problems stem from reporting the easily observed commission costs and ignoring the unobservable market impact costs. First, the impact of commissions hits investment returns by eroding the fund net asset value, not by increasing a fund's management fee. Separate reporting of commissions encourages investors to believe that the charges represent a cost above and beyond the reported management fee. Second, commissions represent only the measurable portion of the trading costs incurred by funds. The market impact of trading activity imposes a further burden on fund returns, inflating the expense of portfolio turnover. By reporting the observable commissions and ignoring the unobservable market impact, SEC-mandated reporting misleads investors into underestimating the impact of portfolio turnover on mutual-fund returns.

Commissions constitute the visible portion of trading costs. Analysis of Lipper data indicates that in 2002, commissions cost actively managed equity mutual funds roughly 0.2 percent of assets.[24] The mutual-fund industry displayed a wide range of trading behavior, as shown in Table 8.9. The most active quartile of assets produced an astonishing weighted-average turnover level of 152 percent, consistent with an implied holding period of less than eight months. The bottom quartile of assets recorded a lethargic, investor-friendly 16 percent turnover, corresponding to an implied holding period of 6.25 years. Not surprisingly, commissions vary directly with the degree of trading activity. Top-quartile turnover consumed 0.46 percent of assets, while bottom quartile turnover absorbed a mere 0.04 percent of funds. Commissions paid by active managers represent a direct transfer from mutual-fund assets to Wall Street brokers, made with the futile hope that trading activity might produce superior results.

Table 8.9 High Portfolio Turnover Imposes Portfolio Costs

	Capitalization-Weighted Turnover (Percent)	Implied Holding Period (Years)	Capitalization-Weighted Commissions (Percent)
First	152	0.66	0.46
Second	64	1.56	0.19
Third	35	2.86	0.12
Fourth	16	6.25	0.04
Number of Funds	9,217		7,470

Source: Lipper, Inc.
Notes: Each quartile includes one-quarter of mutual-fund assets. The number of funds providing data on turnover and commissions differs because some funds fail to report information on commissions. Data reflect fiscal years ending in 2002.

Market impact of trading activity proves more difficult to quantify than the easily observed commission costs. Ted Aronson, principal of a successful money management firm, estimates that actively man-

Table 8.10 Market Impact Takes a Toll on Returns (Percent)

Estimated Capitalization	Estimated Market Commisions	Total Trading Impact	Costs
Largest 500 securities	0.12	0.51	0.63
Second 500 securities	0.25	1.25	1.50
Third 500 securities	0.38	2.34	2.72
Fourth 500 securities	0.56	3.00	3.56
Fifth 500 securities	0.76	3.57	4.33

Source: Aronson, Johnson & Ortiz, LP.
Note: Assumes actively managed portfolio with 100 percent annual turnover.

aged, top-500-securities-by-market-capitalization institutional portfolios with 100 percent annual turnover incur approximately 0.5 percent
drag on performance in noncommission trading costs.[25] Smaller-
capitalization securities cost more to trade. As shown in Table 8.10,
second, third, and fourth cohorts of 500 securities lose between 1.25
percent and 3.0 percent of assets to the Wall Street toll taker. The fifth
rank of securities costs an eye-popping 3.6 percent per year for the hypothetical 100 percent turnover portfolio. In all cases, the take from
market impact exceeds the expense of commissions by a substantial
margin. Market impact matters.

Consider the market-capitalization-weighted cost of market impact.
Aronson's estimates of costs for the largest 2500 securities cover more
than 97 percent of the total market capitalization, with approximately
80 percent of total market value residing in the 500 largest securities
alone. Weighting each quintile by its respective market capitalization
leads to the conclusion that market impact consumes nearly 0.8 percent of assets annually for a 100 percent turnover portfolio. Adding
the estimated capitalization-weighted commission charge of 0.17 percent to the market impact of 0.79 percent leads to a total trading cost
burden of 0.96 percent. The active trader battles a substantial headwind.

Aronson's trading cost estimates apply to a distressingly large part
of the mutual-fund industry. Lipper data indicate that in 2002, 38 percent of equity funds demonstrated turnover in excess of 100 percent.
For nearly two-fifths of mutual-fund capital, Aronson's once-a-year
portfolio churn represents a best-case scenario.

Because the mutual-fund industry's capitalization-weighted aver-

Table 8.11 High Portfolio Turnover Leads to Commission-Related Return Erosion

Fund Type	Capitalization-Weighted Turnover (Percent)	Implied Holding Period (Years)	Capitalization-Weighted Commission (Percent)
Actively managed equity	67	1.49	0.20
Equity index	8	12.50	0.01
Growth	97	1.03	0.28
Value	43	2.33	0.16
Large-capitalization growth	102	0.98	0.25
Large-capitalization value	39	2.56	0.13
Small-capitalization growth	106	0.94	0.41
Small-capitalization value	49	2.04	0.26

Source: Lipper, Inc.
Notes: The data reflect twelve-month periods ending on the respective fiscal-year-end dates of the reporting mutual funds. Data are for fiscal years ending in 2002.

age turnover amounts to 67 percent, to describe the market-wide costs of trading, Aronson's figures (which reflect the assumption of 100 percent turnover) require downward adjustment. Applying the observed turnover rate to the estimated market impact cost leads to the conclusion that market impact of portfolio trades reduced returns by more than 0.5 percent in 2002.

Total transactions costs for playing the active management game create a high hurdle for success. In 2002, reported commissions amounted to 0.2 percent. Estimated market impact totaled 0.5 percent. Trading costs diminished mutual-fund returns by more than 0.7 percent.* Wall Street wins. Mutual-fund investors lose.

---

*The 0.73 percent total trading cost calculation combines the Aronson market impact estimate of 0.53 percent with the Lipper commission observation of 0.20 percent. Using Aronson's assessments for both market impact and commissions leads to a total trading cost estimate of 0.64 percent.

Trading Costs for Style-Based Strategies

Portfolio turnover statistics for growth and value funds correspond to *a priori* assumptions regarding style-based management characteristics. Growth funds pursue investments in the stocks of the day. Traders demand instant gratification, seeking quick execution to guarantee exposure to the favored names. Portfolio managers churn frequently, eliminating yesterday's faded stocks in favor of today's brightly hued alternatives. As outlined in Table 8.11, the frenetic activity of growth fund managers leads to average turnover of 97 percent, substantially above the average turnover for equity funds of 67 percent.[26] Growth fund managers do not own stocks; they rent them for short periods, showing an average holding period of just over one year.

The high turnover of growth-stock portfolios leads to high commission charges. In 2002, growth funds incurred commissions of 0.28 percent of assets, well in excess of the 0.20 percent incurred by general equity funds. High portfolio turnover produces elevated levels of costly market impact, particularly in the case of growth funds. Because growth strategies demand quick execution, Wall Street supplies the desired liquidity, but at a steep price. By selecting securities in a crowded marketplace and requiring immediacy, growth managers operate in an expensive environment.

In contrast to the growth manager's quick trigger finger, the value manager takes deliberate aim. Value funds select investments in out-of-favor areas. Traders accumulate holdings carefully, slowly building positions by taking stock from investors disenchanted with the security's prospects. Portfolio managers buy and sell judiciously, choosing today's ugly duckling that shows the promise of becoming tomorrow's beautiful swan. Turnover for value funds amounts to 43 percent of assets, substantially below the 67 percent for all equity funds and the 97 percent for growth funds.

Low turnover for value-stock portfolios corresponds to low commission costs. In 2002, value-stock commissions amounted to 0.16 percent of assets, falling well below the equity fund average of 0.20 percent and the growth fund average of 0.28 percent. Market impact impedes value funds to a far lesser degree than growth funds. Value-fund traders accommodate the market, buying what others want to sell and selling what others want to buy. From a transactions-cost perspective, value trumps growth.

Size matters in transactions costs. Small-cap growth funds lead the pack in commissions with a charge of 0.41 percent of assets, well above the large-cap growth commission level of 0.25 percent of assets. The same phenomenon exists in the value arena, with small-cap value posting commissions of 0.26 percent of assets relative to the large-cap value level of 0.13 percent. Trading small-capitalization portfolios involves a significant level of costs.

Index funds provide the exception to the mutual-fund rule of ridiculously high portfolio turnover and incredibly burdensome transactions costs. In 2002, index fund portfolio turnover amounted to a modest 7.7 percent, causing commissions to consume a mere 0.007 percent of assets. Ironically, index fund portfolio managers operate in an extremely tough trading environment. The transparency of index fund trades required for full replication and the promptness of execution demanded to match index characteristics combine to increase costs of market impact for index funds. Because market makers see the index portfolio transactions coming, Wall Street stands ready to take more than a fair share of the trade. In spite of the adverse market environment for index fund trading, low turnover causes overall index fund trading costs to remain small. The transactions cost advantage enjoyed by index funds joins a long list of reasons to prefer the rock-solid certainty of market-mimicking returns over the will-o'-the-wisp possibility of market-beating results.

Trading Costs for Index Funds

Turnover matters even in the world of index funds. Well-constructed indices, such as the S&P 500 and the Wilshire 5000, exhibit low turnover, leading to attractive trading cost characteristics and reasonable tax consequences. Poorly constructed indices, such as the Russell 1000 and Russell 2000, experience high turnover, leading to unattractive cost attributes and poor tax outcomes.

The fixed-membership S&P 500 Index includes five hundred companies selected by a committee of Standard & Poor's, a unit of the McGraw-Hill Companies.[27] The Index changes composition when constituent companies exit because of a merger, acquisition, or bankruptcy. Departures from the index require index-fund managers to realize gains or losses and incur costs for security sales and purchases. The S&P committee adjusts the membership of the index on an as-needed basis, maintaining the membership count at an even five hundred.

The Wilshire 5000 provides more expansive exposure to the U.S. equity market than the S&P 500, as the broader index includes all publicly traded stocks for which prices exist. Exit from and entry to the Wilshire 5000 depend on mergers, acquisitions, bankruptcies, spin-offs, and initial public offerings. In contrast to the rigid S&P 500, the flexible Wilshire 5000 mirrors day-to-day changes in the complexion of the market, altering its membership to adjust to new market realities.

Even though the S&P 500 contains far fewer securities than the 5,242 stocks included in the misnamed Wilshire 5000, as shown in Table 8.12, the large-capitalization S&P 500 manages to incorporate 77 percent of the market's aggregate value. Not surprisingly, with such a large percentage of common membership, from a statistical perspective the S&P 500 and the Wilshire 5000 closely resemble one another.

In recent years, turnover of the S&P 500 and Wilshire 5000 registered at similar levels, with trailing three-year turnover rates averaging an annual 4.3 percent and 4.6 percent, respectively. The fixed nature of the S&P 500 membership and the all-inclusive character of the Wilshire 5000 membership create relatively stable index characteristics, leading to modest year in and year out levels of portfolio adjustments.

Factors that drive turnover for the S&P 500 and Wilshire 5000 stem from market-related events. When a company exits the S&P 500 through merger, acquisition, or bankruptcy, a committee-chosen replacement takes the departing company's place. The Wilshire 5000 passively accepts the ebb and flow of company creation and elimination, making as-frequent-as-necessary adjustments to the composition of the index. Bankrupt companies disappear, cash merger deals require redeployment of proceeds, and stock-for-stock transactions lead to elimination of the line item of the acquired company. Public offerings of securities force full-replication Wilshire 5000 index-fund managers to raise cash to acquire newly issued shares, while spinoffs

Table 8.12 Index-Fund Share Turnover Varies Dramatically

Index	Number of Securities	Capitalization			Annual Turnover (Percent)	
		Total (Billions of Dollars)	Percent of Capitalization	Weighted Average (Millions of Dollars)	Year Ending December 31, 2003	Three Years Ending December 31, 2003
Wilshire 5000	5,242	13,300	100	71,500	4.7	4.6
Russell 3000	2,948	12,800	96	56,700	9.7	12.7
Russell 1000	991	11,700	88	61,400	10.7	15.8
S&P 500	500	10,200	77	89,700	2.0	4.3
Russell 2000	1,951	1,100	8	861	18.4	23.4
Russell 2000 Growth	1,294	753	6	876	31.1	36.4
Russell 2000 Value	1,284	738	6	846	30.0	33.3

Source: Prudential Financial Research Benchmark Study: Year-End 2003.
Note: Data as of December 31, 2003.

simply require adding another line to the list of security holdings. In somewhat different fashion, both the S&P 500 and the Wilshire 5000 produce extremely low, investor-friendly levels of portfolio turnover.

In contrast, the Russell 2000 exemplifies an extremely poorly constructed index. Defined as the two thousand securities in size below the one thousand largest securities, as measured by May 31 prices, the index suffers from extraordinarily high turnover. Once a year, in July, the Russell indices undergo a reconstitution, in which the Frank Russell Company assigns the top thousand securities to the Russell 1000 and the next two thousand securities to the Russell 2000. The top three thousand securities constitute the Russell 3000.

The Russell 2000 suffers turnover on both ends of the capitalization spectrum. On the top end, Russell 2000 companies that post sufficient increases in relative market capitalization during the previous year graduate from the Russell 2000 to the Russell 1000. Former Russell 1000 companies that suffer large enough decreases in relative market capitalization devolve into Russell 2000 companies (or, in the case of a dramatic relative decline, disappear from the Russell universe altogether). On the bottom end, Russell 2000 companies that decline sufficiently in relative market capitalization suffer the ignominious fate of exclusion from the index, while rising stars ascend to take their place. Excessive turnover promises the reality of unnecessarily high transactions costs and the potential for needlessly inflated tax bills.

The transparent, rules-based process for the annual Russell reconstitution imposes another set of costs on index investors. As the May 31st date of capitalization ranking nears, sharp-witted arbitrageurs identify those securities most likely to enter or exit the smaller-capitalization end of the index. Knowing that index managers mechanistically buy new joiners and mindlessly sell old exiters, the arbitrageurs buy the stocks likely to enter and sell the stocks likely to leave. When the July reconstitution occurs, the arbitrage activity causes the index fund manager to pay more for purchases and receive less for sales. Russell 2000 index-fund investors suffer.

A more complicated version of the arbitrage occurs at the top end of the Russell 2000 capitalization range. There, reconstitution-induced price movement depends on the relative demand for Russell 1000 and Russell 2000 Index-related portfolios. If demand for Russell 2000 Index funds exceeds demand for Russell 1000 Index funds, stocks graduating from the Russell 2000 to the Russell 1000 face downward price pressure, while stocks falling from the Russell 1000 to the Russell 2000 enjoy upward price pressure. If demand for the Russell 1000 exceeds demand for the Russell 2000, the converse applies. In either case, the index investor suffers from the transfer of wealth to the arbitrage community.

The poor structure of the Russell indices leads to higher-than-optimal turnover. The Russell 1000, which suffers from porosity only on the lower end of its capitalization range, experienced an average turnover of 15.8 percent per year for the three years ending December 31, 2003. The Russell 2000, subject to entry and exit at both ends of its spectrum of holdings, posted an average turnover of 23.4 percent for the same period. Turnover for the Russell indices, with the attendant negative consequences for index fund investors, exceeds by a wide margin the turnover for the better-conceived S&P 500 and Wilshire 5000 indices.

The Russell style-based benchmarks, which measure returns of growth-oriented or value-oriented portfolios, exhibit even greater turnover. Not only do style indices suffer the same size-induced modifications as their more broadly based cousins, but the benchmarks respond to changes in security-specific valuation characteristics. Russell uses price-to-book-value ratios and earnings-growth-rate estimates to rank companies along a growth-to-value continuum. As stock prices, book values, and earnings expectations change from year to year, so do the positions of companies in Russell's growth-to-value rankings. During the annual reconstitution, Russell style indices encounter a multiplicity of turnover-inducing factors.

The Russell 2000 Growth Index posted an average annual 36.4 percent turnover for the three years ending December 31, 2003, exceeding by a modest margin the 33.3 percent level for the Russell 2000 Value Index. Turnover for both of the style indices clocked in substantially above the 23.4 percent rate posted by the plain vanilla Russell 2000. Passive investors who select Russell style-based indices lose a substantial share of the transactions-cost benefits of index-fund investing.

The shortcomings of the Russell indices as vehicles for investment translate into shortcomings as benchmarks for performance measurement. Year-to-year changes in composition cause active managers to face a changing benchmark. Quite unfairly from the manager's perspective, the index changes composition without facing the real-world performance drag of transactions costs. Counterbalancing (and likely overwhelming) the lack of a fair cost accounting, reconstitution arbitrage activity pulls in the opposite direction. By forcing prices up for index entrants prior to entry and forcing prices down for index exiters prior to exit, index-fund arbitrageurs slow the rabbit that active managers chase. The Russell indices provide poor standards for measuring active management success.

The inadequacy of the Russell methodology becomes apparent in a comparison of the returns of the Russell 2000 Index with the returns of a better-structured small-capitalization index. In addition to the well-known S&P 500 Index, the Standard & Poor's Corporation offers two lesser-known fixed-membership capitalization-based indices—the S&P MidCap 400 Index and the S&P SmallCap 600 Index. The S&P 600 SmallCap Index is a close substitute for the Russell 2000. Aside from differences in the number of securities—at year-end 2003 the S&P SmallCap contained 600 stocks and the Russell 2000 contained 1,951 stocks—the two market measures appear remarkably similar. As outlined in Table 8.13, the capitalization size of the index constituents falls in the same general range. A Prudential Financial Research monograph reports that the five-year monthly correlation between the S&P SmallCap and the Russell 2000 registers at an impressively high 96 percent.[28] The two indices measure much the same thing.

The most fundamental difference between the two market measures stems from the dissimilar approaches to index construction taken by Standard & Poor's and Russell. In contrast to the market-driven, high-turnover Russell reconstruction, Standard & Poor's employs a committee-based, moderate-turnover approach to selecting stocks. For the three years ending December 31, 2003, the S&P Small-Cap annual turnover rate of 9.4 percent amounted to less than one-half of the Russell 2000's 23.4 percent annual rate.

Table 8.13 The S&P SmallCap Index Beats the Russell 2000
(Dollar Figures in Millions)

	S&P Small Cap	Russell 2000
Number of companies	600	1,951
Average size (weighted mean)	$1,100	$861
Size range		
Lowest	$69	$14
Highest	$4,900	$2,400
Trailing 3-year turnover	9.4%	23.4%
Trailing 10-year performance	11.6%	9.5%

Source: Prudential Financial Research Benchmark Study: Year-End 2003.
Note: Data as of December 31, 2003.

In spite of strong similarities in the characteristics of the constituents of the S&P SmallCap and the Russell 2000, performance differs greatly. For the ten years ending December 31, 2003, the S&P SmallCap outdistanced the Russell 2000 by a margin of 11.6 percent to 9.5 percent. The surprisingly large performance differential results in

large part from the games played by arbitrageurs during the reconstitution process. The arbitrage profits directly diminish the performance of the Russell benchmark, offering a free ride to managers
evaluated against the Russell 2000. Unless small-cap managers beat
the Russell 2000 return by several percentage points, the managers did
not beat the market at all. Similarly, index fund investors in the Russell 2000 pay the piper. Reconstitution arbitrage represents a deadweight loss to the passive index fund investor. Of course, the
arbitrage-induced performance deficit comes before the excessive
trading costs associated with the ridiculous Russell rebalancing. Sensible investors avoid the Russell mess.

In George Orwell's *Animal Farm,* "all animals are equal, but some
animals are more equal than others." Well-constructed indices, such
as the S&P 500 and Wilshire 5000, provide reasonable measures of
market returns and sensible vehicles for passive investors. Poorly
structured indices, such as the Russell 2000, paint a warped picture of
the market, cause unnecessary trading costs, and accelerate deferrable
tax bills. Serious investors examine closely the turnover in index fund
benchmarks.

Tax Costs of Turnover

In an industry guilty of many crimes against investors, ignoring the
tax consequences of portfolio transactions ranks among the most
grievous. In 2002, roughly 67 percent of mutual-fund assets resided in
taxable accounts. In a long-term upward-trending market, high levels
of portfolio trading activity cause taxable investors to realize gains,
creating a wealth-destroying tax liability. Lack of tax sensitivity by the
mutual-fund community imposes huge costs on investors.

In a 1993 study, Robert Jeffrey and Robert Arnott investigate the
impact of turnover-generated taxes on portfolio returns, concluding
that "the typical approach of managing taxable portfolios as if they are
tax-exempt is inherently irresponsible."[29] Jeffrey and Arnott calculate
the tax burden imposed by portfolio turnover. Using a 35 percent capital gains tax rate and a 6 percent pre-tax growth rate (roughly equivalent to the long-term capital appreciation of U.S. equities), the authors
conclude that even modest levels of turnover create material costs. For
example, as shown in Table 8.14, a turnover rate of 10 percent leads to

a tax bill that reduces returns by more than a full percentage point, a steep price to pay relative to the 6 percent pre-tax rate of appreciation. At the more extreme turnover of 100 percent, after-tax returns fall more than two full percentage points below the pre-tax growth rate.

Table 8.14 Portfolio Turnover Reduces After-Tax Returns (Percent)

Turnover Rate	Pre-Tax Return	After-Tax Return
0	6.0	6.0
5	6.0	5.4
10	6.0	5.0
25	6.0	4.4
50	6.0	4.1
100	6.0	3.9

Source: Arnott and Jeffrey, Journal of Portfolio Management 19, no. 3 (1993): 19.

Recall that the average market-capitalization-weighted turnover for mutual funds registered at 67 percent in 2002.* If investors face a future with 35 percent capital gains taxes and 6 percent pre-tax growth, the tax man would reduce returns by approximately one-third, to around 4 percent per annum.

Of course, turnover does not necessarily represent a deadweight loss to investors. If turnover leads to security selection that results in superior after-tax investment performance, then investors justify the tax-related costs. In the final analysis, the tax consequences of selling winning positions increase in fairly dramatic fashion the hurdles that must be overcome by new entrants to the portfolio.

Taxable Distributions

Investors in mutual funds receive annual distributions of ordinary income and capital gains. Regardless of the investor's holding period for mutual-fund shares, an investor who holds shares on the fund's distribution date faces a tax liability for the fund's full-year distribution.

Mutual-fund tax distributions come in two versions—ordinary income and long-term capital gains. Ordinary income consists of dividends, interest, and short-term capital gains. The self-explanatory

---

*See page 242.

long-term capital gains distribution consists of tax-advantaged allocations of net realized appreciation on security holdings.

In recent years, ordinary-income receipts generated modest tax
burdens for investors in mutual funds. Low-dividend yields, low interest rates, and recurring operating expense deductions combined to
dampen distributions to mutual-fund shareholders. Consider the experience of the two largest equity mutual funds for the decade ending
December 31, 2003. As shown in Table 8.15, ordinary income distributions for Vanguard's 500 Index Fund averaged 1.9 percent of assets
over the past ten years, ranging from a high of 4.8 percent in 1994 to a
low of 1.0 percent in 2000. The actively managed Fidelity Magellan
Fund, with its lower-than-market dividend yield and higher-than-
Vanguard expense ratio, posted a ten-year average distribution of only
0.7 percent, imposing a lower ordinary income tax burden than the
market-matching Vanguard 500 Index Fund.

The story changes when considering long-term capital gains distributions. Index funds realize capital gains or losses only when
prompted by the need to match changes in index composition or to accommodate withdrawals of investor funds. When stocks exit the in-

Table 8.15 Taxable Distributions Impair Investor Returns

(Percent of Assets)

| Year | Vanguard 500 Index Fund | | Fidelity Magellan Fund | |
	Ordinary Income	Capital Gains	Ordinary Income	Capital Gains
1994	4.8	1.5	0.2	3.5
1995	2.3	1.7	0.7	5.7
1996	2.1	0.4	1.3	15.2
1997	1.7	0.8	1.3	5.4
1998	1.3	0.4	0.6	4.2
1999	1.2	0.8	0.5	8.2
2000	1.0	0.0	0.2	3.8
2001	1.1	0.0	0.4	0.8
2002	1.5	0.0	0.7	0.0
2003	1.6	0.0	0.9	0.0
Average	1.9	0.6	0.7	4.7

Sources: Fidelity; Vanguard.
Notes: Vanguard data as of December 31. Fidelity data as of March 31 of the subsequent
year. Percentages represent distributions relative to the average net assets for the relevant
year.

dex, the market-mimicking manager sells the departing security, realizing a gain or a loss on the trade. When investors redeem assets from a mutual fund, the manager sells representative slices of securities to meet withdrawal requests, triggering taxable events.

Fixed-membership index funds, such as the Vanguard 500 Index Fund, tend to demonstrate superior tax characteristics, since managers make relatively few trades to keep current with the relatively static index composition. During the ten years ending December 31, 2003, long-term gains distributions for the flagship Vanguard index fund averaged 0.6 percent of assets, ranging from 0.0 percent to 1.7 percent on an annual basis. Tax bills for long-term capital gains did little to diminish the returns of Vanguard's index-fund investors.

Actively managed mutual funds generally place a greater tax burden on their shareholder base. In an almost inevitably futile quest to beat the market, active fund managers try to buy cheap and sell dear, paying commissions, generating market impact, and creating tax obligations. The record of the Fidelity Magellan Fund, which fell short of the Vanguard 500 Index Fund returns by a margin of 1.8 percent per year for the decade ending December 31, 2003, conforms to the rational investor's active-management-deficit expectations. Fidelity's premier fund posted a deficit before considering sales charges and before considering taxable distributions. For shareholders of Fidelity's Magellan Fund, taxes make a bad story worse.

Over the ten years ending December 31, 2003, Magellan's capital gains distributions averaged a hefty 4.7 percent, ranging from a bear-market low of 0.0 percent to a bull-market high of 15.2 percent. Recall that Vanguard's passively managed fund produced gains distributions averaging only 0.6 percent per year. Fidelity's active management subtracted value twice—once through inferior security selection and once through elevated taxable distributions.

Mutual-fund managers exert little control over distributions of dividend and interest income, which represent the natural consequence of investing in income-producing securities. Realization of capital gains, however, for actively managed funds rests firmly under the control of portfolio managers. Ironically, profits produce losses, as by selling winners, mutual-fund stewards book gains and create far-too-little-considered tax liabilities. Thoughtful investors pay close attention to the tax consequences of active management.

Potential Tax Liabilities

The tax story reaches beyond ordinary income and long-term gains distributions. Investors placing new monies into equity mutual funds frequently buy into a significant potential tax liability stemming from accumulated unrealized capital gains in the fund's portfolio. Even though new purchasers of the fund's shares receive no benefit from the appreciation that led to the unrealized gains, the new investor assumes the associated tax liability. As time passes, if the fund manager realizes the embedded capital gains, the investor receives a tax bill for a proportionate share of the gain. In contrast, if the fund manager offsets the embedded gains with future losses the investor loses the opportunity to benefit from prospective application of the losses. In either case, the purchaser of an embedded-gain mutual fund loses.

The magnitude of the potential tax liability gives careful investors pause. Table 8.16 contains a ten-year time series of embedded tax liabilities for investors in Fidelity's Magellan Fund and Vanguard's 500 Index Fund. Ironically, the most tax-sensitive funds carry the burden of the largest potential tax liabilities. Because tax-conscious fund managers attempt to avoid realizing gains, the resultant low turnover strategy leads to an accumulation of unrealized gains. As a consequence, the Vanguard 500 Index Fund posts a consistently high proportion of unrealized gains, averaging 28.1 percent of assets for the decade ending December 31, 2003. Notice the correlation between fund returns and unrealized gains. Strong returns correspond to increases in unrealized gains, while weak returns correspond to decreases in unrealized gains. Bull market investors face the highest risk of buying into hidden tax liabilities.

Active management exacerbates tax problems. Taxable holders of Fidelity's Magellan Fund suffered from a triple capital appreciation deficit. First, investment gains failed to match the market, as evidenced by the 1.5 percent per year shortfall relative to the Vanguard 500 Index Fund. Second, long-term capital gains distributions burdened investors with tax liabilities on an annual average of 4.7 percent of assets relative to the index fund's 0.6 percent of assets. Third, in early 2004, Magellan Fund investors faced higher potential tax liabilities, buying into unrealized gains of 25.4 percent of assets relative to Vanguard's 17.8 percent of assets. The tax characterstics of Fidelity Magellan increased the pain felt by the fund's already humbled investors.

Table 8.16 Potential Tax Liabilities Threaten Future After-Tax Returns

Unrealized Capital Gains (Percent of Assets)

| Year | Vanguard 500 Index Fund | | Fidelity Magellan Fund | |
	Fund Performance	Imbedded Tax Liabilities	Fund Performance	Imbedded Tax Liabilities
1994	1.2	10.9	8.2	16.0
1995	37.4	26.0	28.4	26.3
1996	22.9	28.1	9.1	19.7
1997	33.2	36.5	45.4	39.6
1998	28.6	42.1	25.6	46.9
1999	21.1	43.1	21.1	48.3
2000	−9.1	34.2	−24.2	27.9
2001	−12.0	22.5	−0.8	27.1
2002	−22.2	−2.7	−24.7	3.4
2003	28.5	17.8	30.4	25.4
Average		28.1		25.9

Sources: Fidelity; Vanguard.
Notes: Vanguard data as of December 31. Fidelity data as of March 31 of the subsequent year. Percentages represent embedded liabilities relative to the average net assets for the relevant year.

The unfavorable tax consequences of embedded tax liabilities that confront new investors create a benefit for existing investors. In essence, the new investor takes on a share of the existing investor's potential tax liability. Of course, new investors soon become old investors, subject to the same beneficial dilution of prospective tax consequences created by new entrants to the fund.

When mutual funds show a net unrealized loss position, the position of old and new investors reverses. Existing investors in net-loss funds anticipate sheltering future gains. New investors buy into valuable tax shelters, diluting the existing investors' position. The odd structural framework that causes new and existing investors to receive disparate tax treatment adds another unknown to the mutual-fund investor's lot.

The bull market–induced flow of assets into mutual funds no doubt masked the issues associated with the massive accumulation of unrealized gains in equity mutual funds. Constant inflows allowed mutual-fund managers to direct portfolios of ever-increasing size, obviating the need to liquidate shares to satisfy investor redemption requests and providing cash to facilitate the trades required to reposition portfolios.

If the pattern of regular inflows of cash to mutual funds ever reverses itself, investors would face a far different set of circumstances. Managers, seeking to meet withdrawal requests or looking to add new portfolio holdings, would sell securities, resulting in realization of gains. The realized gains would cause the remaining fund shareholders to receive taxable capital gains distributions. Taxable investors need to be wary of funds with large accumulated unrealized gains.

The actions of the larger community of mutual-fund shareholders inevitably affect the tax situation of the individual shareholders, creating benefits or causing harm depending on the circumstances of particular investors. Portfolio manager activity provides another factor that influences shareholder tax bills. Taxable investors must consider carefully and skeptically the tax consequences of making commitments to mutual-fund portfolios.

High turnover makes no sense from either an investment perspective or a tax perspective. As a general rule, investment markets exhibit sufficiently efficient pricing such that exploiting those few anomalies that exist requires the patience of a long-term horizon. Taxable investors always prefer deferral of gains, postponing the inevitability of paying the tax man. Aside from the merits of the investment-related and tax-related arguments for low turnover, deliberate portfolio management strategies enjoy the added benefit of limiting the mischief of soft dollars and directed brokerage. Whether expressed in the form of higher taxes or lower returns, excessive trading harms mutual-fund investors.

Investor-Inflicted Turnover Costs

On top of the egregious damage imposed on investors by excessive buys and sells of positions in mutual-fund portfolios, investors add another layer of damage by unproductive redemptions and exchanges of the mutual funds themselves. Instead of taking an appropriate long-term perspective, in a triumph of hope over experience, mutual-fund shareholders all too frequently jump from a demonstrably disappointing fund to a potentially pleasing alternative. Possible costs associated with the fund-to-fund trading activity include adverse tax consequences and avoidable sales charges.

Fund turnover takes place at a startlingly high rate. Investment Company Institute data on mutual-fund redemptions and exchanges indicate that fund outflows average 35 percent of average assets per year, consistent with an average holding period of only 2.9 years.[30] The rate of turnover appears to be relatively consistent. As Table 8.17 indicates, during the last decade, annual churn ranged from a low of 30.3 percent, associated with an average holding period of 3.3 years, to a high of 42.2 percent, associated with an average holding period of 2.4 years.

Table 8.17 Investors Swap Mutual-Fund Holdings with Return-Damaging Frequency

	Mutual-Fund Turnover (Percent)	Holding Period (Years)	Stock Market Returns (Trailing Three Years to June 30)
1994	31.9	3.1	10.4
1995	30.3	3.3	13.7
1996	31.2	3.2	16.8
1997	32.2	3.1	26.7
1998	34.8	2.9	28.1
1999	37.7	2.7	25.8
2000	40.4	2.5	19.1
2001	37.3	2.7	3.5
2002	42.2	2.4	−8.2
2003	32.0	3.1	−10.6
Average	35.0	2.9	

Sources: Investment Company Institute; Wilshire Associates.
Notes: The analysis uses ten years of monthly data from January 1, 1994 to December 31, 2003, measuring redemptions and exchanges relative to average net assets. Monthly turnover of 2.9 percent equates to annual turnover of 35 percent.

Mutual-fund holders hurt themselves by aggressively rotating fund positions. For the roughly two-thirds of fund assets in taxable accounts, a consistent pattern of fund redemptions imposes an expected tax penalty. Note that the trailing three-year equity market returns (reported to correspond to the roughly three-year average holding period) suggest that mutual-fund investors experienced substantial aggregate gains in each of the years from 1994 to 2000. The data indicate that mutual-fund investors needlessly realized substantial amounts of taxable gains by redeeming or exchanging equity fund shares.

Two sources of uncertainty cloud the conclusion that taxable investors suffer by their own hand. First, turnover activity may be concentrated in tax-deferred accounts, leading to no current tax consequence from redemptions and exchanges. Second, turnover activity may be motivated by rational harvesting of losses instead of irrational realizing of gains. Given the general lack of sensible behavior on the part of the investing public, both explanations prove unlikely.

In particular, turnover maintains a fairly steady pace regardless of whether loss-harvesting opportunities appear abundant or scarce. The tax-sensitive investor would avoid turnover in years with historical market gains, including the period from 1994 to 2000, and would embrace turnover in years with market losses, namely 2002 and 2003. No such pattern shows itself. In fact, during the first quarter of 2000, fund turnover amounted to a sample-period high of an annualized 51.4 percent, implying an average holding period of less than two years. With trailing three-year market gains of 19.1 percent, so broadly based that losing funds scarcely existed, only the most unbelievably inept investor found losses to realize. In contrast, during the 2001 to 2003 period of modest or negative returns, when investors might realize losses, mutual-fund holdings exhibit below-average turnover. Investor behavior before and after the market peak proves damaging to the rational-investor hypothesis.

Aside from adverse tax consequences of redemption and exchange activity, investors who churn portfolios pay greater fees. The more than 60 percent of mutual funds purchased from the brokerage community face the highest risk of fee-induced diminution of assets. Up-front loads represent the most transparent threat. Investors who redeem shares to purchase a load fund dig deeper into a hole that proves tough to escape. Deferred sales charges represent a far less transparent threat. Unscrupulous brokers encourage clients to switch funds before contingent charges lapse, leading to a payday for the broker and an empty pocket for the investor.

The mutual-fund industry implicitly contributes to the problem of churn. Morningstar's backward-looking star system subtly encourages fund holders to trade up to a five-star offering. Brokerage firm incentives explicitly reward brokers who repeatedly collect up-front loads and deferred sales charges. Investors find the deck stacked against them.

Mutual-fund turnover statistics tell a depressing tale. Above and beyond the tax damage done by portfolio managers, investors inflate their tax bills by excessive trading of funds. Fund churn increases the likelihood that investors incur deferred sales charges and raises the possibility of facing a fresh round of up-front loads. Counterproductive turnover of fund shares diminishes investor wealth.

SUMMARY OF VISIBLE ACTIVE MANAGEMENT COSTS

The costs to play the active management game consume a material portion of market returns. Consider the median U.S. equity mutual-fund manager. In 2002, management fees amounted to approximately 1.5 percent of assets. Commissions consumed around 0.25 percent. Market impact extracted an estimated 0.60 percent. In aggregate, a total of 2.35 percent of assets disappeared from the median active investor's account, representing a high price to pay to play a zero-sum game.

Note that the annual 2.35 percent fails to include the debilitating costs of up-front sales loads or deferred contingent sales charges. Investors foolish enough to make a direct contribution to the financial well-being of a financial advisor face much worse odds of winning the active management game. Note also that the annual 2.35 percent ignores the adverse tax consequences from portfolio turnover or mutual-fund churn. Investors foolish enough to make unnecessary payments to Uncle Sam carry a heavy handicap into the active management race.

The 2.35 percent of equity assets consumed in 2002 by fees, commissions, and market impact corresponds closely to Rob Arnott's two-decade mutual-fund annual performance deficit of 2.1 percent. The comparison requires a number of caveats. First, the burden of fees, commissions, and market impact may have changed over the years. While SEC data suggest reasonable stability in mutual-fund management fees over the past two decades, no reliable historical data exist on the costs associated with portfolio turnover. Nonetheless, the striking similarity of the 2–percent plus active management costs and the 2–percent plus performance deficit represents something other than mere coincidence.

If the aggregate mutual-fund performance deficit corresponds to the aggregate active management cost, one reasonable explanation implies that mutual-fund portfolio managers as a group exhibit no active management skill. Skillful security-selection on the part of active equity managers produces returns above the market return. Since active management constitutes a zero-sum game, mutual-fund managers win only if another set of market participants lose. Conversely, inept security-selection on the part of active equity managers produces returns below the market return. In the zero-sum game of active management, underperforming mutual-fund managers subsidize the gains of another set of market participants. Because the costs of playing the active management game correspond closely to the long-term performance deficit, it appears that mutual-fund managers produce results neither better nor worse than the aggregate of the other equity market players. Mutual-fund managers apparently engage in enormous efforts simply to spin their wheels.

Active management of mutual-fund assets makes little sense. Before management fees, before commissions, before market impact, before sales loads, before contingent fees, and before taxes, investors in actively managed mutual funds face a coin flip. After all fees and expenses, investors experience a performance deficit. Rational mutual-fund investors avoid active management.

CHAPTER SUMMARY

Management fees and trading costs represent the most important battlegrounds in the contest between fiduciary responsibility and profit maximization. In the arena of active management, investor interests suffer a resounding defeat. Profits win and responsibility loses.

Sales loads constitute an affront to investors. A sales load leads to certain-return diminution that no-load investors avoid. In fact, evidence suggests that the size of the load corresponds to the load fund's performance deficit. In spite of widespread recognition of the superiority of no-load funds, load funds remain extremely popular, driven by the brokerage community's fee-induced marketing greed.

Even without the daunting hurdle of a sales load, investors in actively managed funds face a tough track. In 2002, the median fund lost approximately 1.5 percent to management fees, around 0.25 percent to commissions, and an estimated 0.60 percent to market impact. Total active management costs, amounting to about 2.35 percent, provide a handicap too substantial for all but the most skillful or most fortunate.

Index funds provide a clearly superior alternative. Expense ratios for Vanguard's 500 Index Fund amount to less than one-fifth of the dollar-weighted expense ratio for general equity funds. Security-trading commissions for Vanguard's fund total 0.005 percent of assets, representing one-fortieth of the dollar-weighted average. Market impact for Vanguard's 7 percent turnover registers at an estimated level of 90 percent below the market impact of the universe of actively managed equity funds. Low management fees, low commissions, and low turnover give index funds a huge edge.

Yet, not all index funds meet the litmus test of investor suitability. A number of widely known funds suffer from poor structures that lead to excessive turnover, high costs, and low tax efficiency. Careful investors choose broad-based, well-structured index funds.

Tax consequences of trading certainly matter to investors, as more than two-thirds of mutual-fund assets reside in taxable accounts. Taxes clearly matter little to portfolio managers, as excessive levels of turnover result in unpleasantly frequent and indefensibly large distributions of gains to investors. The virtually unrecognized scandal of managing taxable assets as if they were tax deferred receives far too little attention from regulatory authorities and the broader investment community.

From a tax perspective, index funds once again provide a significantly better option. Even though passive replication of a market index falls short of total tax efficiency, the low turnover of an index fund produces after-tax results superior to nearly all actively managed portfolios.

The strong correspondence between the mutual-fund industry's two-decade 2.1 percent annual performance deficit and the year-2002 2.35 percent cost of active management suggests that the mutual-fund industry exhibits no stock-picking skill. As a group, mutual-fund managers earn a gentleman's C for unimpressively average performance. By paying grade-A fees for grade-C performance, mutual-fund investors receive a failing mark.

Investor education represents the only reliable means to address the forbidding mutual-fund landscape. The profit-seeking behavior of the mutual-fund industry places the interests of investors in conflict with the goals of fund management companies. High management fees, bloated pools of assets, and tax-insensitive trading combine to inflict serious damage on investor interests.

The highly visible issues associated with conflicts between principals and agents place the mutual-fund investor at a huge disadvantage. Unfortunately, the story continues with a range of less-transparent forces that further diminish return-generation prospects for mutual-fund investors.

9

Hidden Causes of Poor Mutual-Fund Performance

The mutual-fund-investing public faces an array of performance-damaging practices that serve to all but guarantee disappointing results to investors. High fees top the list, as indefensible up-front loads, excessive management fees, counterproductive 12b-1 fees, and gratuitous incentive fees collectively puncture investor hopes for excess returns. Inappropriate levels of portfolio turnover impair pre-tax returns and gut after-tax returns. Bloated pools of assets under management provide handsome streams of fees to mutual-fund management companies and create insurmountable obstacles to returns for mutual-fund investors. Visible characteristics of mutual funds provide more than ample reason to avoid actively managed funds.

Unfortunately for investors, a range of less visible practices serve to undermine further the aspirations of shareholders. Ill-disclosed compensation arrangements between brokerage firms and fund management companies cause investors to receive tainted advice. Stale-price trading provides a mechanism to inflate fund company profits. Soft-dollar kickbacks harm investor interests and inflate the bottom line for mutual-fund companies. Hidden characteristics of mutual funds provide additional reasons to avoid actively managed funds.

A significant portion of the mutual-fund quest for profits stems from legal, albeit unseemly, behavior that proves opaque to much of the investing public. In the 1920s and 1930s, Wall Street dealers benefited from the ability to trade against small investors in the distribution of open-end funds. In the 1940s, 1950s, and 1960s, mutual-fund companies increased profits by allowing large investors to take advantage of stale prices to make excess profits. In the 1970s, 1980s, 1990s, and 2000s, fund companies increased their take through widespread use of soft dollars and continued sanctioning of mutual-fund timing strategies. Decade after decade, the mutual-fund industry abetted strategies that favored dealers and large players, simply because the favoritism, however outrageous, served to increase mutual-fund industry profits.

Even more regrettable than corporate gains from legal shenanigans, a number of mutual-fund companies profited from illegitimate activity. Throughout the history of the mutual-fund industry, investment companies flouted not only common sense, but rules, regulations, and laws in efforts to boost the bottom line at the expense of individual investor interests. Fund companies violated offering document terms, allowing late trading by favored clients and facilitating market timing by hedge fund operators. Mutual-fund complexes ignored SEC regulations, employing soft dollars to purchase prohibited goods and services. In a depressingly large number of situations, mutual-fund companies crossed the line, moving from immoral acts to illegal behavior. The mutual-fund management company quest for profits, whether licit or illicit, trampled individual investor interests year in and year out.

Examining the history of the mutual-fund industry leads to the disheartening conclusion that legislation and regulation prove no match for the greed-inspired creativity of mutual-fund companies. Sometimes, as in the case of 12b-1 fees and soft dollars, the regulators create the problem by providing explicit authorization for investor-unfriendly practices. In other cases, authorities fail to act in the face of widespread understanding and acknowledgment of fund company abuses. Finally, in those instances where regulators get it right, the fund management industry finds new mechanisms to pursue old abuses. Mutual-fund managers win. Mutual-fund investors lose.

FIDUCIARY RESPONSIBILITY VERSUS THE BOTTOM LINE

Prior to the 2003 mutual-fund market-timing and late-trading imbroglio, Paul Haaga, Jr., a senior executive of Capital Research and then-chairman of the Investment Company Institute, characterized the industry as "scandal free," bragging that "Trust is the reason why our relationship with investors has not been broken by the bear market of the past three years. Our shareholders trust that their mutual funds are being managed with their best interests in mind." For his statement, made three months before the mutual-fund scandal broke, respected *New York Times* columnist Gretchen Morgenson awarded Haaga "The Pride Goeth Before a Fall Award."[1] Scandal-plagued investors in mutual funds received no award.

Upon reflection, Haaga mused that "the phrase 'scandal-free' never should have been used. It wasn't the proper message. It's like saying, 'Hey, send us your money and we probably won't steal it.'"[2] Such expressions of high ethical standards provide cold comfort to mutual-fund investors.

Haaga's protestations of mutual-fund integrity exhibit clear ignorance of mutual-fund history. From the very first day that the very first mutual fund offered shares to investors, fund management companies took great pains to show an investor-friendly face to the world. Even as fund managers paid lip service to fiduciary responsibility, the competition between generating management company profits and serving investor interests resulted in a clear victory for the bottom line. Fund management companies produced profits from a variety of sources, ranging from legitimate, transparent fee arrangements to underhanded, opaque kickback schemes. An examination of the abuses perpetrated throughout the life of the mutual-fund industry unequivocally shows an investor-friendly mask covering the true, venal face of the industry.

PAY TO PLAY

When mutual-fund investors buy shares from brokerage firms, hidden incentives often cause brokers to push particular families of funds. In a flagrantly investor-unfriendly practice, the brokerage community charges outside families of mutual funds (Capital Group, Fidelity, Federated, Dreyfus, et al.) for the privilege of being a preferred provider, producing an underhanded means of extracting yet another level of fees from sales of mutual funds. In exchange for payments to brokerage firms, the mutual-fund families obtain special access to the broker's sales force, creating incentives for brokers to push the preferred funds and tainting the advice that clients receive from their brokers. In polite financial circles, the contemptible practice goes by the euphemism of "revenue sharing"; more direct observers use "pay to play."

The payments by the mutual-fund companies create a substantial conflict between the broker's interest and the client's interest. Instead of choosing from the broadest array of mutual-fund offerings, the broker narrows the menu to the firms that pay to play. Consider the case of Edward D. Jones, characterized by the *Wall Street Journal* as "one of the nation's largest distributors of mutual funds."[3] Jones boasts 5.3 million customers who hold more than $115 billion in mutual-fund shares. The firm's website claims that the firm focuses "on seven preferred mutual-fund families that share our same commitment to service, long-term investment objectives, and long-term performance."[4] According to the *Wall Street Journal*, the preferred fund families enjoy an extraordinary position, as during broker training "Jones gives them information almost exclusively about the seven 'preferred companies' . . . generally discourag[ing] contact between brokers and sales representatives from rival funds."[5]

The Jones website fails to disclose the payments it receives from fund companies to buy favored status for their products. Amounting to $86 million in 2002 and $90 million in 2003, the thinly veiled bribes purchase a much-coveted position in an elite group of funds that Jones brokers peddle to clients, even as the brokers discourage clients from selecting mutual funds outside of the select seven.[6] According to Boston financial consultant Cerulli Associates, 90 to 95 percent of Jones's fund sales involve the companies on the preferred list.

Capital Research & Management Company's American Funds confirms that it makes payments to Jones to "get access" to the firm's brokers. A firm spokesman justifies the payments as a means "to meet with the individual financial advisors [to] explain our products and our funds."[7] Evidently the meetings prove productive. Jones ranks as the top seller of American Funds.

In the case of the generally strong-performing American Funds, investors might wonder about the harm of payments for preferred treatment. In the case of Putnam Investments, another of the Jones "preferred mutual fund families," the harm shows in high relief. Not only did Putnam produce poor results in the aftermath of the 2000 stock market bubble, but the firm generated the disappointing returns while engaging in scandalous behavior, including market timing of the firm's funds by the firm's fund managers. What "commitment to service" did Jones have in mind when it selected Putnam as a preferred provider?

Of course, while ethical lapses and weak investment performance add injury to the insult of pay-to-play kickbacks, strong investment performance fails to justify the egregious activity. Payments from mutual-fund companies to brokerage firms certainly bias a broker's advice to clients. Pay to play blackens the reputation of every party that touches the practice.

The pay-to-play system pervades Jones's corporate culture. According to the *Wall Street Journal,* fund companies on the preferred list "pay for Caribbean cruises and African-wildlife tours for Jones brokers," during which "fund-company representatives make sales pitches to a captive audience." More than one-half of the firm's brokers sell sufficient quantities of the preferred funds to qualify for the semiannual boondoggles.[8]

In spite of Jones's neck-deep involvement in the slimy world of pay to play, the firm responded to the mutual-fund scandal by striking a sanctimonious pose. A full-page advertisement in the November 6, 2003, *New York Times* contained a reproduction of a letter to SEC chairman William Donaldson from Jones's managing partner John Bachmann and chief operating officer, Douglas Hill. Disingenuously claiming to be "completely unaware that the 'anything goes' mentality of the late 1990s had infected a few fund managers," the letter asserts that "investors are entitled to transparency. They should know what they are paying and what we, as the broker, are receiving."[9] Shame on Jones for failing to consider its own compromised position before offering ethical advice to others.

Pay to play represents a deadweight loss to investors. Clients of Edward D. Jones receive no benefit from the enormous sums that the firm receives from mutual-fund management companies. In fact, clients suffer from broker restrictions on fund choice and higher fees to offset the burden of mutual-fund company payments. Pay to play presents yet another reason for sensible investors to avoid broker-marketed mutual funds.

Payments for preferred product placement taint most of the mutual-fund industry's largest players. Of the five largest mutual-fund groups, four engage in pay to play. The coldly legalistic prospectus language, extracted from the mutual funds' Statements of Additional Information and reproduced in Table 9.1, tells a chilling tale of payola for placement. Fidelity, Capital Group, AIM/Invesco, and Pimco play the dirty game. Only Vanguard, which does not market funds "through intermediary brokers or dealers," provides a safe haven for investors.[10]

Prior to the fall of 2004, instead of making direct cash payments to compensate Wall Street brokerages for preferential marketing treatment, mutual-fund companies sometimes employed the twisted, tangled web of directed commissions. Directed commissions result from a fund manager paying a higher-than-market price to trade. The fund manager then directs the broker to use the premium to purchase any of a number of goods and services. When used to satisfy pay-to-play obligations, directed commissions caused mutual-fund shareholders to bear the costs of pay to play in the form of higher trading expenses (and lower investment returns). Directed brokerage serves no legitimate purpose. In the case of using directed brokerage to pay for product placement, the practice took on an even more offensive aura.

In a minor respite from the unrelenting scandal of pay to play, only three of the five largest fund groups employed inflated commissions to meet pay-to-play obligations. Capital Group, manager of the American Funds, joined Vanguard in eschewing the investor-unfriendly practice of using investor assets to thwart investor interests.* (Of course, Capital Group continued to use its corporate assets

---

*Even though in 2003, Capital Group halted the practice of using directed brokerage to reward brokers for sales of its funds, the March 25, 2005, *Wall Street Journal* reports that Capital Group ". . . faces an enforcement action brought by the National Association of Securities Dealers for using trading commissions paid out of fund assets to compensate brokerage firms that sold its funds." Capital Group disputes the NASD's claims. Moreover, according to the April 1, 2005 *Wall Street Journal,* the SEC is investigating whether Capital Group failed to achieve best execution in trades where directed brokerage compensated other dealers for product placement. The company is "cooperating with the SEC investigation."

Table 9.1 Four of the Five Largest Fund Groups Pay to Play

Fund Manager	Fund	Pay-to-Play Language	Directed Brokerage Language
Fidelity	Magellan	. . . FMR may pay significant amounts to intermediaries, such as banks, broker-dealers, and other service providers, that provide [distribution] services . . .	. . . FMR is authorized to allocate portfolio transactions in a manner that takes into account assistance received in the distribution of shares of the fund or other Fidelity funds . . .
Capital Group	American AMCAP	. . . American Funds Distributors, at its expense, currently provides additional compensation to investment dealers . . . American Funds Distributors may also pay expenses associated with meetings that facilitate educating financial investment advisors and shareholders about the American Funds that are conducted by dealers . . .	. . . when the investment advisor places orders for the funds' portfolio transactions, it does not give any consideration to whether a broker-dealer has sold shares of the funds managed by the investment advisor . . .
Vanguard	Index Funds	. . . the Funds do not market their shares through intermediary brokers or dealers . . .	. . . Because the Funds do not market their shares through intermediary brokers or dealers, it is not the Funds' practice to allocate brokerage or principal business on the basis of sales of their shares . . .
AIM/ Invesco	AIM Funds Group	. . . [sales] activities include . . . supplemental payments to dealers and other institutions . . .	. . . AIM may target levels of commission business with various brokers . . . based upon . . . sales of the Funds . . .
Pimco	Pacific Investment Management Series	. . . The Distributor makes distribution and servicing payments to participating brokers and servicing payments to certain banks and other financial intermediaries . . .	. . . Pimco may also consider sales of shares of the Trust as a factor in the selection of broker-dealers to execute portfolio transactions for the Trust. . .

Sources: Fidelity Magellan Fund Statement of Additional Information, *21 May 2003: 12, 31;* AMCAP Fund, Inc. Statement of Additional Information, *1 May 2004: 20, 44;* Vanguard Index Funds Statement of Additional Information, *28 April 2003: B-26;* AIM Funds Group Statement of Additional Information, *3 March 2004: 36, 63;* Pacific Investment Management Series Statement of Additional Information, *13 March 2003: 49, 62.*
Note: Funds are ranked by assets under management as of December 31, 2003.

for payola purposes.) Fidelity, AIM/Invesco, and Pimco reserved the right to use their shareholders' funds to grease the dirty palms of the brokerage industry. In fact, Fidelity articulated a particularly offensive variation on the theme, suggesting that excessive commissions paid by Magellan Fund shareholders might be employed to compensate brokers for "distribution of shares of . . . other Fidelity funds."[11] Magellan Fund shareholders bore the burden of costs that undermined their investment position as well as costs that undermined the position of other Fidelity fund shareholders. Mutual-fund companies inhabit a bizarre world.

In an apparent improvement in the mutual-fund regulatory framework, in August 2004 the SEC barred mutual funds from using directed commissions to compensate Wall Street firms for promoting the sale of fund shares. SEC chairman William Donaldson noted that using fund assets for distribution "clearly presents a conflict of interest"[12] and "presents opportunities for abuse."[13] Mutual-fund industry lobbyist Investment Company Institute (ICI) "voiced its strong support," calling the rule "a milestone that will benefit fund investors and strengthen the operating integrity of mutual funds."[14] Wall Street's mouthpiece, the Securities Industry Association (SIA), "expressed its support" for the rule, noting that it "will help to eliminate potential conflicts of interest in mutual fund sales."[15] Evidently, the mutual-fund industry, Wall Street, and the regulatory authority collaborated to promulgate a regulation to benefit the investing public.

In reality, the rule accomplishes nothing. The investor-hostile practice of pay to play continues. Mutual-fund companies simply need to find other sources of funds to satisfy their odious obligations. The investor-damaging activity of directed brokerage continues. Mutual-fund companies simply need to find other ways to deploy their ill-gotten gains. By ignoring the root causes of investor abuse, namely, pay to play and directed commissions, the SEC follows a time-worn path of taking half measures that fail to do the job.

The supporting statements of the ICI and the SIA for the pay-to-play directed-brokerage ban raise serious concerns about the past behavior of mutual-fund management companies and the brokerage industry. In press releases endorsing the ban, both trade organizations note the conflicts of interest in employing inflated commissions to purchase shelf space for funds. Yet prior to the SEC's August 2004 ruling, the mutual-fund industry and the brokerage industry embraced the idea of using client monies to pay kickbacks. Nobody forced Fidelity, Capital Group, AIM/Invesco, and Pimco to pay to play. Nobody forced Fidelity, Capital Group, AIM/Invesco, and Pimco to use directed brokerage for pay to play. The words of the ICI and the SIA clearly damn the past practices of their members. The eleventh-hour conversion of the dirty scheme's trade associations masks an ulterior agenda.

In fact, the SEC, the ICI, and the SIA engaged in an elaborately choreographed charade that produced a public impression of regulatory improvement, yet left a private reality of business as usual. By fashioning a rule that attracted industry endorsements, the SEC failed as the "investor's advocate." Even worse, by creating the illusion of advancing investor interests without the accompanying reality, the SEC provided an outright disservice to investors. The more things change, the more they stay the same.

Some idea of the scope of the pay-to-play payola program comes from the number of dealers that receive payoffs from the Capital Group's American Funds. The May 2004 list, reproduced in Table 9.2, includes the financial services elite: national brokerage giants Merrill Lynch and Smith Barney, regional brokers Legg Mason and Raymond James, insurance players AIG and MetLife, and banks UBS and Wachovia. The Capital Group disclosure contains both a straightforward list of corporate players and less-transparent identification of little-known subsidiaries. For instance, Deutsche Bank and A. G. Edwards appear under their well-recognized names, while John Hancock registers as Signator and Mass Mutual shows up as MML Investors Services. The vast majority of large commercial banks and substantial insurance companies appear nicely disguised, listed as little-known financial advisory subsidiaries. Regardless of the clarity of disclosure, pay-to-play schemes clearly infect vast numbers of the financial services community.

Even though investor interests suffer from the repugnant practice of revenue sharing, the SEC simply opts for disclosure. As if clear, comprehensive disclosure were not a sufficiently weak remedy, the "investor's advocate" requires only the most general, uninformative description of revenue sharing. In a February 2000 court case involving issues surrounding revenue sharing, a prospectus in question merely stated that "significant amounts from the advisors own resources are paid . . . to broker-dealers and other financial intermedi-

Table 9.2 The Capital Group's Pay-to-Play Partners Include a Long List of Financial Securities Giants

Banks	Insurance Companies
Citigroup (Smith Barney)	AIG (American General/Franklin Financial)
Deutsche Bank (Deutsche Bank Securities)	AIG (SunAmerica Group)
National City Bank (NatCity Investment)	Ameritas Life (The Advisors Group)
PNC Bank (JJB Hillard)	AXA Advisors
Regions Financial (Morgan Keegan & Company)	CUNA Mutual (CUNA Brokerage Services)
Royal Bank of Canada (RBC Dain Rauscher)	Guardian Life (Park Avenue Securities)
Society National Bank (McDonald Investments)	ING Group (ING Advisors Network)
UBS (UBS Financial Services)	Jackson National (National Planning Holdings)
US Bancorp Piper Jaffray	Jefferson Pilot (Jefferson Pilot Securities)
Wachovia	John Hancock (Signator Investors)
	Lincoln National (Lincoln Financial Advisors)
Financial Advisors	Mass Mutual (MML Investors Services)
Cadaret, Grant & Company	MetLife (MetLife Enterprises)
Cambridge Investment Research	Minnesota Life (Securian/C.R.I.)
Capital Analysts	Nationwide Life (1717 Capital Management Company)
Commonwealth Financial Network	Ohio National Life (O. N. Equity Sales Company)
Hefren-Tillotson, Inc.	Pacific Life (PacLife Group)
Investacorp	Penn Mutual (Hornor, Townsend & Kent)
Linsco/Private Ledger	Penn Mutual (Janney Montgomery Scott)
National Financial Partners (NFP Securities)	Principal Life (Princor/PPI)
Securities Service Network	Protective Life (ProEquities)
	The Phoenix Companies (WS Griffith Securities)
Investment Banks	Western Reserve Life (InterSecurities)
A. G. Edwards & Sons	
Baird (NMIS Group)	**Industrial Companies**
Edward Jones	GE
Ferris, Baker Watts	(GE Independent Accountant Network)
Legg Mason Wood Walker	
Merrill Lynch	
Raymond James Group	
Stifel, Nicolaus & Company	

Source: AMCAP Fund, Inc. Statement of Additional Information, *1 May 2004.*
Notes: In cases with parenthetical listings, the corporate parent appears with the Capital Group's named disclosure in parenthesis. In cases without parenthetical listings, the Capital Group's named disclosure appears.

aries for their own distribution assistance." The SEC supported the
adequacy of the disclosure, stating that the purpose was to "inform
customers of the nature and extent of a broker-dealer's conflict of interest" and that "disclosure with precision is not necessary," even
though "a broker-dealer customer that has invested in a fund typically
cannot tell from the prospectus whether his broker-dealer received
any such payments."[16] Mealy-mouthed, SEC-approved disclosure fails
to serve investor needs.

In a variation on a theme, consultants and plan administrators responsible for defined-contribution retirement plans frequently engage
in the practice of revenue sharing. According to consulting firm Wat-
son Wyatt Worldwide, roughly 90 percent of 401(k) plans ask asset
management firms for fees in exchange for placing the firms' offerings
on the plan's menus.

The pay-to-play nature of retirement-plan revenue sharing harms
investors by obfuscating important financial arrangements and limiting the menu of investor choices. While revenue sharing may cover legitimate expenses incurred by plan administrators, sponsors, and
brokers, only by happenstance will the revenues shared match the expenses incurred. In fact, the market-sensitive revenue sharing almost
certainly will not match the relatively fixed administrative costs. The
more than likely outcome results in a revenue stream that becomes a
profit center.

Because revenue sharing biases decision makers toward high-cost
funds and away from low-cost funds, the practice compromises the
list of alternatives offered to participants. Not surprisingly, Vanguard,
the king of low-cost investment products, suffers. As reported in the
New York Times, Vanguard's director of institutional sales said he had
been contacted by brokers who wanted to include Vanguard funds in a
menu of 401(k) alternatives. "When brokers realize they won't be compensated for placing our funds in a plan, they typically hang up on
us."[17] Revenue sharing represents yet another tool for the financial es-
tablishment to extract funds from the individual investor in exchange
for limiting the investor's alternatives.

At some point in the future, the SEC no doubt will investigate the
murky arrangements between investment brokers and mutual-fund
companies, concluding that revenue sharing practices impair investor
interests. If regulators attempt to control payments for preferential

treatment, the fund companies will find other means to gain special status and the brokers will find other mechanisms to profit at the expense of clients. In any event, investors purchasing mutual funds from the pay-to-play crowd face another layer of fees and experience further discontinuity of interests in the investment process.

PRICING GAMES

In March 1924, MFS Investment Management launched the first mutual fund in the United States. Managed by Merrill Griswold, chairman of the fund management company, the Massachusetts Investors Trust provided individual investors of modest means the opportunity to invest in a diversified, professionally managed portfolio. The offering of MFS's mutual fund marked the beginning of an era filled with promise and fraught with peril.

In the late 1920s and throughout the 1930s investors in open-end mutual funds faced a staggering array of costs associated with buying, holding, and selling funds. For example, today open-end fund investors buy and sell shares at net asset value, executing both purchase and sale transactions at the fair market value of the portfolio. Prior to passage of The Investment Company Act of 1940, distributors posted bid prices (at which they were willing to buy) and ask prices (at which they were willing to sell). The substantial difference between bid and ask prices constituted a source of nearly riskless profits to the distributor and a source of unavoidable costs to the investor.

Two-Price System

In addition to transparent up-front loads, ongoing management fees, and transaction-related bid-ask spreads, investors in the 1920s and 1930s confronted a murky "two-price" system that worked to the great advantage of dealers and to the enormous disadvantage of investors. The two-price system, "employed by almost all open-end investment companies," provided special trading opportunities to fund managers, dealers, and distributors, allowing generation of riskless and nearly riskless profits.[18] The less well-informed and less well-advantaged individual investor suffered.

In the 1920s and 1930s, for some portion of the trading day, distributors typically offered mutual-fund shares at the previous day's "liquidating value" (the then-current term of art for net asset value) plus a sales load. The 1940 Securities and Exchange Commission *Report on Investment Trusts and Investment Companies* cites the example of Dividend Shares, Inc., offered through Calvin Bullock. The distributor marketed Dividend Shares at the previous day's liquidating value "plus a premium of 8-2/3 percent of the offering price" (i.e., slightly less than 9-1/2 percent of liquidating value).[19] The offering price remained good until noon on the offering day. In essence, for the entire morning of any given trading day distributors offered Dividend Shares at the previous day's price.

Even though the stale-pricing mechanism theoretically allowed individual investors to make profits by trading at yesterday's prices, the nearly 9.5 percent load effectively eliminated the possibility of individual investors exploiting profitable arbitrage opportunities. Dealers, however, faced no such hurdle, as load-free trading allowed them to take advantage of the system.

Beyond the ability to trade load free, dealers enjoyed a hidden, critical advantage in stale-price trading. According to the prospectus for Dividend Shares, Calvin Bullock informed dealers of the next day's offering price "approximately one-and-one-half hours after the close of the New York Stock Exchange . . . while the previous offering price is still in effect." The prospectus then helpfully outlined the arbitrage opportunity available to dealers:

> . . . dealers and investors may defer purchasing shares at the then effective price when it appears that the price to become effective the next business day will be lower, and conversely, may purchase shares at the then effective price when it is known that the price to become effective the next day will be higher.[20]

The prospectus failed to disclose that dealers could profit from short positions in fund shares when the price had already fallen. With foreknowledge of the next day's price, dealers that enjoyed no-load access to mutual funds generated arbitrage profits at the expense of information-poor and load-hindered individual investors.

In a quaint, albeit unseemly, foreshadowing of 2003's foreign-fund stale-pricing scandal, 1930s-vintage mutual-fund dealers exploited a transcontinental time differential. The SEC Report noted the "added advantage afforded dealers . . . located in the eastern part of the country to sell such shares in the western part of the country," concluding that "the dealer has all the afternoon to trade against the two prices."

For many years, mutual-fund investors remained blissfully ignorant of their informational disadvantage, as "prior to December 31, 1935, the prospectuses of open-end investment companies contained no description of the two-price system and its operation." The SEC asserted that the investor "was not aware that the dealer and distributor could make indirect profits, . . . that the two-price system resulted in a diminution of the asset value of outstanding shares, . . . [and] that information vital to a prospective purchaser was previously omitted."[21]

After year-end 1935, the SEC required disclosure of the two-price system, allowing sophisticated mutual-fund investors to understand the opportunity available to dealers to take advantage of the system. Disclosure failed to inhibit dealer activity. Finally, the Investment Company Act of 1940 eliminated the two-price system, forcing fund management companies to find new methods of fleecing mutual-fund investors.

SEC-Mandated Stale Prices

To the continued disadvantage of individual investors and in spite of the Investment Company Act of 1940's proscriptions, large investors found ways to exploit the newly revised mutual-fund pricing mechanisms. Even though the SEC *Report on Investment Trusts and Investment Companies* recognized that "if both the sales and redemption prices were based on the closing asset value on the day of the receipt of the order, many abusive trading practices of distributors and dealers which existed or were possible under the two-price system could be eliminated," the 1940 Act failed to institute such a system. Instead, to the detriment of the individual investor, the 1940 Act accommodated "the objection commonly invoked against this method of pricing," namely that "dealers could not sell shares during the day without a firm or specific price."[22]

In requiring that buyers and sellers trade at the most current available price, the Investment Company Act of 1940 eliminated the unjustifiable spread between bid and ask prices in secondary trading of open-end mutual-fund shares and banished the two-price system that gave dealers riskless profits at the individual investors' expense. However, gallingly bowing to investment industry pressure, the 1940 Act failed to mandate pricing at the current trading day's close ("forward pricing"), opting to retain pricing at the previous trading day's close ("backward pricing"). Arguing that backward pricing served investor interests by allowing mutual-fund purchasers to trade at a known price, the fund industry failed to point out that stale pricing allowed larger, more aggressive traders to profit at the expense of the ordinary mutual-fund investor.

Throughout the 1940s, the 1950s, and most of the 1960s, stale mutual-fund pricing allowed exploitative traders to pick the pockets of long-term investors. While the 1940 Act eliminated the two-price system's opportunity for dealers simultaneously to buy at today's price and to sell at tomorrow's, market players retained the ability to trade at yesterday's price today. When markets rallied, traders profited by buying mutual-fund shares at yesterday's discounted price. Orders placed immediately before the closing bell on a big up day provided the investor with a significant profit-making opportunity. By hedging the cheaply acquired mutual-fund position with higher-priced market-traded assets, the mutual-fund timer accepted little risk in taking unfair advantage of other mutual-fund shareholders.

Aside from the short-term players' direct dilution of long-term holders' returns, the activity of market timers interfered with mutual-fund portfolio management activities. An SEC report observed that "speculative trading practices can seriously interfere with the management of registered investment companies" by forcing mutual-fund managers to maintain cash balances to accommodate speculative flows or, worse yet, to incur transactions costs when buying and selling securities to facilitate speculative activity.[23]

Mutual-fund holders lost twice. Market timers directly diminished returns through extraction of ill-gotten profits from trading activity. Fund managers indirectly diminished returns by holding cash that flowed from market-timer purchases and by generating cash that facilitated market-timer sales. Stale pricing worked against the interest of long-term investors.

In spite of the costs suffered by investors, fund management companies, driven by profits, welcomed the high-volume traders. More assets under management translated into more fees for management. Profits trumped returns.

In 1968, after more than four decades of easy profit opportunities for mutual-fund timers, the SEC promulgated Rule 22c-1 requiring that mutual funds employ "forward looking" pricing. The regulators finally addressed head on the pricing problem that had bedeviled investors from the first days of the mutual-fund industry's existence. Even though as early as the 1930s the SEC clearly understood the nature of the problem and the character of the solution, the regulatory authority waited decades to implement the fix. Unfortunately, as with the Investment Company Act of 1940, the regulators addressed only the most visible aspects of abuse, without eliminating the roots of the problem.

Despite the fact that SEC Rule 22c-1 dealt with the most glaring features of stale pricing, the issue persisted for funds that contained infrequently traded assets and overseas-listed security positions. In the case of less liquid securities, such as corporate bonds and small-capitalization equities, when markets make broad moves, less than current prices for the less liquid securities at the 4:00 P.M. mutual-fund pricing deadline create a disconnect between the fair-value reality and stale-price closing mark. In the case of foreign markets, when U.S. markets make broad moves after the overseas markets close, the anticipated correlation between the active U.S. markets and the dormant foreign markets creates a disconnect between the fair-value expectation and the stale-price closing mark. In the 1970s, 1980s, 1990s, and into the 2000s, big-time traders exploited stale prices, buying funds when breaking market events suggested that true values exceeded posted closing prices. Large mutual-fund companies aided and abetted the practice, attracted by the fees produced by the market timers' activity.

By the turn of the twenty-first century, stale-price trading activity had reached a fever pitch. Scandalous schemes fell into two broad categories: late trading and market timing. Late trading involved clearly illegal transactions that violated the SEC's 1968 Rule 22c-1, which required execution of trades prior to the daily 4:00 P.M. determination of fund net asset value. Bank of America mutual-fund executives led the parade of shame by allowing hedge fund operator Canary Capital Partners to engage in late trading of a number of the bank's mutual funds. Market-timing activity per se violated no laws, but proved problematic on two counts. First, the actions of market timers clearly impaired returns of long-term shareholders, raising questions regarding the faithful exercise of fiduciary responsibility on the part of the mutual fund's management and board of directors. Second, many mutual-fund offering documents contain fund policies that discourage or prohibit market timing. Allowing or facilitating actions contrary to representations contained in a fund's prospectus constitutes a criminal offense.

Many mutual-fund companies entered into explicit arrangements with market timers, allowing the disruptive activity in exchange for promises from market timers to place "sticky" money in designated funds. In fact, David Brown of the New York State Attorney General's Office said "it just blew me away" that a fund company employed form-letter contracts to arrange market-timing deals, even though the fund's offering documents explicated rules to combat market timing.[24] The pacts between mutual-fund companies and market timers often established ratios between longer-term investments and market-timing capacity to ensure, in the words of one Janus Capital Group employee, "that there are enough static assets so that we are making a decent profit for all of the trouble we are put through."[25]

"In general, the CEOs of these companies knew [about the alleged wrongdoing]. The senior people knew," according to David Brown.[26] The SEC charged Ray Cunningham, president of Invesco Funds Group, with playing a direct role in the firm's relationship with market timer Canary Capital Management. According to the regulaters, John Carifa, president of Alliance Capital Management, and Bruce Calvert, chairman of Alliance's board, participated in discussions of market timing trades and "sticky asset" arrangements with market timer Daniel Calugar.[27] In fact, Carifa once calculated that Alliance "stood to earn $1.8 million from Calugar's business."[28] The explicit involvement of fund companies' most senior executives in market-timing deals speaks volumes regarding the dominance of profit-seeking behavior over fiduciary responsibility.

Consider the misdeeds of Daniel Calugar's Security Brokerage. In market-timing activity, mutual-fund companies received financial rewards that paled in comparison to the aggressive trader's ill-gotten gains. Calugar's profits stemmed from more than two years of market-timing activities at Alliance Capital Management and Massachusetts Financial Services (MFS), involving transactions totaling between $400 million and $500 million. According to the SEC, in "prospectuses provided to investors, Alliance discouraged market timing and MFS prohibited it." Part of Calugar's market-timing arrangement involved an explicit agreement with Alliance for up to $220 million of market-timing capacity in what the SEC termed "an extensive *quid pro quo* scheme." Calugar profited to the tune of $175 million.[29] Alliance and MFS made single-digit millions.[30] Not only did these senior executives at Alliance and MFS sell investors down the river, the firm's excuses sold the investors cheap.

Some mutual-fund executives took the abomination of market timing to deeper depths by taking direct personal action to damage investor portfolios. Twenty Putnam Investments employees, including six portfolio managers, market timed the firm's funds.[31] When employees pursue market-timing strategies in funds for which they exercise control, the crime of insider trading enters the picture. According to the SEC, Putnam's portfolio managers enjoyed access to current portfolio holdings, valuations, and transactions not readily available to all fund shareholders. Trading on material, nonpublic information adds criminal insult to the financial injury of market timing. On October 28, 2003, Putnam earned the dubious distinction of becoming the first mutual-fund company formally charged with securities fraud in the unfolding scandal.[32]

Mutual-fund chief executives foolishly miscalculated the risks and rewards of exploiting market-timing strategies for personal gain. Richard Strong, founder, chairman, and chief executive of the eponymous Strong Financial Corporation, resigned his posts after facing accusations that he made profits of more than $600,000 by market-timing his firm's funds.[33] Reality proved worse than expected. Strong ultimately admitted to executing market-timing trades in forty accounts distributed across ten funds, including the Strong Discovery Fund, which he managed. In 2001 alone, Strong made 510 trades in his firm's mutual funds. Overall, he reaped as much as $1.8 million in tainted profits, more than three times the initial estimate.[34]

Legal authorities and regulators skewered Richard Strong. New York State attorney general Eliot Spitzer charged Strong with "massive violation of fiduciary duty," while SEC director Stephen Cutler characterized Strong's actions as "betrayal of the highest order." The government's settlement included the unusual requirement that Strong apologize, enduring what Spitzer called "public humiliation." Even in the face of overwhelming evidence, the case's resolution contained the regulators' usual concession that Strong neither admitted nor denied the allegations.[35]

Of the $175 million in fines and penalties levied in the Strong Financial scandal, fully $60 million came from Strong personally. In spite of the hefty fine, the greatest damage to Strong's finances came from a loss in value for his roughly 90 percent stake in Strong Financial. Suffering from a tangible loss in assets and an intangible loss in reputation, Strong's violation of fiduciary standards reduced the value of the firm by hundreds of millions of dollars, giving new meaning to the phrase "penny wise, pound foolish." By hitting up fund investors for relatively modest market-timing gains, Strong dramatically impaired the value of his firm's franchise.

Perhaps even the apparently massive penalty paid by Strong proved insufficient to match his transgressions. Warren Buffett wrote in his 2003 Annual Letter to Shareholders: "At least one miscreant management company has put itself up for sale, undoubtedly hoping to receive a huge sum for 'delivering' the mutual funds it has managed to the highest bidder among other managers. This is a travesty. Why in the world don't the directors of those funds simply select whomever they think is best among the bidding organizations and sign up with that party directly? The winner would consequently be spared a huge 'payoff' to the former manager who, having flouted the principles of stewardship, deserves not a dime."[36] Of course, had the directors of Strong Financial Corporation followed Buffett's advice, Richard Strong's hundreds of millions of dollars of personal profits from the sale of his firm would have disappeared. Maybe Richard Strong got off easy.

Gary Pilgrim and Harold Baxter, co-founders of Pilgrim Baxter & Associates, each found a method to gain at the expense of their investors. According to the SEC, Harold Baxter passed inside information to the president of Wall Street Discount, a brokerage firm that in turn provided the data to market-timing clients. Gary Pilgrim one-upped Baxter by secretly establishing and financing Appalachian

Trails, a hedge fund that began market timing Pilgrim Baxter mutual funds in 2000. Gary Pilgrim actually managed one of the mutual funds subjected to timing activity, the PBHG Growth Fund. Even as Growth Fund investors suffered losses of 20 percent in 2000 and 35 percent in 2001, Pilgrim profited personally. From March 2000 to December 2001, Appalachian Trails produced $13 million of market-timing profits, of which $3.9 million accrued to Gary Pilgrim. Showing no honor among thieves, Pilgrim allegedly told Baxter nothing of the Appalachian Trails chicanery.[37]

The market timing by Appalachian Trails represented only a portion of Pilgrim Baxter's alleged misdeeds. The SEC and the New York State attorney general charged that between 1998 and 2001 the firm allowed twenty-eight investors to deploy in excess of $600 million in market-timing monies. In announcing the June 2004 settlement with regulators, the SEC's Ari Gabinet asserted, "Pilgrim Baxter & Associates was an early and popular haven for some of the best-known and most-active market timers. The firm allowed these timers to make millions at the expense of ordinary shareholders, who saw the value of their investments in the PBHG Funds plummet." Pilgrim Baxter & Associates agreed to a $100 million settlement, while neither admitting nor denying guilt.[38]

Stale pricing of mutual-fund shares provided market-timing opportunities for bad actors during the entire history of the mutual-fund industry. In the 1920s and 1930s, stale pricing underlay the investor-unfriendly two-price system. In the 1940s, 1950s, and 1960s, stale pricing resulted from backward-looking pricing mechanisms that allowed investors to trade today at yesterday's prices. In the 1970s, 1980s, 1990s, and 2000s, stale pricing occurred in mutual funds holding securities that traded in different time zones or that traded infrequently, or both. Over the decades, opportunities for profit from stale pricing persisted, even as the targets for ill-gotten gains changed.

The most straightforward solution to the problem of market timing involves fair pricing of mutual-fund shares. Instead of using prices known to differ from true values, fund managers possess the legal ability to adjust asset values to reflect reality. In fact, in April 2001 the SEC mandated that mutual funds employ fair value pricing after any "significant event" likely to result in stale prices. As the *Wall Street Journal* opined, "the industry's response was less than wholehearted."[39] In spite of the uncharacteristically constructive efforts of the SEC, mutual-fund companies and market timers continued to exploit stale pricing of funds.

As long as mutual funds have existed, individual investors have suffered from the greedy, exploitative tactics of market timers, aided and abetted by the fund management industry. First, dealers fleeced investors using the two-price system. The Congress intervened. Then, big-time traders took advantage of backward pricing. The SEC intervened. Next, fund companies and favored clients employed stale prices to generate undeserved gains. As legislators and regulators reacted belatedly and ineffectively, the game changed, but the outcome remained the same. Big shots won. The little guy lost.

SOFT DOLLARS

The history of the less visible, more complex use of soft dollars provides an even more worrisome tale. Prior to May 1, 1975, Wall Street operated under a system of fixed commissions that set rates far above the costs of executing trades. Competitive forces caused brokerage firms to circumvent the fixed prices, by providing rebates to favored customers in the form of soft dollars. Soft dollars, in essence a kickback from broker to trader, funded both investment-related and non-investment-related goods and services.

Think about the implications of soft-dollar trades for mutual-fund investors. Paying inflated commissions to trade securities, for whatever purpose, reduces investment returns. The reduction in return comes straight from the investor's pocket. The benefit, in the form of goods and services, accrues directly to the fund manager. Because the costs of soft-dollar goods and services would otherwise have come from the fund's management fee, soft dollars represent nothing other than a well-disguised increase in management fees. Wall Street benefits at Main Street's expense.

The T. Rowe Price Statement of Additional Information, dated March 1, 2004, describes the soft-dollar game. "Under certain conditions, higher brokerage commissions may be paid in return for brokerage and research services. . . . Such services may include computers and related hardware. T. Rowe Price also allocates brokerage for research services which are available for cash. . . . The expenses of T. Rowe Price could be materially increased if it attempted to generate additional information through its own staff. To the extent that research services of value are provided by brokers or dealers, T. Rowe Price is relieved of expenses it might otherwise bear."[40] Investors learn of T. Rowe Price's soft-dollar policies through carefully constructed, legally correct prose buried on pages 90 and 91 of an infrequently read disclosure document. Even though T. Rowe Price presumably satisfies legal requirements with its disclosure, the firm compromises investor interests with its soft-dollar usage.

After May Day 1975, when the SEC abolished the system of fixed commissions, the raison d'être for soft dollars vanished. Price competition would set brokerage commission rates. Under-the-table kickbacks could disappear. Unfortunately for mutual-fund investors, fund managers realized that soft dollars transferred research-related expenses from their accounts (management fee income) to the investors' accounts (trading expenses). As a result, the mutual-fund industry enthusiastically defended the use of soft dollars.

Instead of banning soft dollars, in 1975 Congress created a safe harbor for their use by amending the Securities Exchange Act of 1934. Perverting a piece of legislation originally designed to protect the investing public, Congress bowed to pressure from Wall Street and explicitly allowed fund managers to deplete investor assets, legitimizing soft dollars by instructing the SEC to define appropriate use. Why do market participants tolerate the inefficiencies involved in paying inflated prices for trading services and then receiving rebates in the form of goods and services? The answer lies in the lack of transparency of the process, which allows mutual-fund companies to profit in an opaque manner. Were the soft-dollar charges as transparent as the highly visible management fees, the investment management industry would have no use for the concept.

When the Securities and Exchange Commission examined the soft-dollar issue in the mid 1980s, the commission not only missed an opportunity to eliminate the scourge of soft dollars, it actually expanded the epidemic. In wonderfully bureaucratic prose, the SEC noted that its 1986 report addressed "industry difficulty in applying the restrictive standards" on soft-dollar usage by "adopting a broader definition of 'brokerage and research services.'"[41] In other words, if the restrictions bind, loosen the constraints. The SEC's 1986 soft-dollar regulations favored the advisor over the advisee.

The SEC again failed to protect mutual-fund investors in 1998. The regulator's *Inspection Report* dryly notes "the widespread use of soft dollars," as "almost all advisers obtain products and services other than pure execution from broker-dealers and use client commissions to pay for those products and services." The report recognizes that "advisers using soft dollars face a conflict of interest between their need to obtain research and their clients' interest in paying the lowest commission rate available and obtaining the best possible execution." The report details instance after instance of questionable use and outright abuse of soft dollars, including payment "for office rent and equipment, cellular phone services and personal expenses, employee salaries, marketing expenses, legal fees, hotels and car rental costs."[42] Wall Street's definition of research bears little correspondence to *Merriam-Webster's.*

In spite of the fundamental, irreconcilable conflict of interest in soft-dollar use and in spite of the long litany of soft-dollar abuse, the 1998 *Inspection Report* concludes only that the SEC "should reiterate and provide additional guidance, consider adopting recordkeeping requirements, require more meaningful disclosure and encourage firms to adopt internal controls." Instead of protecting investor interests, the SEC defended Wall Street's gravy train.

While the substance of the 1998 *Inspection Report* argued for abolition, the SEC wimped out. Faced with a concerted lobbying effort by interested parties—including mutual-fund companies, Wall Street firms, and the normally sensible trade association of research analysts—and a lack of pressure from individual investors, the self-styled "investor's advocate" opted to tighten regulation instead of taking the high road of total eradication. A cynic might argue that the SEC acts on highly visible, easy-to-understand investor protection issues, while allowing low-profile, difficult-to-comprehend abuses to remain.

One of the most obscene soft-dollar abuses involved payments that rewarded brokerage firms for distributing mutual-fund shares. Deep in the 1998 *Inspection Report,* the SEC observed that "as mutual fund distribution becomes increasingly competitive, [soft dollar variant] step-out trades have become an additional incentive used by fund advisers to reward broker-dealers for selling fund shares."[43] By using soft dollars to pay for fund distribution, the offending mutual-fund company hurt its investors thrice: once by using soft dollars to inflate fees; once by impairing performance through bloating assets under management; and once by biasing broker advice to investors.

The mutual-fund scandal of 2003 led to calls for soft-dollar reform. In December 2003 the Investment Company Institute, in a foxy attempt to guard the chickens, called for restrictions on the use of soft dollars, including a ban on the use of brokerage commissions to reward dealers for distributing funds. Finally, in 2004, six full years after identifying the practice, the SEC banned the use of inflated commissions to satisfy revenue-sharing obligations.

Even though the SEC banned the use of directed commissions to fulfill pay-to-play charges, the SEC failed to disrupt the use of directed commissions for other purposes and failed to halt the practice of revenue sharing using other funds. Since directed commissions and pay to play continue to plague mutual-fund holders, the regulator's response accomplished nothing.

Industry apologists achieved victory, but failed to cover themselves in glory. The ICI's mealy-mouthed letter to the SEC cited "appearance of a conflict of interest" and "potential for actual conflicts" when the reality of conflict stared straight into the eyes of observers.[44] In a *Wall Street Journal* commentary, Paul Haaga, Jr., senior executive of Capital Research and Management Company* and chairman of the Investment Committee Institute, trumpeted his organization's call for major reforms.[45] In decrying the "longstanding practice" of using soft dollars and the pay-to-play character of directed brokerage, Haaga showed himself to be a twenty-first-century version of Captain Louis Renault, who in the film "Casablanca" is "shocked, shocked to find that gambling is going on in here," even as the croupier hands Renault his winnings. True to the script, the SEC's August 2004 reforms did nothing to stop the casino's activities.

---

*Capital Research and Management Company manages the American Funds. Both organizations are part of the Capital Group Companies. See Table 9.2 for a list of the Capital Group's pay-to-play partners.

CHAPTER SUMMARY

The history of the mutual-fund industry contains example after exam-ple of conflicts resolved in favor of mutual-fund company profits at the expense of individual investor returns. When fiduciary responsi-bility to investors competes with corporate desire for profits, profits win.

Wedges between investor and corporate interests come in trans-parent and less transparent forms. Intolerable up-front loads, deferred sales charges, excessive annual management fees, inappropriate mar-keting fees, and excessive portfolio turnover stare investors in the face. Beneath the surface, investors suffer from murky brokerage sales practices, exploitative stale-price trading activity, and contemptible soft-dollar usage.

For the vast majority of mutual-fund investors, the future appears dim. Regulators identify abuses, deal superficially with the most high-profile issues, and move on to other matters. Meanwhile, the mutual-fund industry finds new ways to place profits above investor interests. Even if the SEC eliminates pay-to-play revenue sharing, enforces fair-value pricing mechanisms and bans soft dollars, the mutual-fund in-dustry, as it has from its beginning in 1924, will employ its endless creativity to find visible and less visible means to take advantage of in-dividual investors.

10
Winning the Active-Management Game

As a general rule, the corporate bottom line wins the battle between a mutual fund's obligation to serve as a fiduciary to investors and that fund's quest to produce profits for its owners. Every improvement in net income for a mutual-fund organization diminishes the account of the mutual-fund investor. In the case of excessive management fees, indefensible distribution fees, high portfolio turnover, and bloated portfolio size, the causes of disappointing results stare investors directly in the face. In the case of product placement payments to brokerage firms, stale-price trading activity, and soft-dollar kickbacks, the damage to investor portfolios remains largely hidden from view. Mutual-fund shareholders operate in a challenging environment.

Some rays of hope shine through the dark clouds that obscure investor aspirations. The vast population of the fund industry contains a small subset of truly talented investors who deserve the trust associated with managing the assets of others. Within that small subset, a handful of mutual-fund managers transcend the pure pursuit of profit, placing the selfless service of investor needs above the selfish search for personal gain. In particular, in those rare instances in which mutual-fund managers own a significant stake in the funds that they manage, the manager transmutes from agent to principal, dramatically increasing the odds of serving investor interests. Mutual-fund owners increase the chances of success by choosing to invest with management companies that place investor interests front and center.

For those intrepid investors hoping to identify a market-beating mutual fund, assessing the manager's personal characteristics tops the list of investment criteria. Active-management success depends on investing with individuals who exhibit the integrity to pursue the often uncomfortable policies that lead to generation of superior investment returns. For example, structuring concentrated portfolios and owning out-of-favor securities generally prove both helpful to investment success and hurtful to personal reputation. Mutual-fund investors face the difficult problem of evaluating the character of fund managers, a task that involves tough, qualitative judgments regarding information that proves nearly impossible for the individual investor to gather.

Not only do mutual-fund investors seeking to beat the market need to identify courageous portfolio managers willing to go against the grain of conventional wisdom, but prospective investors must find fund management organizations that place investor interests ahead of corporate profits. In the financial markets that sit at the heart of the capitalist system, investors face enormous challenges in setting out to identify investment management companies that value fiduciary responsibility more than the bottom line. Limiting assets under management represents one of the most powerful statements regarding the primacy of investor interests over personal profit. Unfortunately, in the asset-gathering mutual-fund world, managers who exhibit prudence in capping or closing funds constitute the rare exception to the profit-maximizing rule.

Investors might sensibly consider placing money with fund management companies that demonstrate high degrees of co-investment by the firm's portfolio managers. A manager's desire to take on the role of principal, expressed by significant side-by-side participation in fund performance, signals an unusual coincidence between the interests of investors and the incentives of fund managers. Unfortunately, the value of the co-investment signal may be short-lived. If co-investment becomes a litmus test for investors, fund managers will no doubt increase personal fund holdings, trumpeting the salutary effects of sharing investment outcomes. Side-by-side investment may morph from an indication of aligned interests to a precondition for gathering assets.

A final caution awaits the hopeful market beater. Even after identifying an extraordinarily talented team willing to act in investor interest by pursuing superior returns, a harsh reality intrudes. The standard prospectus boilerplate language defines the problem: "Past performance provides no guarantee of future results." People change. Markets change. Circumstances change. Even with all of the stars properly aligned, the most carefully considered decisions sometimes prove wrong.

Of the 9,000 or 10,000 mutual funds in the United States, a mere several dozen merit the consideration of thoughtful investors. Managed by a handful of maverick mutual-fund families, the meritorious funds stand nearly alone in a vast wasteland. The overwhelming number of mutual funds fail to meet the fundamental criterion of fidelity to fiduciary principles, as pursuit of profit overwhelms responsibility to investors. In the final analysis, almost all mutual funds represent a good idea gone bad.

DESIRABLE MANAGER CHARACTERISTICS

Many try, but few succeed in winning the active-management game. Security selectors who attempt to beat the market operate in a brutally competitive atmosphere. Surrounded by highly qualified, highly motivated, highly compensated competitors, the active investment manager struggles to identify and exploit an edge that leads to superior results. Personal characteristics play an enormous role in determining which of the market players prevail.

Great investment managers pursue the business with a passion bordering on obsession. The most successful practitioners sometimes marvel (in private moments) that they are paid to practice such an intellectually stimulating profession. Because the range of influences on markets defies description, nearly every aspect of life provides grist for the investment manager's mill. Active managers who allow the markets to permeate their lives enjoy a greater likelihood of investment (if not personal) success.

Stamina helps investors keep pace with a nearly inexhaustible supply of inputs. Superior information represents a necessary, albeit not sufficient, condition for superior results. Successful investors work harder to gather greater quantities of data than their unsuccessful counterparts. Information comes from more and better company visits for the green-eyeshade investor or from more and better numbers for the quant jock.

Raw intelligence assists in the process of drawing conclusions from the accumulated data, placing the information in a context that leads to successful investment strategies. Yet, because market prices already incorporate conventional wisdom, simply grasping the current environment proves far from sufficient to generate superior returns. To thrive in the money management world, investors require out-of-the-mainstream, nonconsensus insights.

Courage of conviction stands investment managers in good stead, as willingness to initiate and hold out-of-favor positions plays a critical role in taking advantage of true investment wisdom. All too often, the difficulty of maintaining a contrarian stand turns what should have been profits into losses.

Market-beating managers express their insights in concentrated portfolios that differ dramatically from the character of the broad market. Steadfastness proves absolutely necessary when managing a concentrated portfolio. In the inevitable periods that produce disappointing results, managers either hold on, allowing for the possibility of ultimate vindication, or bail out, locking in the certainty of disappointment. Certitude in defense of well-considered investment positions plays an instrumental role in investment success.

Superior investors love to win. But those looking to entrust their funds to others take care to understand the game being played. By identifying investors who define winning as beating the market, fund shareholders vastly increase the chances for success. On the other hand, by placing money with fund managers who define winning as maximizing fee income, fund shareholders face almost certain disappointment.

Unfortunately, precious few mutual-fund investors enjoy the opportunity to gather direct evidence regarding a portfolio manager's integrity, passion, stamina, intelligence, courage, and competitiveness. The information most necessary for selecting superior investment managers remains inaccessible to nearly every market participant.

External advisors provide little help. Investment advisory services, such as Morningstar, produce rankings based predominantly on quantitative characteristics, doing an elegant job of explaining what was and a lousy job of identifying what will be. Even if fund advisory services focused on the character traits of fund managers, investors might legitimately wonder if the consultants got the "soft stuff" right.

The inability of nearly all mutual-fund investors to assess the qualitative aspects of fund management teams produces a nearly insurmountable impediment to investment success.

Contractual agreements provide little help in forcing fund managers to look after investor interests. Regardless of the strictures contained in rules and regulations, market participants respond to economic incentives. Compensation schemes and management contracts fail to ensure principal-oriented behavior on the part of investment managers, forcing investors to consider the personal goals of fund managers when evaluating investment opportunities. Aside from the rare circumstances where mutual-fund managers own substantial positions in the funds they manage, economic incentives clearly point to pursuit of asset-gathering, benchmark-hugging strategies. The shareholder's best bet for alignment of interests lies in identifying managers with an unusual set of personal aspirations.

Mutual-fund shareholders stand to benefit by engaging managers that consider satisfying client interests to be a high priority even if economic incentives dictate otherwise. The challenges of producing risk-adjusted excess returns pale in comparison to the ease of gathering assets to inflate the management company's bottom line. Increasing assets under management and charging high fees lead to higher corporate income at the expense of lower investment results. By placing risk-adjusted investment returns ahead of personal gain, managers behave ethically.

The most fundamental strategy to mitigate conflicts between principals and agents lies in engaging agents who behave as principals. Agents may be motivated to serve the interests of clients by a combination of economic incentives and ethical imperatives. While the ethical character of investment managers generally fails to produce hard evidence for prospective fund holders to evaluate, some economic incentives provide clues for fund investors to uncover and assess.

Perhaps the most powerful incentive for an agent to serve client interests stems from substantial side-by-side investment. Co-investment (say, by a mutual-fund manager in the fund itself) places the agent (fund manager) on the same page as the principal (fund shareholder), as the fact of co-investment actually transforms the agent into principal. Many high-quality investment managers pride themselves on "eating their own cooking."

Co-investment works best when fund managers own substantial portions of a portfolio's assets. Consider the case where managers own 99 percent of assets and outside investors own one percent. Clearly, in this instance, generating investment returns trumps assessing management fees, since fees coming from outside investor assets do not even register on the radar screen.

In situations where fund managers own a less than overwhelming position in the fund's portfolio, the rational economic calculus considers the level of assets under management in light of the trade-off between higher income from asset gathering and lower investment returns from asset-induced performance drag. In the extraordinarily unusual case of high levels of co-investment, side-by-side positions create a powerful coincidence of interests between managers and investors. Unfortunately, the vast majority of mutual funds contain precious little side-by-side capital. More often than not, from a manager's perspective, the seeming certainty of higher fee income wins out over the nebulous possibility of lower investment returns.

While superior outcomes generally result from intertwining the interests of principals and agents through high levels of co-investment, in some instances problems result. In cases where fund shareholders and managers operate with different time horizons, dissimilar tax circumstances, or divergent risk preferences, manager investment decisions may not serve shareholder interests. When making investment decisions, mutual-fund shareholders ought to evaluate the investment horizon, tax position, and risk characteristics of mutual-fund managers, attempting to identify a good fit. Regardless of potential deviations in investment goals between fund managers and fund shareholders, more co-investment generally beats less.

Even if the economics of co-investment fail to drive investment managers to focus on generating investment returns, side-by-side investments play an important behavioral role in aligning interests. Significant co-investment by fund managers signals an orientation toward sharing investment outcomes with fund shareholders. The psychological bond created by co-investment may be as important as the economic impact.

Because high levels of co-investment represent as much an attitudinal connection as a financial alignment between fund managers and shareholders, cautious investors take care not to overestimate the benefits of side-by-side commitment. If high levels of fund investment by portfolio managers become a widely employed litmus test for fund investment, mutual-fund executives will rush to invest in their funds, trumpeting the alignment of interests produced by their personal commitments. At that point, co-investment becomes a cost of doing business, a means to the end of collecting management fees. In a world unaware of the benefits of co-investment, high levels of side-by-side financial commitment send a powerful signal. Once the requirement of co-investment becomes widely employed, the signal loses its power. In any case, side-by-side investment currently represents a rare piece of objective evidence, available to the average fund investor, that illuminates the behavioral biases of portfolio managers.

SOUTHEASTERN ASSET MANAGEMENT

Southeastern Asset Management, sponsor of the Longleaf Partners mutual-fund family, exhibits a number of extremely attractive, investor-friendly behavioral attributes. Begun unpropitiously in April 1987, a scant six months prior to the worst one-day collapse in stock market history, the Longleaf Partners Fund, managed by the team of O. Mason Hawkins and G. Staley Cates, provides a prime example of high-quality individuals devoting their careers to practicing what they preach.

Principal Orientation

In the 1998 Longleaf Partners Fund's letter to shareholders, Hawkins and Cates articulate ten guiding principles for managing investor assets. The first principle, "We will treat your investment in Longleaf as if it were our own," expresses a commitment to bridge the gap between the principal-shareholder and the agent-manager. The promise of Longleaf Partners to step into the shoes of the mutual fund's shareholders causes the firm's portfolio managers to stand apart from the vast bulk of participants in the mutual-fund business. For example, as part of the firm's commitment to serve investor interests, Southeastern cites its decision not to accept soft-dollar kickbacks, a policy that the firm called "unique in the industry."[1] By articulating the guiding tenet that Southeastern's managers strive to act in investor interests, the firm sets the stage for the investor-friendly principles that follow from that premise.

Clear Strategy

A firmly held, carefully expressed investment strategy contributes mightily to the likelihood of portfolio management success. The investment managers at Longleaf Partners promise to "choose our common stock investments based on their discount from our appraisal of their corporate intrinsic value, their financial strength, their management, their competitive position, and our assessment of their future earnings potential."[2] Using a price-to-fair-value ratio to measure the relative attractiveness of individual securities, Longleaf portfolio managers view the market from the perspective of a strict valuation discipline. When well-managed companies trade at a significant discount to fair value, the managers express considerable enthusiasm for their portfolio's prospects, encouraging shareholders to commit funds. When discounts to fair value shrink, managers exhibit caution, allowing cash positions to rise.

During the early years of the firm's history, the thoughtful approach to markets worked well. Longleaf Partners Fund produced returns of 15.3 percent per annum from the April 1987 inception to December 1995. The result outperformed the S&P 500's 12.6 percent per annum return for the same period, satisfying aspirations of investment manager and mutual-fund investor alike.

During the next five years, the story changes as the Southeastern portfolio managers labored under the pressures produced by an underperforming contrarian portfolio. In the twelve months ending with March 2000, the Longleaf Partners Fund lagged the S&P 500 by nearly 27 percentage points. In the previous five years, the annual deficit relative to the S&P 500 amounted to more than 12 percentage points per year. Few investment managers proved more out of synch with the new era than Southeastern.

Shareholder questions from the firm's 1999 annual report illustrate the pressures confronting Southeastern: "Is something wrong at Longleaf?" "Why are you avoiding the Internet growth stories?" "Will Longleaf ever invest in technology?" "Why aren't you worried about your results?" Even though Hawkins and Cates publicly answer the last question by stating that "the best collection of assets we have ever held, at the best prices . . . should produce significant future returns," the senior executives of Longleaf Partners must have lost at least some sleep over the firm's performance.[3] The April-1987-inception-to-date results, market-beating as recently as 1998's year end, showed more than 1 percent per annum deficit relative to the S&P 500 at December 31, 1999. The excesses of the Internet mania turned a once distinguished record of superior performance into an apparently run-of-the-mill showing.

Yet the March 31, 2000, Longleaf Partners Funds letter to shareholders contained several well-timed warnings: "Historically, those who owned stocks which sold at large premiums to their underlying business values paid dearly; or worse, speculators who chased the good performance and bought those companies as they approached their peaks had dismal results; [and] following a comfortable consensus of owning everyone's favorite stocks almost always hurts financial health in the long run."[4] While other fund managers abandoned investment discipline to participate in the new era of Internet investing, Southeastern stayed faithful to its portfolio of old economy companies that traded for a fraction of the firm's estimate of fair value.

In spite of the firm's rational approach to markets, Longleaf Partners Fund's inability to match the manic bull market returns caused substantial numbers of investors to defect. During the period from June 30, 1999, to June 30, 2000, more than $1 billion of investor capital fled Longleaf Partners Fund, representing nearly 30 percent of the fund's December 31, 1999, net assets. Helping to define the market top, Longleaf's departing investors left at the moment of maximum opportunity.

In a shameful sideshow to the main event, Morningstar contributed to the exodus of investors from the Longleaf Funds. In spite of Longleaf Partners' dramatic underperformance, even as late as June 1999, the fund enjoyed a five-star rating from Morningstar. Yet, with perfectly pathetic poor timing, in December 1999, Morningstar reduced the Longleaf Partners Fund rating to a middling three stars. Just when investors needed the forward-looking vision to maintain their position, Morningstar's rearview-mirror image showed them the door.

Hawkins and Cates understood the importance of a stable ownership base, noting in the June 1998 semi-annual report that "the right kind of shareholder is more important to a mutual fund than to an individual corporation. We think Longleaf has a nonpareil group of owners. Our partners are unequalled in their average size, ownership duration and moral support. Longleaf shareholders understand buying undervalued and qualifying businesses one at a time, minimizing taxes, and having a long-term time horizon."[5] Without steadfast investor support, the best investment firm in the world cannot produce superior results for clients.

Even though Longleaf Partners Fund could no longer serve the investors who had departed, the firm rewarded investors who remained for maintaining a tough, out-of-the-mainstream position. From the end of the first quarter of 2000 through the end of 2003, the fund returned nearly 16 percent per annum, outpacing the S&P 500's negative return by 22 percentage points annually. More important to the firm's long-term fund shareholders, April-1987-inception-to-date performance exhibited a dramatic edge relative to the S&P 500, trouncing the passive benchmark by an annual margin of 3.9 percent. Hewing to a sensible, carefully considered set of investment principles, the wild ride notwithstanding, ultimately produced substantial rewards for both Southeastern and its loyal band of shareholders.

Long-Term Focus

Longleaf portfolio managers "invest for the long term, while always striving to maximize after-tax returns and to minimize business, financial, purchasing power, regulatory and market risks."[6] Instead of playing a high-turnover, frenetic, beat-the-market game that inevitably imposes a sizable tax burden on investors, the investors at Southeastern serve shareholder interests by managing assets in a tax-sensitive fashion. Of course, more than altruism motivates Longleaf's managers. Hawkins and Cates note that "as owners we tally our compounding success after paying taxes."[7]

Portfolio Concentration

By recognizing the "importance of concentration," portfolio managers "choose only [the] best ideas," ensuring that positions "have a meaningful impact on the overall portfolio."[8] Rejecting the cynical, closet-indexing ploy practiced by a host of asset-gathering mutual-fund complexes, the investors at Longleaf Partners take the business risk of constructing a less diversified collection of positions. Concentrated portfolios require evaluation over a longer time horizon than do more broadly diversified offerings. Because performance depends on a relatively small number of positions, the deviation between portfolio results and market returns looms large. In the inevitable periods of underperformance, the managers of concentrated portfolios face the business risk of losing clients. Yet with superior active managers, concentration pays huge dividends, as astute stock selection influences results in a dramatic fashion, thereby increasing the likelihood of satisfying investor hopes for superior performance.

Stable Client Base

Southeastern recognizes the importance of attracting sophisticated mutual-fund investors who share the firm's investment philosophy. If performance-chasing hot-money players abandon the Longleaf funds at an inopportune time, the fund withdrawals damage the exiting shareholders, the remaining shareholders, and the Longleaf Partners portfolio managers. Little wonder that Hawkins and Cates emphasize the importance of populating the firm's investor base with individuals who operate with a sufficiently long time horizon.

Fully five years prior to the mutual-fund scandal of 2003, Longleaf Partners articulated the principle of "discouraging short-term speculators and market timers." In an action that brings shame to nearly all of the rest of the mutual-fund industry, Hawkins and Cates wrote that "during 1998, we worked closely with third party clearing firms and our transfer agent to identify market timers. We have compiled a large list of investors and advisors who are prohibited from trading in any of our funds. Inflows from a person whose time horizon is less than three years do not benefit our investment partners."[9] While managements of other mutual funds cut deals for sticky assets with market-timing vermin, Longleaf Partners strove to eradicate the pests.

Fair Fee Arrangements

Sensitive to the fee-induced erosion of investor assets, Longleaf Partners states that the firm "will not impose loads, holding periods, exit

fees, or 12b-1 charges." The 1998 annual report notes simply that "low
expense ratios and no surcharges are in shareholders' best interests,"
concluding that "we will not raise or add fees." Amazingly, Southeastern on occasion takes the extraordinary step of reducing fees. In September 2003, Longleaf Partners International Fund announced a
decrease in annual management fees from 1.5 percent to 1.25 percent
for assets in excess of $2.5 billion, suggesting that "it is fair that we
share some of the economies of scale with our partners."[10] The reduction in fees clearly represented no ploy to attract assets on a discounted basis. Less than six months later, Southeastern closed the
International Fund to new investors.

Substantial Co-Investment

The firm's principals demonstrate conviction by investing substantial
personal assets side by side with investors, stating "we will remain
significant investors with you in Longleaf."[11] Co-investment at Southeastern registers at a truly impressive level. At the end of 2003,
Longleaf trustees, employees, and their relatives owned more than
$400 million of Longleaf fund shares, representing around 4 percent
of the firm's $10 billion of mutual-fund assets. Southeastern Asset
Management's prohibition on employee investments outside of the
firm's mutual funds reinforces the principal orientation of the firm.

   In spite of the generally beneficial implications of side-by-side financial co-investment, high levels of co-investment may represent
more of an attitudinal orientation than a financial incentive. Consider
the case of the Longleaf Partners Fund. Suppose the asset-induced
performance drag of adding $2 billion of assets diminishes expected
investment returns by 1 percent. If Southeastern's managers were to
focus exclusively on the bottom line, they would weigh the certainty
of an increase of $15 million in management fee income (gross of ex-
penses) against the possibility of a decrease of $4 million in returns on
their $400 million personal stake. The cynical calculus leads to unbri-
dled asset growth. Of course, the expected return lost by adding $2 bil-
lion of assets may be more or less than 1 percent, perhaps leading to a
different conclusion on the part of fund managers. Yet the fact remains
that in spite of the extraordinary co-investment level of Southeastern
Asset Management's principals, a lack of clarity exists regarding the fi-

nancial consequences of asset gathering. The trade-off between higher fee income and lower investment return produces mixed signals.

Regardless of the net result of the profit-maximization equation, Southeastern's magnificent co-investment speaks to the firm's unrivaled principal orientation. The side-by-side commitment of the firm's principals adds another line item to the list that demonstrates Southeastern's fidelity to investor interests, even at the expense of management firm profits.

Limits on Assets under Management

In another remarkably investor-friendly policy, when Southeastern Asset Management sees diminished investment opportunities, the firm closes its funds to new investors. In September 1995, citing "our inability to find qualifying businesses managed by capable individuals at prices sufficiently discounted from our corporate appraisals," Mason Hawkins and Staley Cates closed their flagship Longleaf Partners Fund.[12] As evidence of the lack of investment opportunity, cash constituted 26 percent of the fund's $1.76 billion in assets.

At the same time that Longleaf Partners closed with less than $1.8 billion in assets, the world's largest actively managed mutual fund— Fidelity Magellan—boasted more than $50 billion in assets. Even though Magellan took the size prize by a country mile, Longleaf led in the performance derby by a respectable margin. Trailing five-year performance for Memphis-based Longleaf clocked in at 24.3 percent, comfortably ahead of the Boston-based Magellan result of 22.9 percent. Both actively managed funds handily beat the five-year S&P 500 Index return of 17.2 percent.

Had Southeastern decided to market the 1995 Longleaf Partners Fund track record, the firm certainly could have amassed tens of billions of dollars in assets under management. With each $10 billion contributing a potential $75 million in revenues to the management company, Hawkins and Cates required only fifth-grade math to understand the impact on their personal finances. Yet, instead of pursuing personal profit, the fund managers closed their flagship fund, reducing the impact of size-induced performance drag.

In the letter announcing the decision to close the fund, Hawkins and Cates noted that investors had benefited from economies of scale during the fund's early stages of asset growth. At inception in 1987, Longleaf Partners Fund's expense ratio stood at 1.50 percent. By 1995, the ratio declined to 1.06 percent as a result of efficiencies associated with managing a larger pool of assets. As part of the rationale for closing the fund, the portfolio managers observed that further increases in assets under management will produce "proportionately much less benefit" to the expense ratio, once again illustrating Southeastern's focus on shareholder interests.

The reduction in the expense ratio represents another example of Southeastern placing investor interests above the profit motive. Instead of allowing economies of scale to drive down expenses, the managers could have quietly maintained the percentage-of-assets charges, generated greater cash flow, and garnered greater profits for themselves. Instead, Southeastern transferred a significant portion of the benefits of increasing scale to its customers.

Slightly more than three years after closing Longleaf Partners Fund, in October 1998, Southeastern reopened its flagship offering, noting that "investment opportunities exceeded the Fund's cash levels and new inflows could enhance all shareholders' returns." The door to new investors closed again, less than a year later in June 1999, as Southeastern found "few new investments that meet the Partners Fund's criteria."[13] Continuing its opportunity-sensitive policies, the Longleaf Partners Fund reopened in February 2000 to facilitate acquisition of "compelling" investments.[14] The news release announcing the opening of the fund observed that the expense ratio had declined to 0.92 percent of assets, providing further evidence of Southeastern's investor orientation.

The years during which Southeastern closed the Longleaf Partners Fund certainly constrained the size of assets under management. At the end of 2003, the fund held twenty stocks in a portfolio valued at $7.7 billion. In contrast, the Magellan Fund owned 224 stocks in a portfolio of $68 billion. Yet Southeastern's investment disciplines, including portfolio concentration and asset growth restraint, paid off in a big way. At year-end 2003, trailing five-year returns for Longleaf Partners Fund amounted to 10.8 percent per annum. Over the same period, the bloated Magellan Fund, with its too broadly diversified portfolio, returned −1.1 percent per year, failing to match the −0.6 per-

cent annual return of the S&P 500 Index. Even though Magellan generated revenues for Fidelity far in excess of Longleaf Partners' financial
contribution to Southeastern, Hawkins and Cates provided the greater
service to investors.

In contrast to the closing and opening of Longleaf Partners Fund in
response to the ebb and flow of investment opportunities, the Longleaf Partners Small-Cap Fund closed to new investors on August 1,
1997 without reopening. Mason Hawkins cited "concerns that the
core investment positions were being diluted and that the prospect for
finding good business stakes had diminished."[15] Not even a year after
closing the small-stock fund, Hawkins and Cates noted that "even if
volatility or a market correction present buying opportunities," the
fund "will likely remain closed to new investors to maintain our
small-cap focus and our concentration strategy."[16] In a story of man
bites dog, investor interests trump profits!

The practice of closing funds to limit assets under management to
a level appropriate to the investment opportunity certainly benefits
existing shareholders. Unfortunately, as a behavioral signal for
prospective investors, willingness to close a fund constitutes a mixed
blessing. In a frustrating financial-world catch-22, closing a fund eliminates access for new investors. Interested parties face the unhappy
prospect of waiting, perhaps futilely, for a closed fund to reopen. In
the case of Longleaf Partners Fund, Southeastern's large-capitalization
offering, the wait might be marked in years. In the case of the Longleaf
Partners Small-Cap Fund, new investors may never gain the opportunity to invest. As of the end of 2004, the fund had been closed for
more than seven years.

If the principals of the Longleaf Partners Funds believe they no
longer possess ability to add value in a particular investment vehicle,
the firm exits the business. In September 2001, stating that "the structure of the real estate sector mutual fund no longer provides shareholders the best vehicle for compounding capital in real estate
investments," Southeastern Asset Management closed the Longleaf
Partners Realty Fund, a mutual fund with more than $500 million un-
der management.[17] Foregoing a management fee of 1 percent, the firm's
managers walked way from $5 million in annual fees, expressing ex-
traordinary fidelity to investor interests.

Shareholder Communication

Southeastern's final principles deal with commitments to shareholder services and candid communication. While asset-gathering mutual-fund companies invariably provide easy access to offering documents that prospective shareholders must receive prior to making an investment, auxiliary documents that contain sensitive information—such as the statement of additional information (SAI)—frequently prove more difficult to obtain. In a February 2004 survey of websites of the top ten mutual-fund groups as measured by size, only one fund family provided online access to its SAI. Capital Research's American Funds' Investment Company of America garnered points for investor-friendly disclosure of the fund's SAI. Included in the poor disclosure hall of shame were AIM's Premier Equity Fund, Fidelity's Magellan Fund, Franklin's Income Fund, the Janus Fund, Oppenheimer's Main Street Fund, Pimco's Total Return Fund, Putnam's Fund for Growth & Income, T. Rowe Price's Equity-Income Fund, and Vanguard's 500 Index Fund. Consistent with Southeastern's broad-based investor-friendly policies, the firm's commitment to candid communication with shareholders allowed access to the SAI with a simple click of the mouse.

Summary

Southeastern's status as a privately held independent company proves critical to the firm's ability to serve investor interests. Were Southeastern Asset Management a subsidiary of a financial services conglomerate, the firm would face pressures to contribute to the parent company's bottom line. Were Southeastern a publicly traded company, the firm would owe a duty to provide profits to shareholders. Only when operating in the context of a privately held, portfolio-manager-controlled, independent company do for-profit managers possess the ability to consider serving the interests of investors without worrying about the implications for the income statement. Independent companies enjoy the opportunity to choose the degree to which the firm serves investor interests or generates corporate profits.

Southeastern Asset Management exemplifies every fundamentally important, investor-friendly characteristic conducive to active-management success. Portfolio managers exhibit the courage to hold concentrated positions, to commit substantial funds side by side with their shareholders, to limit assets under management, to show sensitivity to tax consequences, to set fees at reasonable levels, and to shut down funds in the face of diminished investment opportunity. Even though all of the signs point in the right direction, investors still face a host of uncertainties regarding Southeastern's future active-management success.

Because people constitute the core of the investment management process, the important questions regarding future performance revolve around personnel. How long will Mason Hawkins and Staley Cates continue to devote the time and effort necessary to produce superior investment results? Have the senior members of the management team attracted, trained, and retained high-quality younger people? Are the economic rewards distributed fairly among the professionals responsible for producing investment returns? Answering critical questions regarding the experience, motivation, and engagement of the investment team requires a depth of organizational understanding unavailable to the average mutual-fund investor.

Beyond considering the level of continuing commitment of the current management team, the same soft, qualitative characteristics that investors evaluate prior to an initial investment require continual monitoring. Prudent investors consider the character not only of the old guard, but also of the up-and-comers. The task of assessing active investment managers never ends.

Finally, successful mutual-fund investors must understand themselves well enough to know if they possess the conviction to maintain fundamentally sound, yet out-of-favor positions. The nearly 30 percent of assets that investors withdrew from Longleaf Partners at the peak of the market in late 1999 and early 2000 doubtlessly damaged portfolios thrice. First, exiting investors paid taxes on realized gains. Second, the leave-takers suffered poor relative past performance and missed good relative prospective results. Third, departing players likely chased a recent hot-performing fund just as results were about to turn cold. Identifying a winning fund proves helpful only if the investor demonstrates sufficient staying power to reach the finish line.

Signing up for any active-management program, even one as attractively positioned as Southeastern Asset Management's, requires a giant leap of faith. Investors must believe that the future will resemble the past, all the while recognizing the inevitability of change. Fund managers grow old, disengage, exhibit greed, fail to plan for succession. Even if the names on the door remain the same, the firm that produced the top-of-the-charts ten-year record differs from the firm that will produce the next decade's results. People change.

CHAPTER SUMMARY

Even though overwhelming amounts of mutual-fund assets rest under the control of managers who trample investor interests in the race to generate profits, a small proportion of mutual-fund assets enjoy the care and attention of organizations that place investor interests above all else. Sensible investors who wish to hold shares of actively managed mutual funds seek firms with investor-friendly behavioral and structural characteristics. Side-by-side investment and assets-under-management limitations represent behaviors consistent with an investment-return-generating principal orientation. While investors stand to benefit from fund managers who behave well, the prospective mutual-fund purchaser faces a considerable challenge to identify and monitor those mutual-fund managers who exhibit good behavior. Investors must prepare to wade through swarms of B-grade movie bad guys to identify the minuscule number of blockbuster heroes. Perhaps even more daunting, once the investor identifies the rare superstar, questions remain as to whether the next production proves a hit or a flop. Identifying active-management winners represents an incredibly tough assignment.

11
The Exchange-Traded
Fund Alternative

Exchange-traded funds—open-end mutual funds with shares that trade like company stock—provide an intriguing alternative to traditional mutual-fund index investing. Well-structured ETFs share with standard index funds the benefits of diversification, low cost, and tax efficiency. In fact, under certain circumstances, ETFs may exhibit greater tax efficiency than otherwise comparable regular index funds.

The ETF industry began on January 22, 1993, when State Street Bank and Trust, the American Stock Exchange, and Standard & Poor's partnered to issue 150,000 shares of Standard & Poor's Depositary Receipts (SPDRs), a security designed to track the movement of the S&P 500 Index. Known colloquially as Spiders, the shares proved quite popular. From a $6.6 million capitalization on the initial offering in 1993, by December 31, 2003, State Street's Spider had grown to $43.8 billion, representing roughly one-quarter of the $157.4 billion market value of all ETFs.

ETFs exist for every core asset class, including domestic equities, foreign developed equities, emerging market equities, domestic bonds, inflation-indexed bonds, and real estate. Based on breadth of market coverage, investors enjoy the opportunity to create a well-diversified portfolio employing only ETFs.

High-quality investment management firms dominate today's ETF market, with Barclays Global Investors and State Street Global Advisors accounting for nearly three-quarters of the aggregate ETF market value on December 31, 2003. With roots in the practice of passive management of large portfolios for institutional investors, Barclays and State Street bring to the ETF market a long history of providing cost-effective investment management services. In spite of their for-profit orientation, years of operating in the highly competitive institutional index fund management arena forced Barclays and State Street to develop a customer-oriented perspective that carries over into most of their ETF market activities.

The necessity of dealing with the brokerage community constitutes the most serious drawback of investing in ETFs. Generally, Wall Street brokers make money by engaging in activities detrimental to investor interests. Charging high fees for trades, providing poor execution for infrequent traders, imposing assessments for account maintenance, and encouraging excessive trading represent four means that brokers employ to line their pockets at their clients' expense. Regardless of the degree of bad behavior on the part of brokers, payments of commissions on ETF trades dictate a minimum scale for trades, ruling out smaller transactions. Sensible investors pay extremely close attention to the costs of trading and the principal-agent conflicts inherent in the trade execution process.

Trading ETFs poses some significant challenges for individual investors. Even though the ETF structure includes an arbitrage mechanism that tends to keep market price close to fair value, arbitrage activity proves most effective for ETFs that invest in securities that trade in liquid, resilient markets. Arbitrage activity finds further support with ETFs that themselves trade in active, deep markets. Because the arbitrage mechanism sometimes fails to keep price in line with fair value, unsophisticated investors face the possibility of buying ETFs at prices above fair value and selling at prices below fair value.

In addition to a strong roster of sensible offerings, the ETF market contains a number of funds that suffer from high costs or faulty structure or both. For instance, Rydex Global Advisors charges 0.40 percent for an equal-weighted S&P 500 ETF product, while Barclays Global Advisors charges 0.09 percent for a market-capitalization-weighted S&P 500 ETF. Why should investors incur more than four times the expense for essentially identical investment management services? The proliferation of narrow niche products, including individual country funds and specific sector funds, clutters the ETF landscape with generally irrelevant, often confusing choices. Some ETFs track badly conceived indices, providing investors with an unappealing product. Other ETF structures produce static portfolios that fail to respond to changes in index composition, leaving investors with potentially unrepresentative portfolios. Investors must employ the same caution and skepticism in the ETF market as they would in any other aspect of financial services.

Investors should prepare for a more difficult future. The dramatic growth in ETF assets has already attracted the usual Wall Street lowlifes, who have fashioned ways to increase their take. More shoddily structured products and more high-fee offerings stand in the wings. Creative financial engineers have developed a means to offer actively managed ETFs, increasing the level of dysfunctionality in the ETF world. As time passes, the ETF market will increasingly take on the unattractive characteristics of the traditional mutual-fund universe.

ETFs represent a viable alternative to traditional index funds for a broad range of investors. Unfortunately, as in all parts of the financial services world, ETF investors face a set of agency issues that separate the investors from their goals. Addressing the agency challenges with thoughtful selection of funds and careful execution of trades allows investors to fashion a portfolio with attractive investment characteristics that match or exceed the positive attributes of a portfolio of standard index funds.

EXCHANGE-TRADED FUNDS

In little more than a decade, the ETF market grew from its first offering of $6.6 million of Standard & Poor's Depositary Receipts to 134 securities totaling $157 billion of market capitalization at year-end 2003. The ETF market includes a variety of asset types, ranging from domestic, foreign, and global stocks to domestic bonds and TIPS.

U.S. equities dominate the ETF listings, with more than a 60 percent share by number. In terms of market capitalization, as shown in Table 11.1, U.S. stock funds account for nearly 90 percent of total ETF capitalization. In fact, the top five funds—all focused on U.S. stocks—hold a striking 55 percent of ETF assets.

Table 11.1 ETFs Span a Range of Asset Classes

	Number of Funds	Market Capitalization (Millions of Dollars)
U.S. stocks	86	139,088
Foreign developed market stocks	24	11,784
Foreign emerging market stocks	9	2,563
Global stocks	7	307
Real estate	3	1,282
U.S. bonds	5	2,231
TIPS	1	142
Total	134	157,396

Source: Morgan Stanley.
Note: Data as of December 31, 2003.

The ten largest ETFs, shown in Table 11.2, include four funds that provide core asset exposure (Standard & Poor's Depositary Receipts, iShares S&P 500 Index Fund, and Total Stock Market VIPERs for domestic equities; iShares MSCI EAFE for foreign developed equities). The remaining six funds mirror benchmarks that prove either poorly structured (e.g., the Dow Jones Industrial Average and the Russell 2000) or suitable for speculation (NASDAQ 100) or both. In spite of the ETF market's general focus on index funds, the top ten offerings constitute a mixed bag.

Regardless of the presence of a number of poor-quality ETFs, the market offers well-structured, reasonably priced securities that provide exposure to a wide range of core asset classes. Table 11.3 shows a half dozen alternatives for broad exposure to the U.S. stock market, a handful of options for bonds and real estate securities, and one possibility each for foreign developed markets, foreign emerging markets, and TIPS. Barclays Global Investors' iShare offerings dominate the list, taking eleven of fourteen positions. State Street Global Advisors captures second place with two entries, but with responsibility for the mammoth Spider ETF, State Street achieves in size what it lacks in numbers. Relatively recent ETF market entrant Vanguard earns one spot on the roster.

Three firms dominate the ETF landscape, posting a combined market share just short of 95 percent of assets as of December 31, 2003.

Table 11.2 Largest ETFs Dominate the Market

ETF	Index	Trustee or Advisor	Market Capitalization (Millions of Dollars)
Standard & Poor's Depositary Receipts	S&P 500	State Street Global Advisors	43,750
NASDAQ-100 Index Tracking Stock	NASDAQ 100	Bank of New York	25,608
iShares S&P 500 Index Fund	S&P 500	Barclays Global Investors	7,858
Diamonds	Dow Jones Industrial Average	State Street Global Advisors	6,772
Standard & Poor's MidCap 400 Depositary Receipts	S&P MidCap 400	Bank of New York	6,420
iShares MSCI EAFE Index	MSCI EAFE	Barclays Global Investors	5,362
iShares Russell 2000 Index	Russell 2000	Barclays Global Investors	4,509
iShares MSCI Japan Index	MSCI Japan	Barclays Global Investors	2,840
Total Stock Market VIPERs	Wilshire 5000	The Vanguard Group	2,509
iShares Russell 1000 Value Index	Russell 1000 Value	Barclays Global Investors	2,329

Source: Morgan Stanley.
Note: Data as of December 31, 2003.

The two top players—Barclays Global Investors and State Street Global Advisors—share roots as important participants in the world of passive institutional funds management. Barclays and State Street rank among the world's largest asset management firms, responsible for approximately $1 trillion each at the end of 2003. Bank of New York earns a spot in the troika by dint of its involvement with Merrill Lynch's HOLDRs and the bank's own BLDRs, a motley collection of sorry constructs that ill-serve investor interests. The character and culture of the firms that dominate the ETF market provide clues to the likely success or failure of ETFs to satisfy investor needs.

The institutional nature of Barclays' and State Street's money management business provides substantial benefits to ETF shareholders. In the intensely competitive environment for providing commodity-like passive management services to sophisticated institutional clients, Barclays and State Street operate profitably on razor-thin margins. The

**Table 11.3 Core Asset Class ETFs Provide
Useful Portfolio Management Tools**

Asset Class	ETF	Index	Share Ticker	Fair Value Ticker
U.S. stocks	Total Stock Market (VIPERs)	Wilshire 5000	VTI	TSJ
	Russell 3000 (iShares)	Russell 3,000	IWV	NMV
	Dow Jones U.S. Total Market (iShares)	Dow Jones U.S. Total Market	IYY	NLAX
	S&P 1500 (iShares)	S&P 1500	ISI	EIS
	S&P 500 (iShares)	S&P 500	IVV	NNV
	S&P Depositary Receipts	S&P 500	SPY	SXV
Foreign developed market stocks	MSCI Europe Australasia and Far East (iShares)	EAFE	EFA	IEE
Foreign emerging market stocks	MSCI Emerging Markets Free (iShares)	EMF	EEM	EEV
Real estate	Wilshire REIT (streetTRACKS)	Wilshire REIT	RWR	EWR
	Cohen & Steers Realty Majors (iShares)	Cohen & Steers Realty Majors	ICF	ICG
U.S. bonds	Lehman 1 to 3 Year Treasury (iShares)	Lehman 1 to 3 Year Treasury	SHY	SHZ
	Lehman 7 to 10 Year Treasury (iShares)	Lehman 7 to 10 Year Treasury	IEF	IEN
	Lehman 20+ Year Treasury (iShares)	Lehman 20+ Year Treasury	TLT	TLZ
TIPS	Lehman TIPS (iShares)	Lehman U.S. Treasury Inflation-Protected Securities	TIP	TBK

Source: Morgan Stanley, Exchange Traded Funds. Index-Linked ETFs: Quarterly Update, *28 January 2004.*

fair pricing and competition-induced efficiencies carry over from the firms' core asset management businesses to the ETF market, benefiting the retail ETF investor.

From the perspective of Barclays and State Street, participation in the ETF market represents an extension of their core institutional index fund activity. In fact, although reliable data separating retail holdings from institutional positions do not exist, institutions appear to participate actively in ETF trading, requiring that the asset management firms offer a fairly priced product or risk losing market share.* In Barclays' and State Street's ETF world, market forces operate to keep prices at fair and efficient institutional levels, as opposed to unfair and excessive retail levels. Retail investors benefit from riding institutional investor coattails.

In stark contrast to the competitively honed products offered by Barclays and State Street, the ETF market as a whole contains a number of poorly structured funds created by retail-oriented firms. Bank of New York, the third-largest player in the ETF world, serves as trustee for Holding Company Depositary Receipts (HOLDRs) and Baskets of Listed Depositary Receipts (BLDRs), funds that rely more on clever acronyms than on superior investment structure. HOLDRs, a brainchild of Merrill Lynch, consist of static sector funds that shrink when companies disappear, but fail to grow when new companies appear. Ill-conceived as a series of concentrated sector portfolios, HOLDRs allows Merrill Lynch's clients to make inappropriately risky bets.

BLDRs represent the lazy man's approach to foreign and global investing. Instead of rationally exposing investors to the full range of overseas securities, BLDRs own only shares of companies that choose to offer American Depositary Receipts (ADRs), a security that allows foreign shares to trade on U.S. exchanges. ADRs appeal to unsophisticated investors, because shares trade side by side with domestic stocks, obviating the need to deal with foreign currencies and foreign stock exchanges. Clearly, simplicity of execution provides no rationale for limiting investor choice in a professionally managed fund, as

---

*Morgan Stanley estimates that ETF trading stems in roughly equal proportions from institutions and from individuals.

trading in foreign stocks proves no obstacle for even the greenest institutional funds manager.

Perhaps Bank of New York's focus on ADRs arises from ulterior motives. First, Bank of New York receives a fee of .06 percent of assets as recompense for licensing its pathetically unrepresentative ADR index. For context, compare Bank of New York's six-basis-point BLDRs licensing fee to State Street's nine-basis-point Spider total expense ratio. Clearly, paying an egregious licensing fee for a poorly conceived index constitutes a significant payment of something for less than nothing. Second, Bank of New York, a major player in the creation and maintenance of the ADRs that undergird the BLDRs product, no doubt benefits by channeling assets to the ADR market. In a press release celebrating the launch of the BLDRs program, the Bank of New York appeared oblivious to the obvious conflict: "As the world's largest depositary for depositary receipts, we are delighted to be associated with an ETF that offers investors another innovative solution. . . . The BLDRs Fund family broadens the advantages and enhances the visibility of depositary receipts as a convenient and cost-effective way to invest in non-U.S. securities."[1] Owners of BLDRs, with no axe to grind in the ADR market, suffer from exposure to a restricted opportunity set, while Bank of New York double dips.

TRADING ETFS

Because ETFs trade like other securities listed on stock exchanges, investors face the unwelcome prospect of dealing with a brokerage firm to execute trades. Few areas of the securities world exhibit as clearly defined, diametrically opposed conflicting interests as the relationship between a broker and a customer. Brokers succeed by extracting the highest possible fees. Customers succeed by paying the lowest possible fees. Brokers succeed with short-term churning of positions. Customers succeed with long-term holding of positions. Sensible investors evaluate every statement from their broker with unabashed skepticism.

Careful customers exacerbate the inherent conflicts with brokers by behaving in a manner that produces little in profit for the broker. Cost-sensitive investors avoid paying high levels of profitable-to-the-broker fees. Long-term investors avoid executing large numbers of profitable-to-the-broker transactions. Sensible investors generate dismal profits for brokers, placing an additional measure of strain on the already conflicted relationship.

The full service offered by full-service brokers generally impairs the investor's odds of success. Full service includes demonstrably worthless research. Full service encompasses clearly irrelevant broker advice. Full service costs materially more than other trading alternatives. Investors who employ full-service brokers pay a very real something for an extremely costly nothing.

At the other end of the spectrum stand pure-execution services. Self-reliant investors simply place orders and receive executions, avoiding the counterproductive excess of full-service operations. In the realm of pure-execution services, Internet-savvy investors enjoy a cost advantage over their telephone-wielding counterparts.

Broker-assisted transactions fall between the extremes of pure-execution and full-service brokerage. The incremental fees paid for broker-assisted transactions purchase only a human voice. None of the ostensible benefits of full-service brokerage accrue to broker-assisted trades.

Patterns of brokerage charges vary dramatically across the different execution categories. A sampling of trading costs, conducted in August 2004 and summarized in Table 11.4, shows a constant pricing level (regardless of trade size) for pure-execution online trading. The trade-size-invariant pricing reflects the fact that the costs incurred by brokers do not vary with trade size. The cost to trade 100 shares equals the cost to trade 100,000 shares. In the competitive online arena, trade-size-invariant costs result in trade-size-invariant pricing.

Contrast the trade-size-constant pricing for online trades with the trade-size increasing pricing for full-service trades. Even though the difference between trading 100 shares and trading 500 shares consists only of a different number on the trade ticket, A.G. Edwards and Smith Barney charge five times as much for 500 shares as they charge for 100 shares. Full-service brokers use the lame excuse of a larger trade size to extract a larger commission from their clients. Investors foolish enough to trade with full-service firms get what they deserve.

The trading cost survey examines charges for executing trades of Standard & Poor's Depositary Receipts (SPY), illustrating the dramatic differences in levels of brokerage charges. Traditional full-service brokers extract egregious fees. Merrill Lynch leads the parade of shame with charges of $206.79 for trading 100 shares of SPY and $687.53 for 500 shares.

Full-service fees take a sizable chunk from investor assets regardless of trade size. At the top of the scale, Merrill Lynch charges a full 1.9 percent of a $10,900 SPY trade. Even the most attractively priced full-service broker, A. G. Edwards, registers at 0.9 percent. Sentient investors avoid excessive full-service fees.

The picture improves dramatically with online trading. Ameritrade prices execution-only services at $10.99 for a 100-share order, undercutting a Merrill Lynch full-service trade by a factor of more than 18. As a percentage of the hypothetical SPY transaction, Ameritrade clocks in at a modest 0.1 percent.

Larger trades produce more dramatic comparisons. Ameritrade charges $10.99 to trade 1000 shares of SPY, while Merrill Lynch de-

Table 11.4 Investors Face a Wide Range of Trading Costs

Estimated Costs to Trade S&P Depositary Receipts (SPY)

Broker	100 Shares SPY Dollars	Percent	500 Shares SPY Dollars	Percent	1000 Shares SPY Dollars	Percent
Pure execution online						
Ameritrade	10.99	0.10	10.99	0.02	10.99	0.01
TD Waterhouse	17.95	0.16	17.95	0.03	17.95	0.02
Fidelity	29.95	0.27	29.95	0.05	29.95	0.03
Pure execution telephone						
Ameritrade	14.99	0.14	14.99	0.03	14.99	0.01
TD Waterhouse	35.00	0.32	35.00	0.06	35.00	0.03
Fidelity	45.00	0.41	45.00	0.08	67.50	0.06
Broker-assisted						
Ameritrade	24.99	0.23	24.99	0.05	24.99	0.02
Merrill Lynch	50.00	0.46	116.25	0.21	150.00	0.14
Fidelity	55.00	0.50	111.00	0.20	181.00	0.17
Full service						
A.G. Edwards	100.00	0.92	500.00	0.92	976.68	0.90
Smith Barney	110.50	1.01	552.50	1.01	1052.57	0.97
Merrill Lynch	206.79	1.90	687.53	1.26	1081.06	0.99

Sources: Brokerage firm websites; institutional representatives.
Notes: When applicable, charges reflect the lowest account balance. Percentage calculations assume a price for SPY of $109, derived from the average price during the month of August 2004, when the data were gathered.

mands $1,081.06, representing nearly 100 times the Ameritrade charge. As a percentage of value, Ameritrade registers at 0.01 percent compared to Merrill Lynch's 0.99 percent. Self-reliance in the form of pure-execution brokerage avoids the brokers' noise and saves money, producing a win-win for the investor.

Brokerage charges effectively limit sensible trading of ETFs to large transactions. Investor returns suffer little diminution from pure-execution charges of 0.01 percent for a $109,000 1000-share trade of SPY or 0.10 percent for a $10,900 100-share trade of SPY. But, a 10.0 percent charge for a $109 one-share trade of SPY consumes far too much investor capital. ETF trading only makes sense for substantial transactions.

Payment of brokerage fees for ETF trades represents one of the largest drawbacks to ETF investing. By using execution-only services, investors achieve the double benefit of avoiding mindless broker chatter about the stock of the hour and receiving the best possible pricing for trade execution. Prudent investors avoid full-service brokerage firms and execute trades through low-cost, execution-only brokers.

ARBITRAGE MECHANISMS

Most ETF structures contain arbitrage mechanisms that encourage trading activity to keep the market price of the ETF in line with the fair value of the underlying securities. A tight relationship between market price and fair value ensures that market participants trade at realistic prices. ETFs largely avoid the stale pricing problem that haunts standard mutual funds, as continuous pricing of ETF shares during trading hours affords investors the opportunity to trade at fresh market prices. Table 11.3 includes core-asset-class ETF ticker symbols for both market price and fair value.

Even though demand or supply imbalances for particular ETFs may cause the market-clearing price to deviate from fair value, when deviations between market price and fair value reach sufficient magnitude, an arbitrage mechanism allows certain large investors to profit by redressing the imbalances. As a result, markets generally operate effectively throughout the trading day.

So-called authorized participants perform the arbitrage function by buying or selling institutional blocks of ETF shares, usually sized at 50,000 shares for equity ETFs and 100,000 shares for fixed-income ETFs. When the ETF market value exceeds fair value, arbitrage-motivated authorized participants purchase the relatively cheap securities underlying the ETF index, with the objective of creating and selling newly issued ETF shares. Note that the arbitrage activity reduces the gap between fair value and market price as the increased supply of ETF shares serves to drive market price down toward fair value. In the case of market price exceeding fair value, arbitrage activity increases the volume of ETF shares outstanding.

If, on the other hand, ETF fair value exceeds market price, the authorized participants reverse the process. The arbitrageurs sell short the overvalued securities underlying the ETF index and buy the undervalued ETF shares. The authorized participant can then exchange the ETF shares for the underlying securities, using the securities so obtained to cover the short positions. Note that the arbitrage activity reduces the gap between fair value and market price, as the reduced supply of ETF shares serves to drive market price up toward fair value. In the case of fair value exceeding market price, arbitrage activity decreases the volume of ETF shares outstanding.

The effectiveness of the arbitrage mechanism for ETF shares depends on the depth and liquidity of the underlying market for the securities that comprise the ETF, as well as on the depth and liquidity of the market for the ETF shares themselves. Markets that accommodate large trades at narrow bid-ask spreads facilitate arbitrage activity. In contrast, markets that absorb only small volumes at wide spreads frustrate arbitrageurs. Because a tight price/fair-value relationship underpins investor confidence in the fairness of the markets, market depth and resilience play an important role in supporting the ETF market.

MARKET DEPTH

In the world of ETFs, price and fair value correspond most closely when deep and resilient securities markets support the trading of the index fund constituents. If the constituent securities trade in substantial volume at narrow bid-ask spreads, arbitrageurs can assemble quickly sizable positions to employ in price/fair-value arbitrage activity. Conversely, if constituent securities trade sporadically at wide bid-ask spreads, arbitrageurs face a difficult task in executing price/fair-value equilibrating trades.

A snapshot of the ETF markets taken during the week of May 3, 2004, illustrates the effectiveness of the arbitrage mechanism for six core asset ETFs. An examination of the relationship between price and fair value, appropriately weighted by volume, for all of that week's ETF trades measures the effectiveness of markets in producing fair results. Obviously, one week's trades provides only indicative results, but the results appear instructive.

Since equating price to fair value constitutes one goal of an efficient market, any deviation of price from fair value represents a market failure. Consequently, it makes sense to examine the absolute value of differences between price and fair value, allowing positive and negative deviations between price and fair value to receive equal weight. Because the amount of money exposed to trades matters, volume-weighted data allow larger trades to influence the results more (and smaller trades to influence the results less), providing the clearest indication of the degree to which markets operate efficiently.

The data on ETF market efficiency correspond nicely to *a priori* notions of relative market robustness. The Lehman 7 to 10 Year Treasury ETFs—designed to mimic the intermediate portion of the world's deepest and most efficient securities market—produce the smallest volume-weighted deviation between price and fair value, registering at a mere 0.04 percent. As illustrated in Table 11.5, domestic equities and TIPS demonstrate a high degree of market effectiveness, sharing a 0.08 percent differential between price and fair value. As expected, less liquid foreign markets prove less prone to effective arbitrage, with developed markets exhibiting a 0.22 percent gap and emerging markets showing a 0.57 percent deviation.

While the volume-weighted data represent the experience of the community as a whole, the individual trade data matter to the individual traders. During the week of the analysis, basic categories of U.S. bond ETFs traded within a range of minus 0.2 percent to plus 0.3 percent of fair value, TIPS ETFs traded within a range of minus 0.2 percent to plus 0.4 percent, and U.S. stock ETFs traded within a range of minus 0.3 percent to plus 0.2 percent. Foreign developed ETF markets traded in a range of plus or minus approximately 0.7 percent, while foreign emerging markets traded within a range of 2.1 percent, from a deficit of minus 1.6 percent to a premium of 0.5 percent. In the more efficient markets, investors register less concern regarding execution at fair value, expecting that the arbitrage mechanism provides fair prices. In the less efficient markets, careful investors pay attention to effective execution of trades.

Table 11.5 Core Asset Class ETF Price-to-Fair-Value Relationships Correspond to Relative Market Efficiency

Asset Class	ETF	Volume-Weighted Difference Between Price and Fair-Value (Percent)	Price-to-Fair-Value Range		
			Lowest Discount	Largest Premium	Range
U.S. bonds	Lehman 7 to 10 Year Treasury (iShares)	0.04	−0.23	0.34	0.56
TIPS	Lehman TIPS (iShares)	0.08	−0.21	0.38	0.59
U.S. stocks	Total Stock Market (VIPERs)	0.08	−0.33	0.20	0.53
Real estate	Wilshire REIT (streetTRACKS)	0.17	−0.81	0.52	1.33
Foreign developed market stocks	MSCI Europe, Australasia, and Far East (iShares)	0.22	−0.69	0.74	1.43
Foreign emerging market stocks	MSCI Emerging Markets Free (iShares)	0.57	−1.64	0.46	2.10

Source: Bloomberg.
Note: Data cover the week of May 3, 2004.

The size and liquidity of the markets for ETF shares play an important role in the quality of trade execution. One measure of market effectiveness, the bid-ask spread, represents the differential between the price a market maker offers to pay for a security and the price a market maker demands to receive for a security. A wide spread corresponds to a high trading-cost regime. A low spread corresponds to a low trading-cost environment.

During the week of May 3, 2004, U.S. marketable-security ETFs led the low-cost parade, with average bid-ask spreads ranging from 0.06 percent to 0.09 percent of the share price. Foreign developed market and foreign emerging market ETFs clocked in at 0.12 percent and 0.15 percent, respectively. The far-less-liquid real estate ETF, which trades more or less by appointment, brought up the rear with an average spread of 0.31 percent. Table 11.6 contains the details.

Table 11.6 ETF Bid-Ask Spreads Vary Across Asset Classes

Asset Class	ETF	Market Capitalization as of December 31, 2003 (Millions of Dollars)	Average Daily Trading Volume (Thousands of Shares)	Average Bid-Ask Spread (Percent)
U.S. bonds	Lehman 7 to 10 Year Treasury (iShares)	398	174,804	0.06
TIPS	Lehman TIPS (iShares)	142	113,673	0.07
U.S. stocks	Total Stock Market (VIPERs)	2,509	155,216	0.09
Foreign developed market stocks	MSCI Europe, Australasia, and Far East (iShares)	5,362	605,390	0.12
Foreign emerging market stocks	MSCI Emerging Markets Free (iShares)	1,090	142,330	0.15
Real estate	Wilshire REIT (streetTRACKS)	285	17,500	0.31

Sources: Morgan Stanley; Bloomberg.
Note: Average Daily Trading Volume data cover 100 trading days up to January 28, 2004.

Market liquidity plays an important role in ETF pricing. A close relationship between price and fair value depends on the robustness of the markets for the constituent securities of the ETF and for the ETF itself. Fortunately for investors, ETFs for core asset classes exhibit generally attractive liquidity characteristics, providing a reasonably high degree of confidence that market prices reflect fair value.

TAX EFFICIENCY

ETFs exhibit greater tax efficiency than otherwise comparable open-end mutual funds. Tax liabilities arise when mutual-fund portfolio managers, of whatever ilk, sell shares and realize gains, producing taxable distributions to fund shareholders. The ETF arbitrage mechanism provides an opportunity for fund managers to reduce taxable gains distributions.

The tax benefit to ETF investing stems from the in-kind exchanges that constitute part of the price/fair-value arbitrage activity. When ETF fair value exceeds market price, arbitrageurs sell short the overvalued index-constituent securities and buy the undervalued ETF shares. The arbitrageur then exchanges the ETF shares for a basket of the underlying securities. This in-kind exchange involves no tax consequences and provides an opportunity for the fund manager to deliver to the arbitrageur the lowest-cost-basis securities (which represent the highest potential tax liability). The arbitrageur then completes the trade by using the basket of underlying securities to cover the short positions.

As expected, historical data indicate that the S&P 500 Spider ETF demonstrated greater tax efficiency than standard S&P 500 Index Funds. Table 11.7, which covers the ten-year period ending December 31, 2002, shows an average capital gains distribution of 1.87 percent of assets for regular open-end S&P 500 Index Funds relative to a barely visible 0.01 percent of assets for the Spider ETF. Even though the absolute level of the standard index fund capital gains distribution indicates a high degree of tax efficiency, ETFs enjoy an edge in the tax efficiency arena.

Table 11.7 ETFs Exhibit Superior Tax Efficiency
Capital Gains Distributions Relative to Net Asset Value

	ETFs (SPY)	Standard Open-End S&P 500 Index Funds
1993	0.00	1.10
1994	0.00	1.35
1995	0.00	3.85
1996	0.12	2.10
1997	0.00	2.34
1998	0.00	1.67
1999	0.00	1.52
2000	0.00	2.58
2001	0.00	1.76
2002	0.00	0.42
Average	0.01	1.87

Source: Morgan Stanley, Exchange Traded Funds. Index-Linked ETFs: Quarterly Update, *28 January 2004.*

CORE ASSET-CLASS ETFS

Not all ETFs prove useful to investors. Of the 135 ETF issues traded on U.S. exchanges as of January, 2004, only fourteen provide broadly diversified core asset exposure to investors. The remaining 121 ETF offerings expose investors to inappropriately structured benchmarks or risky concentrations of assets or both. Most flawed benchmarks employ structures that involve unnecessarily high turnover, although in some cases the concerns relate to inferior security-selection techniques. Investors find unwelcome asset concentration risk in sector funds, which include portfolios based on capitalization size (small, mid, and large), style characteristics (growth and value), market sector (health care, telecommunications, utilities, etc.), or geography. Sensible investors avoid the vast majority of ETF offerings.

Unfortunately, aggregate investment in non-core ETFs now exceeds the investment in core ETFs. As depicted in Figure 11.1, in the early years of ETF investing, core funds dominated the list of offerings. Wall Street's financial engineers responded to the early success of sensible funds by creating not-so-sensible alternatives. As a result of Wall Street's efforts, non-core ETFs now dominate the market.

Figure 11.1 Core ETFs Lose Ground to Non-Core ETFs

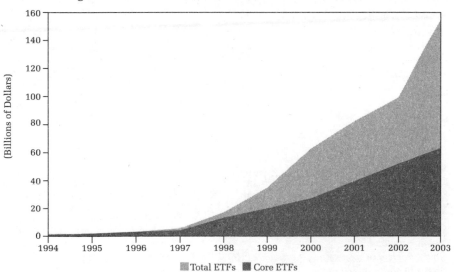

Source: Lipper, Inc.

Core-asset-class ETFs offer investors cost-effective access to broad-based asset classes. As depicted in Table 11.8, core ETFs post average expense ratios of 0.24 percent, or somewhat less than one-half of the non-core ETF expense ratio of 0.49 percent. The combination of low costs and superior structure translates into improved investment results for core-asset-class ETF investors.

Table 11.8 Most ETFs Serve No Sensible Portfolio Purpose

	Number of Funds	Average Expense Ratio
U.S. stock ETFs		
Core	6	0.16
Other diversified	16	0.28
Style	18	0.23
Sector	43	0.52
(excluding real estate)		
Foreign developed market stock ETFs		
Core	1	0.35
Other diversified	1	0.30
Regional	8	0.45
Country	16	0.82
Foreign emerging market stock ETFs		
Core	1	0.75
Other diversified	1	0.30
Regional	1	0.50
Country	6	0.94
Global stock ETFs		
Diversified	3	0.35
Sector	5	0.65
Real estate ETFs		
Core	2	0.30
Other	1	0.60
U.S. bonds		
Core	3	0.15
Corporate	1	0.15
Diversified	1	0.20
TIPS		
Core	1	0.20
Summary		
Core ETFs	14	0.24
Non-core ETFs	121	0.49
Total	135	0.46

Source: Morgan Stanley, Exchange Traded Funds. Index-Linked ETFs: Quarterly Update, *28 January 2004.*
Note: Expense ratios exclude 17 issues of HOLDRs, which assess percentage charges that vary with share price.

Note the dramatic difference between the expenses for core U.S. stock ETFs of 0.16 percent and expenses for U.S. sector ETFs of 0.52 percent. Not only do most sector funds expose investors to inappropriate risks, but investors also end up paying a premium for the dubious product.

The details beneath the aggregate figures suggest that sensible investors pay close attention to individual ETF expense ratios. Consider the characteristics of utility sector ETFs managed by Barclays Global Investors and State Street Global Advisors, as outlined in Table 11.9.

Table 11.9 Similar ETFs Assess Dissimilar Charges

ETF	Index	Investment Advisor	Expense Ratio	Top Ten Holdings (Percent of Assets)
Dow Jones U.S. Utilities Sector (iShares)	Dow Jones U.S. Utilities Sector	Barclays Global Advisors	0.60	Southern (6.3)
				Exelon (6.1)
				Dominion Resources (5.8)
				Duke Energy (5.5)
				Entergy (3.8)
				American Electric Power (3.6)
				Firstenergy (3.5)
				FPL Group (3.2)
				Progress Energy (3.1)
				PG&E (3.0)
Utilities Select Sector SPDR	Utilities Select Sector	State Street Global Advisors	0.28	Southern (7.4)
				Exelon (7.2)
				Dominion Resources (6.8)
				Duke Energy (6.5)
				Entergy (4.5)
				American Electric Power (4.2)
				Firstenergy (4.1)
				FPL Group (4.1)
				PG&E (3.8)
				Progress Energy (3.6)

Source: Morgan Stanley, Exchange Traded Funds. Index Linked ETFs: Quarterly Update, *28 January 2004.*

Even though the two ETF portfolios exhibit such striking similarity that the top ten holdings match perfectly in identity and match nearly in rank order, the two firms come to widely disparate pricing decisions, with Barclays charging 0.60 percent and State Street charging 0.28 percent. State Street's investors enjoy a superior deal.

A similar pricing range exists for four technology sector ETFs, designed to track indices constructed by Dow Jones, Goldman Sachs, Morgan Stanley, and Standard & Poor's. The divergent span of charges, ranging from 0.28 percent to 0.60 percent of assets as outlined in Table 11.10, bears no relation to the common character of the funds' investment mandates and the similar nature of the funds' security holdings. Cisco appears among the top ten positions of all four indices. Microsoft, Intel, IBM, Dell, Hewlett Packard, and Oracle appear in the top ten lists of three of the four funds. With common holdings and nearly identical investment challenges, a rational observer might expect the four technology funds to share similar pricing levels. Yet, pricing clearly differs.

A worrying observation relates to the vintage of the funds. State Street's December 1998 Standard & Poor's Technology Select Fund represents the best buy, as the fund's charges define the floor at 0.28 percent of assets. Barclays' bubble-era Dow Jones U.S. Technology

Table 11.10 Technology-Sector-Focused ETFs Exhibit Material Pricing Differentials

ETF	Investment Advisor	Number of Securities	Launch Date	Expense Ratio
Dow Jones U.S. Technology Sector (iShares)	Barclays Global Investors	250	May 15, 2000	0.60
Goldman Sachs Technology (iShares)	Barclays Global Investors	222	March 13, 2001	0.50
Morgan Stanley Technology (iShares)	State Street Global Advisors	35	September 25, 2000	0.50
Technology Select SPDR	State Street Global Advisors	95	December 22, 1998	0.28

Source: Morgan Stanley, Exchange Traded Funds. Index Linked ETFs: Quarterly Update, 28 January 2004.

Sector Fund came in at 0.60 percent, while State Street's year 2000 offering registered at 0.50 percent. Did the index fund managers take advantage of ETF investors' price insensitivity to raise the rates?

Foreign developed market ETFs provide a classic example of the sum of the parts failing to match the whole. Barclays Global Investors offers a Europe, Australasia, and Far East index-tracking ETF for the reasonable price of 0.35 percent of assets. Barclays also offers individual country funds for thirteen of the twenty EAFE countries, allowing investors to obtain exposure to approximately 90 percent of EAFE's market capitalization by using country funds. Surprisingly, expenses amount to 0.84 percent for each of the country funds, representing nearly two and one-half times the EAFE fund charges. The sum of the parts approach to foreign equity investing represents an expensive alternative.

Strangely, Barclays' country fund expense levels bear no relation to fund-specific characteristics, with charges amounting to the same 0.84 percent for the United Kingdom ETF (25.6 percent of EAFE at December 31, 2003) and the Japan ETF (21.4 percent) as well as the Belgium ETF (1.1 percent) and the Singapore ETF (0.8 percent). No reasonable explanation emerges for the disparity in pricing between the EAFE ETF at 0.35 percent and the constituent country funds at 0.84 percent, particularly since the EAFE whole simply represents the sum of the country parts.

Moreover, Barclays' pricing bears no relation to fund asset levels. In fact, the iShares MSCI Japan ETF boasts a total of $2.8 billion in assets as of December 31, 2003, placing the fund among the top ten of all ETFs by market capitalization. Barclays cannot argue that small size requires premium pricing for the firm's Japanese offering. In contrast to the case of Japan, a scale argument might resonate with the iShares MSCI Belgium ETF and its tiny $11.4 million portfolio, but the Belgian fund charges the same 0.84 percent of assets as the Japanese fund. Perhaps, ignoring its investor-friendly institutional roots, Barclays simply asks what the market bears.

POORLY STRUCTURED ETFS

In a depressing development, several poorly conceived, high-cost ETFs pollute the otherwise relatively pure ETF waters. Rydex Global Advisors* offers an equal-weighted S&P Index Fund for the ridiculous charge of 0.40 percent of assets, relative to the Barclays charge of 0.09 percent for the standard market-capitalization-weighted S&P Index Fund. Not only do Rydex fund investors pay more than four times a fair price for index management services, but the equal-weighted ETF holders face the possibility of adverse tax consequences from the quarterly rebalancing trades required to maintain equal security weights. Table 11.11 displays the sorry story.

PowerShares Capital, with its offerings of equal-weighted funds, provides an even greater disservice to investors by conducting the same tax-insensitive quarterly rebalancing for an even more ridiculous price of 0.60 percent of assets. Beyond the excessive fees, a further troubling aspect of the PowerShares offering relates to the nature of the indices that the firm mimics. According to the prospectus for the PowerShares Dynamic Market Portfolio, the fund "seeks investment results that correspond generally to the price and yield . . . of an equity index called the Dynamic Market Intellidex℠ Index." Intellidex, presumably a compression of intelligent and index, represents a contradiction in terms. By using what a Morgan Stanley research report calls "rules based quantitative analysis" to evaluate and select securities, PowerShares engages in active management, not in passive index replication. The so-called index construction process ranks companies "based on a variety of criteria including fundamental growth, stock valuation, timeliness and risk factors." Belying the assertion that the Intellidex constitutes an index, the prospectus clearly describes an active-management process that seeks to buy growing companies at reasonable prices in a timely fashion without undue risk. By dressing the active-management wolf in passive-management sheep's clothing, PowerShares fools the investing public and sullies the otherwise purely passive character of the ETF arena.

---

*Prior to the launch of the high-priced, badly structured S&P Equal Weight Index, Rydex earned a spot in the Investment Management Hall of Shame for its high-cost, up-front-load REIT Index Fund.

A close reading of the offering documents for Rydex and Power-Shares indicates the potential for further damage to investor interests with the adoption of Rule 12b-1 plans that allow charges of up to 0.25 percent per annum for distribution services. While implementation of the plans remains in abeyance, investors face the threat of a future, quiet increase in costs to fund an asset-gathering activity that benefits only the ETF sponsor.

Table 11.11 Bad Actors Enter the ETF Stage

ETF	Index	Investment Advisor	Expense Ratio (Percent)
Rydex S&P Equal Weight	S&P 500 Equal Weight (quarterly rebalancing)	Rydex Global Advisors	0.40
PowerShares Dynamic Market Portfolio	100 stocks Rules-based, modified, equal-dollar weighted (quarterly rebalancing)	PowerShares Capital	0.60
PowerShares OTC Portfolio	100 NASDAQ stocks Rules-based, modified, equal-dollar weighted (quarterly rebalancing)	PowerShares Capital	0.60

Source: Morgan Stanley, Exchange Traded Funds. Index Linked ETFs: Quarterly Update, *28 January 2004.*

Rydex further chips away at investor interests by reserving the right to use bloated soft-dollar commissions to pay for research services, including "information on the economy, industries, groups of securities, individual companies, statistical information, accounting and tax law interpretations, political developments, legal developments affecting portfolio securities, technical market action, pricing and appraisal services, credit analysis, risk measurement analysis, performance analysis, [and] analysis of corporate responsibility issues . . ." What role does such research play in management of a fund that places 0.20 percent of assets in each of the five hundred constituent securities of the S&P 500? Since research services provide absolutely no benefit to index fund managers, the answer may lie in the fact that such services "may be of benefit to the Advisor in the management of other accounts of the Advisor, including other investment companies advised by the Advisor."[2] In other words, Rydex enjoys the option of using commission payments from trading ETF assets to obtain research that supports the firm's other investment management activities.

In an interesting footnote, Bank of New York (already identified as associated with the unappealing offerings of BLDRs and HOLDRs) serves as administrator, custodian, and transfer agent for the unattractive Rydex and PowerShares funds. The network of relationships between poorly conceived products and promotional producers takes on a self-reinforcing and self-perpetuating character. Once identified, low-quality actors tend to appear in low-quality production after low-quality production.

Unfortunately for ETF purchasers, a number of market participants currently harbor plans for offering actively managed ETFs. Led by the American Stock Exchange, which hopes to benefit from future ETF listings, a group expects to launch in 2005 a number of ETFs that "track the stock picks of individual portfolio managers."[3] Since real-time disclosure of the composition of actively managed portfolios directly undermines the effectiveness of active-management, the American Stock Exchange hopes "to create actively managed ETFs where the holdings are not disclosed," using a process "on which patents are pending."[4] Once active managers join the ETF ranks, investors face a more difficult task in separating the well-constructed, low-cost wheat from the poorly structured, high-cost chaff.

Signs abound that change threatens the heretofore generally attractive characteristics of the ETF market. High-class managers like Barclays and State Street hear the siren song of excessive fees. Low-quality players like Rydex and PowerShares, supported by the Bank of New York, see shareholders as sheep ready for shearing. Even though today the overwhelming majority of ETF assets reside in sensibly structured, fairly priced vehicles, the industry's future may increasingly resemble the traditional mutual-fund industry, where poorly conceived, high-cost products predominate.

CHAPTER SUMMARY

ETFs provide a promising alternative for investors with the assets, the time, and the inclination to take a hands-on approach to portfolio management. By accepting the costs of wrestling with the never-ending principal-agent conflict inherent in any brokerage relationship, investors earn the opportunity to invest in a range of low-cost, high-quality, tax-efficient products.

The ETF market makes no sense for investors who deal with modest pools of capital or who make small incremental trades. The toll exacted by Wall Street for executing trades proves too burdensome for the small investor to overcome.

At this relatively early stage of development, the overwhelming portion of the market value of ETFs (albeit decidedly not the overwhelming number of ETFs) provides exposure to reasonably priced, well-structured, core-asset-class vehicles. The primary reason for the investor-friendly character of the ETF market stems from the institutional index fund management roots of the market's two largest investment firms—Barclays Global Investors and State Street Global Advisors. By managing and pricing ETF products in a manner similar to their core institutional offerings, Barclays and State Street allow retail investors the rare opportunity to purchase high-quality investment services at reasonable prices.

The current state of the ETF market stands in sharp contrast to the sorry shape of the traditional mutual-fund industry, in which the larger numbers of investment firms pursue excessive profit at the expense of serving individual investor interests. Unfortunately, the ETF market appears to be moving down the same investor-hostile path previously trod by the mutual-fund industry. The class acts of the ETF industry cheapen their image by introducing superfluous products for which they impose unjustifiable charges. The bit performers confirm their mediocrity by offering second-rate products for which they assess ludicrous fees. As the ETF market matures, investors face an increasingly unappealing set of alternatives.

AFTERWORD

12
Failure of For-Profit Mutual Funds

Overwhelming evidence proves the failure of the for-profit mutual-fund industry. When the fiduciary responsibility to produce high risk-adjusted returns for investors inevitably comes into conflict with the profit motivation to provide substantial revenues for funds management companies, investor returns lose and company profits win.

Mutual-fund investors consistently fail to achieve investment objectives, because the balance of power in the investment management world skews dramatically in favor of the profit-seeking investment manager. When a sophisticated provider of financial services stands toe to toe with a naïve consumer, the all-too-predictable conclusion resembles the results of a fight between a heavyweight champion and a ninety-eight-pound weakling. The individual investor loses in a first-round knockout.

Investors increase the odds for success by avoiding purely profit-motivated firms and engaging organizations that reduce or eliminate the conflict between seekers of profit and seekers of return. Not-for-profit organizational structures allow investment management companies to focus solely on fulfilling fiduciary responsibilities. Moreover, in the not-for-profit world, the absence of profit margins leads to lower costs for mutual-fund shareholders. On the battlefield of the investment management world, not-for-profit investment managers provide safe passage.

Important subcategories exist within the world of for-profit mutual-fund management, based on the character and quality of ownership. One significant distinction concerns public versus private
ownership. Public entities generally hew slavishly to the search for
profits, while private concerns sometimes promote secondarily the
furtherance of investor interests. Another meaningful distinction can
be drawn between independent management companies and corporate subsidiaries, usually of financial services organizations. While
both independent firms and corporate subsidiaries seek profits, investment management firms that serve a higher corporate authority face a
far wider range of conflicts than firms that concentrate solely on investment management.

Regulations promulgated and enforced by the SEC fail to protect
investor interests. The chronically understaffed and constantly over-
burdened market cop invariably plays a game of catch-up. At the
agency's best, it responds to a high-profile problem, fashions a solution, addresses industry concerns, and implements a watered-down
reform. Meanwhile, industry participants find a way to continue the
targeted practice, carefully avoiding running afoul of the new, albeit
ineffective, regulations. At the agency's worst, it creates a safe harbor
for investor-unfriendly activities. The SEC cannot keep pace with the
superior resources of the mutual-fund industry.

Disclosures mandated by the SEC fail to protect investor interests.
With an institutional culture based on belief in the efficacy of free-
market forces, disclosure represents the regulatory authority's first
(and often last) line of defense against bad mutual-fund industry practices. Disclosure provides no help. In the first instance, few investors
read disclosure documents. In the second instance, even if investors
carefully read the hundreds of pages contained in the readily available
offering prospectus, the not so easily obtained statement of additional
information, and the readily available annual report, few investors
know what to do with the information. Unfortunately for investors,
the SEC aids and abets fund managers in continuing poor practices by
simply requiring the largely unread disclosure, leaving the hapless
(but ostensibly well-informed) investor to twist in the wind.

The only reasonable course for individuals lies in avoiding for-
profit investment management firms and turning away from the siren
song of active-management. After eliminating assets managed by

profit-seeking firms and assets managed with market-beating aspirations, very little remains of today's mutual-fund industry. Overwhelmingly, mutual funds extract enormous sums from investors in exchange for providing a shocking disservice.

FOR-PROFIT VERSUS NOT-FOR-PROFIT STRUCTURES

Nearly insurmountable hurdles confront investors hoping to identify an actively managed mutual fund destined to provide risk-adjusted excess performance. Some obstacles stem from flaws in the ability and character of portfolio managers. Other challenges arise from the conflict between investor aspirations and corporate goals. At every turn of the road, investors face the daunting prospect of making difficult assessments with inadequate information.

Investors face a simpler task in selecting fund management companies with organizational structures likely to serve investor interests. When examining a for-profit investment manager, careful investors consider the behavior of fund managers, assess the publicly disclosed fee schedules, and worry about the hidden charges and kickbacks that reduce investment returns. The savvy mutual-fund investor recognizes the inherent conflict between the profit motive and fiduciary responsibility. In the case of fund management companies organized on a not-for-profit basis, no conflict exists between serving investor goals and generating corporate income. When evaluating a not-for-profit investment manager, investors begin with the comfort of knowing that they sit on the same side of the table as the fund management company. While for-profit fund managers suffer the cognitive dissonance created by divergent goals, not-for-profit fund managers enjoy single-minded focus on discharging fiduciary responsibilities.

When the quest for profits disappears, abuse of investors dissipates. Excessive management fees abate, Rule 12b-1 fees vanish, portfolio turnover declines, and asset gathering stops. Not-for-profit fund management companies avoid product-placement fees, counter market-timing traders, and avoid soft-dollar usage. Alignment of interests between not-for-profit firms and their investors handily beats the disconnect between for-profit firms and their victims.

From a mutual-fund shareholder's perspective, not-for-profit organizations provide a clear-cut financial advantage: for-profit fund management companies charge more than not-for-profit companies for otherwise identical services. Simple arithmetic dictates that generation of profits requires charging fees above the basic costs of providing investment services. The portion of the fee attributable to the fund company's profit margin inures to the benefit of the fund shareholder in the not-for-profit world.

Few significant not-for-profit mutual-fund management companies exist. A check of the top-ten-by-assets fund companies, listed in Table 12.1 as measured at year-end 2003, shows four insurance company subsidiaries, three publicly traded companies, two privately held for-profit corporations, and one not-for-profit entity. The range of ownership structures influences in important fashion the character and quality of investor outcomes.

The publicly traded companies and subsidiaries of financial services concerns pose the greatest threat to investor interests. Shareholders of publicly traded companies demand profits. Corporate parents of money management concerns require contributions to the bottom line. Unfortunately, in case after case after case, the quest for profits drives managers from the obviously acceptable to the debatably legal to the overtly unethical to the demonstrably illegal. A wide chasm separates the interests of mutual-fund shareholders and for-profit entities that serve public corporate parents.

Private for-profit entities encounter a potentially less powerful conflict with their mutual-fund clients. While profits remain the lifeblood of public and private companies alike, top executives of publicly traded concerns see little alternative to single-minded focus on producing net income to satisfy the requirements of a diffuse, dispersed body of shareholders. In contrast, leaders of private entities with a concentrated ownership base enjoy the option of placing greater value on nonmonetary considerations. Some evidence exists that private mutual-fund companies choose greater fidelity to client interests over complete obeisance to the bottom line. For instance, during the early days of the 2003 mutual-fund scandal, the *Wall Street Journal* observed that the three largest fund families, all privately held, exhibited relatively little bad behavior, gaining market share relative to the seven purely profit-motivated firms that followed in the top ten.[1] Yet, in spite of the possibility of better investor outcomes, ultimately for-profit entities—whether public or private—seek

Table 12.1 Ownership of Fund-Management Companies Spans a Broad Spectrum

Fund Manager	Assets at December 31, 2003 (Billions of Dollars)	Parent	Corporate Status
Fidelity	616		Private
Vanguard	615		Not-for-profit
Capital Group	457		Private
Franklin Templeton	191		Public
Pimco	143	Allianz and IAP Life	Subsidiary
Putnam	143	Marsh & McLennan	Subsidiary
T. Rowe Price	118		Public
Janus	96		Public
Oppenheimer	89	Mass Mutual	Subsidiary
MFS	80	Sun Life Financial	Subsidiary

Source: Morningstar.
Note: Excludes money-market assets.

profits. Inevitably, fund-management company profits reduce fund shareholder returns.

Vanguard and TIAA-CREF

Fortunately for investors, two substantial funds management organizations operate on a not-for-profit basis, fostering corporate cultures designed to serve investor interests. Vanguard, with $615 billion of long-term assets under management as of December 31, 2003, and TIAA-CREF*, with $272 billion, adhere to a higher set of fiduciary standards, allowing the companies to place individual investor interests front and center in the funds management process.[2] By emphasizing high-quality delivery of low-cost investment products, Vanguard and TIAA-CREF provide individual investors with valuable tools for the portfolio construction process.

Vanguard's corporate structure, characterized as "unique" by chairman and chief executive officer John Brennan, gives the firm an extraordinary edge in serving investor interests. Because the Vanguard

---

*David Swensen serves as a trustee of TIAA.

Group seeks no profit, "the funds obtain at cost virtually all of their corporate management, administrative, and distribution services." In addition, Vanguard's internally managed index funds receive investment advisory services on an "at-cost basis from an experienced investment management staff employed directly by Vanguard."[3] Vanguard's low costs and impressive economies of scale accrue solely to the account of the firm's shareholders.

Beyond the cost advantages stemming from Vanguard's not-for-profit status, investors enjoy a strong coincidence of interests with the firm's management. In the 2002 annual report for the Vanguard 500 Index Fund, Brennan noted that Vanguard's corporate structure "ensures that our interests are aligned with yours. We have no other constituency to serve."[4] Before the mutual-fund scandal prompted other fund-management company executives to utter empty platitudes, often in response to their own scandalous behavior, Brennan highlighted his requirement that employees "meet the highest standards of ethical behavior and fiduciary responsibility." Brennan's words ring true, in no small part because his colleagues feel no countervailing pressure to produce profits.

The Teachers Insurance Annuity Association and the College Retirement Equities Fund, better known as TIAA and CREF, operate on a not-for-profit basis, placing client interests at the top of the list of firm priorities. Because the bulk of TIAA-CREF's assets take the form of variable annuities, the firm fails to make the top-ten list of mutual-fund managers. Yet, the investment management company ranks as

**Table 12.2 Not-for-Profits Play an Important Role
in the Defined-Contribution Market**

Fund Manager	Assets as of December 31, 2003 (Billions of Dollars)	Corporate Status
Fidelity	360	Private
TIAA-CREF	291	Not-for-profit
Vanguard	180	Not-for-profit
State Street	160	Public
Capital Group	135	Private

Source: "Top Defined Contribution Managers," Pensions & Investments 32, no. 16 (2004): 20.

one of most important providers of defined-contribution services to individuals. Following only Fidelity, as shown in Table 12.2, TIAA-CREF surpasses industry giants Vanguard and Capital Group in managing individually directed retirement accounts.

The roots of TIAA-CREF date to 1918, when the Carnegie Foundation established TIAA to improve retirement income for college and university professors, many of whom in earlier decades left the academy for lives of genteel poverty. In its early years, TIAA provided a conventionally conservative investment vehicle for its participants, with assets invested predominantly in government and railroad bonds.[5]

Andrew Carnegie's brainchild boasts an impressive history of innovation. Recognizing that the post–World War II inflation eroded the returns of nominally denominated fixed-income assets, in 1952 TIAA started CREF, then the world's first variable annuity and today one of the world's largest pools of equity assets. In the 1970s, CREF became "one of the first companies to use an extensive portfolio of international stocks."[6] More recently, the firm added an extremely unusual real estate vehicle that provides retail investors direct access to a well-managed, institutional-quality portfolio of properties. Throughout its history, TIAA-CREF has exhibited a single-minded focus on serving the interests of the firm's participants.

Herb Allison, chief executive officer of TIAA and CREF, articulated the firms' enduring values, noting "TIAA-CREF is a special company. We have been very careful to distinguish between the aspects of our company's products and services that must continually change so that we can better serve our participants and the qualities of our company that must never change. We will remain committed to the values that have always set TIAA-CREF apart—objectivity, low-pricing, high-quality products, sound investment management, and noncommissioned consultants. And in these times of concern over corporate scandals, we will remain committed to the highest standards of integrity."[7]

TIAA-CREF's overly active approach to investing its participants' funds sometimes falls short of success, as measured by the generation of risk-adjusted excess returns. But the firm's laser-like focus on creating low-cost, high-quality investment products increases the odds that clients will win in a very competitive, extremely tough game.

Financial Services Firm Subsidiaries

At the opposite end of the spectrum from the not-for-profit investment managers stand the money management subsidiaries of diversified financial services firms. In addition to the standard list of conflicts inherent in for-profit money management, mutual funds managed in the context of a larger financial services enterprise expose individual investors to a range of additional perils. Material amounts of mutual-fund assets reside in mutual funds managed by diversified financial services firms. As outlined in Table 12.3, Citigroup, Morgan Stanley, and Merrill Lynch supervise the largest amounts of conflict-ridden assets. Yet the asset base of affiliated funds pales in comparison to independent giants such as Fidelity, Vanguard, and Capital Group. Top-five affiliated-fund assets total $234 billion, compared to top-five independent-fund assets of $2 trillion.

**Table 12.3 Mutual-Fund Assets Under Management
at Diversified Financial Services Firms**

Fund Manager	Assets as of December 31, 2003 (Billions of Dollars)
Citigroup	66
Morgan Stanley	64
Merrill Lynch	58
Goldman Sachs	25
J. P. Morgan	21

Source: Morningstar.
Note: Excludes money-market assets.

Consider the possibilities for abuse of mutual-fund assets in the cause of promoting the interests of the diversified financial services corporate parent. The parent company may engage in underwriting securities offerings for clients. If the offering proves difficult to distribute, perhaps the mutual-fund subsidiary could acquire shares to contribute to the success of the offering. Underwriting clients care about after-market performance. If shares perform poorly after the offering, perhaps the mutual-fund subsidiary could acquire a position in the client company to boost the share price. A corporate client of the parent company may need proxy votes to succeed in a contested takeover or to prevail in more mundane corporate governance measures. Perhaps shares held by the mutual-fund subsidiary could vote in a manner designed to satisfy the parent firm's client.*

Conflicts inevitably develop when one arm of the firm wishes to make hard-nosed, fact-based decisions about investments and another arm of the firm wishes to engage in obsequious pandering to clients. Serious investment operations do not belong under the umbrella of multiline financial services organizations.

Problems with divided loyalties date to the earliest years of the mutual-fund industry. Paul Cabot, founder of State Street Investment Corporation and treasurer of Harvard, wrote a hard-hitting article entitled "The Investment Trusts" carried in the March 1929 issue of *The Atlantic Monthly*. Cabot identified "two common abuses to which the investment trust is now being put. First, that of being run for ulterior motives and not primarily for the best interests of the shareholders; second, that of being used as a depository for securities that might otherwise be unmarketable." Cabot went on to note the dangers in the "practice by which a house of issue sells a part of its own underwriting to its own trust," a "temptation" to which "trusts run by banks and brokers are particularly subject . . ."[8]

Cabot testified before a committee of the New York Stock Exchange that abuses in the investment trust arena stemmed from "(1) dishonesty; (2) inattention and inability; (3) greed." In spite of Cabot's clear articulation of widespread problems with investment trusts and impressive evidence to support his allegations, he provided (perhaps

---

*Conflicts of interest between money management activities and other business lines of financial services arise even in the apparently mundane function of voting corporate proxies. According to an August 19, 2003, SEC News Release, on March 15, 2002, the Deutsche Asset Management subsidiary of Deutsche Bank "cast all 17 million proxies on [Hewlett Packard Company] stock it controlled (on behalf of its clients)" against a proposed merger with Compaq Computer. Following entreaties from Hewlett Packard management, funneled through Deutsche Bank's investment banking division, Hewlett Packard management received an opportunity "to make a last-minute presentation to the [Deutsche Asset Management] proxy committee." With knowledge that Hewlett Packard "had an enormous banking relationship with Deutsche Bank," the proxy committee "held a re-vote, and changed its vote in favor of the merger." The SEC fined Deutsche Bank $750,000, not for violating its fiduciary duty in changing its vote, but for failing to disclose the conflict of interest.

even pioneered) the industry's favored solution of "publicity and education." Cabot explicitly stated that all "remedial legislation . . . can do is hamper able management and fail to protect the public."[9]

Cabot's powerful statement regarding investment trust abuse (and not his powerless suggestion about appropriate policy responses) infused SEC commissioner Robert Healy's Congressional testimony regarding the adoption of the Investment Company Act of 1940. To a litany of extensive quotations from Cabot's article, Healy added an evocative reference to investment trusts as "dumping grounds."[10] Ultimately, the Investment Company Act of 1940 prohibited investment companies from purchasing securities subject to an underwriting by an affiliate of an investment company. In a direct if narrow response to widespread well-documented abuse, the 1940 Act addressed a clear conflict of interest.

As time passed and memories faded, the mutual-fund industry lobbied to relax the prohibition on purchasing shares in an offering of securities managed by an affiliate. In 1958, the SEC adopted a rule that allowed investment companies to purchase up to 3 percent of the value of an affiliate's underwriting. By 1979, as more time passed and more memories faded, the SEC increased the limit to 4 percent of the offering. Finally, in 1997, the SEC allowed purchase of up to 25 percent of an offering, responding to "concerns that the dramatic growth in the fund industry, combined with increasing concentration in the underwriting industry, and increasing business affiliations between funds and underwriters, had made the percentage limit too restrictive."[11] Clearly, the SEC responded to concerns of the mutual-fund industry, not to the needs of the investing public.

A description of today's financial services firm-affiliated mutual-fund activities echoes mutual-fund abuses of the 1920s and 1930s. "Funds are used as dumping grounds," according to Mercer Bullard, a former SEC division of investment management official. Says Edward Siedle, former SEC attorney, "You want to show that you are not only able to sell the deal, but you're able to put away the product. The more you can do that, the more your clients are going to be attracted to you." While inadequate granularity of disclosure prevents reaching rock-solid conclusions about financial services firms' conflicts, a *Bloomberg News* study of 108,000 SEC records concluded that investment-bank-affiliated funds owned a "a disproportionate number of shares in companies that were clients."[12] The temptation of the mutual-fund subsidiary's cookie jar proves too great for the parent company to resist.

The history of limitations on mutual-fund purchases of securities in underwritten offerings by affiliates illustrates in high relief the problems with regulatory response to investment company abuses. First, the scope of the rule proves insufficient to deal with the breadth of the problem. The 1940 Act and the SEC deal only with purchases of shares in an underwritten offering, viz., the primary market for securities. Significant potential exists for multiline financial service companies to use the secondary market to promote client interests at the expense of mutual-fund shareholders. Second, the rule retains effectiveness only as long as the issue maintains sufficiently high profile with the public and the regulatory authorities. If the issue poses complexities beyond the comprehension of the public, regulators tend to ignore the problem. If the issue becomes stale, regulators lose interest and allow industry advocates to gain the upper hand. In the final analysis, regulatory authorities oversee preordained industry victories won at the public's expense.

High-Cost Index Fund Management

The active-management cost advantage created by employing a not-for-profit investment manager instead of a for-profit firm proves difficult to measure. In the active-management arena, the pricing edge enjoyed by not-for-profit investment managers stands obscured by the lack of an apples-to-apples comparison. The range of fees levied depends on the nature of the investment strategy, the quality of the portfolio manager, the historical record of performance, the size of assets under management, and other idiosyncratic factors. For-profit fund managers might use any of a number of rationales to justify fee differentials, however ridiculous they might be.

The picture changes completely when considering index-fund-management. Index funds involve passive replication of market characteristics, representing the fund-management world's version of a pure commodity. The execution of index-fund management requires no particular strategy, depends on no specially trained personnel, and produces no newsworthy track record. After funds under management reach an appropriate scale, size ceases to matter. In contrast to the world of active management, passive management produces a simple story.

Economic theory teaches the law of one price, viz., that in freely competitive markets identical goods or services trade at identical prices. In the case of index-fund management, the portfolio management fees charged by various service providers should be identical, or nearly so. Otherwise, rational consumers transfer funds from high-cost providers to low-cost providers, thereby driving the greedy (or inefficient) fund-management companies to reduce prices or exit the business.

Economic theory fails. In a 2002 study, Morningstar identified fifty-seven S&P 500 index funds that charged more than Vanguard's market-leading 0.18 percent annual fee.[13] The average yearly expense ratio of the non-Vanguard index managers amounted to an over-the-top 0.82 percent. Fully twenty companies charged more than 1.2 percent, with one company hitting investors with an unconscionable 2.18 percent. Assets under management in the high-cost funds totaled more than $57 billion, representing far more than chump change.

Had the expensive index funds emanated from a disreputable bunch of bucket shops, investors might conclude that the poor saps who chose the high-cost funds deserved the consequences of paying active-management fees for less than passive-management results. In fact, the roster of high-fee index fund managers includes two of the investment management world's most venerable names—Morgan Stanley Funds and Scudder Investments.

A close look at the Morgan Stanley S&P 500 Index Fund reveals an ugly picture. The firm offers three classes of shares on a stand-alone basis. Class A shares come with the insult of a front-end load, amounting to as much as 5.25 percent of the investment. Class B shares and Class C shares manifest the indignity of a less visible contingent deferred sales charge. All classes of shares come with ridiculously high year-in and year-out expenses.[14]

The Morgan Stanley S&P 500 Index Fund charges "management fees and other expenses" of 0.50 percent per year.[15] In contrast, Vanguard's annual expenses total 0.18 percent for ordinary Investor Shares and 0.12 percent for Admiral Shares, available to "many long-time shareholders and those with significant investments."[16] Morgan

Stanley charges "distribution and service [12b-1] fees" of 0.23 percent for Class A shares and 1.00 percent for Class B and Class C shares.[17] Vanguard charges no such fees.

Table 12.4 Index-Fund Fees Vary Dramatically

Expenses for a $10,000 Investment Producing a 5% Annual Return

	Holding Period			
	1 Year	3 Years	5 Years	10 Years
Vanguard Investor Shares	$18	$58	$101	$230
Vanguard Admiral Shares	12	39	68	154
Morgan Stanley Class A Shares	596	746	910	1,384
Morgan Stanley Class B Shares	653	774	1,018	1,791
Morgan Stanley Class C Shares	252	471	813	1,779

Sources: Vanguard; Morgan Stanley.

The expenses add up. Short holding periods damage Morgan Stanley clients, as up-front or contingent sales charges eviscerate returns. As shown in Table 12.4, one-year holders of Vanguard's Investor Shares pay $18 for a hypothetical $10,000 account, while owners of Morgan Stanley's Class B shares pay $653 for the same service. For ten-year periods, as the brokerage firm's up-front sales charges spread over a number of years and contingent sales charges burn off, the relative difference diminishes while the absolute dollar difference grows. The standard Vanguard account holder pays $230 over ten years. In contrast, the owner of Morgan Stanley's B shares pays $1,791.

Investors who qualify for Vanguard's super-low-cost Admiral Shares fare even better. A five-year holding period costs Vanguard's preferred shareholders only $68, amounting to less than 10 percent of the charge imposed by each of the Morgan Stanley share classes. In well-executed index-fund management, low costs create a clearly defined edge for investors.

Morgan Stanley S&P 500 Index Fund investors fare poorly even when ignoring the impact of sales charges. Table 12.5 tells the discouraging tale. For the five years ending December 31, 2003, Class A shares returned –1.28 percent per year, providing a sizable performance margin over Class B share returns of –2.04 percent per year and Class C share returns of –2.03 percent. Class A shares show better than

**Table 12.5 Even Without the Impact of Sales Charges
Morgan Stanley Fails to Perform**
Total Return for Periods Ending December 31, 2003 (Percent)

	One Year	Five Years
Morgan Stanley Class A Shares	27.82	−1.28
Morgan Stanley Class B Shares	26.84	−2.04
Morgan Stanley Class C Shares	26.91	−2.03
Vanguard Investor Shares	28.50	−0.63
S&P 500 Index	28.67	−0.54
Lipper S&P 500 Funds Index	28.25	−0.88

Sources: Morningstar; Vanguard; Lipper Inc.

Class B and Class C, because the reported results ignore the impact of Class A's front-end load.

Morgan Stanley's indefensible fee structure causes the firm's S&P 500 Index Funds to fall far short of the index return. Over the five-year period, Class A shares posted an annual deficit of 0.74 percent relative to shortfalls of 1.50 percent for Class B shares and 1.49 percent for Class C shares. In contrast, Vanguard's cost-efficient, shareholder-friendly management provided investors with a return of only 0.09 percent less than the index result.

Comparing Morgan Stanley's S&P 500 Index Fund results to other index-fund returns only adds to the firm's shame. Consider the equal-weighted index of thirty leading index funds constructed by mutual-fund data provider Lipper, a Reuters company. By virtue of size, Morgan Stanley Class B shares, the poorest performing of the firm's three share classes, earn a spot on the roster of Lipper's index-fund team. With five-year results that fall 1.16 percent per year short of Lipper's average, Morgan Stanley Class B shares reside decidedly in the fourth quartile. The smaller Class A and Class C shares fail to make the Lipper size cut. However, with results falling 0.40 percent below the mean for Class A shares and 1.15 percent below the mean for Class C shares, had the two classes been included in the Lipper group, they too would have placed in the fourth quartile. In sharp contrast, Vanguard set the standard for the Lipper group, beating the average by 0.25 percent per year and generating returns that no other index manager came close to matching.[18]

Part of Morgan Stanley's index-fund shortfall stems from the inferior nature of the product. The October 30, 2002, Morgan Stanley S&P 500 Index Fund prospectus noted that "the Fund's portfolio is managed by the Core Growth Team."[19] In spite of paying ridiculous fees, for the first six years of the fund's existence, Morgan Stanley clients failed to get a dedicated index-fund management team. In an optimistic development, the September 30, 2003, supplement to the prospectus announced that "the Fund is managed within the Index Team," mitigating one of the many indignities inflicted on Morgan Stanley Index Fund shareholders.[20] Of course, a green index team at Morgan Stanley managing a subscale portfolio poses no competition to the time-tested index-fund managers at Vanguard.

Suppose a client wishes to invest in Morgan Stanley's index funds, in spite of the long list of reasons to avoid the firm's offerings. Investors choosing among Morgan Stanley's Class A, Class B, and Class C shares face a bewildering set of pay-now, pay-later, or pay-now-and-pay-later alternatives. As an example of the complexity, the critical difference between Class B and Class C shares rests on a conversion feature available to Class B shares—but not Class C shares—ten years "from the last day of the month in which the shares were purchased."[21] Evidently, the complexity kerfuffled both Morgan Stanley financial advisors and their clients. In November 2003, the firm paid $50 million in restitution for inappropriate sales practices, including failing to place investors in the appropriate share classes and neglecting to inform investors of special sales incentives.[22]

The SEC allowed Morgan Stanley to employ the usual Wall Street doublespeak, making amends without "admitting or denying wrongdoing." Part of the wrongdoing that Morgan Stanley neither admitted nor denied involved the high proportion of Class B Fund shares sold by Morgan Stanley's brokers. Not surprisingly, because Class B shares carry higher annual fees, they tend to represent the most expensive alternative for investors. In fact, the Morgan Stanley S&P 500 Index Fund prospectus reveals that Class B shares cost more for each holding period presented in the disclosure document—one, three, five, and ten years. In a masterly understatement, the *Wall Street Journal* noted that "Morgan Stanley brokers could end up earning more by putting clients in B shares." In a further observation, damning to both broker and client, the paper noted that some investors did not know that they purchased B shares "until they saw their confirmations or monthly account statements."[23]

Another part of Morgan Stanley's $50 million spat with the SEC concerned the favored status accorded to Morgan Stanley's own funds. The firm paid its brokers higher commissions for sales of home-made products without informing customers of the practice. SEC enforcement division director Stephen Cutler noted: "Few things are more important to investors than receiving unbiased advice from their investment professionals or knowing that what they're getting may not be unbiased. In plain and simple terms, Morgan Stanley's customers were not informed of the extent to which Morgan Stanley was motivated to sell them a particular fund."[24] The Morgan Stanley brokers who pushed the firm's S&P 500 Index Fund took their clients for an expensive ride.

The November 2003 $50 million SEC restitution followed close on the heels of a September 2003 $2 million National Association of Securities Dealers fine. According to the NASD, Morgan Stanley brokers participated in "prohibited sales contests" designed to "promote the sale of Morgan Stanley mutual funds." The press release announcing the censure and fine stated that "between October 1999 and December 2002, the firm conducted 29 contests, [offering] tickets to Britney Spears and Rolling Stones concerts, tickets to the NBA finals, tuition for a high-performance automobile racing school, and trips to resorts." Evidently, Morgan Stanley conducted the contests with a guilty corporate conscience, attempting "to shield this focus on sales of its own mutual funds from the public as much as possible to avoid public relations ramifications." In accepting the fine and censure, Morgan Stanley neither admitted nor denied the charge.[25]

As demonstrated by the case of Morgan Stanley's obscenely priced index funds, profit-seeking mutual-fund companies sometimes abuse investor interests. The question arises as to what market failure causes for-profit mutual funds to disserve their customers. The core of the problem lies in pitting a large, sophisticated financial services company against a lone, uninformed investor. The outcome proves easy to predict. Profits win. Investors lose.

Mutual-fund directors provide no help to the retail investor. Shareholder-oriented directors could negotiate fair, competitive fees for index-fund management. Directors could stop the abuse of charging 12b-1 fees. Directors could exercise the power to assign the contract for managing index-fund assets to a lower-cost provider of higher-quality service, say Vanguard. Instead, a financial-services-firm-oriented board, populated by Morgan Stanley employees and their cronies, actively approves sweetheart contracts that allow Morgan Stanley to profit unreasonably at the expense of the firm's naïve customers. Thievery, even when dressed in the cloak of SEC-approved governance, remains thievery.

In the case of actively managed portfolios, mutual-fund directors enjoy the opportunity to rationalize above-market fees, employing the generally false hope that luck or skill might produce market-beating returns. The world of index-fund management permits no such rationalization. The directors of Morgan Stanley's S&P 500 Index Fund know that shareholder returns inevitably will fall short of the competition as the cumulative effects of unreasonable loads, 12b-1 charges, and excessive management fees take their toll. Profits dominate fiduciary responsibility.

In the world of institutional fund management, buyers and sellers of investment management services deal on reasonably even terms. Buy-side professional staff examine sell-side money managers carefully, performing extensive due diligence and negotiating mutually acceptable contractual terms. Regardless of the ultimate outcome, at least the institutional asset manager signs up for a fair fight.

In the case of the individual investor, the government attempts to remedy the asymmetry in position through legislation and regulation. Unfortunately, the money management industry's heavyweight champion proves too much for the government's Joe Palooka. When the government recognizes money management abuses, the legislative and regulatory apparatus responds slowly and inefficiently. By the time that a set of rules addresses a known abuse, the industry takes the punch and mounts an effective counterattack, finding new means to win the fight. Neither government intervention nor individual initiative prevails against mutual-fund company greed.

LEGISLATIVE AND REGULATORY ACTIVITY

Public awareness of intolerable levels of investor abuse by mutual-fund companies ultimately leads to public outcry, with predictable demands for reform and restitution. The SEC and Congress, as the main players in the regulatory framework, use the tools of regulation and legislation to influence mutual-fund behavior. Unfortunately for investors, regulatory reform rarely proves effective. In most cases, regulators miss a host of complex, off-the-radar-screen problems, and address only the most basic, well-publicized issues. Invariably, authorities react after the fact of the scandal. When regulators confront mutual-fund chicanery, the mutual-fund industry consistently identifies variations on a prohibited-profit-producing scheme, neutering regulatory efforts to control bad behavior. Finally, the oversight process occasionally produces perverse rules and regulations that provide new mechanisms or safe harbors for mutual-fund management companies to employ in their quest to fill the corporate coffers.

Disclosure represents a favored response to the never-ending stream of issues that arise in the management of mutual-fund assets. In fact, the SEC website notes that "the laws and rules that govern the securities industry in the United States derive from a simple and straightforward concept: all investors, whether large institutions or private individuals, should have access to certain basic facts about an investment prior to buying it."[26] While disclosure benefits large institutions with the resources to understand and act on the information, it provides little help to individuals. Mutual-fund managers simply comply with the letter (if not the spirit) of disclosure requirements. Individual investors ignore the information. Abuses continue apace.

Regulations

Investors face recurring problems with the focus and scope of regulatory action. The SEC and the Congress prefer to deal with simple-to-understand and high-profile issues, leaving the more-complicated and out-of-the-limelight abuses to impair investor interests. The issues of late trading and soft dollars in the fund scandal of 2003 illustrate the tendency of regulators to confront the comprehensible and ignore the complex. Late trading—an easily observed, clearly illegal activity—received enormous amounts of regulatory scrutiny. Late trading achieved prominence from the explicit identification of individual culprits, allowing regulators and news organizations to participate in a public spectacle. In contrast, soft dollars—a well-hidden, pervasive drain on investor returns—garnered far less attention. Even though regulators have recognized for decades the inherent conflicts in soft-dollar usage, the Congress and the SEC pay scant attention to the media-unfriendly topic. As a result, mutual-fund companies continue to exploit complex, less readily observed tools to transfer wealth from investors to the fund company bottom line.

Even in those cases where the regulatory authorities confront important abuses directly, the mutual-fund industry counters by finding new methods to thwart investor interests. In the case of stale pricing, dealers in the 1920s and 1930s employed the absurdly venal "two-price" system. Stopped from trading at tomorrow's price today by the Investment Company Act of 1940, the mutual-fund industry employed "backward pricing" in the 1940s, 1950s, and 1960s to trade at yesterday's price today. After the SEC's 1968 prohibition of "backward pricing," mutual-fund management companies profited from stale pricing on a variety of fund types, most notably those holding less-liquid and foreign securities. Throughout the eight decades of the mutual-fund industry, regulators recognized the importance of fair prices and knew the mechanisms needed to produce fair prices. An unfortunate combination of industry pressure and regulatory incompetence allowed the mutual-fund industry to stay several steps ahead of the regulator's restraints.

Aside from the problem of the regulatory stimulus producing a countervailing mutual-fund response, a further issue involves perverse legislative or regulatory actions that damage the position of mutual-fund investors. The use of inflated commissions to create kickbacks for fund companies received a regulatory boost in 1975 when Congress provided legislation that allowed the SEC to define a "safe harbor" for soft-dollar usage. The imposition of marketing charges, which hurt investors directly through the fee-caused reduction in returns and indirectly by the fee-generated increase in assets, received official sanction when the SEC created Rule 12b-1 fees for the mutual-fund industry. Soft dollars and 12b-1 fees show Edward Hyde's face in the Jekyll and Hyde character of the "investor's advocate."

Perhaps in the future, legislators or regulators will get it right and eliminate stale prices, soft dollars, and 12b-1 fees. Even so, the history of the mutual-fund industry proves over and over that regulations provide temporary solutions, at best. The powerful profit motives of the mutual-fund industry and Wall Street combine to produce creative mechanisms to circumvent or to undermine investor-protection measures.

Disclosure

A favorite regulatory bromide involves disclosure of the relevant facts to the investing public. Advocates of frank, full, and ever-increasing disclosure believe that investors thoughtfully evaluate information contained in offering documents prior to making carefully considered investment decisions. Even if investors fail to read and comprehend disclosure documents, the mere requirement of disclosure might prevent fund companies from pursuing outrageous investor-unfriendly activities. Unfortunately, disclosure fails to benefit investors.

Consider the offering documents for the Vanguard U.S. Stock Index Funds. Index-fund management represents one of the investment world's most basic activities. Yet Vanguard's prospectus runs to thirty-seven pages, including the helpful "Glossary of Investment Terms," the six-page "Account Registration Form," and the horizon-expanding "Vanguard Fund and Account Option List." The Statement of Additional Information, dated April 28, 2003, runs another forty-six pages, while the 2003 Vanguard 500 Index Fund Annual Report totals thirty-four pages. Few investors take the time to slog through page after page of financial prose, even if the writing complies with the SEC's "plain English" initiative.[27]

Vanguard makes it easy to obtain the prospectus, because delivery to potential investors constitutes a legal precondition to making an investment. The offering document, available both online and in more traditional formats, provides an introduction to index funds, profiles of various index funds, a description of the investment advisor, and procedures for purchasing shares. Careful investors pay particular attention to disclosure of fund investment objectives, investment strategies, fees and expenses, and historical performance.

Yet the prospectus represents only the starting point. Buried deep in the prospectus, a thorough reader finds mention of a so-called "Statement of Additional Information" or SAI, "incorporated by reference into [and] legally a part of" the prospectus.[28] Even though the main body of the offering document resides on Vanguard's website, available for anyone with Internet access to download, obtaining the SAI requires making a special request and waiting for snail-mail delivery. No wonder Karen D'Amato of the *Wall Street Journal* dubbed the SAI "Something Always Ignored."[29] By employing the U.S. Postal Service to deliver a hard copy of the statement of additional information, with the attendant inefficiencies in production cost, delivery expense, and time lag, Vanguard impedes investors from obtaining sensitive information.

The forty-six-page Vanguard Index Funds SAI contains information about trustee conflicts of interest, ownership of shares, and compensation for services rendered. The disclosure ranges from precise, noting that trustees each receive $108,000 annually for the basic job of overseeing 112 separate Vanguard mutual funds, to vague, showing that trustees hold shares in categories of "None," "Up to $10,000," "$10,001 to $50,000," "50,001 to $100,000," and "Over $100,000." Investors interested in corporate governance learn of Vanguard chief executive officer John Brennan's status as an "Interested Trustee," as well as his shareholding—or lack thereof—in the Vanguard equity funds.[30]

Even though Vanguard generally makes interests of investors paramount, share owners may nevertheless wonder about the firm's security trading policies. Only by careful examination of page B-26 of the SAI do investors detect clues to the firm's involvement in the slimy world of soft dollars. Vanguard equivocally states that "consideration may be given to those brokers who supply statistical information and provide other services" to the funds.[31] In a lame defense of an indefensible practice, Vanguard claims that it "will use its best judgment to choose the broker most capable of providing . . . the best available price and most favorable execution."[32] Yet the utter falsity of equating pure execution with pure execution plus other services remains. Even though Vanguard stands nearly alone as a shining example of an investor-oriented organization, by hiding the soft-dollar disclosure in the SAI, the firm discourages investors from learning about an unappealing aspect of its operations.

Mutual-fund quarterly, semiannual, and annual reports comprise the third volume of the disclosure trilogy. Available on the Internet and back in the realm of the readily obtainable, Vanguard's December 31, 2003 annual report covers a range of useful portfolio information, including information on fee levels, recent performance, and general market conditions. For readers able to deal with small type fonts, the report contains a comprehensive list of security holdings.

Careful investors face the daunting task of examining 149 pages of disclosure documents prior to making a commitment to Vanguard's 500 Index Fund. Information regarding the superiority of indexing flies off the pages of readily available offering documents. More worrisome information lies out of sight, deep in the SAI, masked by less

Table 12.6 Investors Face a Paper Jungle
Mutual-Fund Disclosure Documentation (Number of Pages)

Fund Manager	Fund	Prospectus	SAI	Periodic Reports	Total
Fidelity	Magellan	22	37	40 (Annual) 28 (Semi-Annual)	127
Capital Group	AMCAP	32	70	36 (Annual)	138
Vanguard	500 Index Fund	37	46	34 (Annual) 32 (Semi-Annual)	149
AIM/Invesco	AIM Premier Equity Fund	32	113	29 (Annual) 28 (Semi-Annual)	202
Pimco	Total Return	54	143	39 (Annual)	236

Sources: Fidelity; Capital Group; Vanguard; AIM/Invesco; Pimco.
Notes: Date of Fidelity prospectus (5/28/04), SAI (5/28/04), annual report (3/31/04) and semiannual report (9/30/03).
Date of Capital Group prospectus (5/1/04), SAI (5/1/04) and annual report (2/29/04).
Date of Vanguard prospectus (4/23/04), SAI (4/28/03), annual report (12/31/03), and semiannual report (6/30/04).
Date of AIM/Invesco prospectus (4/30/04), SAI (3/3/04), annual report (12/31/03), and semiannual report (6/30/04).
Date of Pimco prospectus (7/30/04), SAI (7/30/04), and annual report (3/31/04).

than forthright prose. If the class act of the mutual-fund industry receives poor marks for some aspects of its disclosure, what grades can garden-variety mutual-fund families expect?

The most fundamental problem with disclosure concerns the individual investor's inability to wade through dozens and dozens of pages of densely worded documents. In terms of paper-consumption capacity, all top mutual-fund firms inundate investors with overwhelming amounts of material. As shown in Table 12.6, Pimco leads the cohort with a grand total of 236 pages. Fidelity, the piker of the group, registers a still impressive sum of 127 pages. Perhaps a fund manager most effectively hides embarrassing information by burying it deep in a fund's disclosure documents.

Distribution methods for the SAI call into question a number of mutual-fund companies' commitment to disclosure. Vanguard, AIM/Invesco, and Pimco forced investors to call to request the SAI and then wait to receive it via snail mail. Costly, inefficient methods of distribution speak volumes about a firm's desire to inform investors. While in the future the SEC may mandate online access to SAIs, the one-time reluctance of the mutual-fund industry to share required disclosures with investors represents a long-lasting black mark on the industry's reputation.

Disclosure falls short as a mechanism to protect investor interests. Few investors devote the time and energy necessary to benefit from the contents of disclosure documents. Even if an investor gathers and studies the relevant materials, many issues remain beyond the grasp of all but the most accomplished student of markets. Disclosure manages at the same time to be unduly voluminous and hopelessly ineffective.

CHAPTER SUMMARY

The fundamental market failure in the mutual-fund industry involves the interaction between sophisticated, profit-seeking providers of financial services and naïve, return-seeking consumers of investment products. The drive for profits by Wall Street and the mutual-fund industry overwhelms the concept of fiduciary responsibility, leading to an all too predictable outcome: except in an inconsequential number of cases where individuals succeed through unusual skill or unreliable luck, the powerful financial services industry exploits vulnerable individual investors.

The ownership structure of a fund management company plays a role in determining the likelihood of investor success. Mutual-fund investors face the greatest challenge with investment management companies that provide returns to public shareholders or that funnel profits to a corporate parent—situations that place the conflict between profit generation and fiduciary responsibility in high relief. When a funds management subsidiary reports to a multiline financial services company, the scope for abuse of investor capital broadens dramatically. In contrast, private for-profit investment management organizations enjoy the option of playing the role of a benevolent capitalist, mitigating the drive for profits with concern for investor returns. Yet investor interests take center stage only in the not-for-profit world.

Investors fare best with funds managed by not-for-profit organizations, because the management firm focuses exclusively on serving investor interests. No profit motive conflicts with the manager's fiduciary responsibility. No profit margin interferes with investor returns. No outside corporate interest clashes with portfolio management choices. Not-for-profit firms place investor interests front and center.

Fortunately for investors, two substantial funds management organizations adhere to high fiduciary standards, adopted in the context of corporate cultures designed to serve investor interests. Vanguard and TIAA-CREF both operate on a not-for-profit basis, allowing the companies to make individual investor interests paramount in the funds management process. By emphasizing high-quality delivery of low-cost investment products, Vanguard and TIAA-CREF provide individual investors with valuable tools for the portfolio construction process.

Ultimately, a passive index fund managed by a not-for-profit investment management organization represents the combination most likely to satisfy investor aspirations. Following Mies van der Rohe's famous dictum—"less is more"—the rigid calculus of index-fund investing dominates the ornate complexity of active fund management.

Pursuing investment with a firm devoted solely to satisfying investor interests unifies principal and agent, reducing the investment equation to its most basic form. Out of the enormous breadth and complexity of the mutual-fund world, the preferred solution for investors stands alone in stark simplicity.

Appendix 1
Measuring Investment
Gains and Losses

Most investors measure performance simply by examining rates of return. If the return proves adequate in absolute terms or if the return provides sufficient margin in relative terms, the investor declares victory. Simple assessment of rates of return tells the entire story in cases without intermediate cash flows, that is, in cases when all funds are committed up front.

In situations where investors make periodic cash flows, the timing of those flows influences the outcome in important ways. Yet examining the simple rate of return fails to account for the impact of the intermediate cash flows. Measurement of the dollar value of investor gains and losses proves instructive in cases where interim contributions or withdrawals alter investor exposures. By separating gains (and losses) attributable to investment performance from contributions (and withdrawals) caused by investor activity, the net investment gains (or losses) can be calculated. If investors contribute funds at low prices and withdraw funds at high prices, the analysis will show aggregate gains. Buying low and selling high works. Conversely, if investors make purchases at higher prices than sales, the analysis will show aggregate losses. Buying high and selling low hurts.

Because mutual-fund managers do not disclose information on assets under management on a daily basis, assessing the mix between investment performance and investor flows requires making assumptions regarding the timing of investor inflows and outflows. The calculation of the dollar value of technology fund losses employed annual data regarding assets under management and quarterly data regarding performance. The analysis distributed the non-performance-induced change in assets (namely, the investor inflow or outflow) throughout the quarterly periods between the known annual points. In the absence of distributing the cash flows throughout the year, as clearly occurs in the real world, too much of the annual change in assets appears to result from investment performance. By assuming that investor contributions (or withdrawals) occur quarterly, the analysis much more closely resembles reality.

Appendix 2
The Arnott, Berkin, and Ye
Study of Mutual-Fund Returns

The examination of two decades of mutual-fund performance by Robert Arnott, Andrew Berkin, and Jia Ye in *"How Well Have Taxable Investors Been Served in the 1980s and 1990s?"* published in *Journal of Portfolio Management,* Summer 2000, deserves a prominent place in investment literature because of the thoroughness and care with which the authors conducted their work. The study garners special kudos for considering tax issues and for including failed fund results. Another noteworthy aspect of the study concerns the use of an investable alternative—Vanguard's 500 Index Fund—as the standard for measuring success and failure. The use of Vanguard's passively managed account provides the advantage of employing an individual investor's real-world investment alternative, albeit with the disadvantage of not matching the mutual-fund industry's market-capitalization characteristics.

Few serious studies of mutual-fund performance address the knotty issue of after-tax returns. By gathering data on mutual-fund distributions and collecting information on historical tax rates, the authors enable the calculation of the tax impact on investment returns. The sheer magnitude of the task no doubt prevents others from pursuing similar studies. The authors leave only the mind-numbing complexity of state taxes for future study.

The Arnott team examined "all equity-oriented mutual funds with at least $100 million in assets in 1979, 1984, or 1989, including funds that subsequently disappeared." By gathering data on funds that closed their doors or merged into other funds, the authors bring a critical dose of the reality of failure to what would otherwise represent a too-rosy picture of fund performance.

Table A.1 Failure Takes Its Toll on Performance

Pre-Tax Performance Relative to Vanguard 500 Index Fund
(Percent per Annum)

Period	Shortfall including Survivorship Bias	Shortfall without Survivorship Bias	Impact of Survivorship Bias
10 years	3.1	3.5	0.5
15 Years	3.5	4.2	0.7
20 Years	1.8	2.1	0.4

Source: Arnott et. al., Journal of Portfolio Management 26, no. 4 (2000).
Notes: Totals may not add due to rounding. Data reflect periods ending December 31, 1998.

In the Arnott study, of the 195 equity-oriented mutual funds with over $100 million in assets in existence in 1979, thirty-three funds, or 17 percent of the total, disappeared during the two-decade course of the study. The remaining 162 survivors produced a 1.8 percent per year deficit relative to the results of the Vanguard 500 Index Fund. By unearthing the returns of the thirty-three funds that disappeared, Arnott and his colleagues discover that the performance deficit increases to 2.1 percent annually. Table A.1 details the impact from inclusion of the returns from the disappearing funds. Correcting for survivorship bias, the tendency of surviving mutual funds to produce better returns than disappearing mutual funds makes a material difference in reported mutual-fund results.

The use of Vanguard's 500 Index Fund allows Arnott to make an apples-to-apples comparison between passively managed and actively managed funds. Unfortunately, a capitalization-size bias related to the use of the large-capitalization Vanguard 500 Index Fund introduces a potential source of error to the study. The Vanguard 500 Index Fund mimics the returns of the S&P 500, a measure dominated by large-capitalization securities. Because mutual-fund managers choose from all available securities, not just those in the S&P 500, a broader measure of the market provides a fairer benchmark. The Wilshire 5000, a misnomer because the index actually contained 7,234 stocks as of December 31, 1998, captures nearly every publicly traded security in the United States, constituting a fairer standard for measuring active-management results.

Over the period of the Arnott study, relative performance of smaller and larger capitalization securities explains a portion of the return differential between the Vanguard 500 Index Fund and the broad group of mutual-fund managers. For the two decades ending December 31, 1998, the S&P 500 outperformed the Wilshire 5000 by 0.3 percent per annum, indicating that larger stocks earned a premium return relative to the more extensive universe of securities from which mutual funds create portfolios. As shown in Table A.2, ten-year and fifteen-year periods show even larger advantages for large-capitalization stocks.

Table A.2 Performance of the S&P 500 versus the Wilshire 5000
(Percent)

Period	S&P 500	Wilshire 5000	Difference
10 years	19.0	18.1	0.9
15 Years	17.7	16.7	1.0
20 Years	17.5	17.2	0.3

Sources: Bloomberg; Wilshire Associates.
Note: Data reflect periods ending December 31, 1998.

In those parts of the Arnott study that present returns without survivorship bias, the measured underperformance of active managers likely overstates reality by a margin approximately equal to the performance differential between the S&P 500 and the Wilshire 5000. For example, because Arnott removed survivor bias from the data in Table 7.2 and Table 7.5, the data exaggerate the size of performance shortfalls measured against a fair benchmark. In those parts of the study that calculate the odds of winning and losing along with the average margins of victory and defeat, survivorship bias enters the picture. (This part of the study excludes funds that disappear, because the authors need a full-period record to calculate the results.) Consequently, the data in Table 7.3 and Table 7.6 overstate the odds of winning, inflate the average margin of victory, and understate the average margin of defeat. A cursory examination of the numbers suggests a form of rough justice, namely that the capitalization bias (0.3 percent per year for twenty years in favor of investors) approximately offsets the survivorship bias (0.4 percent per year for twenty years against investors). Regardless of the nuances, the fact remains that long odds face the investor who hopes to beat the market.

Robert Arnott, Andrew Berkin, and Jia Ye produced a well-constructed study that adds immeasurably to understanding of mutual-fund performance. By considering tax consequences of mutual-fund active-management activity and dealing with the return inflation of survivor bias, the authors point to a powerful conclusion: sensible investors embrace passively managed index funds.

Notes

INTRODUCTION

1. John Maynard Keynes, *The General Theory of Employment, Interest and Money* (London: MacMillan and Co., 1936), 158.
2. Whitehouse.gov, "Specifics on The President's Plan to Strengthen Retirement Security," 2 February 2002.
   http://www.whitehouse.gov/news/releases/2002/02/20020228-1.html.
3. Paul A. Samuelson, "The Backward Art of Investing Money," *Institutional Investor*, October 2004: 114.

OVERVIEW

CHAPTER 1: SOURCES OF RETURN

1. Roger G. Ibbotson and Paul D. Kaplan, "Does Asset Allocation Policy Explain 40, 90, 100 Percent of Performance?" *Financial Analysts Journal* 56, no. 1 (2000): 32.
2. John Y. Cambell, Martin Lettau, Burton G. Malkiel, and Yexiao Xu, "Have Individual Stocks Become More Volatile? An Empirical Exploration of Idiosyncratic Risk," *Journal of Finance* 56, no. 1 (2001): 25.
3. Ibid., 9, 25-26.
4. James M. Poterba, "Taxation, Risk-Taking, and Household Portfolio Behavior," NBER Working Paper Series, Working Paper 8340 (National Bureau of Economic Research, 2001), 2.
5. Accf.org, "ACCF Testimony: Capital Gains Taxation and U.S. Economic Growth," 2 September 2004. http://www.accf.org/December99test.htm.
   Cbo.gov, "Effective Federal Tax Rates Under Current Law, 2001 to 2014," 2 September 2004. http://www.cbo.gov/showdoc.cfm?index=5746&sequence=1.
   Poterba, "Taxation, Risk-Taking, and Household Portfolio Behavior," NBER Working Paper Series, Working Paper 8340 (National Bureau of Economic Research, 2001), 3–4.

PART 1: ASSET ALLOCATION

CHAPTER 2: CORE ASSET CLASSES

1. Ibbotson Associates, *Stocks, Bonds, Bills, and Inflation 2004 Yearbook* (Chicago: Ibbotson Associates, 2003): 28.
2. Jeremy Siegel, *Stocks for the Long Run* (New York: McGraw Hill, 2002): 6.
3. William N. Goetzmann and Philippe Jorion, "A Century of Global Stock Markets," NBER Working Paper Series, Working Paper 5901 (National Bureau of Economic Research, 1997), 16.
4. Robert Arnott, "Dividends and the Three Dwarfs," *Financial Analysts Journal 59*, no. 2, (2003): 4.
5. James K. Glassman and Kevin A. Hassett, *Dow 36,000: The New Strategy for Profiting from the Coming Rise in the Stock Market* (New York: Random House, 1999).
6. Siegel, *Stocks for the Long Run,* 210.
7. "Jack's Booty," editorial, *Wall Street Journal,* 10 September 2002.
8. Leslie Wayne and Alex Kuczynski, "Tarnished Image Places Welch in Unlikely Company," *New York Times,* 16 September 2002.
9. David Leonhardt, "Reining In the Imperial C.E.O.," *New York Times,* 15 September 2002.
10. Stephanie Strom, "In Charity, Where does a C.E.O. End and a Company Start?" *New York Times,* 22 September 2002.
11. Ibid.
12. Gretchen Morgenson and Patrick McGeehan, "Wall St. and the Nursery School: A New York Story," *New York Times,* 14 November 2002.
13. Steve Lohr and Joel Brinkley, "Microsoft Management Tells Workers There Will Be No Breakup," *New York Times,* 26 April 2000.
14. Jathon Sapsford and Ken Brown, "J.P. Morgan Rolls Dice on Microsoft Options," *Wall Street Journal,* 9 July 2003.
15. Data from Wilshire Associates.
16. Ibbotson Associates, *2004 Yearbook,* 224, 234.
17. Carole Gould, "Better Understanding of Bonds," *New York Times,* 27 August 1995.
18. Publicdebt.treas.gov, "Treasury Calls 8-1/4 Percent Bonds of 2000–05," http://www.publicdebt.treas.gov/com/com114cl.htm.
19. Bureau of the Public Debt. Press Release of January 15, 2004: "Treasury Calls 9-1/8 Percent Bonds of 2004–09."
20. Treas.gov, "Key Initiatives," http://www.treas.gov/offices/domestic-finance/key-initiatives/t ips.html.

21. Data from the Investment Company Institute. Foreign equity category includes International Equity, Emerging Equity, and Regional Equity, but excludes Global Equity.
22. Stephen J. Brown, William N. Goetzmann, and Stephen A. Ross, "Survival," *The Journal of Finance* 50, no. 3 (1995).
23. Data from Bloomberg; LehmanLive; National Association of Real Estate Investment Trusts.
24. National Association of Real Estate Investment Trusts, "Forming and Operating a Real Estate Investment Trust," http://www.nareit.com/aboutreits/formingaREIT.cfm.
25. Green Street Advisors, "REIT Share Price Premiums to Green Street NAV Estimates," http://www.greenstreetadvisors.com/premnav.html.
26. PR Newswire, "Wells Real Estate Fund Launches New Wells REIT II Offering of Up to $7.76 Billion," 2 December 2003.
27. Financial Advisor Magazine, "Frontline News," http://financialadvisormagazine.com/articles/nov_2003_frontline.htm l.
28. Wells Investment Securities, Inc., *Prospectus for Wells Real Estate Investment Trust, Inc.,* 26 July 2002: 50.
29. Ibid., 59.
30. Ibid., 13.
31. Ibid., 21.
32. Ibid., 57.
33. Ibid., 6.
34. Ibid.
35. *Inland Western Retail Real Estate Trust, Inc.* Prospectus, 15 September 2003, 46.
36. Terry Pristin, "Commercial Real Estate; So-Called Private REIT's Are Gaining Ground, and Their Share of Critics," and *New York Times,* 4 August 2004.
37. TIAA-CREF, *College Retirement Equities Fund Prospectus, 1 May 2003: 27.*
38. The Vangard Group, *Vanguard REIT Index Fund Investor Shares Prospectus,* 25 November 2003: 3.
39. Wells Real Estate Funds, Wells STP REIT *Index Fund Prospectus,* 25 November 2003: 3.

CHAPTER 3: PORTFOLIO CONSTRUCTION

1. John Maynard Keynes, *Monetary Reform* (New York: Harcourt, Brace, 1924): 88.
2. Robert J. Shiller, *Irrational Exuberance* (Princeton: Princeton University Press, 2000): 142.

CHAPTER 4: NON-CORE ASSET CLASSES

1. Marie Nelson, "Debt Ratings," *Moody's Investors Service,* 23 July 2003.
2. "WorldCom's Credit Rating Sliced to Junk by Moody's," *Bloomberg,* 9 May 2002.
3. Sharon Ou and David T. Hamilton, "Moody's Dollar Volume-Weighted Default Rates," *Moody's Investors Service,* March 2003.
4. Data from Moody's Investors Service.
5. Data from Lehman Brothers.
6. Nelson, "Debt Ratings."
7. Ibid.
8. Aaron Lucchetti, "Bond Investors May Unlock More Information: Rule-Making Group is Expected to Require Price Reporting of Munis 15 Minutes After Trade," *Wall Street Journal,* 11 February 2004.
9. Lawrence Harris and Michael S. Piwowar, "Municipal Bond Liquidity" (13 February 2004). http://ssrn.com/abstract=503062, 6.
10. Ibid., 53. "The MSRB is currently implementing a real-time transaction reporting and dissemination system. It is scheduled to go into operation in January 2005." The benefits to individual investors remain unclear. First, individuals might face difficulty in accessing the information, particularly since the currently available day-old data seem to have found only a narrow audience. Second, dealers may find ways to thwart dissemination of the data since they continue to maintain an interest in operating a nontransparent market that allows maintenance of wide spreads.
11. Aaron Lucchetti, "Muni Bonds Can Cost More to Trade than Stocks," *Wall Street Journal,* 12 February 2004.
12. Harris and Piwowar, "Municipal Bond Liquidity," 1.
13. Andrew Bary, "Paying the Piper," *Barron's Chicopee* 74, no. 15 (1994).
14. Bary, "Paying the Piper," *Barron's Chicopee.*
15. Jeffrey M. Laderman and Gary Weiss, "The Yield Game," *Business Week,* 6 December 1993.
16. Laura Jereski, "Mortgage Derivatives Claim Victims Big and Small," *Wall Street Journal,* 20 April 1994.
17. Bary, "Paying the Piper."
18. Data from Lehman Brothers.
19. Kevin Mirabile and Rosemarie Lakeman, *Observations on the Rapid Growth of the Hedge Fund Industry* (Barclays Capital, 2004): 2.
20. Data from Cambridge Associates' proprietary online Benchmark Calculator®.
21. Ibid.
22. Estimated numbers, based on data collected by Cambridge Associates. Controlled capital is defined as current net asset value of the ag-

gregate partnerships plus aggregate undrawn capital. All data refers to the U.S. market only.

23. Randall E. Stross, *eBoys: The First Inside Account of Venture Capitalists at Work* (New York: Ballantine Publishing Group, 2000): 182.
24. Ibid., xv.
25. Estimated numbers, based on data collected by Cambridge Associates. Controlled capital is defined as current net asset value of the aggregate partnerships plus aggregate undrawn capital. All data refers to the U.S. market only.

PART 2: MARKET TIMING

CHAPTER 5: CHASING PERFORMANCE

1. Thomas E. Weber, "All Star Analysts 1999 Survey: Internet," *Wall Street Journal,* 29 June 1999.
2. David Streltfield, "Analyst With A Knack for Shaking Up Net Stocks," *Washington Post,* 2 April 2000.
3. Rabin, Murray & Frank LLP, New York: *Class Action Complaint for Violations of Federal Securities Law,* April 2003, http://securities.stanford.edu/1027/DCLK03-01/20030425_f01c_032927.pdf.pdf, 12. As Blodget articulated a $400 price target for Amazon.com shares at CIBC/Oppenheimer, Merrill Lynch's head Internet analyst Jonathan Cohen called for a $50 price level. In January 1999 Cohen left Merrill Lynch. One month later, Blodget replaced Cohen.
4. Jeanne Lee, "Net Stock Frenzy," *Fortune,* 1 February 1999.
5. Tom Lauricella, "Merrill's Web Fund to Log Off after Brief Life," *Wall Street Journal,* 4 May 2001.
6. "Merrill Internet Fund Attracts $1.1 Bln, Closes Mutual Funds," *Bloomberg,* 27 March 2000.
7. Patrick McGeehan, "Investing: Funds Watch; Trying to Energize an Internet Portfolio," *New York Times,* 5 March 2000.
8. Lauricella, "Brief Life."
9. Patrick McGeehan, "Trying to Energize an Internet Portfolio."
10. Merrill Lynch, *Prospectus for Merrill Lynch Internet Strategies Fund,* 14 March 2000. The fee example assumes an investment of $10,000 and a 5 percent annual return. Class A and Class D shares carry maximum sales charges of 5.25 percent. Class B and Class C shares carry maximum deferred sales charges of 4.0 percent and 1.0 percent, respectively. All classes of shares charge 1.0 percent management fees. Class B and Class C shares charge 1.0 percent distribution (12b-1) fees, while Class D shares charge 0.25 percent 12b-1 fees. All classes of shares charge other expenses of 0.27 percent. Merrill Lynch Inter-

net Strategies Fund investors face an unpalatable combination of outlandish up-front charges and unreasonable recurring fees.

11. Oppenheimer Funds advertisement, *Wall Street Journal,* 7 April 2003.
12. Charles Schwab advertisements, *Wall Street Journal,* 10 April 2000.
13. Ibid.
14. Ibid.
15. Charles Schwab advertisement, *Wall Street Journal,* 6 June 2003.
16. Ibid.
17. Neil Weinberg, "Holier than Whom?" *Forbes,* 23 June 2003.
18. Karen Damato, "Longleaf Leaves Schwab," *Wall Street Journal,* 2 May 2003.
19. Schwab advertisement, 6 June 2003.
20. Data from Financial Research Corporation.
21. Morningstar.com, "General FAQ,"7 November 2004. http://www.morningstar.com/Help/DataFAQ.html.
22. Ian McDonald, "Mutual-Fund Ratings Come Under Fire: Those Five-Star Funds Don't Necessarily Outperform their Lower-Ranking Peers," *Wall Street Journal,* 15 January 2003.
23. Council of Economic Advisers, *Economic Report of the President,* 102.
24. Morningstar.com, 7 November 2004.

CHAPTER 6: REBALANCING

1. John Ameriks and Stephen Zeldes, "How Do Household Portfolio Shares Vary with Age?" Working Paper (New York: TIAA-CREF Institute).
2. Martin L. Leibowitz and P. Brett Hammond, "The Changing Mosaic of Investment Patterns," *Journal of Portfolio Management* 30, no. 3 (Spring 2004).

PART 3: SECURITY SELECTION

1. Robert D. Arnott, Andrew L. Berkin, and Jia Ye, "How Well Have Taxable Investors Been Served in the 1980s and 1990s?" *Journal of Portfolio Management* 26, no. 4 (Summer 2000).

CHAPTER 7: THE PERFORMANCE DEFICIT OF MUTUAL FUNDS

1. Investment Company Institute, *2004 Mutual Fund Fact Book:* 1, 59, 105.
2. Ibid. 79–80.

3. Terry K. Glenn, Investment Company Institute, "ICI Chairman's Report at the 2001 ICI General Membership Meeting," 17 May 2001.
4. Arnott et al., "How Well Have Taxable Investors Been Served?" 85–86.
5. Alicia H. Munnell, Kevin E. Cahill, and Natalia A. Jivan. "How Has the Shift to 401(k)s Affected The Retirement Age?" *Center for Retirement Research,* no. 13, September 2003.
6. Arnott et al., "Taxable Investors," 89.
7. Investment Company Institute, *2004 Mutual Fund Fact Book,* 25.
8. Arnott et al., " Taxable Investors," 86.
9. Warren Buffett and Thomas Jaffe, "What We Can Learn from Phil Fisher: A Talk with Philip Fisher," *New York Times,* 19 April 2004.

CHAPTER 8: OBVIOUS SOURCES OF MUTUAL-FUND FAILURE

1. Mark Hulbert, "Do Funds Charge Investors for Negative Value Added?" *New York Times,* 8 July 2001.
2. Matthew Morey, "Should You Carry the Load? A Comprehensive Analysis of Load and No-Load Mutual Fund Out-of-Sample Performance," *Journal of Banking and Finance 27,* no. 7 (2003): 1245–1271.
3. Data from Lipper Inc.
4. Standard and Poor's, "S&P Research on Fees Shows Cheaper Funds Continuing to Outperform Their More Expensive Peers," Press Release, 29 June 2004.
5. Securities and Exchange Commission, Division of Investment Management, *Report on Mutual Fund Fees and Expenses* (Washington, DC.: GPO, 2000), 59–60.
6. Ibid., 15.
7. Ibid., 18.
8. Kara Scannell, "Closed, but Open for Business; Mutual Funds That Prohibit New Customers Still Can Charge Fees to Cover Advertising Costs," *Wall Street Journal,* 16 December 2003.
9. Ibid.
10. Data from Numeric Investors L.P.
11. Data from Morningstar.
12. Granum Capital Management, *Granum Value Fund,* 1 March 2004: 4.
13. Data from Investment Company Institute. See John D. Rea, *Distribution Channels and Distribution Costs,* Investment Company Institute, Perspective, vol. 9, no. 3 (Washington, DC, 2003), 3.
14. Securities and Exchange Commission, *Mutual Fund Fees,* 46–47.
15. Ibid., 43.
16. Ibid., 44.
17. Principal Life Insurance Company, *Prospectus for Principal Mutual Funds,* 1 March 2004.

18. The Vanguard Group, *Prospectus for Vanguard U.S. Value Fund*, 29 January 2004: 1–3.
19. Ibid., 7.
20. John Freeman and Stewart Brown, "Mutual Fund Advisory Fees: The Cost of Conflicts of Interest," *Journal of Corporation Law* 26, no. 3 (Spring 2001): 627–640.
21. Data from Lipper Inc.
22. Kara Scannell, "Quarterly Mutual Funds Review; Bad Market, Good Bet: Our One-Year Winner Draws a Flush," *Wall Street Journal*, 9 April 2001.
23. Christopher Oster and Theo Francis, "Quarterly Mutual Funds Review; Second-Quarter Champions Focus on Small-Cap Stocks and Distressed Companies," *Wall Street Journal*, 7 July 2003.
24. Data from Lipper Inc.
25. Data from Aronson, Johnson & Ortiz, LP.
26. Data from Lipper Inc.
27. Standard & Poor's, "Results for: S&P 500," *The McGraw-Hill Companies*, http://www2.standardandpoors.com/NASApp/cs/ContentServer?pagename=sp/Page/IndicesIndexPg&r=1&1=EN&b=4&s=6&ig=48&i=56&si= 138&xcd=500.
28. Prudential Equity Group, LLC, "The Year-End 2003 Benchmark Study," 19 February 2004: 135
29. Robert D. Arnott and Robert H. Jeffrey, "Is Your Alpha Big Enough to Cover Its Taxes?" *Journal of Portfolio Management* 19, no. 3 (1993): 16.
30. Data from Investment Company Institute.

CHAPTER 9: HIDDEN CAUSES OF POOR MUTUAL-FUND PERFORMANCE

1. Gretchen Morgenson, "A Year's Debacles, from Comic to Epic," *New York Times*, 28 December 2003.
2. Staff Reporter, "Haaga Eats His Words on Scandal," *Institutional Investor*, December 2003: 12.
3. Laura Johannes and John Hechinger, "Conflicting Interests: Why a Brokerage Giant Pushes Some Mediocre Mutual Funds; Jones & Co. Gets Payments from 'Preferred' Vendors," *Wall Street Journal*, 9 January 2004.
4. Edward Jones, "Mutual Funds," http://www.edwardjones.com/cgi/getHTML.cgi?page=/CAN/products /mutual_funds.html.
5. Johannes and Hechinger, "Conflicting Interests."
6. "NASD Considering a Fine for Edward D. Jones," *New York Times*, 31 March 2004.
7. Johannes and Hechinger, "Conflicting Interests."
8. Ibid.

9. Edward D. Jones, advertisement, *New York Times,* 6 November 2000: A12.
10. The Vanguard Group, *Statement of Additional Information for Vanguard Index Funds,* 28 April 2003: B-26.
11. Fidelity Investments, *Statement of Additional Information for Fidelity Magellan Fund,* 21 May 2003: 12.
12. "S.E.C. Orders Mutual Funds to Cease Incentive Pay," *Bloomberg News,* 19 August 2004.
13. John Poirier, "SEC Bars Mutual Fund Payoffs to Brokers," *Reuters,* 18 August 2004.
14. Investment Company Institute, press release, "ICI Supports SEC Action on Directed Brokerage, Portfolio Manager Disclosures," 18 August 2004.
15. Sec. gov, William H. Donaldson, "Speech by SEC Chairman: Opening Statement on Final Amendments to Rule 12b-1 at Open Commission Meeting," (Washington DC, 18 August 2004),
    http://www.sec.gov/news/speech/spch081804whd.htm.
16. Tom Lauricella and Deborah Solomon, "SEC Defended Fund-Broker Compacts in Past," *Wall Street Journal,* 22 January 2004.
17. Lynn O'Shaughnessy, "A 401(k) Picks a Mutual Fund. Who Gets a Perk?" *New York Times,* 15 February 2004.
18. Securities and Exchange Commission, Division of Investment Management, *Investment Trusts and Investment Companies,* Part 3, *Abuses and Deficiencies In the Organization and Operation of Investment Trusts and Investment Companies* (Washington, DC: GPO, 1940), 860.
19. Ibid.
20. Ibid.
21. Ibid., 867.
22. Ibid., 870.
23. Securities and Exchange Commission, Release No. 5519. "Adoption of Rule 22c-1 Under the Investment Company Act of 1940 Prescribing the Time of Pricing Redeemable Securities for Distribution, Redemption, and Repurchase," 16 October 1968.
24. Tom Lauricella, "Quarterly Mutual Funds Review; Scandal Reaches Far and High; It Took Many Bad Apples to Taint Fund Industry's Reputation Amid Continuing Probes of Share-Trading Abuses," *Wall Street Journal,* 8 January 2004.
25. Ibid.
26. Ibid.
27. Tom Lauricella, "Alliance Officials Knew of Timing; Vice Chairman Included E-Mails About Details of Market-Timing Account," *Wall Street Journal,* 17 December 2003.
28. Lauricella "Quarterly Mutual Funds Review."

29. *Securities and Exchange Commission v. Daniel Calugar and Security Brokerage, Inc.,* United States District Court for the District of Nevada, Case No. CV-03-1600-RCJ-RJJ (2003): 3, 6.
    http://www.sec.gov/litigation/complaints/comp18524.pdf.
30. Lauricella, "Quarterly Mutual Funds Review."
31. John Hechinger, "Putnam Is Firing Nine More Workers for Improper Trades," *Wall Street Journal,* 17 December 2003.
32. Deborah Solomon, John Hechinger, and Tom Lauricella, "Milestone for 'Timing' Scandal; Putnam Is First Mutual-Fund Firm to Face a Regulatory Complaint," *Wall Street Journal,* 29 October 2003.
33. Staff Reporter, "Richard Strong Quit as Chairman and CEO of Strong Financial," *Wall Street Journal,* 3 December 2003.
34. Christopher Oster, "A Fund Mogul's Costly Apology; Strong Agrees to Pay $60 Million and to a Lifetime Industry Ban as Part of Rapid-Trading Deal," *Wall Street Journal,* 21 May 2004.
35. Ibid.
36. Warren E. Buffett, Berkshire Hathaway, *Annual Letter to Shareholders,* 27 February 2004: 8.
37, Tom Lauricella, "Pilgrim and Baxter Face Charges; Mutual-Fund Firm's Founders Are Accused of Breach of Duty, Civil Fraud by SEC and Spitzer," *Wall Street Journal,* 21 November 2003.
38. Ian McDonald, "Moving the Market: Pilgrim Baxter Settles for $100 Million," *Wall Street Journal,* 22 June 2004.
39. Editorial, "The Price of Mutual Funds," *Wall Street Journal,* 19 November 2003.
40. T. Rowe Price, *Statement of Additional Information,* 1 March 2004: 90–91.
41. Securities and Exchange Commission, Office of Compliance, Inspections and Examinations, *Inspection Report on the Soft Dollar Practices of Broker-Dealers, Investment Advisers and Mutual Funds* (Washington, DC: GPO, 1998), 9.
42. Ibid., 3–4.
43. Ibid., 30.
44. Laura Johannes and Christopher Oster, "Commissions on Fund Sales Draw Scrutiny," *Wall Street Journal,* 15 December 2003.
45. Paul G. Haaga, "Mutual Integrity, Mutual Trust," *Wall Street Journal,* 15 December 2003.

CHAPTER 10: WINNING THE ACTIVE-MANAGEMENT GAME

1. Longleaf Partners Funds Trust, *Longleaf Partners Funds Annual Report,* 31 December 1998: 1–2.
2. Longleaf Partners Funds Trust, *Longleaf Partners Fund Quarterly Report,* 30 June 2003: 1.

3. Longleaf Partners Funds Trust, *Longleaf Partners Funds Annual Report,* 31 December 1999: 1.
4. Ibid., 1–2, 4–5.
5. Longleaf Partners Funds Trust, *Longleaf Partners Funds Semi-Annual Report,* 30 June 1998: 2.
6. Longleaf Partners Funds Trust, *Partners Fund Fact Sheet,* 30 June 2003: 1.
7. Longleaf, *Annual Report,* 1998: 2.
8. Ibid., 3.
9. Ibid., 4.
10. Longleaf Partners Funds Trust, *Longleaf Partners Fund Quarterly Report,* 30 September 2003: 4.
11. Longleaf, *Annual Report,* 1998: 2.
12. Longleaf Partners Funds Trust, *Longleaf Partners Fund Quarterly Report,* 30 September 1995: 2
13. Longleaf Partners Funds Trust, press release, "Longleaf Partners Fund managed by Southeastern Asset Management, Inc. will close to new investors on June 1, 1999," 13 May 1999.
14. Longleaf Partners Funds Trust, press release, "Longleaf Partners Fund reopened on February 1, 2000," 1 February 2000.
15. Longleaf Partners Funds Trust, press release, "Longleaf Partners Small-Cap Fund managed by Southeastern Asset Management, Inc. will close to new investors on August 1, 1997," 30 June 1997.
16. Longleaf Partners Funds Trust, *Longleaf Partners Fund Quarterly Report,* 31 March 1998: 12.
17. Longleaf Partners Funds Trust, *Longleaf Partners Fund Quarterly Report,* 30 September 2001: 3.

CHAPTER 11: THE EXCHANGE-TRADED FUND ALTERNATIVE

1. The Bank of New York, press release, "NASDAQ Introduces the BLDRs Family of Exchange-Traded Funds Based Upon The Bank of New York ADR Indexes," 13 November 2002.
2. Rydex ETF Trust, *Statement of Additional Information,* 24 April 2003: 16.
3. Tara Siegel Bernard, "Next Up for AMEX," *Wall Street Journal,* 15 July 2004.
4. Tara Siegel Bernard, "Actively Managed ETFs Near," 9 August 2004. http://smartmoney.com/bn/smw/index.cfm?story-20040809033633.

AFTERWORD

CHAPTER 12: FAILURE OF FOR-PROFIT MUTUAL FUNDS

1. Yuka Hayashi, "Big Fund Firms Post Strong Inflows; Fidelity, American Funds, Vanguard Increase Business Despite Industry Scandal," *Wall Street Journal*, 1 December 2003.
2. Data from Morningstar; TIAA-CREF, *2003 Annual Reports*, 31 December 2003.
3. The Vanguard Group, *Vanguard U.S. Stock Index Funds. Investor Shares and Admiral Shares. Prospectus*, 23 April 2004: B-18, B-25.
4. The Vanguard Group, *Vanguard 500 Index Fund Annual Report*, 31 December 2003.
5. TIAA-CREF, "Company History," 2004, http://www.tiaa-cref.org/newroom/history.html.
6. Ibid.
7. Herb Allison, "Opening Remarks," CREF Annual Meeting, 15 December 2003.
8. Paul C. Cabot, "The Investment Trust," *Atlantic Monthly* 268, no. 3 (March 1929): 404.
9. Ibid., 405–406.
10. Senate Committee on Banking and Currency, *Investment Trusts and Investment Companies. Part 1*, 76th Cong., 3rd sess., 2–5 April, 1940, 38–39.
11. Securities and Exchange Commission, *Exemption for the Acquisition of Securities During the Existence of an Underwriting or Selling Syndicate*, File No.: S7-7-96, 31 July 1997: 7.
12. David Dietz and Adam Levy, "Wall Street's 'Dumping Ground,'" *Bloomberg Markets*, June 2004: 40, 43.
13. Data from Consumer Federation of America.
14. Morgan Stanley, *Prospectus for Morgan Stanley S&P 500 Index Fund*, 30 October 2003.
15. Ibid.
16. Vanguard, *Prospectus*, 23 April 2004.
17. Morgan Stanley, *Prospectus*, 2003.
18. Data from Lipper Inc.
19. Morgan Stanley, *Prospectus for Morgan Stanley S&P 500 Index Fund*, 30 October 2002.
20. Morgan Stanley, *Supplement to the Prospectus for Morgan Stanley S&P 500 Index Fund*, 30 September 2003.
21. Morgan Stanley, *Prospectus*, 2003: 19.
22. Tom Lauricella, "Morgan Stanley Settles, but Woes Linger. Deal to Set Aside $50 Million for Clients Resolves SEC Charges, but Mutual-Fund Probes Continue," *Wall Street Journal*, 18 November 2003.
23. Ibid.
24. Ibid.

25. National Association of Securities Dealers, News Release, "NASD Fines Morgan Stanley $2 Million for Prohibited Mutual Fund Sales Contests," 16 September 2003.

26. Sec.gov, "The Investors Advocate: How the SEC Protects Investors and Maintains Market Integrity," *Securities and Exchange Commission*, http://www.sec.gov/about/whatwedo.shtml.

27. Securities and Exchange Commission, *A Plain English Handbook: How to Create Clear SEC Disclosure Documents* (Washington, DC: GPO, 20 August 1998), 2.

28. The Vanguard Group, *Vanguard U.S. Stock Index Funds Prospectus*, 20 January 2004: 68.

29. Karen Damato, "Mutual Funds' Best-Kept Secret," *Wall Street Journal*, 23 January 2004.

30. The Vanguard Group, *Vanguard Index Funds Statement of Additional Information*, 28 April 2004: B24–B26.

31. Ibid., B-26.

32. Vanguard, *Prospectus*, 23 April 2004: B-26.

Index

About the Author

David F. Swensen, Yale's chief investment officer, manages more than $14 billion in Endowment assets. Under his stewardship during the past two decades Yale generated returns of 16.1 percent per annum, a record unequalled among institutional investors. Highly regarded by his peers and competitors, Mr. Swensen's admirers include former Morgan Stanley investment strategist Barton Biggs, who called Swensen a "philosopher prince in a profession saturated with self-promotional paranoids."

Prior to joining Yale in 1985, Mr. Swensen spent six years on Wall Street—three years at Lehman Brothers and three years at Salomon Brothers—where his work focused on developing new financial technologies. At Salomon Brothers, he structured the first swap transaction, a currency exchange involving IBM and the World Bank. Mr. Swensen authored Pioneering Portfolio Management: An Unconventional Approach to Institutional Investment (Free Press, 2000).

Mr. Swensen serves as a trustee of TIAA, a trustee of the Carnegie Institution of Washington, a trustee of The Brookings Institution, and the treasurer of the Hopkins Committee of Trustees. At Yale, he is a fellow of Berkeley College, an incorporator of the Elizabethan Club, and a fellow of the International Center for Finance. Mr. Swensen teaches students in Yale College and at Yale's School of Management.